How To Fix Your Finances

How To Fix Your Finances
A Guide To Personal Financial Planning

Stephen Lofthouse

JOHN WILEY & SONS

Chichester • New York • Brisbane • Toronto • Singapore

Published by   John Wiley & Sons Ltd,
                Baffins Lane, Chichester,
                West Sussex PO19 1UD, England

                National   01243 779777
                International   (+44) 1243 779777

Other Wiley Editorial Offices

John Wiley & Sons Inc., 605 Third Avenue,
New York, NY 10158-0012, USA

Jacaranda Wiley Ltd, 33 Park Road, Milton,
Queensland 4064, Australia

John Wiley & Sons (Canada) Ltd, 22 Worcester Road,
Rexdale, Ontario M9W 1L1, Canada

John Wiley & Sons (Asia) Pte Ltd, 2 Clementi Loop #02-01,
Jin Xing Distripak, Singapore 0512

This book is intended to provide a general guide to financial
planning. It should not be construed as specific advice for
any individual. No mention of a company or product should
be construed as a recommendation for any reader. Whilst every
effort has been made to ensure the accuracy of the material
contained herein, neither the author nor publisher is liable for
any loss resulting from any action taken, or not taken, on the
basis of that material, in any circumstances. Readers should
be aware that many financial products and investments can
go down in value and you may not get your money back. The
income from many financial products and investments may decline.

Library of Congress Cataloging-in-Publication Data

Lofthouse, Stephen.
    How to fix your finances : guide to personal financial planning / by Stephen Lofthouse.
    p.   cm.
Includes bibliographical references and index.
ISBN 0-471-96702-5 (pbk.)
1. Finance, Personal.   2. Investments.   I. Title.
HG179.L554   1996   96–3434
332.024–dc20   CIP

British Library Cataloguing in Publication Data

A catalogue record for this book is available from the British Library

ISBN 0–471–96702–5

Typeset in 10/12pt Sabon by Footnote Graphics, Warminster, Wilts
Printed and bound in Great Britain by Redwood Books Ltd, Trowbridge, Wilts
This book is printed on acid-free paper responsibly manufactured from sustainable forestation,
for which at least two trees are planted for each one used for paper production.

Contents

Preface

This book was written for three types of reader. Primarily it was written for private investors who wish to fix their finances and are willing to put some thought into the process, rather than just be sold products by financial sales staff. The book provides a very broad treatment of financial planning, covering the financial issues that most people encounter. It also includes some advanced material for the more experienced investor. Advanced material, or very specialized material, is always flagged, with advice for some readers to skip it. If you are a private investor, read the first page of Chapter 1 to decide if you should read this book.

The second type of reader who will find this book useful is the professional financial planner. This book covers much of the syllabuses of the major professional financial adviser qualifications, albeit in an informal manner. Would-be planners studying for examinations will find this book to be a useful supplement to their study guides. The material on stockmarket investments such as gilts and equities is more detailed than required for some qualifications. Financial planners will find that the chapters on the stockmarket will extend their knowledge. The third type of reader who will find this book useful is the young stockbroker who advises private investors. Some of the chapters report recent research on picking stocks and markets which is normally found only in academic works. Other chapters will extend a stockbroker's knowledge about non-stockmarket investments.

This book differs in important ways from other personal finance books. More than any other, it looks at the fundamentals of investing. When you sort through the product providers' hype, financial products all boil down to combinations of cash, bonds, shares, and maybe property. You will plan your finances better if you understand the characteristics of these basic assets, their risks and returns.

Many financial products attempt to do several things at once, to mix insurance and investment, or to provide a balance of risk and return, and so on. Often you get a much better deal by separating investment and insurance, and by combining different assets yourself, rather than by buying an expensive package. To do this you need to understand the fundamentals of investing.

In recent years there has been widespread criticism of financial advisers. Anybody who understands the fundamentals will have a much better chance of knowing whether they need advice, and if so what sort of advice, and whether it is competent.

Finally, I am grateful to Richard Bisson, Bridget Boyle, Miles Buckinghamshire, Richard Haas, Jill Hanson, and Jane Raybould for reading all, or part, of this book, and providing comments. They commented in a private capacity, are not responsible for any of the views I've expressed, and do not necessarily agree with them. Despite my best efforts, inevitably there will be mistakes in this book, both of fact and judgement: I'd be grateful if you would point them out to me, care of the publisher.

The book was completed on 1 December 1995, but some material has been updated whilst the book was being prepared for publication.

Stephen Lofthouse

1

Why You Should Read This Book

Advice is less necessary to the wise than to fools, but the wise derive most advantage from it.

Francesco Guicciardini

I think you will benefit from reading this book. So many people have taken ill-judged financial actions, or hold financial beliefs that are just plain wrong, that the odds are that you will benefit enormously. Check the points listed below:

- Most people put off financial planning—but the rewards from investing early are high (Chapter 3).

- Most people turn to banks and building societies for general financial advice—but most of these are "tied" and don't have to give you independent advice. They only have to tell you of a suitable product they have, rather than the best product available on the market (Chapter 10).

- Few people thoroughly check savings rates or the merits of different cheque accounts—but there are huge differences between accounts and the information is readily available (Chapter 5).

- Many people use credit cards to borrow—but the costs are far higher than they think and, in general, debt is for dummies (Chapter 3).

- Most people who have life insurance as protection have whole-life insurance—but for many people term insurance would be a better buy (Chapter 23).

- British investors show a strong preference for cash-based investments. Two-thirds either believe that cash performs better than shares over long periods or are "don't knows". But the historical evidence is that shares have massively outperformed cash—although they are riskier (Chapters 4 and 21).

- Many people have bought gilt unit trusts—but gilt unit trusts are more expensive, riskier and tax-disadvantaged relative to an individual gilt (Chapter 19).

- Insurance investment products are lousy value if surrendered early—and most are (Chapter 23).

- Most mortgages that have been taken out in recent years have been endowment mortgages—but repayment mortgages are more suitable for people who might have to surrender their endowment early, and PEP mortgages are probably better value, if riskier, than endowment mortgages (Chapter 24).

- Most financial advisers claim to be able to pick the best investment managers—but there is scant evidence that consistently good investment managers exist (Chapter 14).

- Only about 4% of the population top-up their pensions with an AVC—but boosting your pension is a great investment (Chapters 27 and 28).

- Most people die intestate—but a will is an essential part of financial planning (Chapter 33).

If any of these points surprise you, you will benefit from reading this book—it will help you fix your finances. If you haven't understood some of the terms I've used, don't worry, they are all discussed later in this book. You can get instant information on most terms by turning to the Glossary at the end of the book. Treat it as your jargon buster.

TAKE RESPONSIBILITY FOR YOUR FINANCES

Why do so many people make poor financial decisions? An important reason is that most people don't take responsibility for their finances, and don't try to understand financial planning. As a result they act in ignorance or rely on financial advisers. Unfortunately, many advisers have been poorly trained. Also, all advisers are really sales personnel and have their own interests, as well as yours, in mind. If you don't believe this, just think of all the publicity there has been in the national press concerning the pensions transfer scandal and the £3 billion compensation the financial services industry will have to pay. Or think of all the household names in the financial services industry that have had to retrain their salesforce—e.g., the Halifax, Norwich Union and Nationwide—and all those that have been fined by their industry regulator. Table 1.1 shows just some of the well-known firms that have been fined.

Noting the many large and well-known financial service companies that have had to retrain their staff, *The Independent* commented: "The problems we are seeing in the industry confirm what many observers have been saying for years, that the sharp-suited men and women who knock on our doors trying to sell us insurance, investments and pensions are often abysmally trained and know little if anything about savings and investment. Training alone is clearly not the solution, however. No matter how well salesmen are taught, ultimately they have to make their living by selling the company's products. If they don't sell, they earn no commission and the company's training costs are wasted. Put in that situation, the temptation for many is to forget whatever they have learnt about good, honest advice. Commission disclosure ... will help but even this will do little to protect the financially illiterate from the financially unscrupulous. Caveat emptor [let the buyer beware] will have to remain the guiding principle...." (p.25, 26 July 1994).

Caveat emptor is the guiding principle of this book. You have to take responsibility for your finances. Of course, you can't do everything. Some things are simply too hard to understand in detail, and you will need some help. But if you take responsibility for your finances, and put some effort into understanding the financial planning process and the investment basics, you will be in a better position to achieve your

Table 1.1 Rapped by Regulators

FIRM	FINE	FIRM	FINE
Aegon Life	£225 000 + £20 000 costs	Irish Life	£300 000 + £85 000 costs
Cannon (now Lincoln Cannon)	£50 000	LAS	£145 000
Canterbury Life	£80 000	Laurentian Life	£70 000
Colonial Mutual	£130 000	Legal and General	£180 000 + £220 000 costs
Commercial Union	First fine, £50 000; second, £105 000 + £25 000 costs	Liberty Life	£80 000
Cornhill	£150 000 + £45 000 costs	London & Manchester	£80 000
Crown Life	£130 000	London Life	£50 000 + £35 000 costs
GA Life	£50 000	Manlife	£65 000 + £35 000 costs
GRE	£100 000	Norwich Union	First fine, £50 000; second, £300 000 + £25 000 costs
Greig Middleton	£200 000	Premium Life	£300 000 + £21 500 costs
Homeowners Friendly Society	£125 000 + £30 000 costs	Prosperity Life	£75 000
Independent Order of Foresters	£200 000 + £17 200 costs	J. Rothschild Assurance	£140 000
Interlife	£160 000	Scottish Widows	£120 000

goals and use advisers wisely, and selectively. Your assets will reflect your needs, and not a salesperson's monthly sales target.

FINANCIAL PLANNING

Financial planning sounds complex and not something that you can do yourself. But it is reasonably straightforward if you ask—and answer—some simple questions. The simple questions, and the financial planner's version of the same questions, are listed below:

1. Where do I want to get to? What are my financial goals?
2. Where am I now? What is my net worth and what is my cash flow?
3. How do you get from here to there? What will be my financial plan?
4. Am I on track? Have I implemented my plan and am I monitoring whether it is meeting my goals and whether my goals are changing?

Although I have set this up as a four-step process, in practice you will often go back and forth. You may set unattainable goals, but when you go through steps two and three this should be apparent, and you will naturally go back to step one and change your goals.

This process is just common sense, and you probably use it for some decisions already. For example, you might have decided you would like to visit America in two years' time. You might set yourself the financial goal of raising £2000 for the trip (step one). You check the piggy bank and find you have no savings at all (step two). This means you will have to save all the money. You might decide to save £79 per month, and put the money into a building society account or a cash unit trust (step three). You do that and periodically ask yourself whether you still want to go to America, and whether £79 per month, plus interest, will build to £2000. And you might check whether your account is giving the highest rate of interest or whether you should shift to a different type of cash account or a different product provider (step four). That's a basic financial plan.

A full financial plan would be a little more complex as it would look at all your financial goals and have more elements. The components of a full financial plan would cover:

1. Cash-flow and personal debt management: handling your daily income and expenditure
2. Emergency planning and insurance: setting aside enough cash to cover the unexpected and making sure you are protecting what you already have
3. Tax planning: ensuring that you keep as much of your money as you can from the Inland Revenue, and that you are allowing for the varying tax treatments of different types of investments
4. Investment strategies: selecting the appropriate assets and in the correct proportions to meet your goals given your attitude to risk
5. Estate planning: drawing up plans so that as much as possible of your assets is conserved and passed on to the people or charities that you want to benefit

This book provides much of the knowledge you need for financial planning and will get you organized. You can get good results, and avoid paying unnecessary fees and commissions. You will have to sit down and work out where you are and where you want to go. Most people don't like doing that. But any good adviser will make you do it, so you might as well do it now.

One advantage you have in getting actively involved in your financial planning is that nobody knows your needs better than you. It is true that at first sight there is a baffling array of financial products, but in most cases these are just fancy packaging of the basic investments, i.e., cash, fixed interest investments, shares and property. In the rest of this book I guide you through the field. If you take responsibility for your finances you will better understand the risks and rewards of your investments. People who rely on experts seldom have much understanding of the risks they are taking. However, sometimes you will need advice and when you do, I say so.

Different readers will have different levels of knowledge. I've tried to cover all important topics so some chapters will be too elementary for some readers. Those readers should just skip the offending chapters. Some chapters will be a demanding read, even for experienced investors, and you may find some chapters to be a bit theoretical. Don't skip those chapters—this is a practical manual, and anything that might appear theoretical is included because it has a big impact on how you should act in the real world.

The order of the chapters is a mixture of the order you might do things in your planning and what makes good sense for exposition. Thus, while life insurance is something many people will wish to consider early in their planning, my discussion appears over halfway through the book. I think you will understand life insurance much better after a discussion of shares, rather than before, so I have put it late in the book. And you will only understand an endowment mortgage after you've read about insurance. So buying a house appears even later in the book.

KEEPING UP TO DATE

Making the right financial decision depends on your personal circumstances, financial resources, goals, attitude to risk and so forth. These are things that I discuss. But it also depends on knowing what is available, and which company is offering the best terms. For some products you will need an adviser to help you, but in other cases you can get the information yourself. A book will always be out of date when you get it because of the time it takes to print and distribute it. The general analysis it gives may have lasting value, but you need to look elsewhere for up-to-date product information. There are two invaluable publications to help you find out what is available and on what terms, *Moneyfacts* and *Which?*

Moneyfacts is a monthly magazine which provides the most comprehensive listing of what is available, and on what terms, for a wide range of products. Equity investments (shares) are, however, excluded. *Moneyfacts* does not recommend particular products. *Which?*, the monthly magazine of the Consumers' Association, appraises a range of products, including financial products, and does pick the best buys. The two magazines complement each other, and both should be available in your local public library. Both are available on subscription, although single issues of *Moneyfacts* are available in some book shops. Subscription details are shown in READ 📖 WRITE 🖹 RING ☎ at the end of the chapter.

Throughout the book you'll find READ 📖 WRITE 🖹 RING ☎. At the end of each chapter in which that appears, you'll find a section giving you references to published material, or addresses or telephone numbers you can write to or ring to get further information. I have also put references to material I quote in this section, rather than clutter the pages with footnotes.

A brief selection of some of the information contained in *Moneyfacts*, and by no means a substitute, appears on Channel 4's Teletext service. A service similar to *Moneyfacts*, which you may see referred to in the press, is *Blay's Guides*. A few specialist libraries have a copy of Blay's monthly *MoneyMaster*, but the major product is a screen-based product which some financial advisers subscribe to. A selection of the information appears on BBC 2's Teletext service.

If you follow the approach set out in this book, you don't need to read about the economy and follow the endless stream of press share tips. However, new products appear, tax rules change, interest rate changes make some investments more or less attractive, and so on. If you want to keep up-to-date the following publications are worth reading:

● The weekend personal finance sections of the national newspapers, including *The Financial Times*

● The weekly *Investors Chronicle* (£2.00)

● The monthly *Moneywise* (£2.40)

It is not necessary to read all three: you may find that if you consistently read the financial section of your usual newspaper you will have as much information as you need.

If you are interested in product advice geared to the professional market, the two key publications are: *Money Management* and *Planned Savings* Both are monthly and available on subscription, or from large newsagents at £4.50 and £4.50 per copy respectively.

I often give references to articles in *Which?*, *Money Management* and *Planned Savings* in READ 📖 WRITE 📧 RING ☎. They were the most up-to-date articles in November 1995, but there may be a more recent article. Many products are written up on an approximately annual cycle.

That's the background. In Chapter 2, we get down to work.

READ 📖 WRITE 📧 RING ☎

◆ Subscription details: *Moneyfacts*, Laundry Loke, North Walsham, Norfolk, NR28 OBD. Tel: 01692 500765. £48.50 annual subscription. *Moneyfacts* also offers a fax service, which I mention at various points in this book. *Which?*, Subscription Department, PO Box 44, Hertford, SG14 1SH. £14.75 quarterly subscription.
◆ The four- and five-point financial planning outlines on pages 3 and 4 are adapted from B. Cohen with A. Diamond, *The Money Adviser*. Toronto: Stoddart, 1994, p.2.

2

Assessing Your Financial Health

Before everything else, getting ready is the secret of success.
Henry Ford

To plan your financial future, the first thing you have to do is to establish where you are. Until you know that, there is no way you can rationally plan. When companies publish their Annual Reports and Accounts, they present three different sorts of accounts—a profit and loss account, a cash flow statement and a balance sheet. It's a good idea if you produce two of these accounts for yourself—a personal cash flow statement and a personal balance sheet.

A personal cash flow statement will show you what cash you get in and where you spend it. From that you can decide how to cut back if you are in debt, or how much savings you will have to invest. Even if you have more money coming in than going out, you may want to save more, so your cash flow statement will help you decide where your expenditure might be trimmed.

Your balance sheet will show you what assets (things of value) you have, and what liabilities you have (what you owe), and what the balance is. This is your net worth. If you have too many liabilities, you may want to reduce them before acquiring more assets. By having a list of your liabilities, and what they are costing you, you can decide which ones to pay off first.

Most readers will be about to skip on to another chapter. Fair enough, nobody enjoys this exercise. However, people who have been forced to do it either out of necessity after being made redundant, or by a bank making it a condition of a loan, have nearly always reported that the exercise was an eye-opener. For many it becomes a habit, even when their circumstances take a turn for the better.

KEEP RECORDS

I'm going to sneak something in here. It's worth a chapter to itself, but if I had a chapter called "record keeping", the only people who would read it would be the obsessive control freaks who already keep good records. Your financial life, however, will be much easier if you keep good records. You need records to be able to carry out the tasks required in this chapter, you need records when things go wrong, you need records to complete your tax return and you need records when you draw up a will, which is a must-do activity (as I explain in Chapter 33). So, why not take the opportunity of getting your records on a sound footing now?

There are two sorts of records you need. The first consists of names and addresses, and the second consists of storing bits of paper. How exactly you do these two things is up to you. You might keep your names and addresses on a computer, or hand-written on a few sheets of paper. If you use a computer, make sure you keep a back-up diskette copy, and that somebody else knows how to use your computer and find the right file. If you write your list, an address book would be ideal since you are less likely to lose it than sheets of paper, and it will be easy to enter new addresses and delete old ones. You can keep your paper records in a shoe box, in some folders in a drawer, or a smart filing cabinet. Some, such as your home's deeds, should be kept in a safe, either yours or your bank's. It's up to you how you arrange these matters.

What should you keep? At least the following:

- Your national insurance number.

- Cheque book stubs (filled out), credit card receipts and ATM (automated teller machine/hole in the wall machine) receipts. When you get your bank statement, or credit card bill, match up the receipts and stubs and dispose of them unless you need credit card receipts for expense claims or for your tax return. If there is an error, complain. Keep a record of your standing orders and Direct Debits. Keep your bank statements and credit card bills for at least a year. Record your bank account number and branch, similarly building society account number and branch. Keep a record of your ATM card number but memorize your PIN (personal identification number). If you lose your cheque card, credit card and so on, you will need to notify the relevant company by telephone immediately—record the number.

- Your employer's address and the address of the personnel department or other office that handles your pension and other benefits. If you die, your employer may pay a lump sum to whoever you have nominated. If your circumstances change, be sure to inform the personnel department.

- Copies of all your insurance policies and renewal dates. Record your account number and the companies' names and addresses. If you have used an insurance agent, record the agent's name and address.

- Where your will is kept and the name and address of the lawyer who drew it up. Record who your executors will be, and their addresses.

- The names and addresses of all financial advisers, such as accountant, stockbroker, independent financial adviser, etc.

- A list of where all your personal papers are kept. Some may be in your shoe box, but where are your home deeds, stocks and shares, and does your accountant keep some of your tax records? If you have PEPs, TESSAs, etc., record the names of the firms involved and your account number. Some firms offering TESSA accounts give you a passbook, but others simply send a letter. If you lose your letter, you will find it hard to contact the company. If you are hit by a bus and die, the existence of your account may not be discovered.

- Keep a record of the latest value of any assets for which you receive a statement, e.g., your half-yearly PEP statement.

- Keep all your dividend and interest statements until you have agreed your tax return with the Inland Revenue. You might like to keep your tax returns and supporting documents for six years.

- If you move home, you will have to notify your change of address. In some cases, e.g., your bank, it is obvious who you write to. For shares that you hold, you will have to notify the appropriate company registrar. Its address appears on the share certificate, and on dividend vouchers. You might like to note it when you get your share certificate or first dividend.

- National Savings gives you a Holder's Number when you buy various National Savings products. Record it, and also the Register Number for any Government Stock bought through the Post Office (you will get a different number for each type of stock).

- The addresses of all the properties you own, and the address of your mortgage lender. Keep the certificate of net interest paid that you will receive, as you will need it for your tax return.

- Make a list of all the debts you have (e.g., hire purchase agreements) and the names and addresses of the firms. List all sums owed to you and by whom, and their addresses.

- Keep a note of the address for correspondence on your Council Tax.

- Keep your gas, electricity and water bills and receipts for a couple of years. The first two are useful for checking changes in your fuel consumption.

- Keep telephone bills for your tax return if you work from home.

You will need a lot of the information you have brought together for the tables shown later in this chapter.

YOUR CASH FLOW STATEMENT

Solvency is entirely a matter of temperament and not of income.
Logan Pearsall Smith

To work out your cash flow statement you should complete Table 2.1, or a modified version that suits your circumstances. You will probably protest that you don't need to do this. Let me expand on what I said in the first paragraph of this chapter. Only if you have a cash flow statement can you find out what you are spending your money on. You need to know that if you want to get out of debt, find more money to invest, work out if you can afford a special treat (visit the kids in Australia?), decide whether you can pay for your children's higher education, decide whether you can take a lower-paid or part-time job to reduce stress, calculate what the financial consequences are of having another child, look at the option of retiring early, assess the financial consequences of redundancy, or divorce, or the consequences of telling the boss where

Table 2.1   Personal Income and Expenditure Statement

CATEGORY	SELF	SPOUSE	JOINT
INCOME			
Employment			
• Pay			
• Bonus			
• Commission			
Self-employment			
State benefits			
Pensions			
Dividends			
Rent (which you receive)			
Interest (which you receive)			
TOTAL INCOME			
TAXES			
• Income Tax			
• National Insurance			
• Capital Gains Tax			
TOTAL TAXES			
NET INCOME (INCOME – TAXES)			
LIVING EXPENSES			
Housing			
• Mortgage or rent			
• Gas			
• Electricity			
• Other Fuel			
• Water			
• Repairs and garden maintenance			
• Contents Insurance			
• Building Insurance			
• Furniture			
• Council Tax			
Food and household items			
Meals outside the home			
Tobacco/alcohol			
Clothes			

Table 2.1   *Continued*

CATEGORY	SELF	SPOUSE	JOINT
Telephone			
Newspapers/magazines/books			
Transportation			
• Car payments			
• Car insurance			
• Road Tax/MOT			
• Petrol			
• Parking, Tolls, Fines, AA/RAC			
• Fares			
Medical/Dental			
• Insurance			
• Bills			
• Prescriptions			
Holidays			
Entertainment			
• TV/video /licence/satellite subscription			
• Clubs			
• Other			
• Pocket money			
Gifts: birthdays/anniversaries/Christmas			
Life or Term Insurance			
School Fees			
SAVINGS PLANS			
TOTAL LIVING EXPENSES			
NET INCOME LESS EXPENSES			

to shove … well, you know. For some of these things you need a statement of your net worth as well. For example, you may not be able to save anything but still be able to visit Australia if you have saved in the past and have substantial assets. I look at net worth, or net assets, shortly.

I've headed Table 2.1 "self" and "spouse". Spouse could, of course, be partner. If you are not married, however, there may be some tricky implications. I look at those in Chapter 29.

Getting all the data for Table 2.1 may prove difficult if you haven't been keeping records. There are four ways of tackling the problem. First, you can just give it your best shot by using my headings. Second, you can go through bank statements/credit card statements for a year. A month will pick up most items, but you will need a year to pick up the annual TV licence, car tax, home insurance, etc. Third, you can visualize what you do: "go to work, get weekly ticket, buy paper, arrive outside office, buy coffee and roll ..." and estimate the cost of each item. Fourth, you can record your expenditure for a week or whatever, as you incur it. You'll be astonished how much is frittered away, and how often some offices have collections for girls you've never met who are leaving to have babies, and so on.

Once you know what your position is, if you have some goals you can adjust your expenditure or your income to achieve them. You may feel you want to save more but somehow you never do. Here's how to do it. **Don't treat savings as a residual.** Don't let the fertility of the girls in the typing pool determine your savings. **Save first.** Write into your cash flow statement a sum for savings and save before you spend. When you get your pay, write a cheque immediately and put it away in your high interest savings account. If you don't trust yourself to do that, join a scheme whereby your savings are automatically deducted from your salary. Or join an investment trust or unit trust savings scheme whereby you make an automatic monthly payment to them. (I discuss all of these investments in later chapters.) If you are in debt, work out how much you should repay each month and treat that as your savings goal. Make your monthly debt repayment before you do anything else.

Saving more, or paying off debt, will involve spending less. I make some comments on this later in the chapter.

Review your cash flow statement every time your salary is reviewed or there is a big change in your life.

NET WORTH

To build up your net worth you need to save, but to achieve your long-run goals, the disposition of your net worth is the key. You have to blend a variety of investments that offer different degrees of risk, return and liquidity. Your cash flow statement tells you what cash is sloshing through your accounts and how much is left at the end of the year, or how much you are in debt. Your net worth tells you how much your total assets exceed your liabilities. Your cash flow is the money into and out of your piggy bank. Your net worth is the value of the piggy bank. If you save, your net worth will tend to grow. If you run up debts, your net worth will tend to fall or become negative. Notice I said "tend". You might find yourself saving and being worse off. This could happen if home prices fall and you lose more on the value of your home than you add in new savings. Over the years, however, new savings will push up your net worth unless you make a string of silly investments.

You should value your net worth once or twice a year, but no more. Don't redo the numbers every time the stockmarket slides or spurts. Your stockmarket investments are long-term. If you keep looking at your volatile investments you will start trading in and out—a very unprofitable activity.

You should complete Table 2.2, or your own version of it, noting both your own and your spouse's assets and liabilities. You should also make a note of the rate of interest on each liability. If you pay off some of your liabilities, you should go for the

Table 2.2 Personal Balance Sheet

ASSETS			LIABILITIES		
MONETARY ASSETS			SHORT-TERM LIABILITIES		
Short-term			Unpaid Bills		
● Bank Accounts			● Taxes		
● Building Society			● Rent		
● Cash Unit Trusts			● Gas		
● Premium Bonds			● Electricity		
● Other			● Water		
Long-term			● Credit Cards		
● National Savings			● Overdraft		
● TESSA			Hire Purchase		
● PEPs			● Car		
● Shares			● Other		
● Bonds			Total Short-term		
● Life Insurance: Cash Value			LONG-TERM LIABILITIES		
● Annuities: Cash Value			Mortgage		
● Pension Plans			Bank Loan		
● Other			Total Long-term		
Total Monetary Assets			TOTAL LIABILITIES		
FIXED ASSETS					
Home					
Furniture					
Car					
Other					
Equity in Own Business					
Total Fixed Assets			NET WORTH (i.e., Total		
TOTAL ASSETS			Assets Less Total Liabilities)		

most expensive (on an after-tax basis) first. Don't be discouraged if you don't have many assets, the exercise is still worth doing. Also, you have the chance to plan your investment strategy from a clean slate.

A couple items in Table 2.2, life insurance and pensions, are tricky to value. You should make sure you take these items into account, but how you value them is up to you. You'll have a better idea after reading the relevant chapters later in this book. The point is that your pension can be valued as the pool of money that will generate your pension. People with personal pensions may think in these terms. Most of us, however, think in terms of how much per week we will get—say two-thirds of our salary at retirement. But putting your weekly pension into the table isn't consistent with how the other assets are recorded, e.g., your total bank account, not just the interest. For now, just fill in the other items and carry a subjective notion of whether you are pension and insurance rich or poor.

ACTION

I do not know what your goals are, or your current financial situation. I therefore cannot offer you specific advice. You may be in great financial shape, and your goals readily attainable. But most people usually find that a few adjustments are necessary. You may need to review your goals, you may want to find more rewarding invest-ments (the subject of most of this book), you may feel that you need a better-paid job (or simply a job, if you have been made redundant), or you may feel that you need to cut down your expenditure to pay off debts or to save more.

Many people feel financial planning should enable them to spend more, not less. However, if you are building up debts, you will have to spend less. And even if you are not, you may wish to spend less so that you have more to spend in the future. The merit of spending less is worthy of a section to itself.

HOW TO SPEND LESS (OR BETTER)

Thrift is care and scruple in the spending of one's means. It is not a virtue, and it requires neither skill nor talent.

Immanuel Kant

If you are in debt, you just have to bite the bullet and stop spending on some major items. The best strategy is to avoid getting into debt and to change your expenditure pattern gradually. Here are some suggestions:

- The easiest option if you are not in debt is to do nothing new but save all of your annual pay rise or bonus. What you've not had you won't miss.

- Don't buy on credit.

- Buy a cheaper car. It will still get you from A to B and will have cheaper insurance, cheaper repairs and use less petrol.

- Quit smoking. It's better for your health, and your family's health, and it will also save you a lot of money.

- Buy in bulk whenever possible, and buy own-label (retailer) brands. You don't have to do this on everything, but do you really need an expensive brand of toothpaste, shampoo, shaving foam, aspirin, socks, underwear, etc.?

- Buy in the sales if you don't have to go into debt to do so, and you would buy the item if it wasn't in a sale.

- Some people go shopping as a form of entertainment. That's OK if you don't end up buying things you don't need, but if you do, find a new form of entertainment.

- Use public facilities: the parks, libraries, and swimming pool (instead of joining a health club).

- Wear things out. Does it really matter that the oatmeal sweater in perfect condition at the back of the wardrobe is in last season's shade? Surely the whole meaning of your life isn't just a fashion statement.

- Take care of what you have.

- Think economy. If you have a utility room, buy a thermostat and set the washing machine to come on in the middle of the night when electricity is a third of the day-time price. If you are sitting in one room, don't heat the whole home, at least not to the same temperature. Don't leave all the lights in the home on.

- Read *Which?* every month (in the public library?) to find the best value brands and discover lots of good tips.

I know, at best this all sounds worthy but dull. If you do draw up a plan, make it one that suits your temperament, and your family's, so that you can keep to it. Build in a little mad money or you won't stay the course. Try to view all this as spending better, rather than spending less. If you decide to do nothing, fair enough but, as I will show in the next chapter, the investment return from spending better is very high.

3

Investment Arithmetic

Annual income twenty pounds, annual expenditure nineteen nineteen six, result happiness.
Annual income twenty pounds, annual expenditure twenty pounds ought and six, result
misery.

Charles Dickens

Don't worry about the title, you don't have to do any sums, I've done them for you.
The goal of this chapter is to show you by vivid illustrations how powerful compounding is over long periods, how harmful inflation and taxes are, and how costly
debt really is. Most people will know the points I'm going to make, but few people
realize the dramatic investment implications. Certainly most investors behave in a
way that suggests that they haven't factored these simple points into their investment
strategy. So, come with me on an arithmetical adventure. It will be fun, and you'll be
amazed.

THE POWER OF COMPOUNDING

'Tis money that begets money.
Proverb

An important factor in achieving success in financial planning is to start early. The
reason for this is the power of compounding. Compounding is most easily thought of as
the process of re-investing income so as to earn income on that income. If you have
£100 and the rate of interest is 10%, if you invest for a year, you will have £10 of
interest at the year end. If you reinvest that, at the end of the second year you will
get £10 of interest on your original £100, but you will also get £1 interest on the
previous year's £10 of interest. In the second year you will therefore get a total of
£11 of interest. In the following year you will get even more. This is the power of
compounding.

Although most people think of compounding in terms of interest, it applies equally
to re-invested dividends, or indeed any form of income. It also applies to increases in
capital.

To see compounding in action, look at Table 3.1. There I start with £1000 and
compound it at 5%, 10%, 11% and 15% over a 45-year period, i.e., about the length
of a working life. To reduce the numbers in the table, I've shown only the first ten
years and the last ten. Three things are worth noting:

1. Money subject to compound interest grows to a large sum if left for a long period. This point doesn't need explanation—just look at any of the totals, all achieved by a single investment of £1000.
2. The money value of the increase is not much in the early years, but is very large in the latter years. To see this, look at the 5% column. The value of the first year's interest is £50 (£1050–£1000). Now look at the value of the investment in year 45 and subtract year 44's value from it. Interest in the final year is £428 (i.e., £8985–£8557).
3. Even modest differences in interest rates lead to substantial differences in the value of the investment. It is not surprising that interest at 15% produces a much higher value in year 45 than does interest at 5%. But look at the final year values for the 10% and 11% interest rates. The final year value for the 10% rate is only two-thirds that of the value for the 11% rate. You may find that surprising. It means that if you can cut your investment purchase costs by just 1%, with unchanged returns, there will be a big impact. When investing, remember that costs kill returns.

I used a computer to complete Table 3.1, but you might find the "rule of 72" a handy rule of thumb for doing quick sums in real life—if you hate sums, skip this paragraph. The rule tells you how long it will take for an investment to double at a specific rate of return, and consists of dividing 72 by the rate of return. Thus, an investment earning a return of 10% will double in about 7.2 years (72 ÷ 10 = 7.2). As you can see from Table 3.1, that looks about right (i.e., £1000 is worth £1949 after 7 years). If you are mentally agile you can work out complex sums with the rule. Thus,

Table 3.1   Value of £1000 Invested at Various Rates Over Various Periods

Year	Year-end value of £1000 invested at these rates:			
	5%	10%	11%	15%
1	1050	1100	1110	1150
2	1103	1210	1232	1323
3	1158	1331	1368	1521
4	1216	1464	1518	1749
5	1276	1611	1685	2011
6	1340	1772	1870	2313
7	1407	1949	2076	2660
8	1477	2144	2305	3059
9	1551	2358	2558	3518
10	1629	2594	2839	4046
36	5792	30913	42818	153152
37	6081	34004	47528	176125
38	6385	37404	52756	202543
39	6705	41145	58559	232925
40	7040	45259	65001	267864
41	7392	49785	72151	308043
42	7762	54764	80088	354250
43	8150	60240	88897	407387
44	8557	66264	98676	468495
45	8985	72890	109530	538769

an investment earning 5% will double in about 14.4 years (72 ÷ 5), and again in 28.8 years (14.4 × 2), and again in 43.2 years (14.4 × 3), i.e., £1000 becomes £2000, then £4000, and then £8000. So if you had to guess the value of £1000 compounding at 5% for 45 years, as in Table 3.1, you could guess it would be over £8000. If this stuff is your idea of fun, there is also a rule of 113, which is explained in the Glossary.

The benefit of beginning early

The advantage of starting early can be illustrated by the story of Sally and Harry. Sally leaves university at 21 years of age, and discovers investing. She starts saving at the rate of £1000 per year. Her savings compound at 8% per annum tax-free. Harry also leaves university at the same time and at the same age, but he discovers sex and drugs and rock and roll. In their late 20s, Sally meets Harry, they fall in love and get married. They decide to start a family, so Sally quits work and stops saving at age 30. She leaves her savings to continue to grow, but she no longer adds to them. Harry, faced with family responsibilities, starts saving at age 31. He saves £1000 per annum and also earns 8% per annum.

If you look at Table 3.2 you can see how much Sally and Harry's savings grow to at age 65. Sally invested £10000 and her investment is worth £231324, whereas Harry invested £35000 and it is worth £186102. (To make the table less overwhelming, I've omitted the rows for ages 36 to 54.) You may think there is something odd with my example, but there isn't, at least, not with the maths. Why sensible Sally should marry horrible Harry is another matter. What is clear is that the sooner you start saving, the better.

Even small sums benefit from compounding

People often think that investing only makes sense if you have lots of money to begin with. But that's not true. Compounding works on any starting sum. If we take a zero off Sally's annual investment and make it £100, but leave everything else unchanged, all we have to do is take a zero off her total in Table 5 to see what a small saver would have achieved. It's the same impressive percentage increase.

BEWARE OF INFLATION AND TAXES

Inflation is as violent as a mugger, as frightening as an armed robber and as deadly as a hit man.

Ronald Reagan

While compounding of investment returns builds up your capital, inflation and taxes erode it. I'll look at the effect of each separately, and then jointly.

Inflation: the unofficial tax

Inflation is a sort of unofficial tax. The Inland Revenue doesn't administer it, but it erodes your wealth just as effectively as the taxes administered by the Revenue. When

Table 3.2   The Benefit of Beginning Early

	SALLY		HARRY	
Age	Annual Investment	Year-end Value	Annual Investment	Year-end Value
21	1000	1080	0	0
22	1000	2246	0	0
23	1000	3506	0	0
24	1000	4867	0	0
25	1000	6336	0	0
26	1000	7923	0	0
27	1000	9637	0	0
28	1000	11488	0	0
29	1000	13487	0	0
30	1000	15645	0	0
31	0	16897	1000	1080
32	0	18249	1000	2246
33	0	19709	1000	3506
34	0	21286	1000	4867
35	0	22988	1000	6336
55	0	107148	1000	78954
56	0	115720	1000	86351
57	0	124977	1000	94339
58	0	134975	1000	102966
59	0	145773	1000	112283
60	0	157435	1000	122346
61	0	170030	1000	133214
62	0	183632	1000	144951
63	0	198323	1000	157627
64	0	214189	1000	171317
65	0	231324	1000	186102

inflation is high, everyone is aware of its effect, but when it is low, people tend to ignore it. Table 3.3 shows the effect of various rates of inflation on £1000 over a 45-year period. (Once again, to avoid overwhelming you with numbers, I've omitted some years, in this case 11 through to 35.) Table 3.3 shows what £1000 saved at age 20 will be worth in today's money when you are 65. As you can see, not much. At 10% inflation, year in and year out, your £1000 has only the purchasing power of £9 today. But even 3% inflation, which many people would consider to be not worth bothering about, reduces your £1000 to the purchasing power of £254 today. In other words, over your working life, 3% inflation is sufficient to reduce your purchasing power to a quarter of what it is worth today.

Looking at the effect of inflation alone does not tell the full story. You should allow for the fact that your capital will be earning a return. Indeed, with a bank account you will probably get a higher rate of interest when the rate of inflation is high. In other words while inflation will be reducing your wealth, interest may be compounding at a fast rate to partially, or totally, offset the effect of inflation. You must always look at inflation in conjunction with investment returns. The important issue is what is your real rate of return, i.e., your return after allowing for inflation:

Table 3.3   Effect of Various Rates of Inflation on the Value of
£1000

Year	Rate of Inflation		
	3%	6%	10%
1	970	940	900
2	941	884	810
3	913	831	729
4	885	781	656
5	859	734	590
6	833	690	531
7	808	648	478
8	784	610	430
9	760	573	387
10	737	539	349
36	334	108	23
37	324	101	20
38	314	95	18
39	305	90	16
40	296	84	15
41	287	79	13
42	278	74	12
43	270	70	11
44	262	66	10
45	254	62	9

Real return = nominal or stated money return *minus* rate of inflation.

For example, if your nominal return is 12%, and inflation is 10%, your real return is 2%. If your nominal return is 8%, and inflation is 10%, your real return is minus 2%.

The problem with inflation is that while some investments' returns tend to adjust to varying inflation rates, some investments' returns don't. In particular, fixed income investments pay an unchanging money return. If the rate of inflation picks up, these investments then pay a lower real return, or even a negative real return. I discuss this in Chapter 19.

Is inflation normal?

I have shown why many investors are right to worry about the effects of inflation. But to say that inflation can be a problem if it occurs, is not the same as saying it will occur. Generals are often said to be prepared to fight the last war and unprepared for the next. Investors can be the same. You must decide whether there will be rapid inflation, or even 3% inflation, in the future. What I can do is tell you whether inflation is as common an occurrence as you may think.

Everybody knows that when Mrs Thatcher was elected in 1979 she made a big point about the need to combat inflation. And those of us old enough to remember life before Thatcher know that inflation was a problem in the 1970s. But was it a problem before that, or indeed after? Table 3.4 gives the answers.

As you can see, periods of modest inflation have been followed by periods of more

Table 3.4 Average Inflation Rates
(Geometric average)

Years	%
1900 to 1913	1.3
1914 to 1918	15.3
1919 to 1939	−1.2
1940 to 1945	4.3
1946 to 1949	2.6
1950 to 1959	4.3
1960 to 1969	3.5
1970 to 1979	12.5
1980 to 1989	7.4
1990 to 1993	5.1

Source: MacFarlane and Mortimer-Lee
(1994, p. 157)

rapid inflation, which in turn have been followed by more modest inflation. Indeed, at the start of the century, a period of rapidly rising prices was followed by a period during which prices actually fell. If we go back to the 1800s, prices rose at the start of the century, but the trend was then erratically downwards for the rest of the century. Despite this long period of decline, over the first 300 years of the Bank of England's life (it was founded in 1694), prices have risen 67-fold.

So, is inflation normal? Yes, prices have risen 67-fold over the last 300 years. No, there have been periods, including much of one century, during which prices fell rather than rose. So what should you do? If you can forecast inflation over the short run, this may dictate your investment strategy. If you are investing for decades, e.g., if you are 20 years old and saving for a pension which you may still be enjoying in 60 years' time, it probably makes sense to play the historical odds and invest in at least some assets that offer returns that are not fixed for ever in money terms, even if that involves some other risks (which I discuss in Chapter 4). You may want to invest in some that offer full inflation protection.

Taxing times

Investment returns can be quoted pre-tax and after-tax. Most returns are quoted before tax and this seems right, because different investors pay different rates of income tax and some may be liable to capital gains tax whereas others won't. However, what concerns investors is the return from an investment that they get to keep, the after-tax returns. This means you have to know what your tax rate is, and for most people the relevant concept is your marginal tax rate as opposed to your average tax rate. I discuss income and capital gains tax in Chapter 8, but I will give a simplified explanation of average and marginal tax rates here.

If you divide your total tax bill by your income you will get your average tax rate. If you earn £30 000 and pay £6000 tax, your average rate of tax is 20% (£6000 ÷ £30 000 × 100% = 20%). But your tax is calculated on the basis of various tax bands with different rates, nil, 20%, 24% and 40%. As you earn more, you pass through each band paying tax on part of your income at each rate. A single person earning £30 000 would have reached the 40% band, and any additional income, say from overtime or investments, would be taxed at 40%. The rate of tax on any additional (or marginal) income is the marginal tax rate, i.e., 40% in this example. It is the marginal tax rate that is relevant when assessing investments. In my example, an extra £1 of investment income would be taxed at 40%, even though the average rate is 20%.

In Table 3.5, I show various tax rates and various before-tax returns. (I've omitted the 24% rate because this isn't charged on most savings, as I explain in Chapter 8.) If you don't pay tax, your before-tax and after-tax returns are the same. If your marginal tax rate is, for example, 40%, a before-tax return of 12% is worth only 7.2% after tax. Currently, the top rate of tax is 40%, but I've added a 60% rate as well, a rate that applied in 1988 and before. You can see the effect.

For the purpose of showing how income tax erodes returns, I've covered sufficient ground. However, it is useful for later chapters to cover a related issue here. Some investments, notably various National Savings products, are paid tax-free. Make sure you don't confuse "tax-free" with "without deduction of tax". The latter means no tax has been deducted but you have to tell the Inland Revenue that you received an income, and it will demand payment of tax at the appropriate rate for your total income. Tax-free means no tax is payable.

To compare a tax-free rate to the rate on a typical investment which is subject to tax, you have to "gross-up" the return—i.e., work out the pre-tax return that, when subjected to tax at your marginal rate, would give you the tax-free rate. Table 3.6 does this for various tax-free rates and various tax rates. For example, a tax-free return of 6% would, for a 40% taxpayer, be the same as a gross return of 10% from which tax had to be paid. For somebody paying tax at 20%, the grossed-up equivalent would only be 7.5%. Tax-free rates are thus much more attractive to high taxpayers than to low taxpayers.

Table 3.5   Effect of Various Tax Rates on Returns

Marginal Tax Rate	Before-Tax Return					
	2%	4%	6%	8%	10%	12%
	After Tax Return					
0%	2.00	4.00	6.00	8.00	10.00	12.00
20%	1.60	3.20	4.80	6.40	8.00	9.60
40%	1.20	2.40	3.60	4.80	6.00	7.20
60%	0.80	1.60	2.40	3.20	4.00	4.80

Table 3.6   Taxable Return Required at Various Tax Rates to Match Tax-Free Rates

Marginal Tax Rate	Tax-free Return					
	2%	4%	6%	8%	10%	12%
	Taxable Return Equivalent					
0%	2.00	4.00	6.00	8.00	10.00	12.00
20%	2.50	5.00	7.50	10.00	12.50	15.00
40%	3.33	6.67	10.00	13.33	16.67	20.00

If you want to make your own calculations, the grossing up formula is:

$$\frac{\text{Tax-free yield}}{1 - \text{applicable tax rate expressed as a decimal}} = \text{grossed up yield}$$

so, with a 20% tax rate and a tax-free 6% yield, the grossed up rate is:

$$\frac{6\%}{1 - 0.20} = \frac{6\%}{0.80} = 7.5\%$$

When thinking about taxes you also have to consider capital gains tax (CGT), a tax on the increase in value of your capital. I discuss CGT in Chapter 8 but it is worth saying here that everybody has a £6300 exemption from CGT (in 1996–97) so it is often worth taking some investment returns in the form of capital gains, rather than income, because you may reduce the tax you pay.

The killer combination: inflation and taxes

I've shown how inflation erodes your wealth and how income tax reduces your returns. What happens if we combine the effect of inflation and taxes? Table 3.7 shows the high returns required to overcome both. Look at the 40% tax and 3% inflation combination. If you got return of 5% before-tax, the after-tax return would be 3%, exactly the same as the rate of inflation. Thus to offset 3% inflation if you have a 40% marginal tax rate, you need to earn a return of 5% to stand still. To make a real after-tax return, you need to earn more. Look at the break-even return required for a 40% taxpayer during a period when inflation is 15%: it's 25%. If there were a 60% tax band, the required return to stand still in real terms would be an unbelievable 37.5%.

Table 3.7 Return Required at Various Tax Rates to Offset Inflation

Rate of Inflation %	Tax Rate		
	20%	40%	60%
1	1.25	1.67	2.50
2	2.50	3.33	5.00
3	3.75	5.00	7.50
4	5.00	6.67	10.00
5	6.25	8.33	12.50
6	7.50	10.00	15.00
7	8.75	11.67	17.50
8	10.00	13.33	20.00
9	11.25	15.00	22.50
10	12.50	16.67	25.00
11	13.75	18.33	27.50
12	15.00	20.00	30.00
13	16.25	21.67	32.50
14	17.50	23.33	35.00
15	18.75	25.00	37.50

For some investments, such as bank deposits, things are as bad as Table 3.7 implies. No allowance is given for the fact that part of your return is just to offset the effect of inflation. For others the problem is not so bad. In the case of shares, for example, the return comes as a mixture of capital gains (or losses) and dividends. Before the capital gains are taxed, an allowance is given for the rate of inflation between the acquisition date and the disposal date. The exact effect of inflation and taxes will depend both on your tax rate and the type of investment. I discuss this again in other chapters.

DEBT IS FOR DUMMIES

Be not made a beggar by banqueting on borrowing.
Ecclesiasticus

If you have read Chapter 2 and worked out your spending plan, and your expenditure exceeds your income, it is time to spend less. It's true that theoretically you could get a better job and you could get better investment returns but, in the short-term, and possibly even the long, the obvious solution is to spend less. You could allow debts to build up, but that is a road to disaster. The sort of people likely to read this book will probably build up debt via bank overdrafts and credit cards. The rates on these vary. Authorized overdrafts tend to be the lowest cost, while unauthorized overdrafts can bear penal rates. The rate on credit cards varies widely. I look at bank accounts and credit cards in Chapters 5 and 6. Here I just want to explain why debt for consumption is, in general, for dummies. Debt for investments such as education and home purchase is a different matter.

In Table 3.8, I show what return your investments have to earn to pay off your debts. I use three rates of interest, 15%, 25% and 35%. Few people will be borrowing at 35%, but it was a common enough rate on credit cards just a few years ago. Currently, a borrower could easily be paying either of the other two rates. I also show various tax rates. Now, to take an example, if you borrow at 25%, to pay that back from an investment when you are in the 40% tax bracket, you will have to find an investment giving a before-tax return of 42%. If you know of one, please write to me. The fact is, there are no investments that you can guarantee will pay off your debts if you borrow at 25%.

Now you might say my example is pretty silly. Nobody has both debts and investments. But you would be wrong. People do it all the time. Finance professors call it the separate pools of money fallacy. Many people keep some money in their building society account for their holiday or a rainy day, and build up debt on a credit card. The building society pays them a few per cent of taxable income, while they pay their credit card company an extraordinarily high rate. The sensible thing to do is to pay off, or reduce, the debt by selling any investment not paying, in my example, a before-tax return of 42%.

There is another way of looking at Table 3.8. If you really have no other pools of money, to pay off the credit card bill you will have to earn the sum owing. You will pay tax on your earnings. So to use the previous example again, if you borrowed £100 to buy something, and you pay income tax at 40%, you will need to earn £42

Table 3.8   Required Return to Repay Borrowings At
Various Interest Rates and Tax Rates

Marginal Tax Rate	Interest rate		
	15%	25%	35%
	Required investment return:		
20%	19%	31%	44%
25%	20%	33%	47%
40%	25%	42%	58%

of taxable income to pay the credit card company interest. In other words you are buying goods at a premium of 42% over the shop price. If you buy at that price you will not only be in debt, you will end up with fewer goods than you would have had if you had cut back in the first place. People get into debt to have more of what they want—but it always gives them less.

Most people whose expenditure exceeds their income say that they simply can't spend less. That's never true. If they continue to build up debt, the courts will eventually tell them to stop. At that point most people find they can cut back. But it is a painful lesson. Look around, you will always be able to find somebody poorer than yourself who seems to manage. You *can* spend less.

Should we all try to spend less? Well, it depends exactly what is meant by "spend less". What I mean by spending less is that it will often be sensible to spend less now so that you can consume more in the future, when you are old, for example, or spend the money later on your children. It is a good idea to be conscious of what you spend so that you can get better value, and be able to spend any money you save by shopping better, on other things. For example, it may seem worth doing some of the things I suggested at the end of Chapter 2 if it means you can go on holiday to a foreign country. Let's assume you want £1000 to go on holiday. You could get this by earning more, getting it from investments, or by spending less on other goods and saving the difference. Let's imagine you can invest at 7%, but you pay tax. How much money must you have invested to earn your £1000 holiday money? Table 3.9 provides the answer, and also the answers for more modest sums.

If you want £1000 and you can invest at 7%, and you pay tax at 40%, you need a staggering £23 810 invested. For most people, spending less on day-to-day bills would be a more realistic way of raising the money.

Good debt

Some debt is worth taking on. Some employers give interest-free loans, e.g., to buy an annual season ticket. Annual tickets are cheaper per journey than daily or monthly tickets. If your firm gives you a free loan to buy one, take it. During the sales, and sometimes at other times, some expensive items are sold with an option to pay over six months with no interest added. That's a good deal too. And, as I mentioned before, it's OK to borrow for education or to buy a home. These are investments. I know a lot of people have got into difficulties as a result of buying a home, but that's a consequence of borrowing too much, and I discuss that in Chapter 24.

Table 3.9   Capital Required, Earning 7%, To Provide Various
Sums

Marginal	To get this much		
Tax Rate	£100	£500	£1000
	You would need the capital shown below		
20%	£1786	£8929	£17857
40%	£2381	£11905	£23810

THE BOTTOM LINE

The message is simple. Compounding returns has a dramatic effect on the value of savings and investments. The higher the rate of return and the longer the period, the greater will be the growth in your investments. So, save as soon as you can, and remember, no sum is too small to save. I have shown how inflation can erode wealth and how taxes reduce returns. The effect of both can be reduced in some circumstances and for some investors. However, both influence all investment planning. Variable inflation makes fixed money return investments risky. Whenever it is possible to hold an investment that is attractive in its own right in a form that escapes tax, the opportunity should be grasped. Of course bad investments remain bad investments, even if they are tax-free. In general, don't use debt, live within your means, and look for the best value when you spend. For many middle-aged people this will be depressingly similar to what their mother told them. But she was right.

READ 📖 WRITE ✑ RING ☎

♦ Table 5 is adapted from G. G. Watters, *Financial Pursuit*. Toronto: FKI Financial Knowledge, 1988, p. 17.
♦ Table 7 and other inflation data are taken from: H. MacFarlane and P. Mortimer-Lee. "Inflation over 300 Years", *Bank of England Quarterly Bulletin*, May 1994, 156–162.

4

Risk, Return and Your Financial Goals

In investing money the amount of interest you want should depend on whether you want to eat well or sleep well.

                                                                    J. Kenfield Morley

One of the first steps in financial planning is establishing your goals. I can't tell what they should be, because they are your goals and not mine. I can, however, give you a list of some common financial goals which may help you think sensibly about yours.

Some people will want to live it up while they are young on the grounds that they might not live to a ripe old age, and if they do they may hope the State will look after them. Other people will want to postpone current expenditure to ensure that if they live a long time they will not be scrimping in old age and afraid to turn on the heating in winter. Which is right? It depends on *your* values and assessment—not mine or those of a financial adviser. Because most people underestimate the power of saving early and the length of time they may be a pensioner, and overestimate the generosity of the State, this book stresses a prudent, long-term planning approach. But you should follow the course you feel comfortable with.

SOME COMMON FINANCIAL GOALS

Many people have financial goals which require them to:

- Set aside some money for emergencies
- Buy insurance to protect existing assets, e.g., contents and buildings insurance
- Save for an anticipated marriage
- Save for a special holiday
- Save to buy a car
- Buy a home
- Pay off debts
- Buy life insurance
- Buy permanent health insurance
- Pay off the mortgage as fast as possible

- Save for school fees or higher education
- Achieve a comfortable retirement
- Invest for long-term security
- Be in a position to look after elderly parents
- Make a will

Of course, these goals are quite general, although it is easier to see whether you have met some more than others. For example, either you have insured your home contents for the proper amount or you haven't. But what does saving for a holiday mean? A vague good intention is not enough for most of us. To achieve our goals we have to put them in a specific form. Unless we decide we need to save £2000 over two years to go to America, and set out how we plan to do this, most of us will not achieve our goals. So, while I can't say what your goals should be, I can say that you are much more likely to achieve them if you put them in very specific form so that you can monitor whether you are on track or not.

FACTORS AFFECTING INVESTMENT SELECTION

It would be a reasonable response to the above discussion to say, "Who needs a whole series of goals? All I want is to have a pile of money, so just tell me the best investment and I'll put everything into that." Unfortunately there is no such thing as the "best" investment. First, some of the goals are concerned with protection (keeping what you have), rather than investment (growing what you have). Second, all investments offer a different combination of risk and return, are taxed in different ways and have other differences. These all need to be taken into account.

I will concentrate on investment here. When you make an investment decision, you need to take into account:

- Your financial goals
- The expected rate of return from your planned investment
- The expected risk of that investment
- The tax treatment of the investment
- Your investment horizon
- Your attitude to risk

I'll look at each of these, but I'll discuss financial goals last. What follows is important stuff. If you master only two chapters in this book make them this one, and Chapter 21. So, get a beer, Prozac, or whatever, and put your thinking cap on.

Rate of return

One factor you will focus on in your investments is the rate of return. For many investments what you are faced with is an expected rate of return rather than a guaranteed return. If you buy a government fixed-interest stock (or gilt) you know the return when you buy it. You know the return from a fixed-term deposit with a building society when the terms of the deal require you to make a deposit of at least some specified amount for some specified period for a guaranteed yield. But for most investments you don't know the return.

When you deposit money in a bank or building society instant access savings account you assume you will get your deposit back, but the rate of interest you earn will usually fluctuate and can't be predicted exactly. When you put money in the stockmarket there is no way of knowing what the return will be in any year. And in my gilt example, the return is only fixed if you hold the stock to redemption (this is explained in Chapter 19). If you have to sell it at short notice, the return could be quite different. And if you have to break a fixed-term investment with a building society, there will usually be some kind of penalty, so even here the return is only an expected return. Again, who knows what the return from buying a home will be in the next few years?

While it is hard to forecast the return from many investments, you can see what the return has been in the past, and that can serve as a guide to your expected return. It won't be the return every year, but over a period of years it might be close. So let's look at the returns from three of the most important types of investments, gilts, equities (i.e., shares), and cash. (Gilts and equities are discussed in Chapters 11 and 19: if you don't know too much about them, don't worry for now and just focus on the returns.) Most of the data I quote are taken from stockbroker Barclays de Zoete Wedd's annual returns publication (*Equity-Gilt Study 1995*). The returns I discuss are what you would have got if you had bought the entire market, e.g., all the shares quoted. Of course, actual portfolios may have done better or worse, but in this chapter (and again in Chapter 19), I focus on returns from the market as a whole.

You can look at financial returns data in a variety of ways. Two of these are especially important, and I mentioned them in the last chapter, nominal and real. Nominal just takes the numbers as they are, whereas the real return allows for inflation. Sometimes I talk about nominal returns and sometimes about real. Investors normally look at stockmarket indices and annual returns in nominal terms, but real returns are better for decision-making.

Since the end of the First World War up to the end of 1994 (but excluding the Second World War) the real returns from equities, gilts and cash have been as shown in Table 4.1 overleaf. Remember, this is the return over and above the rate of inflation.

Table 4.1 reports the geometric mean for each asset. Geometric means are a way of calculating an average, and are especially useful in calculating financial returns. You can either take my word for this or torture yourself with the explanation in the appendix to this chapter. The important point is that equities have trounced gilts and cash in the return stakes. Over the entire period, equities have earned nearly 8% more than inflation per annum, before taxes. So, does everybody buy equities? On the contrary, the British investor prefers cash investments. When the market research firm *Mintel* asked the person in the street where they would invest £500 for a long period, five years or more, most thought in terms of cash-based products, especially TESSAs and building society accounts. When asked whether shares gave a better return than money put in a building society account, about a third thought they did, a third didn't, and a third didn't know. Yet the evidence is clear—over long periods shares have handsomely outperformed cash and gilts.

In Table 4.2, I present data for the last 12 years. There are two reasons for showing

Table 4.1   Real Returns From Equities, Gilts and Cash
1919–94 (excluding World War Two)

Asset	Real Return Per Annum % (Geometric Mean)
Equities	7.90
Gilts	1.64
Cash	1.85

Source: Barclays de Zoete Wedd, (1995, p. 5)

Table 4.2   Real Returns for Equities, Gilts and Cash
1983–94

Asset	Real Return Per Annum % (Geometric Mean)
Equities	11.70
Conventional Gilts	5.82
Index-linked Gilts	2.11
Cash	5.32

Source: Barclays de Zoete Wedd, (1995, p. 17)

this. The first is to show that returns have been especially high in the last decade or so, and the second is to introduce data on index-linked gilts. (Conventional and index-linked gilts are discussed in Chapter 19.)

If you compare Table 4.2 with Table 4.1, you'll see that returns in the last few years have been very high for equities, conventional gilts and cash compared to the entire period since the First World War. It would not be surprising were returns over the next decade to be lower than over the last. But that doesn't mean returns will be awful. What it does mean is that you should be wary of treating recent returns as an indicator of likely future returns.

With regard to index-linked gilts, these were introduced in 1981, but were restricted to pension funds. In 1982, private investors were allowed to buy them, but there were few available. Table 4.2 shows data for the period for which there has been a more broadly-based market.

The message from the data that I've shown is that equities have provided much the best returns from the major types of investments. When you buy a packaged product, whether it is insurance, personal pension, unit trust, or whatever, it will usually just be some combination of cash, gilts and equities. Different products will have different mixes. So, are equities, or packaged products consisting primarily of equities, the best investment? Not necessarily, for I haven't discussed risk.

Risk

Risk has many aspects. Investment professors have tended to focus on a particular aspect which I will discuss, but I think investors should bear in mind all the dimensions.

One way of looking at risk is to consider the likelihood that the return we expect from an investment is not attained. In other words look at the return from an investment over a period of years—if it jumps around a lot the investment is risky. You can

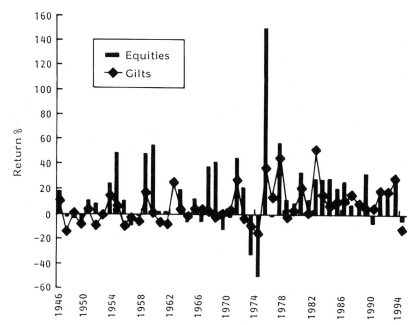

Figure 4.1   Annual Returns From UK Equities and Gilts: 1946–94. Source: Drawn from data in Barclays de Zoete Wedd (1995, p. 54)

never be sure that the return you expect is the return you will get. In Figure 4.1, I show the returns from UK equities and gilts since the Second World War.

As you can see, annual equity returns have been all over the place. The formal way of saying this is that returns have been volatile or highly variable. Statistician-speak is that the data has a high standard deviation. Gilt returns have jumped around a lot too, but nowhere near as much as those of equities. It would seem reasonable to say equities are riskier than gilts and a lot riskier than cash (not shown in the graph) which never has years of negative nominal returns. This seems fair enough. Equities have given investors the best return, but at the cost of investors having to bear substantial risk. In general we would expect risk and return to be related in this way.

Do risky assets always give the best return? Of course not. If they always did, there would be no risk. You hope to be rewarded for bearing risk, but in any given investment period you might really suffer. Remember: no gain without pain. As you can see, the high average return from equities comes from some spectacular returns outweighing some terrible years. In fact, although equities have trounced cash on average (Table 4.1), in 30 of the last 76 years cash has beaten equities.

Not getting the return you expected is a sensible measure of risk, but it is useful to look at what causes return volatility and also at some other aspects of risk. Here are some important sources of risk:

- **Business risk**: this is the risk resulting from the nature of a firm's business. It will be affected by the state of the economy and the firm's sensitivity to changes in the state of the economy, the nature of the industry which it is in (e.g., whether it is regulated, highly competitive, undergoing technological change, etc.), its operational gearing and so on.

- **Financial risk**: this is the risk resulting from a firm's capital structure. For example, if a firm has borrowed lots of money—it would be said to be highly geared or, in America, highly leveraged—it may be very profitable in good times. But it may struggle if interest rates rise, or if trade drops off, and it has to pay large amounts of interest out of smaller revenues.

- **Liquidity risk**: this is the risk that you can't get out of an investment when you want to, or that you can only get out by taking a big cut in the fair market price. It may take you a year or two to sell your home and you may have to slash the price even then: homes are illiquid investments. If you want to sell ICI shares you can always do so at a fair price on the stockmarket. They are very liquid. The shares of a small company, however, may not be liquid.

- **Default risk**: this is the risk that you will not get all of your investment back. This risk will be related both to the soundness of the underlying business or government (e.g., when considering government bonds), and also the security's rank in claims on assets. For example, when a firm goes bust, the creditors will have their claims met before the shareholders.

- **Interest rate risk**: changes in interest rates affect the value of most investments. When rates rise, bond prices fall, as explained in Chapter 19. Equities are also adversely affected by rising interest rates. With cash it's the other way round: high interest rates are good news for investors.

- **Inflation risk**: this is the risk that your investments will not keep up with inflation. As I said before, if you earn a return of 8%, so your £100 grows to £108, that seems like good news. But if inflation is 10%, you will need £110 to buy what £100 used to buy. Your £108 isn't such good news. Inflation risk is a major worry for fixed-interest investors. Their income doesn't go up, even if prices in the shops are soaring.

- **Political risk**: all investments are affected by the government. Tax rates can be changed, some investments can be given special tax treatment, some industries are subject to regulation, and so on.

- **Currency risk**: this applies to all investments that involve foreign currencies. If the exchange rate changes, the value of the investment is affected.

You may feel that with all these risks, you would be better off keeping your money under the mattress. Alas, that wouldn't escape the inflation risk, and anyway I'd just introduce another category of risk—fire and theft. There is no escaping the fact that *all* savers and investors have to bear risks. Fortunately there are various strategies for reducing risks, and I discuss these in Chapter 21.

Taxes

The relationship between risk and return sometimes gets distorted by taxes. What you should be interested in is your after-tax return. Because some investments are favoured by the tax laws (e.g., government and most corporate bonds are, for private investors, exempt from capital gains tax), or some assets held in a special way are favoured (e.g., shares held in a PEP—see Chapter 20—are tax exempt), you will have to factor tax considerations into your financial planning.

Investment horizon

The length of time you plan to invest your money makes a big difference to the way you will want to invest it.

Over the years, the stockmarket has given the best return. Putting your money in a bank has not given nearly as good a return. But think back to my example of saving £2000 to go to America in two years' time. It wouldn't make sense to feed the money into the stockmarket via a savings plan: who knows where the market will be in two years? It could be much higher, but it could turn out that your money is only worth £1500. Much better to be sure, and put your money into some form of high interest account.

On the other hand, if you start saving at age 21 for your retirement, putting money in the stockmarket makes good sense. Nobody will be able to tell you what you will earn, and you will no doubt see a number of huge swings in the market, but over the next 40 to 45 years you have a reasonable chance of coming close to your expected return, i.e., somewhere around the average return of the last 50 years. I say more about this in Chapter 21.

Attitude to risk

We all know that some people love roller coasters, and some hate them. People differ in their attitude to risk. Some people are happy taking risks and some aren't. When the stockmarket slumps, some people just shrug, and say it will come right, others panic and tell their stockbroker to get them out at any price. There is no point in having investments that scare you, even if they provide a good return. Indeed, if they scare you, they won't provide a good return. The nervous investor always sells after the market has fallen, and buys after it has risen. Your attitude to risk should affect your selection of investments.

YOUR FINANCIAL GOALS

It is time to come back to your financial goals. Often it will be true that your goal will be to make a pile of money. But not always. As we saw, there is a trade-off to be made between risk and return. To get a chance of obtaining the best return you may need to take unacceptable risks. Some investments pay a steady income, others have a fluctuating income. Some put the value of your investment at risk, whereas others don't. Some are favoured by the Inland Revenue, others are not. Some investments are more suitable for the short-term, while others are more suited to the long-term. You really can't say your goal is simply to make a pile of money, you do need to carefully think about the variety of financial goals you have.

Factors affecting your goals

Your goals will be affected by your attitude to risk, your age, family circumstances and commitments, your income, and the assets you already have. You may find it helpful if I list some common goals for people who fall into some broad categories. I'm afraid I slip in the word "should" quite often, but it's just my values being expressed. Do what's appropriate for you.

Children will usually be provided for by their parents and will not have an income. Nor are young children able to manage money wisely. Nonetheless, it can be tax-efficient to give money to children (as is discussed in Chapter 30), and it is a good idea to give pocket money at an early age to enable them to experience the problem of making choices with limited funds. It is also good if they have some investments, even if only a few pounds in the National Savings Ordinary Account, so that they learn about the effect of compounding and having money which is saved for the future rather than simply spent.

Young and single adults will usually have low incomes and just be establishing themselves. They should look after what they have (e.g., with contents insurance) and be setting up the financial foundations for their lives. Many will be trying to get as much education as possible. They will be opening cheque accounts and getting credit cards. They should try to establish a good credit record. Many will start saving, although the purpose will vary (e.g., to buy a car, get married, go on holiday). It is tough to save when you have a low income, but young single people should try to save at least 10%. Some people who have received higher education may have some debts. They should be paying these off although, as discussed in Chapter 30, State education loans are a cheap form of debt. Young people should try to get a job that has a pension scheme in which they will be included. Everyone should have a will, even if they have few assets and all they can say is whether they wish to be buried or cremated.

Older singles will have done most of the above, but they should start thinking about the consequences of being unmarried and how they will look after themselves when they get old or if they fall ill. They might try to boost their pension, or perhaps save a bit extra in a PEP. They should be saving nearer 20% of their income. If they got into debt when younger, they should be getting out of it now. They will probably be buying a home. Unless they have a dependant, they should not have life insurance, but they may want permanent health insurance.

Married couples should establish the ground rules before they get married, whether or not they want a pre-nuptial agreement. Will they have joint bank accounts, indeed joint assets in general? They will need to protect their assets, and will probably want their own home. Life insurance may be desirable, especially if there are children. A programme of regular savings—at least 10% of income—will be required, especially if private or higher education for the children is contemplated. As they get older, and the burden of their children eases, they should be looking to invest for their retirement. Not to have wills is inexcusable.

Young widows, widowers, and the divorced have some similarities, but circumstances can vary quite a lot for this group. Some will have children and some won't. If there are dependants, life insurance may be necessary. Divorced people dependent on their former spouse for some support might take out term insurance on the former spouse. Everyone should know what State benefits they are entitled to and make sure they get them. Some divorced people, usually men, may have to make payments to a former spouse. This is not a goal, but they had better plan how they will make the payments. Many in this group may wish to review their accommodation. Perhaps a smaller home is appropriate, and a source of capital to fund goals. Wills should be reviewed.

Older people tend to turn from net savers to net spenders. They will want to get as much as they can from their savings. They should be collecting pensions, and widows should make sure they are getting all they are entitled to from their spouse's pension scheme. Older people should make sure they get all their State benefits. They may switch their investments from those that produce maximum growth to those that offer more income, but they should be careful about this (see Chapter 25). They probably don't need life insurance. If they have private medical insurance they will probably want to keep up the payments if they can. If they have a lot of capital they may wish to pay for their grandchildren's education. They should have plans for a tax efficient disposal of assets. They should make sure their wills are part of their estate planning strategy. Everybody should have thought about a living will, but this is especially important for this group.

WHAT ARE YOUR GOALS?

You may not be familiar with all of the things discussed (e.g., permanent health insurance or living wills). They are briefly described in the Glossary, and discussed at more length later in the book. Even if you know all the things mentioned, you may still not have been able to list your goals. That's normal. Most people need to know much more about the various financial products available before they can sensibly determine their goals. A sensible strategy would be to work through the rest of this book, and then establish your goals. In Chapter 36, I walk you through the entire financial planning process.

APPENDIX: GEOMETRIC MEAN

I use geometric means in many places in this book and here I explain why. Only investment professionals and statistics fans need read this.

Imagine that an index starts at 100, falls after one year to 50, and then rises to 100 after another year. In other words, the market falls by 50% and then rises by 100%. What is the average change? Most people would say that it was $(- 50\% + 100\%) \div 2 = 25\%$. That's what statisticians call an arithmetic average. But if we were looking at a portfolio that had performed as the index had, an investor would be a bit surprised to be told that the average return was 25%. The portfolio is worth 100, exactly what it was at the start of the period. Arithmetic averages are OK for a rough idea of what happened each year on average, but are hopeless as a measure of a portfolio's return. The correct way to calculate a portfolio return is to calculate a geometric mean.

A geometric mean return is that rate of return that would make the initial investment equal the end investment value. It is calculated by multiplying the returns together, subtracting 1, and taking the nth root, where n is the number of returns. The rates of return have to be expressed as 1 plus the return—e.g., 10% is expressed as 1.1. A worked example will make the definition clearer. Taking my earlier figures, the returns of 100% and –50% would be written as 2 (i.e., 1 + 1) and 0.5 (i.e., 1 – 0.5). These returns are multiplied together and 1 is subtracted from them, then the nth root is taken—which in this case would be the square root as there are two returns. So, we have:

$$\sqrt[2]{(2 \times 0.5)} - 1 = 0$$

Most investors would agree that a geometric mean return of zero was a fair description of the example portfolio's return.

In Chapter 21, I discuss geometric means of various periods, for example 3, 5, 10, 15, 20 and 49 years. The arithmetic is tedious, but similar to that shown above. Thus, a 49-year geometric mean rate of return is calculated by taking 49 annual returns, multiplying them together, subtracting 1, and then taking the 49th root.

READ 📖 WRITE 🖃 RING ☎

♦ The BZW study discussed in the text is Barclays De Zoete Wedd, *BZW Equity-Gilt Study 1995*. London: Barclays De Zoete Wedd Securities Limited, 1995.
♦ The Mintel study cited is "Unit Trusts and UCITS", *Mintel: Personal Financial Intelligence*, 2, 1994.

5

Managing Your Cash

In God we trust: all others must pay cash.
American saying

Chapters 3 and 4 provided some important general information. Both gave good reasons why your investment horizons shouldn't stop at some form of cash-based account. But while your horizons shouldn't stop there, you should, of course, have some cash investments. Here and in Chapter 6, I'm going to look at some practical aspects of managing cash.

The first money management decision most people make is to get an account with a bank or a building society to pay their salary (or other source of income) into, and to draw money out of. For most people this will be an account which has cheque writing facilities. This is usually called a current account in a bank, or a cheque book account in a building society. Cheques are, however, going out of style. Many of us get our salary paid into our accounts by electronic transfer, and we spend it mainly by credit or debit cards, standing orders and Direct Debits, cash and the odd cheque. We may get our cash not by queuing in a bank and giving a cashier a cheque, but from an ATM.

So, when I talk about a cheque account, I really mean the work-horse type of account that lets you collect money and spend it. The purpose of the account is not to make you rich, but make your life easier, although if it can make you a little richer as well, that will be good. Given how much use we make of our cheque account, it is surprising how little thought most people put into selecting an account.

The second thing we need to do when sorting our finances is to have a rainy day fund—a fund that will tide us over emergencies, whose value is guaranteed, and which we can get at immediately. For most people this will be some form of savings or deposit account at a bank or building society. Once again, this fund isn't intended to make us rich, it is intended to make us feel secure. But since we are not going to put so many demands on this account, since we won't have money sloshing in and out all the time, we will expect it to pay a higher rate of interest than our cheque account.

I now consider both of these types of account in more detail.

CHEQUE ACCOUNTS

Among the books with unhappy endings are cheque books.
                                                                                    Anon

When selecting a cheque account you need to ask three questions. Is it convenient? Is it cheap? Does it pay a good interest rate? There is no one best account, it all depends on your needs.

Some people like to do all their banking in a local branch where they know the people behind the counter. If that matters to you, you will need to select from the branches that are either near your home or place of work. If you live in a village, you may be very restricted in your choice.

Some people, me for example, never go into a branch. I have everything set up so that my bills are paid by Direct Debit (discussed below), all my sources of income are paid directly to my bank and building society, and all I need do is get cash from a branch. But I never go inside, I always use an ATM. And I always use whatever ATM that I happen to be passing that belongs to my ATM network. (There are three main ATM networks: Mint, Four Banks, and Link. Any member of the network your bank or building society belongs to will accept your ATM card. Mint includes Midland Bank, NatWest Bank and TSB. Four Banks consists of Bank of Scotland, Barclays Bank, Lloyds Bank and Royal Bank of Scotland. Link has 31 members which include Abbey National, Chelsea Building Society, Co-operative Bank, Girobank, Halifax Building Society, Nationwide Building Society, Woolwich Building Society and Yorkshire Bank.)

If you are like me, overall efficiency is more important than a friendly face. Are standing orders paid correctly? Are tax vouchers forwarded when sent with a dividend cheque by the company making the payment? And so on. On this basis, according to *Which?*, you would be well advised to avoid Barclays and NatWest, and consider Alliance and Leicester, First Direct (the postal bank), Nationwide, The Royal Bank of Scotland, Abbey National and Yorkshire Bank. (I've merged a couple of *Which?* reports in producing this list.)

When you assess whether an account is cheap to operate, you have to look at any interest you receive, less any costs you are charged, e.g., for Direct Debits and cheques. If you don't go into the red, you should be able to find an account that does not levy charges and pays you interest.

The position is very different if you get overdrawn. If you get an authorized overdraft you may be charged an arrangement fee (to agree your right to become overdrawn), interest on the overdrawn amount, a fee per quarter or month for being overdrawn, a transaction charge for every transaction during the relevant billing period (which may be the entire quarter even if you were overdrawn for only a day). If you become overdrawn without prior agreement, you may have to pay for a letter telling you that you have attempted to become overdrawn, but the bank has bounced your cheques and is charging you for each one. Alternatively you may be charged for a letter that tells you that you are overdrawn, and all the charges indicated above (except the arrangement fee) now apply, but at a much higher rate.

There is a good case for arguing that you should order your affairs so that you don't get overdrawn. Overdrafts are very expensive and, as I argued in Chapter 3, debt is for dummies. But if you can't resist getting overdrawn, you should be aware that it is the fees, rather than the interest, that really mount up. You should also be aware that some banks don't charge if you go overdrawn by only £100, and some are less nasty than others about unauthorized overdrafts.

While credit cards (see Chapter 6) get a bad press because of high interest rates, they don't charge an arrangement fee. You may find it cheaper to borrow small amounts for short periods on a credit card than pay an arrangement fee and suffer the other charges levied by your bank or building society.

For people who don't get overdrawn, the question is not how much is charged, but how high is the interest rate offered. At the time of writing, interest rates are low. It may not make too much difference which account you have. But a few years ago, interest rates were high, and there were huge differences in the rates of interest various types of accounts offered. If you think rates may one day be high again, you may wish to think about a high interest cheque account. These accounts pay a higher rate of interest if you keep a minimum sum in the account (that means you can never be overdrawn). In some cases there may be a minimum limit to the amount that any cheque may be written for. There are, however, a large number of accounts that have no minimum withdrawal limits, have a modest minimum deposit (say £1000), and offer all the facilities of a normal current account. People who don't go overdrawn should look at these accounts as an alternative to a normal cheque or current account.

You may say that getting details from each bank and building society is just too much trouble. It is. But all the key factors are collected together in the monthly *Moneyfacts* and good guidance on what to look for is given by *Which?* (See READ 📖 WRITE ✎ RING ☎.) There is no excuse for not looking at these two sources for something you will use so often. Students should consider the special student accounts offered by some banks: details are in *Moneyfacts* (but not in every month's issue).

I haven't spelt out what a cheque book is (or cheque guarantee card), as I'm sure anybody who is reading this book already knows. However, I will say something about Direct Debits since so many seemingly knowledgeable people resist them, or use them for only a few bills. With a Direct Debit you can pay your regular bills automatically by having the sum deducted from your account. "Regular" covers anything from monthly payments (e.g., the mortgage repayments), quarterly (e.g., some utility bills), annual (e.g., the TV licence), to the regular but peculiar (e.g., ten monthly payments per year for Council Tax).

With a Direct Debit all you do is complete a form provided by the organization concerned which will register your instructions with your bank or building society, and then claim payments when due. The amount claimed can be changed automatically *by the beneficiary*, but you have to be given 14 days' notice, so you have time to write to your bank to cancel the Direct Debit if you don't agree with the change. The advantages are that you don't have to remember to pay your bills, and you avoid the hassle of posting cheques or standing in queues to pay a cashier. The downside is that if you run your account close to a zero balance and you forget that a Direct Debit will be made, you may become inadvertently overdrawn.

Direct Debits are cheaper for you (no stamps, etc.), and they are also cheaper for the beneficiary. Many organizations will give you a discount for paying by Direct Debit so that you gain a second way. For example, the average family living in

London would save about £30 by paying the telephone, gas and electricity bills by Direct Debit.

Many people dislike the idea that companies can increase the amount they can draw from their account even if notice has to be given. After all, you might be on holiday when the notice is given. This is true enough, but is it really likely that your local utility company will attempt to steal from you? Even if the wrong amount is taken, you will be able to get it back. Much more likely is a human mistake. Your instruction to cancel may not be acted upon (the bank or building society will recompense you), or your bills might not be paid. This may take a little time to sort out, but far less than the amount you have saved by not queuing to pay bills. Under the Direct Debit Scheme, banks and building societies must give a full and immediate refund of any deduction made in error, and make good any consequential loss such as an overdraft fee. And while you will have to talk to them, it is they that have to sort it out, not you.

SAVINGS ACCOUNTS

Get what you can, and keep what you hae: that's the way to get rich.
                                                                     Scottish proverb

There are three reasons for having a savings account. The first reason is the emergency fund that I mentioned above. Most people who write about personal finance recommend that you keep about three months' income in your savings account for this purpose. Of course, this is just a shot in the dark. It seems like a reasonable sum. If, however, there is a good chance you will be made redundant, you may wish to put rather more into this account. Or if you think your car is about to expire. On the other hand, you may be on a year's service contract, or have an extended family that can be relied on to chip in if you have any problems. So, while I suggest you should have three months' income stashed away, if you have good reasons for having more or less, that's fine. But do have good reasons. "I'll never save three months' money" is not a good reason for having only a week's money saved.

The second reason for having a savings account is as a home for investments. Often one finds that people have a lot more than three months' salary saved, and they have few other investments. In that case, the savings account is more than an emergency fund, it is the home of most of the person's savings. There are two reasons for doing this. One is ignorance of the other opportunities for investment. That's a lousy reason. The other is that the person hates risk, and doesn't want to get involved in investments—such as shares—whose value goes up and down. That's a good reason, although I think misguided because, as shown in Chapters 3 and 21, the tax treatment of cash investments is not attractive when there is inflation and, in the past, shares have been much more profitable investments than bank deposits. And there are plenty of other investments too. For example, if you pay tax, I think you will be taking less risk by investing some in a National Savings Index-Linked Certificate than leaving all your money in a savings account. But it's your money, and if your attitudes make you feel more secure in savings accounts, and you have thought about the alternatives, stick with it—it's right for you.

The third reason for having a savings account comes somewhere between the first two. A savings account is one investment among many. It has its own risk and return characteristics. Sometimes the return will be attractive, sometimes everything else will appear so risky that its low risk characteristics will appear attractive. In this approach, sometimes you will only have your emergency stash in your savings account; sometimes you will have a lot more; and sometimes you will just be saving to spend on a known thing at a known time, e.g., your holiday in the US in two years' time.

If you think about these three ways of using a savings account, you will realize that different accounts will appeal to different people. Indeed, you might want a couple of accounts. That's because of the different factors that affect the return you will get.

Usually the return will be higher:

- The lower the quality of the institution you put your money with

- The larger the sum you deposit

- The longer you tie your money up for

- For regular savings

Most people don't think that banks or building societies can go bust. But they can, and do. Remember BCCI? You might have been smart enough to avoid it, but a lot of people didn't, including some professional investors. Some professionals also got caught in Barings, although they were bailed out of that one by a corporate bidder. In general, large building societies have taken over small ones that have got into difficulties, but large banks have not usually helped out small banks. There are deposit protection schemes that will help you, but the help is strictly limited: 90% of the first £20 000 is protected with both a bank and a building society. If you want to be completely safe, stick with big organizations like the High Street banks and be wary of small organizations offering exceptionally high rates. It could mean they are very efficient, or it could mean that they are desperate to get their hands on deposits. That said, you'll soon notice that some of the best rates are offered by small building societies. It's your decision.

That you get a higher rate the larger the sum you deposit doesn't surprise most people. But many people don't pay sufficient attention to their circumstances. Make sure you save with an institution that offers good rates for the sum you have. If it's only £1000, don't save with someone that gives good rates only after you deposit £5000. And some institutions don't pay more after, say, £25 000. If you have £100 000, see if there are better deals elsewhere.

Some savings accounts require that you invest for a certain period. You may not be able to get your money back before the end of the period. Even if you can, it may only be after suffering an expensive penalty such as the loss of three or six months' interest. Is it worth having one of these accounts? It depends on why you are saving. It doesn't make much sense having your emergency fund in an inaccessible account. If it is accessible subject to loss of interest, this only matters if you draw your money. If you are always dipping in, it won't be worth having such an account.

If you are planning to put most of your long-term investments in savings accounts, it may well make sense to tie your money up for long periods, but do keep your emergency money separate. If you do tie your money up for a long time, be aware that what may look good at the time may look silly later if rates rise during your fixed period. You may feel happier tying your money up for no more than six months, say, rather than five years.

Regular savers can often get higher rates, and the sum saved need not be large. For example, in November 1995, the City and Metropolitan Building Society offered a regular savings scheme for sums of at least £10 per month (maximum £500), which paid 5.5%, gave instant access, and placed no limit on the number of withdrawals per annum. Details of all regular savings accounts are in *Moneyfacts*.

Some savers are attracted to offshore savings accounts. Many of the big banks and building societies offer offshore savings accounts in the Isle of Man, Jersey or Guernsey. These are just like the standard savings account except they usually operate as postal accounts. Rates vary, but are not significantly better than the usual High Street or postal savings account. The main advantage is that tax is not deducted from interest. However, you still have to tell the Inland Revenue each year that you have received interest and pay your usual tax rate. The only benefit is that you will be paying your tax slightly later than you would for a UK account. If you are a non-taxpayer because your income is low, you don't need to go offshore to escape tax because you do not need to have tax deducted from a UK account, as I explain in the next section.

You may find that you do not have to distinguish between cheque accounts and savings accounts. For example, at the time of writing (November 1995), the Chelsea Building Society has a postal Classic Account which pays 5% (rising in two steps to 5.75% for sums over £25 000). This offers a cheque book, an ATM card (which can be used in the US, Canada, Japan and various other countries), Direct Debits and standing orders, but requires that a minimum of £2500 be kept in the account. If you write a cheque that takes you below £2500 the cheque will be honoured, but you only get 1% on your balance until you go above £2500 again. It would be possible to operate this as both your cheque account and your emergency fund savings account.

So, to handle your cash well, you have to know what your objectives are (day-to-day living, emergency stash, long-term savings), how you behave (do you get overdrawn?) and you have to know what products are available. The sensible way to do the latter is to use *Moneyfacts*.

Don't pay tax on your savings if you don't have to

Banks and building societies deduct tax at 20% from your interest. If you are not a taxpayer, you can get your interest paid without deduction of tax. (I discuss tax essentials in Chapter 8.) You will need to complete form R85, which your bank or building society should provide. Table 5.1 contains the income limits for getting interest tax-free for various groups of people. You should include your gross (pre-tax) interest when calculating your income.

For children and students the rules are slightly more complex. For children the maximum income limit is £3765 but if the money in the account was a gift from a parent, and the interest is more than £100, the income is taxed as the parent's, and the account cannot be registered to have interest paid without deduction of tax. If the

Table 5.1 Income Limit For Various Groups For Getting Interest From Banks and Building Societies Without Deduction of Tax—Tax Year 1996–97

	Non-Pensioner Adults	Pensioners under 65	Pensioners 65 to 74	Pensioners 75 and over
Single person	£3765	£3765	£4910	£5090
Married man	£5125	£5125	£7595	£7815
Married woman	£3765	£3765	£4910	£5090
Widow or widower	£3765	£3765	£4910	£5090
Single parent	£5125	na	na	na

Note: the married couples allowance can go to either party, or be split equally. In this table the entire amount has been allocated to the man.

Table 5.2 Gross and Net Returns With 20% Tax

Gross %	Net %	Gross %	Net %
1.00	0.8	8.00	6.4
2.00	1.6	9.00	7.2
3.00	2.4	10.00	8.0
4.00	3.2	11.00	8.8
5.00	4.0	12.00	9.6
6.00	4.8	13.00	10.4
7.00	5.6	14.00	11.2

sum invested came from another source, the £100 limit does not apply. For students the maximum income limit is £3765, excluding student grant or loan.

In Table 5.2, I show the gross and net rates of interest after deduction of 20% tax. For example, a bank might claim to pay 7% gross, but unless you complete form R85, you'll be credited with the net rate of 5.6%.

A savings scam

One thing you should watch out for is the bank and building society scam of closed accounts. Banks and building societies like launching new accounts to exploit the latest marketing wheeze. At the same time, some old accounts are closed to new business, but not closed altogether. If you have such an account, you can continue to operate it. But you may get a terrible rate of interest, perhaps less than 1%. You should always check your account from time to time to see what rate of interest you are getting, and see if there is a broadly similar account with a higher rate of interest.

Bad savings

You will often see little old ladies (and others) collecting stamps for a Christmas Club or to pay the television licence. These are bad forms of savings as no interest is paid, and the money saved has to be used for the specific good, or goods, the scheme is set up for. If the savings card is lost, there is no recompense. Try to persuade older people on low incomes to continue to put the money aside each week, but into a building society, or some other account that pays interest.

TESSAS

TESSAs are Tax Exempt Special Savings Accounts which are cash accounts which pay tax-exempt interest. Everybody who keeps some of their investments in the form of cash should look at TESSAs, and this even applies to people who don't pay tax.

You can open a TESSA if you are aged 18 or over. You can only open one account with a bank or building society (you can, however, switch to another provider at any time). You can deposit up to a maximum of £9000 in the TESSA over the five-year life of the account. A maximum of £3000 may be deposited in the first year and up to £1800 in each later year up to a total of £9000 over the five years. For example you might deposit £3000, £1800, £1800, £1800 and £600. But you could also deposit £50 once, and make no further deposits. (The rules are slightly different when you are reinvesting the proceeds of a TESSA that has matured.)

Interest is credited to your TESSA without tax being deducted. You cannot withdraw any capital from your account before the end of the five years without losing tax exemption. You can, however, withdraw some interest—subject to the rules of your account provider. You can withdraw your interest less 20% provision for tax, without losing the tax exempt status. The tax portion does not go to the Inland Revenue but staysin your account. In other words, TESSAs can be used to provide income and still provide a tax shelter.

An example may be helpful. If you deposit £2000 in a TESSA and you earn 7%, after one year you will get credited with £140. After 20% provision for tax, you will be able to withdraw £112, and £28 will remain in your account, attracting interest in subsequent years, and it is yours when the five-year period is up. If you withdraw too much interest, or part of your capital, the TESSA will be closed and you will lose tax exemption. At that point, the account provider will deduct the 20% provision for tax from all interest earned and pay it to the Inland Revenue. If you are a higher rate taxpayer, you will have to pay a further 20% interest to the Revenue. If you don't pay tax because your total income is less than your allowances, you will be able to reclaim the tax deducted.

TESSAs are attractive because they tend to pay good rates for relatively small sums and you get a tax shelter. If you can't stay the five-year course, the worst that happens is you pay the tax you would have had to pay anyway if you had opened a non-TESSA account, unless the provider imposes penalties (discussed below). If you don't pay tax, there is no special tax benefit from a TESSA, but you may get a better rate of interest because banks and building societies are very keen to attract money that may stay for at least five years.

The only snags with a TESSA are those imposed by the providers. TESSAs have been a great hit with the public, and the providers would like to hang on to your money. They would also like to pay the lowest rate possible. As a result, some providers have introduced penalties if you transfer to another provider (e.g., loss of interest or a fee of £25 or £50), some demand notice to withdraw funds, and some offer bonuses which you only get if you stay with them for the full five years. If you are locked in to some extent, it is easy for a once competitive provider to let its rate of interest become less competitive.

All this makes it hard to select the best TESSA. You can't simply look at the best current rate of interest because that provider may not offer such a good rate in a few years' time. Moreover a low rate may be boosted by a bonus, and a high rate reduced by a penalty. My suggestion is that you look in *Moneyfacts* for a high current rate with a provider that either does not charge penalties for transfer, or make low charges. Then make some diary entries to check rates every six months.

What happens at the end of your five-year savings period? You can take your money, or start a new scheme. You can put up to £9000 into the new scheme from one that has matured, providing you do so within six months of the old TESSA maturing. You have to take out the interest you have earned on your first TESSA. If you miss the rollover opportunity, the first-year limit reverts to £3000. If you take the rollover opportunity but don't put in the full £9000, you can deposit up to £1800 in subsequent years until you have reached £9000.

BORROWING

With the exception of borrowing for education or to purchase a home, borrowing does not seem to me to be a good idea (see Chapter 3). But if you disagree, how should you do it?

I have already discussed overdrafts, authorized and unauthorized, and I discuss credit cards in the next chapter. These sorts of borrowing come as a by-product of things that you may already have (a cheque account and a credit card) without you having originally intended to borrow. Three other types of borrowing that you specifically set up are personal loans, revolving credit accounts and hire purchase.

Personal loans are offered by banks and some building societies to both customers and non-customers. Since rates vary, you should choose the cheapest provider, and not automatically go to your existing bank or building society. Personal loans are set for fixed periods, usually between one to five years and there is often an early redemption penalty (typically two months' interest). The APR will vary with the sum borrowed—it is lower for large sums. For sums around £1000 expect to pay about 19% (November 1995) and for sums of £10 000 around 14%. *Moneyfacts* provides a list of product providers and their rates.

Revolving credit accounts are offered by banks. You can borrow up to about 30 times whatever you pay in each month. You will probably pay the same rate as for a personal loan, but the account is more flexible as you don't have to know how much you want to borrow at any specific point, or for how long, or tell the bank what it will be for. If you are in credit, you will get interest, but it will probably not be a very attractive rate.

Hire purchase (HP) is a type of credit you get at the time you make a purchase in a shop. The shop arranges the credit. Since HP is offered without many checks as to your ability to pay, the default rate is high, and the rate of interest reflects that. If you can borrow in another way, you would be wise to do so.

READ 📖 WRITE ✉ RING ☎

♦ For a useful guide to selecting a bank account see "Break Free From Your Bank", *Which?*, November 1995, 42–47. See also: "How Does Your Bank Rate?" *Which?*, October 1995, 34–38.

♦ For details of all the various bank and building society accounts, their charges, rates of interest and conditions, see *Moneyfacts*. Make sure you look at the current month's issue.

6

Paying with Plastic

FRIEND: My wife had her credit card stolen. DAGWOOD: That's terrible. FRIEND:
It's not so terrible—the thief's been spending less than she did.
                                        Dean Young and Jim Raymond (Blondie cartoon)

Credit, charge, gold, store, affinity and debit cards are all means of "paying with plastic".
Charge, gold, store and affinity cards are forms of credit cards, whereas debit cards
are different. For all of these cards your credit record will be checked before you are
issued with one, so not everyone will qualify. Once you have a cheque account, your
next step is likely to be to get a credit card.

CREDIT CARDS

Credit cards are plastic cards which allow you to obtain goods on credit up to a certain limit. You select your goods, pay with plastic, and the credit card issuer subsequently bills you for all the purchases you have made in a month, and you settle your
bill. You can settle in full, or pay a minimum sum, the higher of £5 or 5% of your
bill. The two major credit cards world-wide are Visa and Mastercard (usually issued
as an Access card in the UK, but bearing the Mastercard logo), which are issued by
numerous banks and building societies, whose terms vary.

Providing you are disciplined, credit cards are wonderful. They save you having to
carry large sums of cash around with you, and save trips to the bank. If you make a
large purchase, you are not constrained by the £100 or £50 cheque guarantee card
limit. If you get a card that is issued free, and you pay on time, you pay no charges. In
fact, you effectively earn interest. The reason is simple. Terms vary, but on some
cards you only pay your bill 25 days after the end of your monthly account period.
That means if you make a purchase on day one, you can get 56 days free credit (i.e.,
31 + 25). Of course, you won't always buy on day one, but if you buy on average
half-way through the month you will get 40 days' credit (15 + 25). Since you can keep
your money in a high interest cheque account earning interest until you have to pay
your bill, effectively you are earning interest when you pay by credit card.

Credit cards can be used to obtain cash advances, but the charge is steep and
should be used as a last resort. They can also be used to purchase goods abroad,
which is very useful for travellers.

In my view you should never use a credit card if you cannot pay the bill. The cost
of borrowing by credit card is very high, currently from around 14% per annum, but

usually much more, and it is madness to borrow at such a rate. The argument is set out in Chapter 3. Some people argue that it's OK to have debt on a credit card. It depends on the purpose. Perhaps you are running up debt to buy in the sales or make investments. Well, if you borrow for a month or so and incur costs of 2%, that may be OK, but if the debt is simply being rolled over from month to month, you are losing money hand over fist. But if you must borrow, credit cards can be cheaper than overdrafts in some circumstances (see Chapter 5).

Which is the best card issuer? The answer is that it depends. Different issuers have different fee structures, and you have to do complex sums which juggle the monthly interest rate charged if you don't pay off your bill in full each month, the period from when interest is charged, annual fees, and the length of the interest-free period. However, if you follow my view and never fail to pay your bill in full and on time, matters are simpler. You can ignore the interest rate and just concentrate on getting a card that is issued free and has a long interest-free period. *Moneyfacts* gives all the important information on the various cards. How can you be sure to pay on time? Easy—set up a Direct Debit: if you have the right bank account, this will cost you nothing.

You might prefer to pay an annual fee for a credit card if the fee is low, it gives AIR MILES or some other freebie, and you will spend a lot on your card. For example, some cards give free AIR MILES which you can use to make free flights. To fly from London to Glasgow requires 700 AIR MILES, and you might get one mile per £20 spent. So, if you plan to spend £14000 on your card, you can get a free flight to Glasgow. Free that is, less the annual fees for however many years it takes you to save the points. If it takes you four years of spending, and you pay a £12 annual card fee, you will have paid £48 plus the interest you could have earned on that, i.e., about the cost of a cheap train ticket to Glasgow.

Some people dislike credit cards because they say that their expenditure gets out of control. Some people don't use them because they think they would lose control if they got a card. If your experience has been bad, it's a good idea not to have a card. If you are just scared that you will get into debt, I wonder if you are right to feel this way. Now the last thing I want to do is to encourage you to get into debt, but credit cards are very convenient. If you have a cheque account, and don't overspend with it, why does a card frighten you? You might feel that with a cheque account the reckoning comes so quickly—because the cheque clears in a few days—that you don't get into trouble. Perhaps you should impose some discipline on yourself: pay your credit card bill by Direct Debit, and then you know you don't have the option of spending more than you could by paying by cheque. Your bank account must be able to foot the bill. Still worried? Don't get a card.

Some people who have cards are not worried, but they should be. They are in trouble, but don't know it. Ask yourself these questions. Do you pay only the minimum each month? Do you never make more than partial repayments? Has your balance been growing? Do you sometimes take a cash advance? If you answer yes to these questions, you have the profile of somebody losing control. Cut your card in two, and figure out how to pay off your debts. If your spouse is the spender, face the problem now, whatever arguments this entails, because you'll have to face it some time, and the lower the debt mountain, the better your chance of fixing it without a court intervening.

Affinity cards

Affinity cards are credit cards which bear the name of a charity, political party or some other specific interest group. When you take out the card a donation is made to the charity (usually £5) and a percentage (usually 0.2%–0.25%) of each purchase's value is donated to the charity. Charities and political parties you can support include: Amnesty International, Age Concern, NSPCC, Save The Children, Labour Party, Liberal Democrats, and Great Ormond Street Hospital. If you want to give to one of these or other organizations, do check that the card is reasonably priced. For example, if you have to pay a £12 annual fee, and you spend £3000 on your card in a year and it gives 0.2% to your charity, you would do better getting a free card and giving your charity £12 because you would be no worse off and it would get £12 per annum, versus £6 per annum (£3000 × 0.2% = £6), plus an extra £5 in the first year. If you ignore my advice about debt and borrow on your card, it's even more important that you calculate the cost of having a good value card versus an affinity card.

Store Cards

Store cards are credit cards issued by a particular store, or group. The main case for having such cards is if the store does not accept other credit cards. The two notable chains that don't accept other credit cards are the John Lewis Partnership (which trades under other names as well, e.g., Peter Jones) and Marks and Spencer. Neither store makes an annual charge. Some stores give some benefits to their card holders. Sears gives a discount (£5 voucher per £100 spent) and Jaeger makes free alterations. Unless there is some special reason such as those given, you are carrying an additional piece of plastic for no good reason. The credit charge may well be higher too. You may get a company publication if you have a store card, but do you need more junk mail? Some stores offer preview evenings. Do you really want that, and would you go?

Some people collect store cards because they have hit their credit limit on Visa or Access. That's a lousy reason—it's time to face reality, not get deeper in debt.

Charge cards

American Express and Diners Club are the charge card market leaders. These are credit cards which require you to pay your bill in full each month. They cost about £40 per annum, and are not nearly as widely accepted as are Visa and Mastercard. The amount you can borrow in a month is, however, unlimited. There is no strong case for having a charge card. Once you have had a credit card for a period, you can probably get your credit limit raised to as high as you can comfortably handle. But people who travel abroad frequently may find a charge card useful. American Express, for example, has competent offices in some strange places, and will cash a cheque from your ordinary bank account with no fuss.

Gold cards

You can get gold credit cards and gold charge cards. The annual fees vary from nothing to £250. The only significant advantages are various types of insurance (which you may or may not find useful), you usually get a higher limit, and an automatic £10 000 overdraft at favourable rates, although this does not apply to the lowest cost cards. If you want to borrow that much without answering your bank's questions, and have flexibility as to when you pay the loan off, a gold card may have merit. But unless you draw large sums, the card won't be good value, because the cost of the card will bump up the effective interest rate you are paying. If you are going to draw say, £2000 for six months, and the annual fee is £100, you will be paying the equivalent of about 10% interest in fees, before normal interest is charged. That rate would have to be very low indeed for it not to be better to have a free credit card and a bank loan. If you intend to borrow you should look at the annual cost of the card in conjunction with the interest charges.

DEBIT CARDS

Debit cards are a kind of plastic cheque. The store swipes your card just like a credit card, but the debit is taken straight from your bank account. Debit cards offer some of the convenience of credit cards in as much as you don't need to keep drawing cash, but they don't give you several weeks free credit. Many of the major grocery stores will give you cash out of their till with no interest charge. You buy £30 of groceries, say, and ask the store for, say, £20 cash. Your account will be debited with £50. You save a trip to the ATM, and there is no £50 or £100 limit on purchases as there is with a cheque card. Debit cards don't bear an annual charge, but they cannot be used in most small shops at present, because they don't have the machine for swiping the cards. Some stockbrokers will allow you to pay for shares by quoting your card number over the phone.

Debit cards are useful for people frightened of getting into debt with a credit card. If you are happy with your credit card, and you have an ATM card, you don't really need a debit card. You may, however, get one automatically with your cheque guarantee card in the form of a multi-function card, but you don't have to use the debit card component.

READ 📖 WRITE 🖃 RING ☎

♦ *Moneyfacts* gives a list of the providers of the various cards discussed in this chapter. For a guide to which cards are best for different types of users, see "Winning at Cards", *Which?*, March 1995, 40–46.

7

Insurance as Protection

You don't need to pray to God any more when there are storms in the sky, but you do have to be insured.

Bertolt Brecht

Once you've sorted out your cash and basic savings you will need to think about insurance. Insurance is a large topic and is covered in a number of chapters. Insurance plays two distinct roles. It can be used as protection to maintain what assets you already have and, in conjunction with an investment, to create more assets for you. In this chapter I look at insurance in its protective role. I discuss life insurance in its protective and investment roles in Chapter 23.

It is useful to think of protective insurance in terms of the following three categories:

- Insurance you must have

- Optional insurance you should have

- Optional insurance you can do without

In the first category there is motor insurance, which if you have a car or motorbike, the law demands you have. Some insurance will be a condition of a loan. You will be forced to have buildings insurance if you have a mortgage. There is nothing to discuss about insurance you must have except to say that you should try to get a good deal.

How do you decide whether optional insurance falls into the second or third categories? The rule is simple if you think about why you have protective insurance. Insurance can't prevent you being burgled, for example, but if you have contents insurance you will be protected against the adverse cost consequences. Why do insurance companies offer insurance policies? To make a profit. For the population as a whole, they charge more than enough to cover the cost of bad outcomes and the cost of administration, and so produce a profit. Why do you buy insurance? Because of your attitude to risk. You may well be paying slightly over the odds for your insurance, but an adverse outcome would be so expensive and disruptive to your life, that it is worth paying.

It follows that you should have insurance when the adverse outcome you are seeking protection against would be very inconvenient indeed, were it to occur. Even if you have paid off your mortgage, and so are not forced to have buildings insurance, you will still want it in case your home is burnt down. You will also want contents insurance. Travel insurance if you go abroad also seems sensible, especially if you go to the US where an illness might be very expensive to treat. Mortgage insurance will depend on your circumstances. There are all sorts of other special insurance that may be relevant for a few people. If you are a cinema "sex goddess" it certainly seems worth insuring your legs, butt, or whatever it is that makes you attractive. An accident could lead to loss of your career.

Insuring your legs is exotic, but nowadays you can insure the most mundane products: washing machines, TVs, microwave ovens, contact lenses, etc. Many retailers sell product insurance when you buy the product, and some make a large part of their profits from the insurance. You don't need it. Think how many appliances you have, and for how many years you will have them. With lots of products over many years, you are likely to have pretty much the average run of good and bad luck.

Some products will turn out to be real lemons, while some will run for years and never go wrong. If they do go wrong, you can pay to get them fixed: it won't bankrupt you. It's not something you need protection against. If you worry about not having the money available, find out what the insurance premium is and put that aside in a high interest savings account. You won't have much money at first, but the product will be under warranty then. By the time it's likely to go wrong, you'll have more or less enough money saved for the repairs. Over the years you will be self-insuring, and you'll get to keep the equivalent of the insurance company's administration costs and profits.

Something that isn't usually thought of as insurance is worth considering. If you join a motoring organization, there may be an optional "get you home" scheme. If you have an accident, and your car can't be driven, it will be delivered anywhere you want. You will be taken back home or given the costs of public transport, or free car hire. You could pay for all this, although it is likely to be expensive, but when you have had an accident you may be so shaken that the ability to call the AA, or whoever, who will then do everything, may seem very attractive indeed.

I now consider some specific types of protective insurance.

BUILDINGS, CONTENTS, CAR AND TRAVEL INSURANCE

I could list all the things to look out for in buying these types of insurance. But I'm not going to. It would make this book even longer, and *Which?* magazine regularly reviews these types of insurance, and tells you what to look for and what to avoid. Further, it shows how much various companies charge and notes the best deals. Some of the policies *Which?* recommends are available direct from an insurance company, while others require you to go to an insurance broker.

You may be happy with your existing insurance, but it is worth checking to see whether you are getting a good deal. At one time I had buildings and contents insurance through an insurance broking subsidiary of my employer at a 20% staff discount. I assumed there was no need to shop around. When I left, I read *Which?* and saved 15% on the discounted level!

MEDICAL AND GENERAL PROTECTION INSURANCE

God works the cure and the physician takes the money.
Spanish proverb

Which? covers medical insurances too, but I think it is worth saying something about them here. There are several types of insurance, and most people don't know as much about them as they know about the insurance policies mentioned in the last section, and they will become much more important in the coming years. This is because of the ageing population structure, and the associated State budgetary pressures, which are discussed in Chapter 25.

What you need to consider are:

- Disability or permanent health insurance

- Critical illness insurance

- Private medical insurance

- Long-term care

- Dental insurance

- General protection insurance:

  – Personal accident and sickness insurance

  – Redundancy insurance

Disability or permanent health insurance

Disability or permanent health insurance (PHI) is much neglected. Many financially aware people have never thought about this type of insurance which is an income protection product which replaces part of your salary if it is lost due to disability. PHI provides you with cover when you are unable to work for a longish period, whether from accident or illness.

Most people seem to figure that they will either have the sniffles or be dead. Unfortunately, there is quite a lot in between: you could easily be off work for a year as a result of a car crash or a heart attack, stroke, and so on. You are more likely to be off work for three months or more than you are to die before you are 65. And, people off work for three months or so are typically off work for a few years.

If you are disabled, you will get some financial assistance from the State and from your firm. The amount from your firm will depend on its generosity and, perhaps, your length of service. Some will pay your full salary for a year or more. Most won't. Simply relying on the State will generate an income of about £50 per week, perhaps over £100 if you have a dependent spouse and two children (see Chapter 26). Recent changes in Invalidity Benefit have greatly reduced State aid. Most people will rapidly drain their savings if they try to maintain their normal living standards, and single people will be very exposed. They don't have a spouse to earn some extra income, or care for them. In broad terms, single people should think seriously about permanent health insurance which, unless they have dependants, they should hold instead of life insurance (discussed in Chapter 23). For married people, it is more a case of it all depends on your circumstances.

PHI is paid until age 60 or 65 (when you would stop receiving a salary). You will not be paid your full salary: whatever State and other benefits you get will be topped up to a maximum (in 1995) of about 75% of your salary. This limit is to discourage malingering. But you'll be better off than you think—National Insurance Contributions are not payable on PHI benefits. You can choose when you start to receive benefits, and the amount you will receive. There is a minimum waiting period of four weeks, but you can defer benefits for up to two years. If you are self-employed, you will probably want the waiting period to be short. If you have a generous employer, you should select a longer waiting period. The amount you receive as a percentage of your income has a maximum limit as mentioned above, but you can select a smaller amount. For example, if your spouse could take up employment if you were disabled, you might select a smaller amount. You may wish your benefits to rise in line with inflation.

Your premium will be higher, the shorter the waiting period, the higher the benefit required, and if there is an inflation escalation. Premiums will also vary depending on your job, whether you are self-employed or not, and whether you are a smoker or not. The self-employed and smokers pay more. Premiums vary with age and sex: older people and women pay more.

Some insurers will pay partial disability benefits or proportionate benefits. The first covers people who go back to work part-time, while the second covers people who have to take up a poorly paying profession.

In the 1995 Budget, the Chancellor announced that certain insurance benefits paid in the event of accident, disability, infirmity or unemployment would no longer be taxable. PHI benefits fall into the tax exempt group. However, if you have a group PHI policy which your employer pays for, the benefit belongs to the employer. If it is passed on to you, it is taxed under PAYE as your earned income. Because of the tax change, if you take out your own PHI, a smaller benefit will provide the same after-tax income as before the tax change. As a result, the 75% of income maximum mentioned above is likely to be reduced.

PHI is undoubtedly "a good thing". The snag is the high cost. As I have indicated, the cost varies with a large number of factors. Moreover, there are huge variations in the premiums that different companies charge. But in broad terms, a typical monthly premium for a non-smoking male clerk with a guaranteed premium policy, and a deferred period of 13 weeks, insuring for a level benefit of £20 000 to age 60 might be £25 at age 30, £40 at age 40 and £65 at age 50. Change the profession to self-employed male winebar owner and a 13-week deferred period and the premiums might be £45, £65, £110.

Buying the right policy is not easy: the permutations appear endless. Be careful to determine whether you will be paid if you can't do your "own occupation", or any job for which you are "suited by education or training", or simply any job. If you think you need PHI you should seek advice from an IFA who specialises in it. (I discuss financial advisers in Chapter 10.) You may wish to read something more on this type of insurance to get a better feel for the variations in costs (see READ 📖 WRITE ✉ RING ☎). To be able to afford any PHI, you may have to accept a lower insured benefit, or a longer deferred period than you might want. You may be tempted to start when you are older, when you think you will be more likely to need the insurance. That could be a mistake. Allied Dunbar has found that a quarter of all claims are made by people under 35, and the average age for a claim is 41.

Should everyone have PHI? Not necessarily. If you have sufficient investments, you might prefer to rely on them for an income. If you are approaching an age when you could draw a pension if necessary (50 in many jobs), you may prefer to put money into PEPs or AVCs (see Chapters 20, 27 and 28). If you are a married man and your wife gave up work to raise children, but will be able to return to work soon if necessary, you may prefer PEPs or AVCs—that way the wife covers any near-term income needs and the investments provide for more distant needs.

Critical illness insurance

Critical illness insurance (CII), also known as dread disease insurance, pays out the sum assured (which can be spent on anything you wish) if you are diagnosed as having a specified illness. The six core illnesses are heart attack, cancer, stroke, kidney failure, major organ transplant, and coronary by-pass surgery. The policy may be a stand-alone, or an option on a whole-life or endowment policy. Comparisons between products are difficult, because the conditions covered vary and the definitions of illness require more medical knowledge than most of us possess. For a list of product providers see READ 📖 WRITE ✍ RING ☎.

The basic problem with this sort of insurance is that while most of us may succumb to a critical illness of some sort, we don't know which it will be. It seems silly to be insured against cancer (as defined in the policy) and then go down with Hodgkin's disease which may not be covered. Surely we want to be protected against everything that stops us earning a living. PHI seems a better bet. Proponents of CII point out that PHI only pays if you cannot continue to work, whereas critical illness pays out even if you can continue to work. Any costs you would incur from the illness can then be met from the policy proceeds. While this is true, you still have to be insured against the illness you actually suffer from. Assuming that you can't afford both, my inclination would be to go for PHI rather than CII.

Private medical insurance

When people think of medical insurance they usually think first of private medical insurance. PHI, however, is more important. Private medical insurance (PMI) is somewhat like PHI but covers medical costs instead of providing an income. PMI covers short-term or acute conditions. To get treatment, referral by your GP is necessary. Emergency treatment will usually be provided by the National Health Service (NHS).

Most people want PMI so that they can jump a NHS queue or get a private hospital room. Some people argue that it also allows choice of the specialist or surgeon involved, but as most of us could not make an informed selection, and as it is unclear how knowledgeable our GP is on specialists, this argument may be a rationalization rather than a reason.

If your firm will pay for PMI, your decision is a simple one of deciding whether to accept the offer. You will have to pay tax on "free" PMI premiums if you earn more than £8500, because it is a benefit-in-kind. Still, it will be a good deal because your employer will pay less than you would as an individual member so that even if you are a 40% taxpayer, you will be paying less than 40% of what it would cost you to buy it yourself.

If you have to pay for PMI yourself, the decision is harder. PMI is expensive. For example, BCWA, one of the major suppliers, was making the following charges in 1995. For the highest form of cover, a civil servant in the 18–29 age group, paying annually by Direct Debit, and taking an optional annual excess of £150, would have paid £507. At age 55–64, the cost was £889. With all the same specifications, the cost for a family with the oldest member in the 55–64 age group would have been £2045.

Although PMI is more expensive for older people, basic rate tax relief can be claimed against income tax by anyone 60 years of age or more (or if one of a married couple is that age).

Some firms offer various budget schemes which reduce the cost, but also reduce the cover. Often you will only get private treatment if you are put on a NHS waiting list of more than six weeks. If you want PMI so that you can have a private room, this sort of cover is not very attractive since you may well end up treated on the NHS.

Even if you are insured you may still end up paying a large medical bill. While you may have all your hospital bills met if you go into hospital, what is covered as an out-patient will be limited—e.g., you might be allowed around £500 each year, in total, for consultations with specialists, radiology, pathology, physiotherapy, etc. A consultation with a neurosurgeon and a MRI (magnetic resonance imaging) scan would consume the entire annual benefit and leave you out of pocket. Older people especially, should be aware that budget policies often give little cover for out-patient care.

Of course, if you want private medicine, you don't have to be insured. You can still be treated privately without insurance, but you will have to foot the bill. If you have healthy parents and look after yourself, and if you have some investments, you may prefer this route.

If you decide to look into PMI, there are a lot of points to consider (e.g., cash limits, hospital banding, no-claim discounts, pre-existing conditions, and age-related increases) and you should consult *Which?* for a guide (see READ 📖 WRITE 🖅 RING ☎). In general, according to *Which?*, the market leaders are not the best buy.

Long-term care insurance

Long-term care insurance (LTCI) is a recent development in the UK, but has been available for a long time in other countries. Whereas PHI provides cover to replace income lost due to illness or disability up to retirement age, LTCI provides a regular income to an individual, or officially recognized care provider, when an individual cannot perform various activities of daily living (ADLs) without professional help. Benefits can last for a specific term, till recovery or to death. The benefits are exempt from tax.

The activities of daily living that provide the test as to whether the benefit is due include washing, dressing, eating, using a toilet, and so forth. The definitions vary from company to company providing LTCI policies, and it may be necessary to be unable to carry out two or more of the ADLs before benefit is paid.

Usually people are only unable to carry out ADLs when they are old, and it is probably unnecessary to be insured before age 60, or perhaps even age 70. Premiums rise with age and are more for women than men. A 60-year-old man might pay about £850 a year for cover of £250 per week.

The problems with this insurance include: there are not many providers; some policies have a fixed period of benefit, which is not especially useful or reassuring; there is no tax relief for people aged 60 or over (unlike PMI); and acute illnesses are not covered (these require use of the NHS or PMI).

Alternatives to LTCI include having investments you can draw on and raising money from your home (see Chapter 24). In my view having investments is a sensible strategy. For some types of health insurance, what you are insuring against is something that you don't know if, or when, it will affect you. Obviously, for most things the odds are greater as you get older. But even young people can have periods of disability because of sports accidents or car accidents, as well as illnesses, and investments are not really an alternative to PHI because young people haven't had enough time to build up a sizeable investment sum.

But problems with ADLs are very much an older person's problem, and older people have had the time to build up investments, including tax-sheltered investments such as PEPs and AVCs (see Chapters 20, 27 and 28). If you have a large pension or a substantial holding of equities, you can utilize them for your health bills if you have them, or having fun if you don't. Unless you do need care, LTCI is a waste of money. But beware. Long-term care is very expensive.

If you enter a nursing home today which charges £15 000 per annum, and this increases in cost by 5% per annum, and your investments grow by 10% per annum tax-free, and you will be in the home for five years, then you will need £70 000 of investments today to meet the bills. Of course, if you start saving early, you will not need to save anything like as much as £70 000: our friend compounding will do a lot of the work. (In the USA, where there is more experience of this type of insurance, the average LTCI claim is for three years, and 95% of claims are for five years or less.) Chapter 25 also discusses long-term care.

Dental insurance

With so many dentists refusing to offer NHS treatment, many people are finding their dental charges increasing. As a result, many people will consider joining some form of dental plan. In general this seems a type of insurance you can skip. What is on offer is long-term preventative care. The more expensive cosmetic treatment will be excluded, and your teeth will have to be brought up to a high standard before you can join. Only a few homes burn down, but whether it will be yours, you cannot forecast, and the consequences are terrible. Buildings insurance seems like genuine insurance to most of us. But nearly all of us will need some dental treatment, so what we are buying is more akin to an instalment payment plan rather than insurance. Why pay for administration costs and the provider's profits? Put some money every month into your high interest account to pay the dentist, and put the extra cost of the administration and profit into your investments.

General protection insurance

There are two main types of general protection insurance:

● Personal accident and sickness insurance
● Redundancy insurance

These policies may be sold separately or together. They are usually packaged together when used as protection for mortgage payments.

Personal accident and sickness insurance pays the sum assured if the policy holder is off work due to an accident or sickness. Generally a lump sum will be paid on death or on suffering various forms of permanent disablement. In addition there may be a weekly payment for temporary disablement and a lump sum to cover medical expenses.

Contracts are usually on an annual basis and past medical conditions have to be disclosed. In general this type of policy is less flexible than permanent health insurance.

Redundancy insurance is one of those things you can't get when you need it most. You need it most when there is a recession because your chances of being laid-off are greater, but insurance companies aren't so keen on offering it then. Also, you probably have a better idea than an insurance company as to whether you are likely to be made redundant. To balance the scales, insurance companies will make you wait for a period after you take out a policy before you can claim, or part of your period of redundancy will not be eligible for benefit, or there will be a maximum benefit period. Insurance companies are not very keen on providing insurance to the young (under 18), the old (over 64), the self-employed, seasonal workers, anyone not in continuous employment in the preceding year, or indeed anyone who might make a claim.

Redundancy insurance can be obtained in universal whole-life policies, or through a mortgage lender. When it is through the latter, the benefits are likely to be quite restricted and relate to the mortgage only.

READ 📖 WRITE ▭ RING ☎

♦ For some basic information on PHI, and a list of providers, see: Linda Drake, "Breaking Down Resistance to PHI", *Planned Savings*, May 1995, 35–49, and Robert Budden, "No Turning Back", *Money Management*, November 1995, 43–54.
♦ For a list of critical illness insurers see: Catherine Williams, "Cover for When the Anaesthetic Wears Off", *Planned Savings*, July 1995, 29–44 and Stephanie Spicer, "Hit and Miss", *Money Management*, August 1995, 33–44.
♦ For a guide to selecting a PMI policy see: "Finding the Best Medical Cover", *Which?*, July 1993, 8–13 and Stephanie Spicer, "Survey: PMI", *Money Management*, December 1995, 57–68.
♦ LTCI providers are listed in Hazel Spink, "Funding the Twilight Years", *Planned Savings*, November 1995, 47–53.

8

Tax Essentials

In this world nothing can be said to be certain, except death and taxes.
Benjamin Franklin

Tax is an important factor in financial planning. It affects how much of your salary you keep, the effective cost of investments, and the return you obtain from your investments. The previous chapters have had to make reference to income tax, and tax considerations come up more and more as the book progresses. Some knowledge of tax is necessary to understand this book, and this chapter aims to set out the tax essentials. Taxation is a specialist subject in its own right, however, and you should remember that this book considers only some aspects of tax. This chapter is intended to give you some basic tax information in the context of a general investment book. It is not intended as a practical guide. You should not make tax decisions on the basis of this chapter.

TAXES, TAXES AND YET MORE TAXES

Investors encounter at least six different types of tax:

- Income tax
- Capital gains tax
- Inheritance tax
- Corporation tax
- Stamp duty
- Value added tax

and, not technically a tax, but one in reality:

- National Insurance Contributions (NICs)

I discuss income tax and capital gains tax here, and postpone discussion of inheritance tax to Chapter 34. National Insurance Contributions are both a tax and confer entitlement to certain State benefits such as pensions, unemployment benefit, and maternity pay. The tax issues are discussed here, and the benefits in Chapter 26. Aspects of the other taxes are briefly mentioned at various points in the book.

Whether you are liable to the various UK taxes is affected by complex rules relating to residence and domicile. These matters are outside the scope of this book. I'm going to assume the reader is resident and domiciled in the UK—most people living in the UK will be.

INCOME TAX

The hardest thing in the world to understand is the income tax.
Albert Einstein

Income tax is an annual tax based on the income you receive in a tax year. Tax years run from April 6th to April 5th in the following year. This book uses the tax rules for 6 April 1996 to 5 April 1997, i.e., tax year 1996–97. Income includes salary, earnings from self-employment, benefits-in-kind (such as a company car), interest, dividends and rent. It excludes receipts from the sale of capital. Some types of income are tax-free, and that which is taxable may benefit from allowances and reliefs. Allowances are entitlements to certain amounts of income that are not taxed or are taxed at a reduced rate. Reliefs are outgoings which can be deducted from your income to reduce the amount of taxable income.

Tax-free income

Some types of income are not taxable. The list is long, but some of the more common forms are:

- The income from PEPs (see Chapter 20)

- The income from TESSAs (see Chapter 5)

- The interest from some types of National Savings products (see Chapter 9)

- The first £70 of interest from a National Savings ordinary account (see Chapter 9)

- Proceeds from certain life insurance policies that have been held for ten years or three quarters of their life (see Chapter 23)

- Venture Capital Trust dividends (see Chapter 31)

- Prizes from lotteries and Premium Bonds (see Chapter 31)

- Certain social security benefits which are tax-free (see Chapter 26)

- The first £30 000 of any payment which is not a contractual obligation received by an employee on loss of office

Allowances

The most important allowances, or amounts of income not subject to tax, or subject to tax at reduced rates, are shown in Table 8.1.

Every adult and child is entitled to a ***personal allowance***. Husbands and wives are

Table 8.1   Income Tax Allowances 1996–97

Personal Allowance (under age 65)	£3765
Personal Age Allowance (ages 65–74)	£4910
Personal Age Allowance (age 75 and over)	£5090
Married Couple's Allowance (under age 65)	£1790 *
Married Couple's Age Allowance (ages 65–74)	£3115 *
Married Couple's Age Allowance (age 75 and over)	£3155 *
Income Limit for Age-Related Allowances	£15 200
Additional Personal Allowance (Single Parent Allowance)	£1790 *
Widow's Bereavement Allowance	£1790 *
Blind Person's Allowance	£1250

* Relief is restricted to 15% for 1996-97

taxed separately, so each has a personal allowance. Thus everybody's first £3765 of income escapes tax.

For married couples there is also a ***married couple's allowance***. This allowance is given to the husband, but the wife can unilaterally elect to have half of the allowance, or the couple can jointly elect to give all of it to the wife. If, in any tax year, either spouse has insufficient income to use that part of the married couple's allowance that has been allocated to them, they should inform the Revenue that the unused portion is to be transferred to the other. The married couple's allowance, and certain others shown in Table 8.1, are restricted to 15%. For example, if you qualify for an allowance of £1790, the tax you are assessed for will be reduced by £268.50 (i.e., £1790 × 0.15).

Older people get increased personal allowances and married couple's allowance—these are *age allowances*. The personal allowances are determined by individual ages, but the age of the elder spouse determines the level of the married couple's allowance. The election to allocate married couple's allowance to the wife only applies to the basic £1790, the age-related excess is allocated to the husband unless an election is made to transfer an unused portion.

As you will see in Table 8.1, there is an income limit for age-related allowances. Your increased personal allowance because of age is reduced by £1 for every £2 your income exceeds £15 200, but your personal allowance can't be reduced below £3765. Thus the age allowance for someone 65–74 is of no benefit when income exceeds £17 490 (because the clawback of 50% of £17 490 less £15 200, or £1145, equals the difference in the personal allowance for somebody 65–74 and somebody under 65 (£4910 – £3765 = £1145)). Above £17 490, the standard personal allowance is effectively being obtained.

The married couple's age allowances are also subject to clawback of £1 for every £2 excess of the husband's income over £15 200 which has not already been taken into account to reduce his personal allowance. The married couple's allowance can't be reduced below £1790.

As a result of these rules, and the allowances shown in Table 8.1, age allowance is of no benefit when income is greater than:

Age 65–74	£17 490
Age 75 or over	£17 850

A married couple's allowance is of no benefit when the husband's income exceeds:

Husband under 65, wife 65 to 74	£17 850
Husband under 65, wife 75 or over	£17 930*
Husband 65 to 74, wife under 75	£20 140
Husband 65 to 74, wife 75 or over	£20 220
Husband 75 or over	£20 580

* may be increased if transitional provisions apply

When the age allowance is operative, the effective tax rate is 36%. This is because after income of £15 200, the age allowance is cut by £1 for every £2 of additional income, and income of £15 200 falls in the 24% tax band. If you get an extra £2 of income you will pay 48p of tax. But if you get age allowance, that allowance will be cut by £1, so you'll pay 24p on that £1, or an extra 24p on your existing income. Earning £2 extra will have put up your tax bill by 48p + 24p = 72p, which works out at a tax rate of 36% (i.e., 72p ÷ 200p). This effect is often called the age allowance trap.

If you receive age allowance you should consider carefully whether extra taxable income will push you into the trap. You may be better off with an investment that produces a somewhat lower return but is tax-free and so doesn't subject you to a 36% marginal tax rate. And you have to watch out for investments where all the return comes in one year, boosting your income in that year.

There are a number of other personal allowances. The **additional personal allowance** can be claimed by anyone bringing up a child, or children, on their own. The **widow's bereavement allowance** is due to widows in their year of bereavement and the following year providing they do not remarry in the period. The **blind person's allowance** can be claimed by any registered blind person.

One of the simplest tax-saving strategies is for married people to split their assets so that both have income, and both can benefit from their personal allowances, and lower and basic rates of tax, if they have sufficient income, so that their joint tax bill is reduced.

Reliefs

Some of the main reliefs are shown in Table 8.2. The reliefs on **pension payments** are especially valuable, and depend both on age and the type of pension. Pensions are discussed at length in Chapters 27 and 28, and the details of the relief are discussed there.

Relief is granted on **mortgage interest payments** on a loan of up to a maximum of £30 000 for a principal private residence. Relief is restricted to 15%. This is a marked reduction in the relief that has been available in the past. It seems only a matter of

Table 8.2   Income Tax Reliefs 1996–97

Pension reliefs	Varies
Mortgage interest relief (ceiling)*	£30 000
Enterprise Investment Scheme**	£100 000
Venture Capital Trust**	£100 000
Payroll giving scheme	£1200
Gift Aid (minimum donation)	£250

* Relief restricted to 15%; ** relief restricted to 20%

time before mortgage interest relief will be eliminated. Most loans are now covered by MIRAS—Mortgage Interest Relief At Source. This means you simply pay the net interest to your lender on the first £30 000 of your loan, irrespective of your tax rate. Thus, if you had a loan of £50 000 and interest came to £4250, you would get tax relief deducted as follows:

$$\frac{30\,000}{50\,000} \times £4250 \times 0.15 = £382.50$$

Details of the *Enterprise Investment Scheme* and *Venture Capital Trust* are given in Chapter 31. The final two reliefs listed in Table 8.2 relate to payments made to charities.

Benefits-in-kind

I have listed some of the main allowances, reliefs and tax-free types of income. These reduce the tax you pay. Benefits-in-kind can increase your tax bill. Benefits-in-kind are non-monetary benefits you receive that nonetheless have a financial value. Common benefits are season ticket loans, private medical insurance (e.g., BUPA), mortgage subsidies, company cars and car fuel. In some cases the value is easily calculated (although the treatment of those earning over £8500 is different from for those earning £8500 or less), in other cases it is more complex. I'll briefly discuss the position of the British obsession, the company car.

The taxable benefit on a company car is 35% of its price, but where business mileage is 2500 miles or more per annum, the benefit is reduced by one third. Where the business mileage is 18 000 miles or more, the benefit is reduced by two thirds. The benefit is reduced by one third if the car is over four years old. If car fuel for private use is paid for by the employer, benefit is assessed on the basis of the car's engine capacity and type of fuel, as shown in Table 8.3.

Not all benefits-in-kind are taxable. Benefits paid for by your employer that are tax-free include:

- Pension contributions into an approved scheme
- Life and sick-pay insurance premiums
- Canteen meals, if available to all staff
- The first 15p a day of luncheon vouchers
- Car parking at work

Table 8.3   Car Fuel 1996–97

Petrol	
1400 cc or less	£710
1401 cc to 2,000 cc	£890
2001 cc or more	£1320
Diesel	
2000 cc or less	£640
2001 cc or more	£820

Table 8.4   Income Tax Rates 1996–97

Rates	%	Applicable to taxable income :
Lower	20	Up to £3900
Basic	24	Next £21 600
Higher	40	Above £25 500

Income tax rates

Once your taxable income is computed, it is taxed on the basis of the rates shown in Table 8.4. (The rates payable by trusts are discussed in Chapter 35.)

Imagine a single man, Mr Bachelor, who earns £35 000 and who has a very uncomplicated life. His only allowance is his personal allowance, he has no reliefs, and no benefits-in-kind. His tax bill will be:

Slice of income	Tax rate	Tax	Notes
£3765	nil	0	personal allowance
£3900	20%	£780	lower rate band
£21 600	24%	£5184	basic rate band
£5735	40%	£2294	balance at higher rate
£35 000		£8258	

The November 1995 Budget made matters slightly more complicated by taxing savings income at the lower rate. The lower rate of tax on savings applies to income such as:

• Interest from banks and building societies

• Interest distributions from authorized unit trusts

• Interest from gilts and corporate bonds

• Dividends from companies

Banks, building societies, companies, etc. paying interest and other forms of saving income under deduction of tax deduct at 20%, and savers not liable to income tax can reclaim the tax paid. For individuals whose income falls within the lower or basic rate tax bands, the tax deducted will match their liability to tax and no further tax on the savings will be due. For higher rate taxpayers, a further 20% (i.e., 40% − 20% = 20%) will be due.

Savings income will normally be treated as the top slice of income. An individual with non-savings income will have the full amount of the lower rate band of 20% to set against the other income. For example, an individual with taxable income (after allowances and reliefs) of £5000, of which £4500 is earned income, and £500 is savings income, will be taxed as follows:

Slice of taxable income	Tax rate	Tax	Notes
£3900	20%	£780	lower rate
£600	24%	£144	basic rate
£500	20%	£100	lower rate on savings
£5000		£1024	

Now consider a 40% taxpayer. The tax liability of an individual with taxable income (after allowances and reliefs) of £27 000, of which £22 000 is earned income and £5000 is savings income will be:

Slice of taxable income	Tax rate	Tax	Notes
£3900	20%	£780	lower rate
£18 100	24%	£4344	basic rate on non-savings income
£3500	20%	£700	20% tax on savings income that falls below basic rate limit of £25 500
£1500	40%	£600	higher rate on remaining savings income
£27 000		£6424	

NATIONAL INSURANCE CONTRIBUTIONS

National Insurance Contributions (NICs) are not technically taxes, but are used to raise revenue just like any tax. NICs are not relevant to most investment decisions, but it is important that you allow for NICs when you calculate how much of your income you keep. Your contribution record is also important as it affects your entitlement to some State benefits. The reason NICs don't affect most investment decisions is that they are not deductions from income for income tax purposes, and pension contributions do not reduce income for the purposes of calculating NICs. It is also worth noting that NICs are not levied on unearned income (i.e., investment income) or on income from a pension scheme, or on permanent health insurance benefits.

There are four main classes of NIC:

- Class 1 paid by employees and their employers

- Class 2 paid by the self-employed

- Class 3 voluntary contributions

- Class 4 paid in addition to Class 2 contributions by self-employed people whose income or profit is above a certain sum.

The rates are shown in Table 8.5.

Class 1 NICs are paid by employees and their employers. If the employee earns less than the lower earnings limit (£61 per week), no contribution is payable. Once the lower earnings limit is exceeded, employees pay 2% on earnings below the limit and 10% on earnings above it, but below the upper earnings limit of £455. Once an employee earns more than £455, no additional employee NIC is charged (although additional employer NIC is charged). A Labour government might remove the upper earnings limit. This would be a way of taxing the better-off without raising taxes!

Both employees and employers pay reduced NICs on earnings between the upper and lower bands if the employer's pension scheme has contracted out of the State scheme. Contracting out is discussed in Chapter 27. Basically contracting out means that the employer's scheme offers you at least as much pension as you would get from

Table 8.5   National Insurance Contributions 1996–97

Class 1 (employed earners)	
Lower earnings limit (per week)	£61
Upper earnings limit (per week—employees only)	£455
Employee: Initial	2%
Standard	10%
Employer: (note 1)	10.2%
Class 2 (self-employed)	
Per week	£6.05
Small earnings exception (year)	£3430
Class 4 (self-employed)	
Rate	6%
Lower profits limit (per year)	£6860
Upper profits limit (per year)	£23 660
Class 3 (voluntary): per week	£5.95

1. Reduced rates of employer's contributions on total earnings apply if weekly earnings are below £210.
2. If contracted-out (see Chapter 27), the rate on earnings between lower and upper earnings limits is reduced by 1.8% for employees and 3% for employers.

the earnings-related part of the State pension scheme and so has opted out of the State scheme. Instead of paying 10% on earnings between the bands, employees in contracted-out schemes pay 8.2%.

For the self-employed, Class 2 and Class 4 rates apply. With Class 2 NICs there is a flat rate of £6.05 per week and an "exception", i.e., exemption, for low earners (below £3430 per annum). In addition, Class 4 rates apply a 6% charge on any portion of earnings between the lower (£6860) and upper (£23 660) limits.

Class 3 contributions are a fixed sum (£5.95 per week) and are a voluntary contribution made by anyone who wishes to establish a contributions record to be eligible for State benefits, especially the full State Basic Pension.

CAPITAL GAINS TAX

Capital gains tax (CGT) is an annual tax on capital gains made by individuals and trusts. You will make a capital gain or loss whenever you dispose of an asset at a price different from that at which you obtained it. Assets can be acquired and disposed of by buying and selling, but also by receiving or giving a gift, by exchange, acquiring or granting a right, and so forth.

In broad terms, anything you own is an asset, including your clothes, home, shares and other investments. However, some assets are specifically exempted from CGT. These include:

• Chattels with a life of less than 50 years

• Your only or principal residence

• Private cars

- Various National Savings products (see Chapter 9)

- Betting winnings

- Gilts (i.e., British Government stocks, see Chapter 19)

- Certain corporate bonds (see Chapter 19)

- Investments held in PEPs (see Chapter 20)

- Investments in Business Expansion schemes made after 18 March 1986 (these schemes are no longer available for purchase)

- Shares in the Enterprise Investment Scheme (see Chapter 31)

- Shares in qualifying Venture Capital Trusts (see Chapter 31)

- Life insurance policies in the hands of the original owner or beneficiaries

You won't be charged CGT on any gains on the above assets: in return, you can't use any losses on these assets to offset gains made on another asset.

To work out your capital gains, you take the value of the item you have sold (or otherwise disposed of) less any selling costs and deduct its initial cost, including any acquisition costs. The cost can be increased by indexation and any gain reduced as a result. You cannot, however, turn a gain into a loss by indexation. Indexation allowance notionally increases the cost of an asset by any rise in the Retail Prices Index (RPI) that has occurred between acquisition (or 31 March 1982 if that is later) and disposal. The intention is for you to avoid paying tax on gains which are purely a result of inflation, and which do not represent a real increase in value.

A simple example may be helpful. If you bought an asset for £1000 and sold it for £1200, and the RPI had increased by 15% during that period, your indexed cost would be £1150 (£1000 × 1.15), and your gain after indexation would be £50 (£1200 − £1150). The gain after indexation is the chargeable gain, the amount relevant for CGT. If you buy shares, then add to them, then sell some, etc. there are strict rules about how you pool your shares and attribute costs to the shares sold.

To calculate your net chargeable gains, you add all your chargeable gains in the tax year and deduct all allowable losses. If you have made an overall loss, this can be carried forward indefinitely. If you have made a profit, CGT may be payable. As shown in Table 8.6, the first £6300 of net chargeable gains is free of tax for individuals, and the first £3150 for most trusts. If your gains exceed £6300 (or £3150), any losses carried forward from earlier years may be deducted from the gain. If a gain still remains, it is added to your taxable income and taxed as if it were income, but the tax is called CGT. However, any chargeable gain can be deferred if the gain is reinvested in qualifying shares. This is discussed in Chapter 31.

If an individual has no income and therefore pays no income tax, CGT will be charged at 20% (and up through the bands if applicable). Unused personal allowances cannot be used to offset CGT.

"Retirement relief" is available when you are 50 or over, or have to retire as a result of ill-health, and are disposing of all or part of a business you have owned for at least a year, or shares in a business you owned for at least a year, in which you worked full-time and held at least 5% of the voting rights. To get the maximum

Table 8.6   Capital Gains Tax 1996–7

Gains	Rate %
Individuals	
First £6300	Nil
Thereafter	taxed as top slice of income
Trusts	
First £3150	Nil
Thereafter	taxed as top slice of income*
Retirement Relief	
Exempt gain	£250 000**
50% exempt on next	£750 000**
Re-investment Relief	***

* Non-discretionary trusts pay CGT at 24%, discretionary and accumulation trusts at 34%. Where the settlor of a trust retains an interest in the trust, the rate is that applicable to the individual (see Chapter 35).

** Minimum qualifying age: 50

*** Any chargeable gain made by an individual, or most trustees, can be deferred if the gains are re-invested in qualifying shares (see Chapter 31).

relief, you have to have owned the shares or business for 10 years. Anybody who might be eligible for such relief should seek expert advice.

CGT planning

There are three points about CGT that are worth noting for tax planning purposes. First, gifts between husbands and wives are not liable to CGT. The asset is acquired by the other party at the initial value, and all indexation allowances are also acquired. Second, CGT is not payable on death, although inheritance tax is. To pay the least amount of both these taxes may require some careful juggling of assets—this is discussed in Chapter 34. Third, it is often worth while to "bed and breakfast", which I explain below.

If you have a share, investment trust (see Chapter 12), unit trust (see Chapter 13) or other asset that has performed very well, you may have a significant capital gain. I'll imagine that you have just one general investment trust and that it has risen from £6000 to £12 000 in value in one year and there has been no inflation. You might wish to continue to hold that share so you don't intend to crystallise the capital gain by a sale—you only pay CGT on realised capital gains.

Say the share again does well in the following year and rises to £17 000 and you decide to sell. Because I've assumed away inflation, there are no indexation calculations to be made, so the capital gain is £11 000 (£17 000 –£6000). With the current annual exemption of £6300, you will have to pay CGT on £4700 (£11 000 – £6300). Had you sold the share in the first year after you had made £6000 profit, and bought it back the next day, you would have made a disposal for CGT purposes, and your £6000 gain would have been covered by your annual exemption. You would have established a new purchase cost of £12 000. If you sold in the following year when the share reached a value of £17 000 you would have a further gain of £5000 which would again be covered by your annual exemption.

By selling your share one day and buying it back the next, a process known as bed and breakfasting, you will have escaped CGT. If you tell a stockbroker you want to bed and breakfast, he or she will sell your share and automatically buy it back for you and probably charge only one commission. On the purchase you will have to pay stamp duty (0.5% of the value of the shares) and suffer the spread between the buying and selling price, but all this will come to a few per cent instead of anything up to 40% CGT. You will also be exposed to the risk that share prices might change overnight, but of course this could work either in your favour or against you. Judicious bed and breakfasting will keep many portfolios of shares out of the CGT net.

TAX-FREE OR TAXABLE?

Many people get in a mess over the tax status of their investments. You need to be careful with the following four descriptions: tax-free income, income paid without deduction of tax, income paid after the deduction of tax, and tax-free in the hands of the investor.

Tax-free income includes that earned on TESSAs (if you follow the rules), PEP income, and the first £70 of interest in a National Savings Bank Ordinary Account. Nobody pays tax on tax-free income.

Income paid without deduction of tax. This doesn't mean you don't have to pay tax—whether you do will depend on which tax band you fall in. If you don't pay tax (and the new income doesn't lift you into the tax bands), such income will be tax-free to you. But if you do pay tax, you must tell the Inland Revenue, which will claim the appropriate amount of tax. Gilts purchased through the Post Office, National Savings Bank Investment Accounts and some offshore accounts are examples of accounts which pay income without deduction of tax, but you must declare the income.

Income paid after the deduction of tax. You may receive income that has had lower rate tax deducted. However, you may have to pay more tax if you are a higher rate taxpayer. If you don't pay tax you may be able to claim back the tax deducted. For example, dividends from UK shares are paid net, having suffered tax at 20%: higher taxpayers will have to pay another 20%, whereas a non-taxpayer will be able to reclaim the 20%. Non-taxpayers can't always reclaim tax deducted, e.g., from Guaranteed Income and Growth Bonds. If some tax is deducted from income, make sure you know whether you might have to pay more, or whether you might be able to reclaim the tax.

Tax-free in the hands of the investor, or some such phrase, is often used to describe the proceeds of some insurance policies. It's true you don't pay tax on the policy proceeds (providing you meet certain conditions), but the insurance company will have been charged income and capital gains tax on the investments. So it's tax-free in your hands, but it has suffered tax.

Make sure you know your tax position for any investment—always read the product literature's small print.

READ 📖 WRITE ✉ RING ☎

♦ This chapter is intended to give you some basic tax information in the context of a general investment book. For practical guidance see: Arnold Homer and Rita Burrows, *Tolley's Tax Guide*. Tolley: Croydon. Look for the most recent edition.

9

National Savings Investments

Saving is a very fine thing. Especially when your parents have done it for you.
Sir Winston Churchill

National Savings (NS) is a product supplier rather than a particular type of investment. NS offers savings accounts, fixed interest products, an index-linked product, and a special type of lottery—Premium Bonds. These products could appear in other chapters where these types of products are covered. On the other hand, while NS is only one among many financial product providers, it is a unique provider:

- NS products are backed by the Treasury and so won't default.

- NS products are available by post, and many from a Post Office. You can get all the forms for any NS product from a Post Office.

- Many products are tax-free and offer very attractive rates for higher rate taxpayers.

- Income is paid without deduction of tax (except for FIRST Option Bonds) and non-taxpayers therefore don't have to reclaim tax that has been deducted.

What I've opted to do is describe most NS products here (gilts appear in Chapter 19 and Premium Bonds in Chapter 31), mainly because they provide an easy transition from straightforward bank and building society savings products to slightly more complex investments, and also because they are so often overlooked by "serious" investors. I hope a complete chapter on NS products will stop you falling into that trap.

In the descriptions that follow, some products carry a number or letter, e.g., 43rd issue. The reason is this. When rates of interest in general change, it is easy to change some NS products' rates. But some products have five-year guarantees. These products are offering either too generous a return, or too miserly a return. NS withdraws these products from sale and reissues them with new terms. Investors holding existing products still get what they were guaranteed. That means that at any time there may be several versions of the same product in existence, all paying different rates of interest. To identify the different terms, the various issues are labelled by a letter or number.

Although NS products are low risk and pay interest (except Premium Bonds), you should be aware that you generally do not get an income from them. With Income Bonds and Pensioner Bonds you do. With Ordinary Accounts and Investment

Accounts you can create income by withdrawing interest once it has been credited to your account. With FIRST Option Bonds you can apply for a part repayment equal to the amount of interest earned. Other products tie you for a number of years, and all the return comes at the end. You can get early repayment to generate income, but this will mean you will get a poor return.

With some planning, you can create an income. You may feel that some of the products that pay out after five years offer a good return. If you are the sort of person who likes the security of NS, and you don't need income now, but will later, you could use the following strategy. Buy a product every year, or maybe every six months. After five years your first purchase matures. You take the gain, or part of it, as income and reinvest the rest. By doing this every year, you are able to generate a continual stream of income, starting in five years' time.

MATCHING PRODUCTS AND OBJECTIVES

I describe most of the products in the next section. Inevitably, my descriptions concentrate on key features and miss out some relevant details. You should read the NS leaflets on each product before investing. You can get them from most Post Offices, or you can contact NS (see READ 📖 WRITE ✑ RING ☎). Since the product descriptions make tedious reading, I show below a few categories of investors and the products that might interest them—I've followed National Savings own literature here—so that you don't have to read the entire chapter. Although the products listed are the most suitable amongst the NS range, there may be better products offered by other suppliers.

Products especially suitable for taxpayers include the tax-free products and the one tax-paid product:

- Fixed Interest Savings Certificates
- Index-linked Savings Certificates
- Children's Bonus Bonds
- Premium Bonds
- FIRST Option Bond

Products especially suitable for non-taxpayers are:

- Children's Bonus Bonds
- Capital Bonds
- Pensioners Guaranteed Income Bonds
- Income Bonds
- Investment Account
- Ordinary Account
- Gilts

Products especially suitable for children are:

- Children's Bonus Bonds
- Capital Bonds
- Investment Account
- Ordinary Account

Products for investors looking for a monthly income are:

- Pensioners Guaranteed Income Bonds
- Income Bonds

Products offering guaranteed fixed money returns are:

- Fixed Interest Savings Certificates
- Children's Bonus Bonds
- FIRST Option Bond
- Capital Bonds

A product offering guaranteed fixed real (inflation-proofed) returns is:

- Index-linked Savings Certificates

PRODUCT DETAILS

This section discusses each of the NS products. Table 9.1 overleaf gives a summary of product features but should be read in conjunction with the appropriate text.

Some products listed have a five-year life. You can hold them for longer than five years, but the terms change. Often you will get paid what is known as the General Extension Rate, currently 3.51%. I point this out where appropriate in the following sections.

43rd Issue Fixed Interest Savings Certificates

These certificates offer a guaranteed fixed rate of interest for five years. The rate increases year by year, so to get the best rate you need to hold them for the full five years. The rate in the first year is 3.75%, and this rises year by year as follows—4.15%, 5.0%, 6.15% and 7.75%. This works out at a compound 5.35% p.a. over the five years. The return is free of income and capital gains tax.

The minimum for each purchase is £100, and the maximum holding is £10 000 (but other issues of these certificates can be held—i.e., if you already hold the 42nd issue, you can still hold £10 000 of the 43rd). You can reinvest up to a further £20 000 from the proceeds of matured Savings Certificates into 43rd Issue Reinvestment Certificates. If you cash the certificates in the first year, you get no interest (unless it is a Reinvestment Certificate), you get the first year interest after one year and thereafter you get interest for each complete period of three months.

Table 9.1   National Savings Products

Account	Term	Gross %	20%	40%	Min £	Max £
43rd Issue Certificates	5 years	5.35	5.35	5.35	100	10 000
9th Issue Index-Linked	5 years	2.5 +RPI	2.5 + RPI	2.5 + RPI	100	10 000
Capital Bond Series J	5 years	6.65	5.32	3.99	100	250 000
Pensioners Bond Series 3	5 years	7.00	5.60	4.20	500	50 000
First Option Bond	1 year +	6.25	5.00	3.75	1000	19 999
First Option Bond	1 year +	6.50	5.20	3.90	20 000	250 000
Income Bond	3 months	6.25	5.00	3.75	2000	24 999
Income Bond	3 months	6.50	5.20	3.90	25 000	250 000
Ordinary Account	none	1.75	*	*	10	10 000
Ordinary Account	none	2.75	*	*	500	100 000
Investment Account	1 month	5.00	4.00	3.00	20	499
Investment Account	1 month	5.50	4.40	3.30	500	24 999
Investment Account	1 month	5.75	4.60	3.45	25 000	100 000
Children's Bonus Bond H	5 years	6.75	6.75	6.75	25	1000
General Extension Rate		3.51	3.51	3.51		

* First £70 of interest per annum tax-free (£140 joint account).

After five years you can cash the certificates or continue to hold them. If you do the latter, it will be on terms which NS will tell you. If you currently hold old certificates that have matured, you should cash them or reinvest them. Issues 1st to 6th pay interest at between 1.1% and 1.8%. Issues 7th to 34th pay the General Extension Rate of 3.51%. If you want to invest for a five-year period, the 43rd Issue gives a better return. If you want to invest for a shorter period you can get a better rate almost anywhere than that from Issues 1st to 6th. For issues 7 to 34, a rate of 3.51% is not enormous, but it is tax-free. However, if you don't pay tax, you should be able to do better elsewhere, but if you are a higher rate taxpayer, you will need to search to do better: 3.51% grossed up at 40% is 5.85%.

9th Issue Index-Linked Savings Certificates

These certificates offer a guaranteed real return for five years. That is to say, your capital will rise by whatever is enough to fully offset any rise in consumer prices (the meaning of "index-linked"), and then give an additional return on top. The rate increases year by year, so to get the best rate you need to hold them for the full five years. The rate in the first year is 1.0%, i.e., you will get whatever the rate of inflation is, plus 1.0%. This rate rises year by year as follows—1.25%, 2.0%, 3.0% and 5.31%. This works out at a compound 2.5% p.a. over the five years. The return is free of income and capital gains tax.

The minimum for each purchase is £100, and the maximum holding is £10 000 (but other issues of these certificates can be held—e.g., if you already hold the 8th issue, you can still hold £10 000 of the 9th). You can reinvest up to a further £20 000 from matured Savings Certificates and Yearly Plan Certificates into 9th Issue Index-Linked Reinvestment Certificates. If you cash the certificates in the first year, you get only your purchase price (unless it is a Reinvestment Certificate), you get the first year's interest and indexing after one year, and thereafter you get interest of 1.0% and indexing for each complete month.

After five years you can cash the certificates or continue to hold them. If you do the latter, it will be on terms which NS will tell you. If you hold old certificates that have matured, your strategy will depend on which issue you hold. The 2nd issue gives only indexing and no interest. Other issue mature certificates are only paying 0.5% plus indexing. If you want to invest for a five-year period, the 9th Issue gives a better return. If you want to invest for a shorter period you have to guess what inflation will be. If you think it will be, say, 3% you will get 3% p.a. on 2nd Issue and 3.5% on other mature issues. This will be tax-free. The same comments that were made at the end of the section on the previous product apply. If you expect inflation to be 4% or more, higher rate taxpayers may be better off staying put.

Series J Capital Bonds

These bonds offer a guaranteed fixed rate of interest for five years. The rate increases year by year, so to get the best rate you need to hold them for the full five years. The rate in the first year is 4.6%, and this rises year by year as follows—5.2%, 6.1%, 7.73% and 9.7%. This works out at a compound 6.65% p.a. over the five years. The return is taxable, but is paid without deduction of tax.

Capital Bonds are similar to Fixed Interest Savings Certificates except for the tax treatment and rate of interest. Taxpayers will get a better deal with the Savings Certificates, and non-taxpayers will get a better deal with Capital Bonds.

The minimum for each purchase is £100, and the maximum total holding in all Series of Capital Bonds (excluding any holding of Series A) is £250000. If you cash the bonds in the first year, you get no interest, after one year you will get the value at the last anniversary of purchase plus interest to the date of repayment, paid at the rate applicable for the previous year. After five years, NS will tell you if any reinvestment or extension terms are available.

Series 3 Pensioners Guaranteed Bonds

Pensioners Bonds are for people aged 60 and over and offer a guaranteed fixed rate of interest of 7.0% p.a. for each of the next five years. Unlike many NS products, the interest is paid out as a monthly income. It is paid directly into your bank, building society or a NS Investment Account on the 19th of each month. The interest is taxable, but it is paid without deduction of tax. The minimum for each purchase is £500. The maximum holding in Series 3 Bonds is £50000 (or £100000 for a joint holding). This is in addition to any holdings of Series 1 and Series 2 Bonds.

You can cash the bonds in early by giving 60 days' notice. You do not get interest during the period of notice. At the end of the five-year period, NS will tell you the guaranteed rate for the next five years.

FIRST option bonds

This is a rather grand name for what is really just a one-year fixed rate of interest product. You have to invest at least £1000, and the maximum holding is £250000. You get interest of 6.25%, or 6.5% if you hold a bond of £20000 or more. (If you hold two bonds of £10000 each, they don't qualify for the higher rate.) Interest is taxable and, unusually for a NS product, basic rate tax is deducted at source—so you actually get 5% or 5.2 % tax-paid. Higher rate taxpayers will have to pay the Inland Revenue a further 20% tax, and non-taxpayers can claim a refund.

Why is this called an option bond? Because you can opt to leave your money for another year! The only benefit of this option is that it reduces the draconian early repayment conditions. If you cash your bond in before the first anniversary you get no interest. If you leave the bond (instead of cashing it in and getting a new one) and then cash it in before the next anniversary, you'll get your anniversary value plus half the fixed rate of interest for the period since the anniversary. If you are not sure when you will want your cash, this is not a very attractive product.

Income Bonds

Income Bonds pay a variable rate of interest monthly. The interest rate is currently 6.25% on investments of less than £25 000 and 6.5% on investments of £25 000 or more. The rate of interest can be changed on six weeks' notice. Income is paid on the 5th of each month, directly to a bank, building society or a NS Investment Account. The interest is taxable, but paid without deduction. The minimum investment is £2000, and the maximum holding is £250 000.

The bonds may be cashed on three months' notice. Bonds held for a year get the full rate of interest; bonds cashed in the first year earn interest at only half the normal rate. Bonds may be held for at least 10 years.

Income Bonds are an alternative for people eligible to buy Pensioners Bonds. Which is better? Income Bonds yield less, but if rates rise a lot, you would be better off with the variable rates of Income Bonds than the fixed rate of Pensioners Bonds. Of course, if rates rise and then fall, you may be better off with Pensioners Bonds. Compared to Income Bonds, Pensioners Bonds have a smaller minimum purchase value, a greater income penalty for early repayment, except in the first year, and a shorter notice period for early repayment. The choice is yours.

Ordinary Account

The Ordinary Account is a basic passbook savings account. It is not a cheque account. You get a passbook and you can make payments and withdrawals at any Post Office. Deposits have to be at least £10, and the most you can save is £10 000. You can withdraw up to £100 on demand, but if you withdraw more than £50 your passbook is retained for checking. You can nominate a Post Office, and after six months of having an account you can then withdraw up to £250 at your nominated office and still keep your book. Larger sums require application to the Glasgow office. For mastering these Monty Python-type rules, what are the rewards?

Interest is paid at a higher and lower rate—currently 1.75% and 2.75% per annum. You qualify for the latter by keeping your account open for a full calendar year, but you only earn the higher rate for those months in which you have more than £500 deposited. You only get interest on complete months; you don't get interest on a deposit in the month it was made or withdrawn. Interest is credited on 31 December.

These rules are so bizarre that Ordinary Accounts are difficult to take seriously. However, the first £70 of interest (or £140 for a joint account) is tax-free. Moreover children can open these accounts, and children aged seven or more can deposit and withdraw money themselves.

Investment Account

The rules on this account are more straightforward. The minimum deposit is £20, and the maximum holding is £100 000. You must give one month's notice to make a withdrawal. The reward is much better. Currently, the rate of interest is 5.0% p.a. for balances under £500, 5.5% for balances from £500 to £24 999, and 5.75% for balances of £25 000 and more. Interest accrues daily and is credited on 31 December.

Tax is payable, but interest is paid gross, so non-taxpayers don't have to reclaim tax. Children can again have their own accounts and most children will be non-taxpayers.

Children's Bonus Bonds: Issue H

As the name suggests, these bonds are for children only. They are issued in £25 units, and a child may not have more than £1000 worth of the current issue. This is in addition to holdings of other issues. The bonds earn 5% interest every year, and at the end of the fifth year pay a 11% bonus, which gives a 6.75% p.a. compound return over the five years. This return is tax free. After five years the bonds may still be held, but on new terms which holders will be told. Once a bondholder is over 16, the next interest rate and bonus offer applies for the remaining length of time up to age 21. The bond earns nothing after the final bonus is paid out on the holder's 21st birthday.

If the bonds are cashed within one year, no interest is earned. Thereafter interest accrues on a daily basis. However, the bonds need to be held for five years to earn the bonus which is not paid pro-rata for shorter periods.

If parents give their children these bonds, there will be no income tax to be paid by the parent even if the income exceeds £100 (see Chapter 30).

British Savings Bonds

These are no longer issued, but if you have any you should cash them in immediately as they do not pay interest. See READ 📖 WRITE 🖃 RING ☎.

READ 📖 WRITE 🖃 RING ☎

♦ For booklets explaining National Savings products go to your local Post Office, call National Savings on 0645 645000 (local rate call), or write to: Sales Information Unit, National Savings, FREEPOST BJ881, Lytham St Annes, FY0 1BR. The interest rates offered may have changed since this book was written. A 24-hour answering service giving current rates is available on the following numbers: London 0171 605 9483/4; Blackpool 01253 723714; Glasgow 0141 632 2766.
♦ In 1995, an advertising campaign was begun which allows investors to buy NS products "off the page", i.e., directly from adverts. Adverts appear in the major national newspapers.
♦ If you hold British Savings Bonds you should surrender them. Write to the Bonds and Stock Office, Blackpool, FY3 9YP for details of what you should do.

10

Regulation and Financial Advice

"Whatever happened to the good old-fashioned City gent?" "He's helping police with their enquiries."

City of London graffito

The financial services industry is heavily regulated. Those who seek financial advice will quickly discover this, but even investors who go it alone cannot avoid encountering some of the consequences of the regulatory framework. In this chapter I first say a little about financial regulation, and then move on to financial advice. Most people are probably willing to sort out their cheque account, savings account, and National Savings products, without any help except, perhaps, from newspapers or books like this. But for stockmarket investments, life insurance, mortgages, and so forth, most people will want to both read about these products, and talk to an adviser. It seems sensible, therefore, to look at the advisers before I tackle those topics.

THE FINANCIAL SERVICES ACT 1986

The most important piece of legislation for investors is *The Financial Services Act 1986* (FSA). The FSA regulates investment business carried out in the UK by individuals or firms. It sets out a statutory framework within which self-regulation takes place. This means that regulation of the financial services industry is by the industry itself, guided by some statutory rules.

Most of the powers contained in the FSA have been delegated to the Securities and Investment Board (SIB). SIB is, in effect, the senior UK financial services industry regulator and you'll see SIB frequently mentioned in the financial press.

The FSA has a very wide scope. Investments covered by the FSA include: company stocks and shares (including those of investment trusts); debentures; loan stocks and bonds; government and local authority bonds; warrants; options; futures; unit trusts; and long-term insurance contracts which have an investment component. The following investment businesses are also covered: dealing in investments; arranging deals in investments; managing investments; giving investment advice; and establishing collective investment schemes, such as unit trusts.

Although the FSA covers a lot of the investment terrain, there is still a lot outside—for example: bank and building society current and deposit accounts; National Savings Bank accounts; protection-orientated insurance; mortgages; custody of assets; and managing your own money. Although these financial activities are not covered by the FSA. Some are covered by other legislation.

Authorization

To conduct an investment business, a firm or individual must be either authorized or exempt from authorization. Investors should expect to see most advisers or investment managers authorized and regulated by one of the following:

- *Personal Investment Authority* (PIA). The PIA was set up to regulate investment business for private clients.

- *The Investment Management Regulatory Organization* (IMRO). IMRO covers investment managers (but not investment advisers, except in special cases).

- *The Securities and Futures Authority* (SFA). The SFA covers stockbrokers, securities dealers, market makers and futures and options brokers and dealers.

- *A professional body* such as an accounting institute or a law society.

Check the regulator All letters and other literature you receive from an investment adviser or firm should show who its regulator is. Even business cards must state the regulator. You might like to look through some of the financial literature you have and find who regulates the firms you deal with. The regulator is usually shown in small print at the foot of a letter and often on the back cover of a document or brochure. You should check that any firm you are thinking of dealing with that you don't know really is authorized. You can do this by calling a special SIB number— 0171 929 3652.

CONDUCT OF BUSINESS RULES

One of the most important consequences of the FSA is the provision of a set of rules that specifies how business should be conducted between a company representative or independent financial adviser and a client. Discussion of all these rules lies outside the scope of this book, but a few of the rules are worth highlighting.

Know your client An authorized firm must know its client so that it can give the appropriate advice or take the appropriate action. To do this a firm must know:

- The client's personal circumstances (e.g., married/single/divorced; whether there are dependants)

- The client's financial position

- The client's attitude to risk

- The client's financial objectives

If you deal with a financial adviser or salesperson and this exercise is done properly, you should expect to be asked, and to have to answer, a lot of personal questions.

You will usually be asked to complete a formal "fact-find" questionnaire (so you might as well go back and complete the tables in Chapter 2 if you skipped over them).

When the adviser makes a recommendation to you, you must be advised of the risks involved. The adviser should be sure that you understand these risks.

There are various types of client and they are treated differently. In broad terms there are professional investors, business investors, experienced investors and private investors (i.e., Joe Public). As you might expect, the last category consists of those with the least knowledge, and to whom advisers owe the highest duty of care. In addition, any of the previous types of investor can fall into the category of execution-only. This means that no advice is being sought, and the client only requires a transaction to be executed. In this case the adviser's duty of care does not apply.

Best advice   Prior to the FSA it was not always clear whether an adviser was independent or worked for a particular company. SIB said that advisers had to get off the fence—they had to polarize, they were either tied, i.e., a company representative, or they were independent. *The independent adviser acts as the client's agent, whereas the company representative acts as an agent of the company.* Both have to give best advice, but it means something different to each.

Best advice is that advice which is suitable for clients when only their interests have been taken into account, based on the information obtained about the client in the fact-find, and using specialist knowledge about financial products. *For the independent adviser, best advice requires a recommendation of an appropriate product and an appropriate product provider.* Since nobody knows how different unit trusts, for example, will perform in the future, different advisers are likely to give different best advice. That's OK if the advisers have used appropriate procedures and knowledge to make a suitable recommendation.

For the company representative, the position is different. While a suitable product must be identified, *the company representative can only recommend the products of the company being represented.* Thus if the representative thinks that for a particular client a high-yield unit trust is suitable, that must be the advice, and such a product should be selected from the company's range. The representative cannot recommend that another company's high-yield fund be bought, even if his own company's fund has been the worst performing high-yield fund in each of the last ten years. If the company does not have a high yield fund, the representative should point out that his company does not have a suitable product and recommend the client visit an independent financial adviser. Whether that happens, or whether the client is sold another product in the provider's product range, is a contentious issue.

It is very important that you identify whether anybody who offers you advice is tied or independent. Almost all the large banks and building societies are tied—you will automatically be recommended their products or where they don't provide the product themselves (e.g., contents insurance) that of another firm which is their tied provider, even if there are better comparable products available. Some banks and societies have independent financial planning subsidiaries. You will only be directed to them if you ask.

Customer documentation   You have to know who you are dealing with and what you are buying. To ensure this you will be given one or more of the following: "terms of business letter", "client agreement", or "discretionary management agreement". When you first meet an adviser, you should be told who the adviser is, who he or she works for, and who the regulator is.

A terms of business letter is a statement of the terms on which an adviser does business. It will cover a number of issues, some of which include: the services to be provided by the adviser; the name of the adviser's regulator; the method of remuneration; whether the adviser can handle client money and, if so, how; a statement as to whether professional indemnity insurance is held. A terms of business letter must be given at the beginning of a meeting or sent to you.

For an ongoing business relationship, and where more than indirect investments such as life insurance, pensions and unit trusts are involved, a client agreement letter is needed (although not for execution-only clients). A client agreement letter will include everything in a terms of business letter, plus additional items. These include: a statement that you will not be committed beyond assets deposited with the adviser; that you will lose the normal cooling-off period rights that apply to many products (i.e., the right to cancel a purchase within 14 days); the circumstances in which cold calls can be made; and how investment advice is to be communicated.

For a full discretionary service by an adviser, a discretionary investment management agreement is required. This will include everything discussed before plus additional items such as: your investment objectives; restrictions on the type of investments; and a warning on the risky nature of certain investments (such as futures and options).

Product information Since 1 January 1995, there have been regulations which affect life insurance-based product information. Products which are affected include endowments, some forms of life insurance and personal pensions. Much more information has to be provided to buyers, in particular:

- The cost of advice you are paying for

- The key features of the product you are buying

- The reason why a product is being recommended

- Projections of returns

- Following purchase, you will receive written confirmation of the most important details

The PIA is planning to introduce a new disclosure regime for unit trusts, certain PEPs and investment trust savings plans, which will take effect from mid-1996. At the time of writing, the details had not been announced, but the information that will have to be provided to buyers will probably include:

- A statement of the initial and ongoing charges in cash terms

- An example, without growth, of the build-up of charges over time

- An example of the ongoing charges which would apply if the investment doubled

Compliance Compliance has been one of the great growth industries of recent years. Every firm in the financial service industry has to have an employee who is the

Compliance Officer. In the smaller firms, the chief executive may double as the Compliance Officer, while in the larger firms there may be a team of specialists who do nothing but compliance.

The compliance officer (often known as "the sales prevention officer" by the sales team) is the point of contact between the firm and the regulator and ensures that staff know the rules they must follow and that they do follow them. The compliance officer is the person you should write to if you have a complaint about a firm. All complaints must be logged, and any letters kept on file. When firms are inspected by their regulators, the complaints file is one of the first things examined. It is worth complaining if you have a grievance. If you feel you do not get fair treatment, write to the firm's regulator: its address is shown in READ 📖 WRITE ✑ RING ☎. If you are still unhappy, there will be an Ombudsman you can turn to.

Compensation   If you lose money through the insolvency of an authorized firm, you can make a claim for compensation against the regulator of the firm. SIB has set up a firm to operate the Investors' Compensation Scheme. Under this, each investor may claim up to 100% of the first £30 000 of any single loss, and up to 90% on the next £20 000, i.e., up to £48 000 for any single loss. A claim may also be made for damages from a firm which has caused a loss by breaching its regulator's rules. There are also Ombudsmen schemes which can compensate investors when firms have acted improperly. The rules vary with each scheme. For addresses see READ 📖 WRITE ✑ RING ☎.

Client assets   Firms may hold client assets only if they are authorized to do so. If firms do hold assets, they must account for them at least every six months. Any client money will be held on trust in a client account at an approved bank. The account will be designated with the name of the firm involved and include the word "client". Thus you may find yourself posting off a cheque written out to "John Smith Financial Advisers Ltd Client Account". Money in such an account is separate from the firm's own account, and cannot be used by the bank to settle any debts the adviser may have.

BENEFITS FROM REGULATION?

There is little doubt that the FSA has introduced a very complex, and expensive, system of financial regulation. A lot of it is clearly good. But some regulations have had odd effects, and it is not always easy to work out the net effect. For example, polarization has meant that the banks and building societies have, in the main, stopped selling other firms' products and now sell only their own. This appears to have reduced choice in the High Street. On the other hand, you could argue that banks always tended to sell mainly their own products so there never was much choice. Now that you know a bank is recommending only its own product you are more likely to seek out an independent financial adviser, and this may introduce more choice. Yet, this isn't quite right either. Surveys show that most UK investors still turn mainly to banks and building societies (and family members) for financial advice.

Despite the FSA, many financial advisers are still too often badly trained and push products that offer them the most commission. My evidence? Just recall the names of the firms that have been fined and had to retrain their sales team. It seems to me that you should be grateful for what the FSA has done, but you would still be wise to take responsibility for managing your own financial affairs. If you use a financial adviser, the onus is still on you to select one with care. I'll now look at some practical aspects of using an adviser.

WHO ARE THE FINANCIAL ADVISERS?

Financial advisers are salespeople. They are out to sell you something, whether a specific product or general advice. There is nothing wrong with salespeople, except their interests are not necessarily yours. And you have to be careful that you are not secretly hoping to be sold a product, instead of having to make a decision yourself. You should make sure that you buy investments, rather than are sold them.

So who are the financial advisers? Apart from informal advisers such as friends and family members, professional advisers include bank managers, building society managers, insurance agents, solicitors, stockbrokers, accountants, and independent financial advisers. There are pluses and minuses associated with getting advice from all of these advisers.

Bank managers   If you live in the country, you may be advised by your bank manager, but most people will see somebody much more junior. You have to remember that the major banks are all tied—they sell their own products or those of one insurance company. The bank may have a subsidiary that offers independent advice, but you must either approach it directly, or ask to be put in touch with it.

Building society managers   As with banks, you are unlikely to deal with the manager but somebody more junior. Apart from the Bradford and Bingley, all the largest societies are tied. Even if you go to the Bradford and Bingley, your choice will be limited to a few firms which its Head Office has selected. It is quite unlikely that the person you deal with will be competent to discuss firms not on the list of recommended firms. They will, however, be able to get a question answered by Head Office. Many people feel more comfortable with building societies than with banks. But there is very little difference in reality.

Insurance agents   Insurance companies do not have a branch structure in the way the banks and building societies do. You either buy their products through other sellers, by post, or through an insurance agent who visits you at home. Insurance agents are tied. This group has attracted the most adverse criticism. They have been poorly trained, charges were hidden and the commission structure guaranteed a conflict between your interests and the agent's. A number of insurance companies have received heavy fines from their regulators and sales forces have had to be retrained. With the new disclosure requirements, and tougher training standards, things may now be changing.

Solicitors   Most people won't get financial advice from their solicitor, but some will. Solicitors may offer financial advice in the context of wills and structuring trusts. You should always be clear as to whether your solicitor expects to be paid by commission or an hourly fee. Also, you should make sure that your solicitor is sufficiently well informed about financial matters. Giving financial advice is not a solicitor's main function, although some have set up financial planning divisions, and do give general financial advice. Solicitors will usually give independent advice and not be tied.

Stockbrokers Stockbrokers execute share transactions but they may also manage money, either as an adviser, or with full discretion. Some brokers are tied to their own in-house, or associated company, pooled funds. This means that if they have full discretion and they buy a unit trust for you, you will automatically get the in-house fund. Some brokers who manage money will only handle shares and bonds and will not handle insurance products, tax planning, etc. Others will offer a full range of financial advice. I discuss stockbrokers at more length in Chapter 22.

Accountants Most people won't get financial advice from their accountant, but some will. Accountants may offer financial advice in the context of annual tax returns or producing company accounts. You should always be clear as to whether your accountant expects to be paid by commission or an hourly fee. Also, you should make sure that your accountant is sufficiently well informed about investment matters. Giving financial advice is not an accountant's main function but, like some solicitors, some have set up financial planning divisions. Accountants will usually give independent advice and not be tied.

Independent financial advisers (IFAs) IFAs often sound like bucket-shop operations. The word "independent" refers to the nature of the advice, and not the legal structure of the adviser. An IFA may well be a one-man band, but some are more substantial companies, and many IFAs belong to networks which provide a variety of back-up services such as on-line computer systems providing up-to-date evaluations of mortgages, insurance and so forth. Because they are not tied, it is always worth considering an IFA. But not every IFA will be competent, and many will have a bias of some sort, towards say, insurance products, and to a particular company's products.

The perfect adviser There is no such thing. When choosing an adviser, you should interview several, and at least one should be an IFA.

GUIDELINES FOR SELECTING AN ADVISER

There is no definitive list of things to look for, or questions to ask. The questions will vary with your needs and the type of adviser. But you should consider the following, some of which relate to the adviser's firm and some to the individual you would deal with:

- Are they tied or independent?

- Who is their regulator? Check with SIB that they are regulated (call 0171 929 3652)

- How does the adviser charge, and what would you have to pay?

- What other costs are there?

- In what areas of investments is the adviser competent?

- How old is the adviser? Are you able to empathize with the adviser?

- Has your adviser passed any professional examinations? Which?

- How long have they been at the firm?

- What information will they want from you?

- What is the financial planning process that the adviser wishes to use? Do you understand it?

- What is their performance record (especially if a stockbroker is offering discretionary investment management)?

- Can the adviser give names of customers who will supply a reference?

- Has the adviser or employer been fined by his or her regulator or suffered any disciplinary measure?

- Is the adviser covered by professional indemnity insurance?

- What information will you receive? What type of reports?

- Will the adviser implement any plans he or she recommends?

For any piece of advice ask:

- How are you paid?

- How much will it cost me?

- What risk am I taking?

- If I follow your advice, could I lose money?

- Why are you advising me to do this?

If you want to find an IFA, how do you go about it? You might find one on the basis of personal recommendation, either from a friend or another professional adviser that you already have, but you should still interview the person to form your own view of suitability. Alternatively you can contact IFAP, which will send you the names of three IFAs in your area. These may not be specialists in what you are interested in, and they may charge by commission or fee. For specifically fee-based advisers you can get details from *Money Management*, and you will get a specialist in whatever you are interested in. If you are interested in pensions you can also contact the Society of Pensions Consultants. The society will tell you which members charge a fee, and which charge commission. In every case, remember that the advisers whose names you receive may not be very good, so do ask them standard questions. For addresses see READ ⬚ WRITE ⬚ RING ☎.

CONFLICTS OF INTEREST

Even when you have selected your adviser, you should remember that there may be conflicts of interest. These may operate unconsciously. The nature of the conflict will depend on the adviser. Insurance salespeople encounter different conflicts from those by stockbrokers, so it is impossible to produce a definitive list. And, even if a particular product is in the salespeople's interest, it may also be in yours. That said, you should be wary of the biases listed below.

Ignoring debt   It nearly always makes sense to pay off credit card and other consumer debt. It sometimes makes sense to pay off a mortgage. Many advisers ignore this. If you pay off debt you not only don't buy a product generating commission for them, you have less cash available to do so.

Ignoring AVCs   For many people, adding to their pension entitlement will make good sense. One of the simplest ways of doing this will be through an AVC in the employer's scheme. Again, many advisers fail to recommend this since you won't be buying a product generating commission, and you will have less cash available to do so.

Too specialist   Many financial advisers are specialists, such as insurance salesmen or stockbrokers. They may claim to review your total financial circumstances, but their recommendations tend to reflect their background.

Commission orientated   Salespeople tend to push the products that generate most commission for themselves. This is a pervasive problem, with some biases fairly obvious whilst others are more subtle. Some examples follow—I discuss the products later in this book:

- For many years, most advisers ignored investment trusts and favoured unit trusts because the latter gave them a 3% commission, while investment trusts gave nothing. Now that some investment trusts pay commission (in certain circumstances), they are more often recommended.

- Whole-life insurance pays more commission than term insurance. Whole-life is consequently oversold.

- For many investors a general international unit or investment trust is an ideal means of gaining exposure to world stockmarkets. Buy, and hold for ever, would be the strategy. In unit trusts in particular, advisers seldom recommend such funds, preferring specialist regional funds. This enables the adviser to recommend shifts in the regional weightings, with every switch earning the adviser 3% and costing the client 3%. In a general international fund, the fund manager makes country switches, and there is no additional charge.

- Building societies and banks have pushed endowment mortgages rather than repayment mortgages partly because of the commission they have earned.

- Many banks and building societies try to tie you to their buildings and contents insurance when you take a mortgage, even though much cheaper third-party insurance is usually available.

GOOD ADVISERS EXIST

You may feel that there are so many words of warning that everybody in the financial services sector must be a crook. That's not true at all. There are good advisers, as well as some poor ones. In anybody's life, buying a home, arranging to provide for your family if you die young, setting up your pension, ensuring that a family firm continues as you want it to, or any number of other financial transactions are important steps worth thinking about carefully. So, if you decide to have a financial adviser, it is worth taking some care trying to find a good one, and being aware of potential conflicts of interest.

READ 📖 WRITE 🖃 RING ☎

♦ For the names of three IFAs in your area, contact: Independent Financial Advice Promotion, 28 Grenville Street, London, EC1N 8SU. Tel: 0171 831 4027. Internet: http://www.demon.co.uk/moneyweb/
♦ You can get details of 850 fee-based advisers from *Money Management's* National Register of Fee-Based Advisers. You have to specify the type of advice you want, as IFAs specialize: The Money Management Register of Fee Based Advisers, Matrix Data Ltd, FREEPOST 22 (SW 1565), London W1E 7EZ. Tel: 01272 769444.
♦ For specialist pensions advice: The Society of Pensions Consultants, Ludgate House, Ludgate Circus, London, EC4A 2AB. Tel: 0171 353 1688.
♦ *Which?* periodically comments, usually unfavourably, on the quality of financial advice— e.g. "How to Get Good Financial Advice", *Which?*, December 1995, 20–24.

SOME USEFUL ADDRESSES

Regulatory bodies

♦ *Securities and Investments Board* (SIB), Gavrelle House, 2–14 Bunhill Row, London, EC1Y 8RA. Tel: 0171 638 1240. To check if a company is authorized: 0171 929 3652.
♦ *Personal Investment Authority* (PIA). 1 Canada Square, Canary Wharf, London, E14 5AZ. Tel: 0171 538 8860.
♦ *The Financial Intermediaries, Managers and Brokers' Regulatory Association* (FIMBRA). Herstmere House, Hertsmere Road, London, E14 4AB. Tel: 0171 538 8860.
♦ *The Life Assurance and Unit Trust Regulatory Organization* (LAUTRO), Centre Point, 103 New Oxford Street, London WC1A 1QH. Tel: 0171 379 0444.
♦ *The Investment Management Regulatory Organization* (IMRO), Broadwalk House, Appold Street, London, EC2A 2LL. Tel: 0171 628 6022.
♦ *The Securities and Futures Authority* (SFA), Cottons Centre, Cottons Lane, London, SE1 2QB. Tel: 0171 378 9000.

Recognized professional bodies

♦ *The Institute of Chartered Accountants in England and Wales*, PO Box 433, Chartered Accountants' Hall, Moorgate Place, London EC2P 2BJ. Tel: 0171 920 8100.
♦ *The Institute of Chartered Accountants of Scotland*, 27 Queen Street, Edinburgh, EH2 1LA. Tel: 0131 225 5673.
♦ *The Institute of Chartered Accountants in Ireland*, Chartered Accountants House, 87–89 Pembroke Road, Dublin 4. Tel: 00 3531 680400.

♦ *The Chartered Association of Certified Accountants*, 29 Lincoln's Inn Fields, London WC2A 3EE. Tel: 0171 396 5700.
♦ *The Law Society*, 113 Chancery Lane, London, WC2A 1PL. Tel: 0171 242 1222.
♦ *The Law Society of Scotland*, Law Society Hall, 26 Drumsheugh Gardens, Edinburgh, EH3 7YR. Tel: 0131 226 7411.
♦ *The Law Society of Northern Ireland*, Law Society House, 98 Victoria Street, Belfast, BT1 3JZ. Tel: 01232 231614.
♦ *The Institute of Actuaries*, Staple Inn Hall, High Holborn, London, WC1V 7JQ. Tel: 0171 242 0106.
♦ *The Insurance Brokers' Registration Council*, 15 St Helen's Place, London, EC3A 6DS. Tel: 0171 588 4387.

Ombudsmen and others

♦ *Investment Ombudsman*, 6 Fredericks Place, London, EC2R 8BT. Tel: 0171 796 3065.
♦ *Insurance Ombudsman*, City Gate One, 135 Park Street, London, SE1 9EA. Tel: 0171 928 7600.
♦ *PIA Ombudsman*, 3rd Floor, Centrepoint, 103 New Oxford St, London, WC1A 1QH. Tel: 0171 240 3838.
♦ *Pensions Ombudsman*, 11 Belgrave Road, London, SW1V 1RB. Tel: 0171 834 9144.
♦ *Banking Ombudsman*, 70 Grays Inn Road, London, WC1X 8NB. Tel: 0171 404 9944.
♦ *Building Societies Ombudsman*, Millbank Tower, London, SW1P 4QP. Tel: 0171 931 0044.
♦ *Inland Revenue Adjudicator*, 3rd Floor, Haymarket House, 28 Haymarket, London, SW1Y 4SP. Tel: 0171 930 2292.
♦ *Registrar of Friendly Societies*, 15 Great Marlborough Street, London, W1V 2AX. Tel: 0171 437 9992.
♦ *Adjudicator for National Savings*, Room 106 G, Treasury Chambers, Parliament Street, London, SW1P 3AG.
♦ *The Investors' Compensation Scheme*, Gavrelle House, 2–14 Bunhill Row, London, EC1Y 8RA. Tel: 0171 628 8820.
♦ *The Complaints Bureau of the Securities and Futures Authority*, Cottons Centre, Cottons Lane, London, SE1 2QB. Tel: 0171 378 9000.
♦ *Legal Services Ombudsman*, 22 Oxford Court, Oxford Street, Manchester, M2 3WQ. Tel: 0161 236 9532.

11

The ABC of the Stockmarket

Of all the mysteries of the Stock Exchange there is none so impenetrable as why there should be a buyer for everyone who seeks to sell.

John Kenneth Galbraith

Nearly everyone in the UK is affected in some way by the stockmarket. Some people own shares directly, if only a couple of hundred pounds in their local electricity or water company which they bought when it was privatized; some own unit trusts or life insurance; and many of us have private pension entitlements. Unit trusts, life insurance funds and pension funds all usually invest in the stockmarket. It's important to understand the stockmarket because, over the years, it has provided some of the highest investment returns—as I showed in Chapter 4—and, whether you know it or not, you probably already have stockmarket investments, albeit held indirectly.

WHAT'S A SHARE?

A share confers part ownership of a company. If you own 100 ordinary shares in BP PLC you own part of that company, albeit only a little part. Specifically, you own 0.00018%, because BP PLC has 5 502 618 748 issued shares (in 1995). It's your equity interest in the company. As a part-owner you carry the financial can if things go wrong, but you get the rewards when things go well.

As with any business, if there are loans outstanding and other contracts, these have to be honoured before the owners get anything. That puts the shareholders in a risky position—they are the last to get anything. Indeed, they can lose their entire investment. But if things go well, all the profit belongs to the shareholders. Not that they are likely to see all of it. The company may well plough most of the profits back into the company in the hope of faster growth, or a more secure future. But shareholders are likely to get some of the profits paid out as a dividend, usually twice a year. A few companies doing well choose not to pay a dividend; firms doing badly may not be able to pay a dividend.

Ploughing profits back into a company is likely to make it financially stronger, and its shares worth more. The reward from an investment in shares comes in two ways: through the dividends you receive and through changes in the value of your shares. Your total return from a share is the combination of both capital changes and income.

WHAT'S A STOCKMARKET?

A stockmarket is simply a market dealing in stocks (i.e., shares) and bonds. It may have a physical location, e.g., Wall Street, or it may be conducted entirely by telephone and computer screens, e.g., the London stockmarket. Whatever the physical nature of the market, most developed countries have some form of official market, and stocks that are dealt on that market are said to be "listed" or "quoted". Various rules have to be met to become listed, some of which relate to financial records. It is generally expensive to be listed, and not all firms have been in business long enough to meet the financial record requirements. This has created pressure in many countries for a junior market where the requirements are less onerous. In the UK there is the USM, or Unlisted Securities Market, and AIM, or Alternative Investment Market. Of course, the vast bulk of tiny businesses owned by one person or a family are not quoted on any stockmarket. And a few large businesses are not quoted either—e.g., Heron and Virgin.

HOW TO READ A SHARE QUOTE

Let's assume you own some BP shares. If you look in a newspaper (in the stock prices section, and then the oil sector) you might find something like that shown in Table 11.1.

Stock quotations consist of two prices, a bid and offer. If you think of these in terms of a market maker, a firm which makes a market in shares, it will want to buy and sell at two different prices to make a profit. The bid price is the price at which it is willing to buy, and the offer price is the price at which it is willing to sell you stock. Newspapers don't show both prices (which would allow you to see the "spread" between the two prices), but show you the middle price, the price mid-way between the two prices. So, the middle price of BP at the close of the trading day before the newspaper was published was 425½p. The spread would have been about 1%. The next column shows how much the price changed from the previous day. The "+/−" column is sometimes shown as "chg". The symbol "..." or "unch" means the price was unchanged. The next two columns show the highest and lowest price for BP during the year to date were 437p and 340p, about 100p apart. The data is actually for the last day of 1994 (the last full year at the time of writing) so the prices were the high and low for the year. You can see the stock ended the year below its high for the year.

If you multiply all the shares in issue by their price, you get the value of the company, or its stockmarket capitalization. With a market capitalization of £23 billion, BP is clearly a big company. The company pays dividends and the gross yield (i.e.,

Table 11.1   Stock Quote for BP

| | Price | +/- | Year | | Market | Yield | |
			High	Low	Cap. £m	Gross	P/E
BP	425½	−1½	437½	340	23 411	2.8	23.3

value of the annual dividends in pence, divided by the share price, times 100) is 2.8%. Gross means that this has been calculated on the assumption that no tax has been deducted, even though dividends are paid out with a credit for tax of 20% having been deducted (which you can claim back if you don't pay income tax). The P/E ratio is the price–earnings ratio. This is useful in assessing the value of a share. Earnings is stockmarket jargon for profits, and is calculated on a per share basis, i.e., all the profits divided by the number of shares. The P/E ratio is simply the price of the share divided by earnings per share. It shows how many years it would take for unchanged profits to equal the value of a company's shares.

Sometimes you will find a symbol next to a stock price. The most common is xd. A symbol always means that the price is subject to some restriction. In the case of xd, which is short for ex-dividend, it means a buyer will not get the next dividend. The share, in effect, is traded as though the dividend had been paid. This gives the company a period to get its records up-to-date so that it is in a position to be able to pay the dividend on the dividend date to those people who held the stock before it went ex-dividend. You will see from the press that a share's price drops on the day it goes xd.

Two other common symbols are xc and xr which stand for ex-scrip and ex-rights respectively. If you invest in pooled funds, which I explain later, you are unlikely to have to understand the mechanics of these events.

Because newspapers publish Friday's prices on Saturday and the markets close at the weekend, come Monday, the papers can either publish the same information again, or change it in some way. I'll use the *Financial Times* as an example. Tuesday to Saturday it reports the information shown in Table 11.1. On Monday it reports a share's price, the percentage change in price over the past week, the net dividend in pence, the dividend cover (broadly speaking how many times the earnings per share exceeds, or covers, the net dividend—the higher the cover, the safer the dividend), the months in which dividends are paid, and the last date the share went xd.

TYPES OF STOCKS

What I have been discussing in this chapter is really a particular class of shares, by far the largest of the various classes, known as **ordinary shares** or, in the USA, common stocks. There are other types of shares.

Preference shares are shares that fall somewhere between ordinary shares and debt. They rank ahead of ordinary shares when it comes to paying dividends or in the event of liquidation. But the dividend is usually fixed. Some preference shares will pay more in good times, and there may be a date for the shares to be repaid, perhaps for more than their original issue price. Sometimes preference shares can be converted into ordinary shares. Most investors can safely ignore preference shares, except for convertible preference shares.

Convertibles may be convertible loan stock or convertible preference shares. A loan stock is part of a company's debt whereas a preference share is part of its capital. Loan stocks are discussed in Chapter 19. With either form of convertible, when it is issued, the interest yield will be higher than the yield on ordinary shares. On a specified date, or during a specified period, the convertible may be switched into ordinary shares on specified terms. Usually the conversion price is some way above the price of the ordinary shares at the time of the convertible issue, i.e., it is at a premium to the then current share price. To make the conversion worth while, the ordinary share price has to rise a lot when the conversion premium is large, and the convertible will tend to trade much like debt issues. If the premium is small, the convertible will trade more like an ordinary share, and with a lower yield.

Many private investors have been attracted to convertibles in the last decade. They feel they get the best of both worlds—the high initial yield of a fixed interest security, and the opportunity to switch into an equity for capital growth. Some commentators feel the opposite is the case and you don't get as much yield as from a pure bond, and you miss out on some of the growth of an equity. Perhaps the fairest characterization is that convertibles are a half-way house between equities and bonds. In my view, convertibles are complex to assess. You need to understand equities, bonds, and the mathematics of convertibles (which I'm not even going to attempt to explain) to come to a sensible decision on a particular convertible. While a convertible fund may well suit some investors who have an income requirement, I doubt that most investors should hold individual convertibles, or bother with the details.

KEEPING SCORE

You may have noticed in the price data for BP that while it was off its high for the year, it was still quite a long way up from its low for the year. So did BP perform well or poorly during the year? To answer that we need some way to keep score. The point is that a share's performance will depend on how the company is prospering, but also on broad economic factors. If interest rates are raised by 4%, say, you would expect the economy to move towards recession (bad for profits and confidence) and interest rates on savings accounts to rise (making dividend yields on shares relatively less attractive). As a result, you would expect the stockmarket to fall. So if your share's price falls, that doesn't mean you've got a bad share, it may just be reflecting market trends. One question you will want to ask is, is it doing better or worse than other shares? There are a number of comparisons you could make within the stockmarket:

- BP versus the market

- BP versus big stocks

- BP versus oil stocks

The most obvious comparison to make is that of BP versus the whole market. The best measure of the market is the FT-SE-A All-Share Index—often just called the All-Share, or FTA All-Share—which consists of over 900 shares and is capitalization-weighted. To see what this means, imagine there are only two shares in the Lilliput stockmarket, Big and Little. Say Big has a market capitalization of £99, and Little has one of £1. Imagine Big's price rises by 10% and Little's is unchanged. If you weight each share equally, then the index would go up by 5% (i.e., $(10\% + 0\%) \div 2 = 5\%$). But that doesn't really represent what happened to the value of the stockmarket. A capitalization-weighted index allows for the value of the two shares. On that basis the index will have risen by 9.9% (i.e., $(10\% \times 99) + (0\% \times 1) = 9.9\%$), which gives a better idea of what happened to the market.

I noted that BP had a large market capitalization. It's one of the biggest companies in the UK. There is a lot of evidence that small firms have given a better total return than big firms over long periods. Perhaps we should not compare BP with the whole stockmarket, but just with big stocks. One index of big stocks in the FT-SE 100—often called Footsie—which is a capitalization-weighted index of the 100 largest shares.

Because the FT-SE-A All-Share is a capitalization-weighted index, its value will be dominated by big stocks. In effect, both the FT-SE-A All-Share and the FT-SE 100 are big stock indices, so it shouldn't make much difference which we relate BP to.

Had we been looking at a small stock, it could make a great deal of difference whether we compared the stock against the market as a whole or an index of small stocks. That's why a number of small stock indices have been developed, and also some medium stock indices. All of the following are mentioned in the press from time to time: FT-SE Mid 250 Index, FT-SE-A 350 Index, FT-SE Actuaries Fledgling Index, FT-SE SmallCap Index, Gartmore MicroCap Index, Hoare Govett Smaller Companies Index and Hoare Govett 1000 Index. I doubt that you need to know the details of each index, but I've provided them in the Glossary.

Getting back to BP, we might expect companies to tend to perform more like companies in the same industry than the market as a whole. Building companies may be having a tough time while oil companies are having it easy. Perhaps we should be looking at BP in relation to other oil companies. Most investment professionals look at the stockmarket in terms of sectors, which are broad industrial groupings. The standard classification is that used in the FT-SE-A All-Share Index, which is shown in Table 20.4 in Chapter 20. For now, all you need to know is that BP is in the "Oil, Integrated " sector, so we could compare BP to that sector.

In Figure 11.1 overleaf, I have shown the price of BP relative to the FT-SE-A All-Share Index, the FT-SE 100 Index and the "Oil, Integrated" sector index. The figure shows that BP outpaced both the big stocks and the market as a whole by about 30% over the course of 1994. Against the oil sector BP also did well, beating the oil index by about 10%.

I've talked about just one share. But it's very risky owning just one share, it could go bust. Most people will want to diversify and hold a number of shares, i.e., build a portfolio. To see how well the portfolio has done over a period, one can compare the portfolio return to the return from other assets—such as bank deposit accounts—or against other shares. When investors talk about being able to beat the market, they usually mean their portfolio has out-performed the FT-SE-A All-Share Index. If an investor specializes in, say, small companies, the "market" benchmark in this case might be an index of small stocks. Every investor would like to beat the market, but whether many can is the subject of Chapter 14.

WHY OWN EQUITIES?

People hold equities for a variety of reasons. Three important reasons are:

- For a high total return
- For a growing income
- To reduce risk and diversify

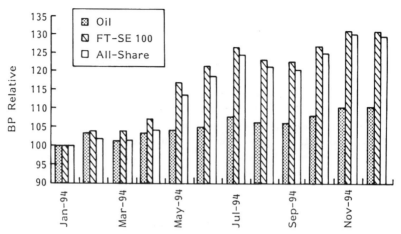

Figure 11.1   BP Share Price Relative to Indices. Source: Datastream

High return   I showed in Chapter 4 that equities have provided a much higher total return—capital growth plus income—than cash or bonds. For most people, investing in the stockmarket has been the easiest way to get a high return.

Growing income   Most people know that bonds, a high interest savings account, or a number of other investments, offer a higher immediate income than equities. Bond yields, e.g., are about twice the level of equity yields. The problem is that bonds offer the same income, year in and year out. And the interest on your savings account can go down as well as up. Equities have been the easiest way to get a steadily growing income. Figure 11.2 illustrates what has happened since the Second World War. In 1946, the yield on equities was only 3.5%. However, dividends have increased in most years—they've fallen in six years between 1946 and 1994—so dividend income has grown over the years. If you had invested £100 in 1946, you would have got an income of £158 in 1994, as a result of dividend growth.

To reduce risk   I pointed out in Chapter 4 that equities were risky in the sense that you don't know in any year what your return will be. The stockmarket could crash. So how can equities be used to reduce risk? The answer is that all investments carry some risk. If you have nothing but bonds, you are very exposed to the risk of rising inflation. If you have just savings accounts you run the risk of having your income decimated if interest rates fall. If you have some equities, you will run some risks, but you will be protected against some others that your other assets may bear. By diversifying into equities when you hold other assets, you will get a better balance of risks. I discuss this at length in Chapter 21.

INVESTING IN THE STOCKMARKET

If you want to invest in the stockmarket you should not hold one or two shares, but a diversified portfolio or fund. That way you reduce your risks. You can construct your

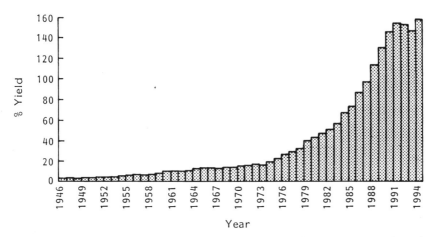

Figure 11.2   Yield on £100 invested in 1946. Source: Drawn from data in Barclays de Zoete Wedd (1995, pp. 48–9)

own fund, have one constructed for you, or buy a ready-made one such as an invest-ment trust or unit trust. And you can have either an active fund or a passive (index) fund. I examine these options in Chapter 15. But as I think most investors who invest in shares should do so through investment trusts and unit trusts, I first explain what they are in Chapters 12 and 13.

READ 📖 WRITE 📄 RING ☎

♦ The data source for Figure 11.2 is Barclays De Zoete Wedd, *BZW Equity-Gilt Study 1995*. London: Barclays De Zoete Wedd Securities Limited, 1995.

12

Investment Trusts

"To give the investor of moderate means the same advantages as the large Capitalists in diminishing the risk of investing."

Foreign and Colonial Investment Trust prospectus, 1868

Most investors should buy an investment trust or unit trust instead of buying individual shares. I justify this view in Chapter 15. In this chapter I discuss investment trusts, and in the next I discuss unit trusts. Both are sometimes referred to as collective investment vehicles, or as pooled funds. In the USA they are referred to as mutual funds. For reasons that will become apparent, investment trusts are sometimes called closed-end funds, while unit trusts are sometimes called open-end funds. The two types of funds have very different legal structures, but their basic objectives are the same. Both types of fund buy portfolios of assets, usually shares, but bonds, cash and other assets too, and provide investors with a means of achieving a diversified portfolio of assets at modest cost.

It is usually argued that unit trusts are easier to understand than investment trusts, and those new to investing should focus on unit trusts. I don't think this is right. Unit trusts usually have fatter fees for advisers and managers than investment trusts so there may be a certain amount of self-interest in this claim. Given my orientation to finding good value, I'm going to begin with investment trusts.

WHAT IS AN INVESTMENT TRUST?

Investment trusts are companies, and they are just like other companies in terms of having a capital structure with shareholders and perhaps some borrowings, having a board of directors, issuing an Annual Report and Accounts, and so on. They are quoted on the Stock Exchange, and their shares are bought and sold in the same way as are those of other companies. Investment trust companies differ from other companies only in their objectives—they don't make anything or provide any services, they just invest in other companies' shares or in other types of assets.

Investment trusts are described as closed-end investment funds because, as companies, they have the typical capital structure of UK companies. UK companies have traditionally had fixed, rather than variable, capital structures. Companies issue a fixed number of shares and, if they wish to change this, they have to get the approval of their shareholders. This can be obtained, but happens infrequently. Shareholders can't get their money back from the company, although they can sell their shares to other investors. All this means that the money being invested is not changed for long periods: the investment fund is "closed".

An investment trust portfolio

As an example of an investment trust portfolio, I have selected one called Majedie. The selection was made at random, and I am not expressing a view as to whether Majedie is a suitable investment for anybody.

The first thing to notice is the strange name. Many investment trusts have strange names, which reflect their history, and you should never assume anything about an investment trust on the basis of its name. Majedie sounds foreign (the name originates from a Malaysian rubber plantation), but 70% of its assets are in the UK. Its distribution of assets is shown in Table 12.1.

You read Table 12.1 as follows. In the left-hand column the types of assets are shown, and the other columns show in which countries the assets are invested in and the total. The first six rows of assets are sectors of the quoted UK equity market. The next row shows unlisted equities. In Majedie's portfolio, 72.4% of the assets are in UK equities, of which the vast majority are in quoted equities; 11.4% are in US equities, and so on. Taking all countries, 99.4% of the portfolio is invested in equities.

The portfolio also holds some convertibles (2.5%), fixed interest stocks (4.7%) and investment in commercial and other property (4.7%) Adding these assets to the equities gives a total of 111.3%. In addition there is cash (1.9%), negative other net assets (–0.4%), the dividend that it is proposed to pay to shareholders (–1.5%), and borrowings in the form of a debenture which is due to be repaid in the year 2020 (–12.4%). These liabilities are the reason that the fixed asset investments can exceed 100%.

Table 12.1   Majedie Investment Trust Portfolio Distribution
(at 30 September 1995)

Asset Type	UK %	USA %	Japan %	Cont. Europe %	Pacific Basin %	Total %
Mineral extraction	6.0	0.5				6.5
General industrials	15.3	6.1	1.1	1.7	1.4	25.6
Consumer goods	11.5	4.0		2.4	0.8	18.7
Services	12.6				0.5	13.1
Utilities	9.9	0.5				10.4
Financials	15.6	0.3	3.1	1.7	2.9	23.6
Unlisted	1.5					1.5
Total equities	72.4	11.4	4.2	5.8	5.6	99.4
Convertibles	2.5					2.5
Fixed interest	4.7					4.7
Investment property	4.7					4.7
Total fixed asset investments	84.3	11.4	4.2	5.8	5.6	111.3
Cash	1.9					1.9
Proposed dividend	−1.5					−1.5
Other net assets	−0.4					−0.4
Debenture stock 2020	−11.3					−11.3
% Total	73.0	11.4	4.2	5.8	5.6	100.0

Source: Majedie Investments PLC. Reports and Accounts, 1995.

This looks like a broadly spread portfolio, but a few shares might dominate the portfolio. In fact, this is not the case. The largest 30 shares constitute only 46% of the portfolio. The largest five stocks (and their percentage of the total portfolio) were: Thames Water (2.4%), BAT (2.4%), BT (2.3%), Shell (2.1%), and HSBC (2.1%).

As you can see, a shareholding in Majedie, or any similar investment trust, would provide a broadly diversified portfolio. This is invested mostly in equities, primarily in the UK, but there is exposure to international equities.

INVESTMENT TRUST OBJECTIVES

There are nearly 300 investment trusts quoted on the London Stock Exchange, and they have a variety of objectives. The Association of Investment Trust Companies (AITC) provides a classification scheme that may make it easier to select a trust that meets your investment objectives. The classification is shown below. It is not particularly good. Majedie is classified as international/general, but the term UK/general probably would give a better feel for its investment distribution. Nonetheless, the following classification is as good a starting point as any other, and once you know the type of fund you are looking for, you can use publications I'll discuss later that show all the investment trusts in each category and how they have performed.

- International: General—general investment trusts with less than 80% of their assets in any one geographical area

- International: Capital Growth—general investment trusts with less than 80% of their assets in any one geographical area which aim to accentuate capital growth

- International: Income Growth—general investment trusts with less than 80% of their assets in any one geographical area which aim to accentuate income growth

- UK: General—investment trusts with at least 80% of their assets in UK companies

- UK: Capital Growth—investment trusts with at least 80% of their assets in UK companies which aim to accentuate capital growth

- UK: Income Growth—investment trusts with at least 80% of their assets in UK companies which aim to accentuate income growth

- High Income—investment trusts which invest in equities and convertibles and aim to achieve a yield at least 1½ times the FT-SE-A All-Share Index yield

- North America—investment trusts with at least 80% of their assets in North America

- Far East: Excluding Japan—investment trusts with at least 80% of their assets in Far Eastern securities and which exclude Japan

- Far East: Including Japan—investment trusts with at least 80% of their assets in Far Eastern securities and which include Japan

- Japan—investment trusts with at least 80% of their assets in Japan

- Property—investment trusts with at least 80% of their assets in listed property shares

- Continental Europe—investment trusts with at least 80% of their assets in Continental Europe

- Pan Europe— investment trusts with at least 80% of their assets in Europe (including the UK) with at least 40% in Continental Europe

- Commodity and Energy—investment trusts with at least 80% of their assets in listed commodity and energy shares

- Emerging Markets—investment trusts with at least 80% of their assets in emerging markets

- Closed-End Funds—investment trusts with at least 80% of their assets in financial shares, including investment trusts

- Smaller Companies—investment trusts with at least 50% of their assets by value invested in the shares of small and medium-sized companies

- Venture and Development Capital—investment trusts which invest a significant proportion of their assets in the securities of unquoted companies

- Split Capital Trust—investment trust companies with more than one class of capital and different rights to capital and income

Twenty years ago, investment trusts were a sleepy back-water. In recent years they have become more fashionable, and there has been a certain amount of financial engineering. There has been a spate of launches of split capital funds (the last category listed above). In my view, most investors should ignore split capital investment trusts: they are discussed in Chapter 32. New funds tend to be launched with warrants attached. Warrants are discussed in Chapter 32.

GEARING

You will recall Majedie had some borrowings, and you may have wondered what the implications are. Investment trusts get their capital from their shareholders and from any debt they take on, whether in the form of short-term or long-term borrowings. If they borrow, investment trust companies are said to be geared. To see the implications, consider the following simple example. Imagine that a company has just been set up with £200 million of capital (its shares), and borrowings of £100 million, and all this has been invested in other companies' shares or equity. The balance sheet will look like this:

	£ million		£ million
Share capital and reserves	200	Equities at market value	300
Borrowings	100		
Total	300	Total	300

If we now assume that the equity market rises by 50%, the equities at market value will rise on the right-hand side of the balance sheet, and all the increase will be

attributed on the left-hand side of the balance sheet to the investment trust shareholders, the owners of the company. The balance sheet will look like this:

	£ million		£ million
Share capital and reserves	350	Equities at market value	450
Borrowings	100		
Total	450	Total	450

Although assets have risen by 50%, because the people who lent money do not
share in this rise (they get a fixed sum, except in special circumstances), the share
capital and reserves has risen by 75% (from £200 million to £350 million). The
shareholders have benefited from gearing. Of course, if the markets fall, the shareholders will suffer from the gearing.

Turning back to Majedie, it isn't quite as geared as it might have appeared. Not all
the money it borrowed has been invested in shares. If you look at the asset distribution,
you'll see some assets take the form of cash and fixed interest investments. They will de-
gear Majedie to a limited extent. (You can take my word for it, or you can rework the
above example with £250 million of equities and £50 million of cash on the right-hand
side of the first balance sheet, and see the implications of a market move.)

Gearing is often indicated by a single number. Gearing of 120 means the shareholders' funds will go up or down 20% more than the trust's assets. Most investors
should probably not buy trusts with gearing of more than 120—beyond that is just
too exciting, or scary. You don't have to calculate gearing as the numbers are published each month, as I discuss later.

NET ASSET VALUE

An important factor in judging the attraction of an investment trust is its net asset
value (NAV) in relation to its price. The net asset value of an investment trust is the
value of its assets less its liabilities. For the first balance sheet above, this would be
£300 million less £100 million, i.e., £200 million. In the case of the second balance
sheet, it would be £450 million minus £100 million equals £350 million. It is usual to
think about net asset on a per share basis, i.e., net asset value divided by the number
of shares. If we assume that each share was issued at £1, there would be 200 million
shares for the company in my example. The NAV per share would be £1 for the first
balance sheet (£200 million divided by 200 million shares) and £1.75 for the second
(£350 million divided by 200 million shares). Whenever I talk of investment trust
NAVs in the rest of this book, it will be on a per share basis.

You don't have to be able to calculate a NAV. Official figures are published every
month for each trust, and estimates appear daily in many newspapers.

WHAT DETERMINES AN INVESTMENT TRUST'S PRICE?

An investment trust's NAV is the value of the assets it holds on behalf of the owner of
a single share. But that's not necessarily the price you'll pay for a share.

An investment trust's share price is set by supply and demand. Because the number of shares is fixed, shareholders can only realize their investment by selling their shares to other investors. Likewise, buyers must find an existing shareholder who wishes to sell. If a trust is very popular, it may be priced at more than the NAV. A less popular trust may trade at less than NAV. In the former case the trust is trading at a premium to NAV, in the latter, at a discount to NAV. For example, if a trust had a NAV of 100p and was trading at 110p, it would be trading at a premium of 10%. If it was trading at 80p, it would be trading at a discount of 20%. Note that in the latter case you have 100p of assets working for your 80p, i.e., 25% more than you paid for.

Usually, investment trusts have sold at a discount to NAV. The size of this discount has varied greatly. At the start of the 1970s it was around 5% on average. It then widened to around 40% in 1976, then moved quickly to about 30% and has since then erratically moved to smaller discounts with the average discount in autumn 1995 about 7%. The narrowing of the discount in recent years has been a consequence of a number of factors:

- Savings plans have been started by many trusts which has brought a regular demand for investment trust shares

- Introduction of commissions for financial advisers so that they have a personal financial incentive to recommend investment trusts as well as high commission unit trusts

- Introduction of wind-up dates for trusts—this means trusts can be liquidated at specific dates at NAV and the proceeds returned to shareholders so that the price and NAV can't get too out of line

- Introduction of new types of trusts such as split capital trusts which have been less prone to selling at a discount

Despite these factors, were there to be a market crash, it is likely that discounts would increase. And if fund managers launch a steady stream of new trusts, they may overwhelm the effect of the factors listed above. Anyone investing in investment trusts should be aware that investment trusts typically sell at a discount to NAV, and this is variable and may increase. It may also narrow or disappear.

The variability of the discount, or less often premium, means there are three ways to make, or lose, money in investment trusts. Asset values may change, the discount or premium may change, or both. For example, a trust may have a NAV of 100p and be trading at 90p, or a 10% discount. If the market rises by 5% and the trust's asset value matches the increase (i.e., 105p), but the discount widens to 20% (i.e., 21p), the share price would be 84p (i.e., 105p – 21p) and the investor would be worse off. What tends to happen is that discounts narrow in a rising market and widen in a falling market. This magnifies the impact of major market moves on investment trust prices.

Is the fluctuating discount a bad thing? Clearly it adds to risk, although if you are a long-term holder, you may be willing to ride out the fluctuations. For savvy investors, wide discounts provide a good buying opportunity. And buying assets at a discount does bring a reward in the form of higher income, even if the discount never changes. For example, if you buy a trust with a net asset value of 100p and the assets produce a 4p dividend or 4% yield, but you only pay 90p (i.e., a 10% discount), you will still get an income of 4p, but this is a yield of 4.44% on a 90p price (i.e., (4p ÷ 90p) ×

100%). The discount has increased your income by 11%. For a trust bought on a 20% discount, your income would be boosted by 25%; a 33% discount boosts your income by 50%.

Discounts and premiums for investment trusts are shown in the *Financial Times* in the "London Share Service" section. More detailed information, available monthly, showing discounts/premiums, asset distribution by country or area, performance record, potential gearing, and so forth is available from the Association of Investment Trust Companies (AITC). The AITC provides a number of booklets that clearly explain investment trusts and their role in various types of financial planning—see READ 📖 WRITE 🖃 RING ☎.

Two things you should be clear on are how discounts/premiums are reported and what performance data relates to. Different publications show discounts and premiums in different ways. Some show premiums with a + sign, whereas others show premiums with a – sign. It doesn't matter which method is used as long as you are aware which it is—read the notes to prices or the table heading carefully. Performance data will normally be shown on a total return basis, i.e., the combination of dividends and capital gains. But the capital gains can be calculated on the share price or the asset value. If the discount has always been the same, the two will be the same, but if the discount has changed, they won't. A trust that has a good share price total return may have achieved this by an average asset performance and a wide discount having been eliminated. This is great for shareholders over the measurement period, but not necessarily indicative of future returns. Indeed, if the discount is unusually narrow, share price performance may not match asset performance in future because the discount may widen. You have to look at both types of performance data (assuming you believe past asset performance is a good guide to the future).

INVESTMENT TRUST CHARGES

You will suffer two types of charge if you invest in an investment trust already trading on the stockmarket. There is an annual management charge, and the cost of buying the trust's shares.

The annual management charge may be anything from about 0.2% of the value of the assets through to 2%. The very large, long-established general trusts tend to have fees of around 0.2% to 0.4%. This charge is deducted from the trust automatically. The more recently launched trusts specializing in narrow or exotic areas, e.g., Latin America, often have fees of up to 1.5%, although some exceed this. In general, however, investment trust annual management charges are lower than those on unit trusts.

The cost of buying and selling investment trusts' shares consist of commission charges (if applicable—see Chapter 16), stamp duty of ½%, and the spread between the buying and selling price, which might be about 1% to 2%, or more.

AN EXAMPLE

I began this chapter with a quote from the first prospectus of Foreign and Colonial Investment Trust, the oldest and largest investment trust. I'll use it to illustrate some of the data you can see in newspapers and the AITC's *Monthly Information Service*.

Table 12.2 Stock Quote for Foreign and Colonial Investment Trust

	Price	+/-	1995		Yield	Dis or
			High	Low	Gross %	Pm(−) %
F&C	152	+1	152	124	1.5	1.9

Table 12.3 Return Data for Foreign and Colonial Investment Trust

	Share price total return on £100				NAV total return on £100			
	1yr	3yr	5yr	10yr	1yr	3yr	5yr	10yr
F&C	112	165	241	528	112	150	216	394
Average	112	164	230	416	112	147	210	337

Source: Extracted from AITC, *Monthly Information Service*, November 1995.

In a newspaper you might see in the investment trust sector on the share price page, something like that shown in Table 12.2.

The table relates to 23 November 1995, so the high/low relates to prices for 1995 up to that date. Recalling my earlier discussion of a stock quote, you can see that Foreign and Colonial's mid-price quote was 152p, having risen 1p the previous day. For the year to date, the stock was at its high, having traded as low as 124p. The gross yield was 1.5%, and the stock was trading at a discount of 1.9% to NAV.

If you had turned to the AITC *Monthly Information Service* for November 1995, you would have found a lot more information on Foreign and Colonial, as at 31 October 1995. Tables 12.3 and 12.4 show some of the information. How has Foreign and Colonial performed? Table 12.3 shows the return on £100 invested for various periods. Total return means both capital gain and dividends have been included. Foreign and Colonial is classified as "International, General" on the basis of its objectives, so I have shown the average return data for this sector too. Looking at the share price total return, we see that Foreign and Colonial has been level pegging with the average trust in recent years, but in earlier years had done spectacularly well. If we look at NAV total return we see much the same, except the earliest years are less spectacular. The share price has performed much better than the NAV. That's because discounts on investment trusts have generally narrowed over the last ten years. The discount narrowing has been greater for Foreign and Colonial than for the typical trust.

In Table 12.4 you can see that the discount is low (1%) for Foreign and Colonial relative to the average (8%) for similar trusts. The danger must be that the discount

Table 12.4 Investment Data for Foreign and Colonial Investment Trust

	Disc/ (+Prem) %	Gearing	Cash and Fixed Interest	Geographical Spread %					
				UK	North America	Japan	Far East	Cont. Europe	Other
F&C	1	112	4	38	22	13	6	15	2
Average	8	111	7	50	15	6	8	11	2

Source: Extracted from AITC, *Monthly Information Service*, November 1995.

could widen. Foreign and Colonial has similar gearing to the average trust. You can see from the asset distribution—geographical spread refers to equities—that Foreign and Colonial has relatively more invested outside the UK than the average general international trust.

TAXATION ISSUES

There are two important taxation issues: how investment trusts are taxed, and how shareholders are taxed. Investment trusts approved by the Inland Revenue under the *Income and Corporation Taxes Act 1988* are exempt from capital gains tax on gains made within the portfolio. The *Financial Times* indicates in the "London Share Service" section whether trusts are approved. Shareholders of approved trusts will be liable to capital gains tax only when they sell their shares, and the tax, if any, is charged on the change in price of the investment trust shares—not its underlying portfolio—after indexation allowance and annual exemption, if the latter has not been used for other assets. Losses may be used to offset capital gains on other assets.

Dividends paid to shareholders carry a tax credit of 20%. Non-taxpayers can reclaim this, but higher rate taxpayers have to pay a further 20% of the gross dividend to the Inland Revenue. Investment trusts don't pay tax on the dividends they receive, so investment trust shareholders aren't taxed twice. If a trust receives interest from a deposit or from a gilt, it will be subject to corporation tax at the full rate (i.e., 33%). However, this can be offset by trust expenses such as interest on borrowings and management charges. Were investment trusts to invest mainly in bonds, the taxation of income they suffer would be disadvantageous to shareholders. Not surprisingly, none do, and there is negligible difference in the income tax suffered by an investor whether individual shares are held directly, or via an investment trust.

READ 📖 WRITE ✉ RING ☎

♦ For further information on investment trusts contact the Association of Investment Trust Companies, Durrant House, 8–13 Chiswell Street, London, EC1Y 4YY. Tel: 0171 588 5347. Fax: 0171 638 1803. Addresses and telephone numbers for all investment trusts are shown in the Association of Investment Trust Companies' *Monthly Information Service*. This also contains details of savings plans, lump sum purchases, and PEPs.
♦ A magazine specializing in investment trusts is the quarterly *Investment Trusts*. Subscription details are available from: IT, 120–126 Lavender Avenue, Mitcham, Surrey, CR4 3HP. Tel.: 0181 646 1031. Your public library may subscribe.
♦ Annual Reports and Accounts can be obtained for many investment trusts by writing to the *Financial Times*. Details of this free service are given in the bottom right-hand corner of the second page of the "London Share Service" feature. You can use the addresses in the AITC's *Monthly Information Service* to contact trusts not in the Financial Times service.

13

Unit Trusts and OEICs

We may not know when we're well off, but investment salesmen get on to it somehow.
Kin Hubbard

Unit trusts provide a means of purchasing a diversified portfolio of assets at a modest cost, just like investment trusts. However, unit trusts have a different legal structure: they are trusts rather than companies. In the case of a unit trust there are three important groups—the investors or unit holders, the managers, and the trustees.

WHAT IS A UNIT TRUST?

A trust is a legal relationship, created by a trust document, whereby assets are placed under the control of trustees for the benefit of beneficiaries. The trustees have to ensure that the assets are managed in accordance with the terms of the trust deed. In the case of unit trusts, the trustees are typically large banks. The beneficiaries are those who can benefit from the trust which, in the case of a unit trust are the unit holders, i.e., people like you and me. The unit trust managers are firms such as M & G, Schroders, Gartmore and so on (and many of the best known also manage investment trusts), and these are responsible for the day-to-day investment management. The managers are the promoters of a trust, and will take the initiative in launching new trusts.

The pool of investments that makes up the unit trust is divided into equal portions, or units. Unit trusts are open-ended in the sense that anyone can buy units from the managers who will create new units for them, or sell back their units for cancellation or liquidation by the managers. The managers make corresponding purchases or sales of investments. Purchasers and sellers of units do not have to deal directly with the manager, they can get an agent such as a stockbroker or independent financial adviser to act for them. I discuss this in Chapter 16.

Most investors who buy a unit trust buy an authorized trust. All trusts that want to advertise direct to the public have to be authorized. Ultimate responsibility for regulating authorized trusts lies with The Department of Trade and Industry, but it has delegated most of its power to the SIB. There are regulations which control which assets can be purchased, what percentage of a fund a single asset can be, how units must be priced, and so on. Unlike investment trusts, unit trusts cannot be geared.

Unauthorized unit trusts are less supervised, although they may be just as well run.

There are two main types, house funds and offshore funds. The latter are discussed in Chapter 31. House funds are funds set up by stockbrokers, merchant banks and others for their own clients, with no attempt made to sell them to non-clients. Some of these funds will be authorized, but not all. They are discussed later.

Unit trusts may largely disappear over the course of the next few years. A new type of pooled investment vehicle, an Open Ended Investment Company, or OEIC (pronounced oik), will be introduced in 1996, and it is anticipated that most unit trusts will convert to OEICs. Because they are not yet in existence in the UK, and because only sketchy details are available (in November 1995), I will give only a brief outline of OEICs in Appendix II to this chapter.

UNIT TRUST OBJECTIVES

Unit trusts hold broadly diversified portfolios in the same way that investment trusts do (see the previous chapter), but they are not geared. The specific portfolio composition will depend on the objective of the fund. As with investment trusts, there is a classification scheme which enables you to find and compare funds with broadly similar objectives. The Association of Unit Trust and Investment Funds (AUTIF) classification in autumn 1995 was as follows:

- Money market (cash) funds—trusts which invest at least 80% of their assets in money market instruments, i.e., cash and near-cash such as bank deposits and short-term fixed interest securities

- UK gilt and fixed interest (UK bond) funds—trusts which invest at least 80% of their assets in UK fixed interest securities including gilts and UK corporate bonds

- Convertibles—trusts which invest at least 60% of their assets in UK, and sometimes international convertibles

- International fixed interest (bond) funds—trusts which invest at least 80% of their assets in fixed interest securities and may invest in most world markets

- UK balanced (managed or mixed) funds—trusts which invest at least 80% of their assets in the UK, but less than 80% in either UK fixed interest securities or in UK equities

- International balanced (managed or mixed) funds—trusts which invest at least 80% of their assets in either equities or fixed interest securities and may invest in most world markets

- UK equity income funds—trusts which invest at least 80% of their assets in UK equities and aim to have a yield in excess of 110% of the FT-SE-A All-Share Index

- UK general (growth and income) funds—trusts which invest at least 80% of their assets in UK equities, aim to have a yield of between 80–110% of the FT-SE-A All-Share Index and provide a combination of growth and income

- UK growth funds—trusts which invest at least 80% of their assets in UK equities and have an objective of achieving capital growth

- UK smaller companies funds—trusts which invest at least 80% of their assets in UK equities which are in the Hoare Govett UK Smaller Companies Extended Index

- International equity income funds—trusts which invest at least 80% of their assets in equities and aim to yield in excess of 110% of the FT/S&P Actuaries World Index

- International growth funds—trusts which invest at least 80% of their assets in equities and have an objective of achieving capital growth. This category includes both broadly diversified international trusts and those which specialize in categories such as emerging markets

- Fund of funds—trusts which can only invest in other authorized unit trust schemes

- Investment trust funds—trusts which can only invest in the shares of investment trust companies

- North America funds—trusts which invest at least 80% of their assets in North American securities

- Europe funds—trusts which invest at least 80% of their assets in European securities. This may include UK securities providing these are less than 80% of the trust

- Japan funds—trusts which invest at least 80% of their assets in Japanese securities

- Far East (including Japan) funds—trusts which invest at least 80% of their assets in Far Eastern securities. This may include Japanese securities providing these are less than 80% of the trust

- Far East (excluding Japan) funds—trusts which invest at least 80% of their assets in Far Eastern securities, excluding Japanese securities

- Australasia—trusts which invest at least 80% of their assets in Australia and New Zealand

- Commodity and energy funds—trusts which invest at least 80% of their assets in commodity or energy securities

- Financial and property funds—trusts which invest at least 80% of their assets in financial sector or property securities

You can find a list of funds falling into each category in AUTIF's *Unit Trusts: The Directory*—see READ 📖 WRITE 🖅 RING ☎.

CHARGES AND PRICES

The price of a unit of a unit trust is the value of a unit's pro rata share of assets plus or minus any charges. Unit trust managers can make three charges:

- Front-end load or charge

- Annual charge

- Exit charge

The **front-end load** is an immediate charge of about 5–6% when you buy. It is used both as a source of profit and as a source of revenue to pay 3%, or thereabouts, to financial advisers who recommend the fund (or simply buy it on your instructions). Some managers have reduced their front-end charge (e.g., Abtrust charges 3½% and Murray Johnstone charges 1%). Many managers have lower front-end charges for gilt funds (e.g., M & G usually charges 5% on its unit trusts, but has no charge on its gilt fund) and it is usual for cash funds to have no front-end charge. Some managers differentiate between their active and indexed equity funds (e.g., Gartmore usually charges 5¼%, but charges nothing on its UK index fund).

The **annual charge** is, as the name applies, an annual charge made on the fund, although it is actually deducted on a daily basis rather than once a year. This charge is seldom less than 1%, and typically is between 1% and 1½%, with 1½ % becoming the norm. This charge also bears VAT. On the higher charging funds, the VAT alone is as much as the total charge made by large investment trusts such as Alliance and Witan. Annual charges are sometimes called periodic charges.

In the past, unit trusts were required to take their annual charge out of income first, and if this was insufficient, to take it from capital. Thus a high-yield UK equity fund would take a charge of, say, 1.5%, or 1.76% after VAT, from an income of, say, 6%, and thus provide an income of 4.24%. A unit trust investing in Japan might also have an annual charge of 1.5%, but the Japanese shares might yield only 1%. In this case, the fund's income would be fully consumed by the manager's charge, and a further 0.76% would be taken from the fund's capital.

Recently, the rules were changed so that annual charges could be taken from capital, even if income was available. To see why, consider again the example above of the high-yield trust. If we assume that the market was yielding 4%, the fund's shares were yielding 50% more. However, after charges, the yield on the fund was only marginally above the market yield. To get a yield on a trust, after charges, that is significantly above the market's yield would involve buying very high yielding shares indeed. Since there are relatively few such shares, the danger would exist of having a very poorly diversified fund. The solution adopted has been to allow managers to take their fees from capital. Thus our high-income fund manager might take 1% from income and the rest from capital.

Although many people get very agitated about consuming capital, the amount being consumed is so small that it hardly constitutes a very great danger. Many investment trusts have been doing this for years. However, taxpayers should note that they are, in effect, converting capital into income, which is then subject to tax. Unit trusts that take all or part of the annual charge from capital are indicated by a letter C in the *Financial Times* in the "FT Managed Funds Service" section.

Unit trusts usually distribute their income twice a year, although some funds, such as Japanese equity funds, distribute only once a year, or not at all if there is no income after charges, and some high-yielding funds make quarterly payments. Unit holders may opt to have the income automatically reinvested in the fund by the manager buying more units with the dividend. Some funds offer accumulation units either as the only form of unit or in addition to the usual sort (often called income units). Accumulation units make no distribution, and any income is added to the assets of the trust. This means that the number of units held does not change, but the price of the units increases at a faster rate than for comparable income units.

An **exit charge** can be made on the sale of unit trusts. For example, you might pay no front-end charge, but be charged 5% if you sell within a year, 4% if you sell in the second year, and so on down to no charge if you hold the fund for more than five years. Exit charges are not common.

Although the unit trust management groups state that unit trust pricing is simple to understand because unit trust prices are based on net asset value, the pricing mechanism is far from simple. Investment trust prices are set by supply and demand, in exactly the same way that any share's price is set. An actively traded share's price may change many times over the course of a day. Unit trusts are valued by the managers once a day at a specific time (the time for each group is shown in the *Financial Times* in the "FT Managed Funds Service" section) and the managers set the price at that time. This price is then unchanged until the next valuation point.

SIB regulations require unit trusts to be priced on a forward or a historic basis. Dealing forward means that any purchase or sale will be deemed to have occurred at the prices established at the next valuation point. For example, if a group values at noon, then anybody dealing at 9.30 a.m. will have dealt at the as yet unknown price set at noon. If somebody deals at 2.30 p.m., the applicable price will be that set at noon the next day. Dealing on an historic basis means that the 9.30 a.m. deal will be executed at a known price set at noon the previous day, while the 2.30 p.m. deal will be executed at a known price set a few hours earlier.

Historic pricing gives scope for investors to take advantage of known market moves. For example, if the market jumps by 5%, perhaps as the result of an unexpectedly good Budget, anybody buying at a price set before the market move is gaining at the expense of existing unit holders. To stop this, managers who deal on an historic basis must deal on a forward basis if they suspect that a revaluation of the fund would show a unit price change of more than 2%. Unit trust investors can insist on dealing forward, even if a manager normally deals on a historic basis. And unit trust managers can insist on forward pricing for transactions that exceed £15 000.

When managers price their units, they are required to follow a SIB formula. I give a detailed explanation in Appendix I of this chapter. Most readers should skip it. The important point that emerges is that the SIB formula allows a spread between a trust's buying and selling prices that is so wide that most investors would be deterred from owning unit trusts. As a result, most trusts price on a narrower spread than the maximum that is permitted.

Although the initial charge is important, the spread between the buying and selling price is the real cost you suffer. That's the amount your investment has to go up for you to get your money back, and what you should focus on. I give an illustration later in the section "An Example".

The basis of unit trust pricing may change soon. Open-ended investment companies (OEICs) will be permitted in the UK in mid-1996 and they will use single pricing. That means they will quote a single price for buying and selling but a sales charge will be added when you make a purchase. Unit trusts are not keen on competing with OEICs if OEICs can use single pricing and unit trusts can't. There is pressure for unit trusts to be allowed to move to single pricing.

BROKER UNIT TRUSTS

Broker unit trusts are unit trusts in which the investment advice is given by a stockbroker or independent financial adviser. The unit trust will form a separate part of a "host company" which provides the administration. Host companies include unit trust groups and insurance companies. The biggest is Old Mutual (formerly Providence Capitol). Broker unit trusts may invest in individual stocks and shares or they may form a fund of funds, i.e., invest in a selection of other managers' funds. For such a fund you will be told that you will be getting the best of the best. Maybe, if it is possible to do such a thing, and the manager has done it—what is certain is that you will be suffering two lots of annual management charges. Many broker funds charge absurdly high annual charges—2.75% is the highest I've seen.

In the past there was so much concern about broker unit trusts that SIB brought in new regulations to control them. The best argument for broker funds is that they are an efficient way of running private client portfolios within a unitized format, and with the tax advantages that offers. While true, you could do the same thing yourself with conventional investment trusts and unit trusts, and probably at a lower cost.

AN EXAMPLE

I'll assume you are interested in buying a general, or balanced, UK unit trust. You might decide to look at one of the biggest, Barclays Unicorn General, and to look at both price and performance data.

In a newspaper, in the unit trust prices section, or the managed funds section, you might find something like that shown in Table 13.1 for 23 November 1995.

Instead of an alphabetical listing of funds, similar to an alphabetical listing of shares, you will find an alphabetical list of management groups. After locating Barclays Unicorn, you may find that its funds have been classified into various groups, and within the appropriate group you will find the fund you are interested in. As you can see in Table 13.1, you could sell the fund for 294.6p, buy for 315.4p, the price rose by 1.2p the previous day, and the gross yield was 2.58%. Somewhere you will be told whether the pricing is historic or forward. In this example the "F" after the words "Barclays Unicorn" indicates forward pricing. The initial charge on this fund is 5.25%, but if you spent 315.4p to buy one unit and then sold it for 294.6p, you would lose 20.8p on the spread, or 6.59% of your original investment. Watch the spread—rather than the initial charge.

AUTIF doesn't publish performance data, so you have to turn to specialist magazines such as *Money Management* and *Planned Savings*. For the period to 29 September 1995, you might have found data like that shown in Tables 13.2 and 13.3. In Table 13.2 you can see that the fund has been a below-average performer in the most recent periods, but has been better than the average fund over the long term. Notice that neither Barclays nor the average fund has been able to return as much as the FT-SE-A All-Share Index.

Table 13.1   Price Data For Barclays Unicorn General Unit Trust

Fund	Sell p	Buy p	Change p	Yield %
Barclays Unicorn Ltd. F				
Balanced Trusts				
General	294.6	315.4	+1.2	2.58

Table 13.2 Return Data for Barclays Unicorn General Unit Trust (periods to 29/9/95)

	Return per £1000				
	1 year	2 years	3 years	5 years	10 years
Barclays General	£1072	£1087	£1428	£1910	£3357
Average Fund	£1096	£1111	£1452	£1837	£3184
FT-SE-A All-Share	£1188	£1228	£1585	£2132	£3865

Source: HSW in *Money Management*, November 1995.

Table 13.3 Return Data for Barclays Unicorn General Unit Trust (periods to 29/9/95)

	1 year	2 years	3 years	5 years	10 years
Barclays General Ranking	78	70	50	26	19
Total Number of Funds	99	97	92	85	62

Source: HSW in *Money Management*, November 1995.

In Table 13.3 you can see how Barclays Unicorn General ranks. For example, in the most recent year there were 99 funds in the "UK General" group, and Barclays Unicorn General ranked 78th.

TAXATION

Authorized unit trusts are not liable to capital gains tax on gains made within the fund. Unit holders will only face a capital gains tax charge when they sell units, and this will benefit from indexation allowance and the £6300 exemption. With regard to income, authorized trusts are treated as companies. Income that has already been taxed is not taxable in the hands of the trust, and other income, after the deduction of expenses, is taxable at a special rate of corporation tax of 20%. Distributions made by trusts are deemed to be made net of tax at 20%, in the same way as individual share dividends are made. Non-taxpayers can reclaim the 20%, and higher rate tax-payers must pay a further 20% to the Inland Revenue.

One odd taxation feature is that gilts are exempt from capital gains tax for individuals, but if held in a unit trust, any capital gain from the gilts will increase the price of the units and this increase is, on sale, subject to capital gains tax.

APPENDIX I—PRICING A UNIT TRUST

Unit trusts are priced in accordance with a SIB formula. The approach is outlined here by means of examples shown in Tables 13.4 and 13.5: the examples are shown on a per unit basis. Novice investors should skip this appendix.

The price at which an investor can buy units is the buying price. This is calculated in the following way. All the assets in the fund are valued at their lowest offer price, i.e., the lowest price they could be bought at. In Table 13.4 I assume that this is 50p. To that is added stamp duty which is charged at ½% of the value of the assets. Brokerage commission is also added, and this will typically be less than 0.2% on UK shares, and rather more on foreign shares. (Investment

Table 13.4 Buying Price Calculation

	Pence
Lowest market dealing offer price	50.0000
+ Stamp duty (0.5%)	0.2500
+ Brokerage costs (0.25%)	0.1250
+ Accrued income (say 1.0000p)	1.0000
= Appropriate price/creation price	51.3750
+ Initial charge (6%)	3.0825
= Total	54.4575
Rounding charge to four significant figures	0.0025
Maximum buying price per unit	54.4600

Table 13.5 Selling Price Calculation

	Pence
Highest market dealing selling price	49.0000
− Brokerage costs (0.25%)	0.1250
+ Accrued income (say 1.0000p)	1.0000
= Total	49.8750
Rounding charge to four significant figures	0.0050
Minimum selling price/cancellation price per unit	49.8700

trusts and unit trusts deal at institutional rates, which are much lower than the rate at which a private investor can deal at. I've assumed an average of 0.25%.)

I explain in Chapters 11 and 19 that when equities are traded, dividends are paid on an all or nothing basis, while gilts are traded on an accrued income basis. Unit trusts are like gilts in that income is accrued. Whatever dividends or interest have been received since the last unit trust distribution belong to the unit holder up to the point the units are sold. Accordingly, we have to add accrued income to our construction of the buying price. This calculation will net out the accrued annual management charges. Next, the manager adds the initial or front-end charge. This will vary from trust to trust. I've assumed 6%. Finally, a charge is added to round up the price to four significant figures. In the example in Table 13.4, the buying price comes to 54.46p.

The selling price is the selling price of units. To calculate this we take the highest price at which the assets can be sold, and subtract brokerage costs. Accrued income is added in, and a rounding-down charge is subtracted. On the basis of a 2% price spread on the underlying assets (i.e., there is 2% difference between the bid and offer prices) and the same assumptions that were made before, Table 13.5 shows that the selling price is 49.87p.

The difference between the bid and buying price in my example is about 8.8%. So, if you bought at the buying price and immediately sold at the selling price, you would lose 8.8%. It would be lower with a smaller front-end charge, and higher if the bid–offer spread is greater than I assumed, as it would be for a fund investing in smaller companies. Thus the maximum possible spread under the SIB formula will vary with each fund. For some funds it may be as much as 12%.

Most investors would be reluctant to invest if the market had to rise by the sort of amounts I have mentioned just for them to break even. As a result, managers usually quote buying and selling prices that are not at the extremes permitted by the SIB. They aim for about a 5% to 6% spread. If there is persistent buying, the managers will price the fund near the buying price end of the range, while if there is persistent selling, they will price at the selling end. Table 13.6 shows my hypothetical fund priced according to the maximums set by the SIB, and on a buying and selling basis with a 5% spread.

If a fund moves from a buying basis to a selling basis, the price at which you can sell will fall without any movement in the price of the underlying assets. This will typically amount to a few

Table 13.6   Possible Buying/Selling Prices for a Unit Trust

Buying/Selling Prices (p)	Basis
54.46–49.87	SIB permitted spread
54.46–51.74	Buying basis
52.49–49.87	Selling basis

per cent, but could be up to 6% or more on a smaller company fund. Thus, although unit trusts are priced in relation to net asset value, there is a similar problem to that encountered with investment trust discounts. You may suffer a fall in the value of your unit trusts without any movement in the value of the underlying assets. The size of the effect, however, is small compared to the possible size of investment trust discount movements. Relative to investment trusts, unit trust prices are based on net asset value.

APPENDIX II—OEICS

An OEIC is an Open-Ended Investment Company and while such entities already exist in Europe, they will be permitted to be formed in the UK for the first time in mid-1996. Technically an OEIC will be a company with variable share capital—an open-ended company. The corporate code governing OEICs will be a special free-standing code, outside of the Companies Acts. An OEIC will thus be like an investment trust in as much as it will be a company, but like a unit trust in as much as it will be open-ended. As far as most private investors are concerned, the major difference between investment trusts and unit trusts is that the former are open-ended and the latter closed-ended. This difference will carry over between investment trusts and OEICs. For most investors, OEICs will just be revamped unit trusts.

The reason that the change will be undertaken is that while the UK has a well-developed fund management industry, unit trusts do not appeal to most Continental Europeans. They are not familiar with the legal concept of a trust, and prefer a company structure. The different buying and selling prices of unit trusts is also not a familiar concept on the Continent—European funds have a single price. It is hoped that OEICs will appeal to the European market. Up to now, many UK fund managers that have wanted to sell into Europe have established operations in Dublin or Luxembourg.

As part of the attempt to appeal to Europe, OEICs will use single pricing. Although single pricing will introduce a single buying and selling price, buyers will have to pay an additional sales charge and may have to pay a redemption charge. Other costs can be added to the price in existing European OEICs. In short, you will buy and sell at different prices: single pricing is a misnomer. The calculation of the single price is not simple either, being an average of the bid value of the underlying portfolio, less commission, and the offer price, plus commission, and stamp duty. But no doubt OEIC marketing people will pretend it's simple.

OEICs will probably mainly be set up as umbrella funds, i.e., a particular group's funds will all be under the umbrella of one company structure and you will be able to switch easily from, say, a North American fund to an Emerging Markets fund. With a unit trust, each fund is a separate legal entity.

Unit trust regulation will probably be changed to allow single pricing. Despite this, it is generally thought that most unit trusts will convert themselves into OEICs.

READ 📖 WRITE ▭ RING ☎

♦ The Association of Unit Trusts and Investment Funds (AUTIF) publishes *Unit Trusts: The Directory*. This shows all UK authorized unit trusts managed by its members, classified by objective and providing information on charges, minimum purchase sums, savings plans, etc.

The address and telephone number of each manager is shown, and further information can be obtained from the managers. To see a fund's actual investments, ask for the latest "Manager's Report". AUTIF also publishes leaflets on a variety of topics such as school fees, PEPs and so on. AUTIF, 65 Kingsway, London, WC2B 6TD. Tel: 0181 207 1361.

♦ Addresses and telephone numbers for all unit trust groups are shown in the *Financial Times* in the "Managed Funds" section.

♦ Appendix I is partly based on pp18–20 of *The Unit Trust Year Book 1995*. London: Pearson Professional, 1995.

14

The Strange World of the Efficient Market

Is it not strange that desire should so many years outlive performance?
William Shakespeare

Now that you know a bit about the returns from shares, and how you can get a well-diversified portfolio cheaply by buying an investment trust or unit trust, the obvious thing to do is to buy the best shares or trusts. But it's not that easy. One of the strangest, but most important, notions in investments is that of the efficient market. The efficient market theory states that security prices fully reflect all available information. If everything that is known is reflected in a share's price, there will be no mispriced securities and neither you, nor a highly paid investment manager, will be able to beat the market.

Most investors will find the material in this chapter strange. It may seem less plausible than the existence of UFOs. However, I hope you will persevere with the chapter. First, the ideas in it have a profound effect on the way I think you should manage your money. Second, most financial planning books do not cover this material, and do not seem to be aware of its importance. As a result, many of their assumptions and assertions are false. If you find the chapter too weird, skip to the last section, which gives an overview.

THE EFFICIENT MARKET THEORY

Prior to the 1950s it was believed that traditional investment analysis could be used to outperform the stockmarket. In the 1950s academic studies began to appear that led to the efficient market notion. If we assume that people who invest are keen to make money, we should expect them to grab every potentially profitable opportunity. The moment there is a chance to make money they will act, and prices will rise or fall in response to their purchases and sales, and shares will then be priced so that there is no opportunity to make further profits. Shares will be priced at their intrinsic value. This does not mean all shares have to offer the same anticipated return—investors may well want additional returns from especially risky shares—just that every stock will be priced at whatever seems the proper price allowing for its risks.

For this argument to hold, there will have to be an abundant flow of information, prices will have to respond quickly to changes in information, investors will have to

Table 14.1   Three Versions of the Efficient Market Theory

Version of Theory	Information Impounded in Prices
Weak-form	Past prices of securities
Semi-strong form	All publicly available information
Strong-form	All public and private information

make rational decisions, and it must be possible to deal easily, frequently and cheaply. These conditions seem to be met by the major stockmarkets. As a result of all our assumptions, it would seem that stock prices should fully reflect all available information. Of course when new information comes along, prices may well change.

In a famous article, Professor Fama divided work on the efficient market into three increasingly wide categories depending on the information assumed to be reflected in prices. In the weak-form hypothesis, security prices reflect all security market information including all past prices, trading volumes, etc. In the semi-strong hypothesis, all publicly available information is reflected in security prices. In the strong-form hypothesis all public and private information (i.e., information not generally available, such as that which company executives might possess about their companies) is impounded in prices (see Table 14.1).

Most investors dismissed the theory when it was first proposed. Chartists and technical analysts look at past prices to deduce what will happen to future prices. This approach can have no value according to the weak-form efficient market theory. Fundamental research (i.e., research on economic and financial factors) fares no better if the semi-strong form hypothesis is correct. Now for the extremely well-paid security analysts, fund managers and brokers' salespeople, this is pretty threatening stuff.

The efficient market school seemed to win the argument at first, not so much because the evidence was very strong, but more because there was persuasive evidence that went against the then prevailing belief that charts and sound fundamental analysis were self-evidently useful. The general academic view appeared to be that the weak-form hypothesis was true, the semi-strong form was mainly true and the strong-form probably was not true.

Even though questions could be raised about the meaning of some of the studies, any reasonable person would have to have conceded that the evidence was sufficiently strong that the onus was now on investors to prove any claim that they could outperform the market. It appeared that the market was reasonably efficient, information was quickly incorporated into prices and there was little evidence that suggested that there were more fund managers with good records than chance alone might allow. Indeed, some academics gave the impression that about all that could be said for investment management was that it was an indoor job that paid well and involved no heavy lifting.

SECOND THOUGHTS

From the late 1970s onwards, a spate of studies appeared that suggested that the market is less than perfectly efficient. For example, studies of specific events, especially related to corporate announcements, suggest that the market is broadly efficient and quickly reflects certain types of information. But some types of information, for example profit figures that are better or worse than expected, appear to take months to be fully reflected in prices.

A large number of variables such as the size of a firm (small is better), and its price–earnings ratio (low is better), have been related to returns. In other words, if you simply bought small companies you would, over a period of years, have beaten the market. This may mean that the market is not completely efficient, or it may mean that characteristics such as small size and low price–earnings ratios are associated with high risk. I think the former explanation is the correct one.

There is some evidence of return predictability. This means that if equity market returns have been poor for a period of years, they are likely to reverse and be good. Equity market returns are also related to the market dividend yield and the price–earnings ratio. But these findings are not very robust, and there is some dispute as to whether they contradict the efficient market theory.

Is there scope to outperform?

At a practical level, what the evidence suggests is that the stockmarket is not completely efficient. This holds out the hope that a clever investor can outperform. However, we might expect that relatively few investors in reality will be able to outperform. Some of the findings mentioned may result from human decision-making suffering from various biases. There is no reason to expect fund managers—or you—to be exempt from them. For example, investors have a tendency to extrapolate past company success into the future, despite profits having a large random component. They attribute company managers with too much ability to control events and too readily believe the future will be like the past. They therefore consistently pay too much for past growth. High price–earnings shares are usually those that have grown fast in the past. If they don't grow as fast in the future, low price–earnings shares, i.e., companies that haven't grown very quickly in the past, are likely to prove better investments. But most investors find this hard to accept.

Again, some clients, especially pension fund trustees, may act in a manner that stops fund managers from outperforming. For example, clients may require managers to be prudent, and not buy companies with known difficulties, even if these are over-discounted in the price, i.e., even a lousy company can be attractive if the price is low enough. And they may emphasize short-term consistency of results, which may rule out strategies that may work over a long holding period but will suffer periods of underperformance (of unknown duration).

And it should be remembered that most big portfolios are managed by investment organizations. Even if there are good managers, you may not be able to benefit from this if the good managers move to other firms, get promoted out of fund management to become bureaucrats, and so forth. Organizational problems, such as those related to rapid growth or change of ownership, may also lead to good managers taking their eye off the ball.

Finally, even if the market isn't perfectly efficient, it may be sufficiently efficient so that after the cost of dealing and management charges, private investors can't beat the market.

All in all, it would not be surprising if fund managers were unable to beat the market. So, how well do managers perform?

The performance record

A good way of deciding whether a manager is any good is to look at the consistency of his or her performance. Does the manager beat the benchmark or other funds more often than not? We have to be careful in this comparison. Think of a coin. It's an equal odds bet as to whether a coin, when it's flipped, will show a head or a tail. If I flipped a coin six times, say, you would expect it on average to show three heads and three tails. But you would not be at all surprised if sometimes it showed four or more heads. If you think of heads as "winners" and you saw four heads out of six flips of a coin, you would not conclude that it was a "winning" coin. You would put it down to chance. In fact there is a formula that can be used to calculate the likelihood of any number of heads appearing in any number of flips.

If we look at the number of UK pension fund managers who have achieved above-average performance in each of five years, who have achieved above-average performance in four out of five years, and so on, and then compare this to the odds of flipping a coin and getting five heads, four heads and so on, we find that the outcomes are much the same. Thus, while some fund managers do appear to show consistency of performance over a few years, the numbers are generally no greater than would be expected if the outcome was determined purely by chance.

What about the funds private investors buy? The best study of the performance of pooled investment funds is by Professor Malkiel, who studied the US market over the period 1971–91. He looked at all general equity mutual funds in the US. He found no evidence that the funds could on average beat the market. He did find, however, that there was some consistency of good and bad performance in the 1970s. If you bought a past winner, the odds were in your favour that you would do well in the next period. But, before you say "told you so", during the 1980s, there was no evidence of consistency in performance—indeed, in the late 1980s, winners did especially poorly.

Some people figure they can follow "hot" managers for a while and then switch when the manager goes "cold". This would involve huge transactions costs (and great skill). What about taking a long-term view? Say you bought the 20 best funds over the period 1970–80, and held them over the period 1980–90. That way you would avoid switching costs. Malkiel found that in the first period, the funds that turned out to be the best, beat the average fund by over 9%, in the second period—when you would have owned them—they underperformed by 0.69%. The average fund, in turn, underperformed the market by 2%. Of course, advisers claim to pick the best of the best, the most consistent of the winners. Malkiel tested this by examining the "Honor Roll Funds" in the highly regarded *Forbes* magazine. The funds didn't outperform over the long-run.

Malkiel's advice was that most investors would be better off looking for a low-cost index fund (something I discuss in the next chapter) rather than trying to find "hot" managers. I think that's good advice for the UK too.

THE PSYCHOLOGY OF EXTRAORDINARY BELIEFS

Most people dismiss academic studies. Real world investor performance is the name of the game. In the real world, when we think of fund manager performance, we are not likely to go to dull statistical analysis for our evidence on performance. We tend to draw on more striking evidence such as the record of winners like Warren Buffett, George Soros or Peter Lynch. These names are known around the world. This tendency to draw on vivid examples, which spring readily to mind, has been called *the availability heuristic* (or shortcut). Because the famous names are so available, one is likely to conclude that consistent outperformance is generally possible, despite the rarity of famous investors.

You might be able to name firms that have beaten the market. They advertise in the newspapers. Sure, but note that of the more than one thousand public funds how few are advertised. Note also that when funds advertise their performance, they all use different periods, sometimes a year, sometimes five, sometimes since launch. Sometimes they compare themselves against an index, sometimes against other funds, or often just against building society deposits. Some include a big number 1, but this can refer to being first, or being first quartile (i.e., top 25%) or even the manager's address. While all this data is available, it does not give you a true idea of the odds of there being winning firms. That, of course, is the idea.

In fact, one out of five UK pension fund managers has outperformed the average manager either every year in a period of five years, or in four of the five years. Many people will assume that these statistics obviously give the lie to the view that fund managers can't outperform, since there does appear to be some consistency to the performance of the best fund managers. You may agree. Actually I'm just restating what I said before, when I said managers didn't consistently outperform. The performance just cited is exactly the odds of getting either four or five heads in five coin flips. The problem is that most of us have a mistaken notion of what a random pattern looks like. Most people expect a random pattern to be apparent in both the total data and in every bit of it. Thus a coin sequence of H-T-H-T-H-T is seen as random, but H-H-H-T-T-T is not. A random pattern will in fact have many short runs, and a few long runs. Because my "one out of five" statement focuses on a run of good performance, most people will find it hard to see this as consistent with random outcomes. And it is exactly this sort of data that most people focus on. When a manager performs well for a few years, most people just won't believe that it could be chance. And there is another reason for this.

Treating fund managers' performance results as analogous to flips of a coin is clearly an unusual way of discussing people who can tell you how they achieved their success. Efficient market theorists do not deny that self-seeking, goal-orientated, behaviour is involved: that is precisely why the market is efficient. Because everyone tries so hard, there are no winners. But the very efforts of fund managers make it unlikely that they, or clients, will see chance as determining their fate. The reason is that people have a tendency to explain outcomes in terms of a cause. Randomness does not seem to count as a cause.

An American psychologist, Ellen Langer, distinguished between chance events and skill events. In a skill event, there is a causal link between behaviour and the outcome, while in the case of chance events, it's just luck that determines the outcome. Do people recognize the distinction? Langer thought they didn't. Most people have a concept of a "just world" that requires outcomes to be related to causes. When faced with chance, people often act as though it's controllable. When asked to throw a low number on dice, many people throw the dice softly. They have an *illusion of control*.

In tasks involving skill, people tend to prepare for the task, familiarize themselves with the activity, practice, think of strategies, and so on. Langer set up a series of experiments involving purely chance events but she encouraged or allowed the subjects to engage in skill behaviours. By so doing, she expected to induce a skill orientation, or an illusion of control—an expectation of success greater than the true probabilities justified. In one experiment, lottery tickets were sold in two offices. The tickets cost a dollar and the prize was to be the total sum raised, which participants were told would be about $50. Half the purchasers were simply given a ticket, whereas half selected their ticket (a "skill" behaviour). The ticket seller then tried to buy tickets back on the grounds that somebody in the other office wanted into the lottery, but there were no tickets left. The average price requested by those given a ticket was $1.96, but $8.67 by those who had selected their tickets.

Now the obvious feature of the fund management business is that it involves so many of what we assume are skill behaviours. If, in what are clearly chance events and/or produce chance outcomes, people can believe that they are involved in skill events, we should expect fund managers, their clients, and journalists to believe that fund management is not a chance situation. But that doesn't mean the results will be different from chance.

Finally, according to attribution theory, we tend to attribute actions taken by people in terms of situational causes or dispositional causes, i.e., in terms of external or internal factors. In general, people strongly prefer to attribute outcomes to people rather than situations—this has been described as the *fundamental attribution error*. This approach to attribution makes it likely that if a fund management firm outperforms for a few years, its success will be attributed to its skill as a manager, rather than to chance.

When we fail in our objectives, however, we do tend to attribute that to the situation. Most of us have heard a manager who held a stock that fell on poorer than expected results explain that "The company misled the market"; not the manager's fault. Again, when the particular investment style a manager uses is working, the manager takes the credit. But when it isn't working, "The poor results are to be expected as value shares are out of favour by the market for the time being"; it's the situation. In short, we too readily discount bad results we might achieve, and too readily attribute good results, achieved by ourselves or others, as caused by dispositional factors.

CHAPTER OVERVIEW

I've outlined the efficient market theory which, in essence, says that if a lot of people chase profits in the stockmarket, prices will end up at a level where there is no scope to do better than the market. The evidence for the efficient market is not strong enough to say it's true, but strong enough to say that it will prove hard to beat the market. There are certainly opportunities to beat the market, as I discuss in Chapters 17 and 18. However, whether a private investor will be able to use the opportunities that exist to beat the market is another matter. You have the option of spending a lot of time trying to do so (and probably failing) or you can give your money to a professional to manage.

I've looked at fund managers' performance. We saw in Table 13.2 that the average unit trust underperformed the market in every period shown. The UK's big institutional pension managers show no more consistency in beating the market than the odds of a coin turning up heads several times in a row. US mutual funds show a more mixed record, but it's not clear that you can achieve superior returns by buying the funds of managers who have been good in the past. You may do better by buying a cheap index fund, which I discuss in later chapters.

Most people find the above arguments so hard to accept that I looked at some psychological explanations of how people can maintain beliefs that are contradicted by the evidence. I think the best assumption the private investor can make is that it will usually be sensible to act as though the efficient market theory is true. I don't think it really is, but it's not clear that there are managers who consistently take advantage of any inefficiencies. The implications of this are spelt out in the next chapter.

READ 📖 WRITE 🗐 RING ☎

♦ This chapter draws on Stephen Lofthouse, "Why Active Management is Popular: The Psychology of Extraordinary Beliefs", *Journal of Interdisciplinary Economics*, 7, 1996, 41–61. The article contains full references to the studies discussed.
♦ The US study by Malkiel is: B. G. Malkiel, "Returns from Investing in Equity Mutual Funds 1971 to 1991", *Journal of Finance*, 50, 1995, 549–572.

15

Portfolio Management Options

A plausible impossibility is always preferable to an unconvincing possibility.
Aristotle

In the previous chapter, I showed that the efficient market theory asserts that all relevant information is reflected in share prices. Profit-orientated investors will ensure that shares are priced at their intrinsic value. The implication of the efficient market theory is that it is unlikely you'll be able to beat the market.

How much faith you have in the efficient market theory should determine your approach to managing investments. Funds may be managed passively or actively. A passive—or index fund—manager simply aims to match the return on some appropriate index whereas an active manager aims to beat the market. Passive managers assume that:

- The market does not misprice securities or assets

  or

- The market does misprice securities and assets, but managers are not able to take advantage of the mispricing

Passive managers set up their funds to match an index. They either buy all the shares in the index (and in the proportion that they make up the index), or they buy a sample, which may consist of hundreds of shares. Once the shares have been bought they are simply held. As a result, transaction costs are low, and annual fund management charges are low.

As an illustration of an index fund, consider Malvern UK Index investment trust. At 30 June 1995, Malvern had net assets of over £70 million. These were invested in 263 shares with the aim of matching the performance of the FT-SE-A All-Share Index. At the time, this consisted of 913 shares. Malvern's indexing procedure was as follows. For the 100 largest shares it employed full replication. Thus, if one of these shares was, say, 3% of the All-Share, Malvern would buy enough so that its holding was exactly 3% of its net assets. For the next 250 largest shares, Malvern held only a sample, which it selected by a technique known as optimization, with the goal of matching the performance of the 250 shares. Finally, for the smallest 8% of the market, Malvern held a small sample of shares and seven investment trusts that specialize in small companies. Given that Malvern exactly matched 100 shares that made up 71%

of the All-Share, and sampled both medium and small companies, we should expect Malvern to closely track the market. That's the goal of an index manager.

Active managers aim to beat the market and assume that:

- The market misprices securities and/or assets

and

- They are able to recognize the mispricing

For private investors to be able to benefit from this, two other conditions are necessary:

- It must be possible to select superior managers
- Those managers' fees and transaction costs must not offset any value they add

FUND MANAGEMENT OPTIONS

You have four options when it comes to buying shares and putting together a portfolio:

1. Do it yourself
2. Give it to an active manager to run as part of an actively managed pooled fund (i.e., an investment trust or a unit trust)
3. Give it to a passive manager to run as part of an indexed pooled fund (i.e., an indexed investment trust or an indexed unit trust)
4. Give it to an active manager to run as a separate portfolio for you

I look at each option in turn.

Manage your own portfolio

I don't think you should select individual company shares, I think you should buy pooled funds. The reasons for not buying shares are:

- It's not clear that most people—let alone part-time investors—have the ability to beat the market.
- Managing a portfolio is a time-consuming task. Your portfolio is supposed to provide unearned income to enhance your quality of life, not give you a second job. Even if you can beat the market, it may not be worth it if you have to spend 20 hours a week working on your portfolio. And completing your tax return will be a chore.
- To get adequate diversification you will need to buy a lot of shares, at least 20–30. Unless you have at least £100 000, and you are using a discount broker, your deals will be small and your cost of dealing high. Costs kill performance.

Pooled funds

I think you should buy a pooled fund or, preferably, funds. The advantages of pooled funds are:

- They provide instant diversification, hold many shares, and sometimes many different markets and asset classes.

- You can get good diversification for as little as £250 (see Chapter 16).

- It's easier to buy funds than shares with regular monthly savings.

- Pound cost averaging (discussed in Chapter 21) is a much safer strategy with a diversified pooled fund than a single share.

- The tax reporting burden is eased if you buy and hold a pooled fund. You only have to report its dividends, and not all the dividends of all the shares it holds for you. Capital gains tax computations will be easier to handle as you won't be endlessly switching in and out of different shares.

- Administration in general will be easier as the fund will handle things like stock dividends, share splits, rights issues and new issues for you.

- You will have to keep an eye on the performance of your fund, but otherwise you can ignore all that boring stuff in the papers about the number of new housing starts, the retail sales figures, etc., which you need to know about if you are selecting individual shares.

- You can buy many funds without going near a stockbroker, as I explain in Chapter 16.

- Many small shares are illiquid and it can prove to be costly or difficult to get out of them quickly. Most pooled funds can readily be sold, even those specializing in hard to trade smaller companies.

- There is a tax break with pooled funds that you don't get with shares. You don't pay CGT on share sales within the fund, but only when you sell the fund.

Active versus passive pooled funds

In the above discussion I've put the case for pooled funds. I've not distinguished between passive funds or actively managed ones. Nor have I distinguished between pooled funds with different legal structures such as investment trusts and unit trusts. I'll discuss these matters in the next chapter. It will suffice to say here that there is a strong case for the private investor having some form of pooled fund. Those that believe the arguments about the efficient market, or the evidence on fund performance, will be drawn to index funds, while those that don't will be drawn to active funds.

Have your own managed portfolio

Many private clients don't want to manage their own portfolio, but hate the idea of pooled funds. They want their own actively managed portfolio and get a stockbroker to do it. I think this is a lousy idea:

- It's not clear that most people, including stockbrokers, have the ability to beat the market.

- Even if some can, they won't work for you for nothing. And have you ever wondered about the ability of the person managing your money? Do you know who he or she is? I bet that unless you have got lots of money, the grey-haired person you gave your money to is the person who wins accounts, the young person hovering in the background ("my assistant") is the one who will actually manage it. If these people are so good, why are they not managing large institutional funds?

- Brokers tend to charge much higher rates of commission when managing your money than you would pay a discount broker, or a pooled fund will pay when it deals. A pooled fund may deal at 1½% less than the rate a broker will charge you. Your broker is unlikely to be good enough to recoup this loss for you.

- You may be attracted by the quality of the firm's research department. But the institutional sales-team will have told their institutional clients the gist of this research over the telephone long before the written version lands on the desk of a private client portfolio manager. By the time your portfolio's composition is affected by the research, the market price may have changed to reflect the research.

- Completing your tax return will be a chore.

- The heroes in a broking firm are not those whose clients beat the market, but those who generate the most commission. Your interest and the manager's interest do not always coincide.

I've spoken here of stockbrokers as though they were the only people to manage accounts. They aren't—you can get your money managed by a merchant bank, High Street bank or a boutique fund manager. The points made above obviously need to be adjusted slightly for each type of manager, but the general thrust of the points will remain valid. Sometimes investors select a stockbroker as their manager because they think a broker will build a "racier" portfolio. That's a mistake. All competent fund managers should attempt to build the portfolio that matches your objectives. All should be able to build a high-risk portfolio, or a conservative high-income portfolio, or whatever you specify.

If you decide to give your money to someone to manage for you, the least you should do is ask some of the questions listed on pages 84–85. Address them both to the manager, and to the assistant, since that's who you may be getting. In particular, demand a performance record. (I doubt that any performance record will tell you very much, but anyone who selects an active manager must believe that the record matters, and so should examine it.) Don't accept any confidentiality nonsense. You want to see performance data, not know whose account it is taken from. Don't accept the record of a "model portfolio", i.e., one that does not really exist, and which won't have true dealing costs subtracted. And don't accept the record of a pooled fund, unless the manager actually manages it. It is common for firms' institutional managers and private client managers to be completely separate, and the institutional managers to manage the investment trusts and unit trusts. These funds' records tell you nothing about how your portfolio is likely to perform. Even if the manager does manage the pooled fund, be suspicious. If it's good, buy the pooled fund instead of having your account managed.

Never mind the fees, feel the performance

Anyone who has talked to a financial adviser, or read the financial press, will sooner or later encounter something to the effect that you shouldn't worry too much about fees, it's performance that really matters. Of course, it is true that if fees are 1%

higher than average, while performance is 2% or so better than average, this will more than compensate. But the problem is that it is not clear that anybody consistently turns in superior performance, or if they do, that it is possible to know who they will be in advance. In short, from an efficient market viewpoint, it makes more sense to argue that since we don't know who will perform well, and we are unsure that it is even possible, the only thing we can sensibly do is assume that performance will be much of a muchness and avoid high fees since they are a certain drag on returns.

A LOOK AHEAD

Here's the plan for the next few chapters. In Chapter 16 I look at how you might construct an equity portfolio using pooled funds: it's a very practical chapter.

Chapters 17 and 18 are for experienced investors. Despite what I've said about the merits of funds, experience shows that many readers will still want to construct their own individual share portfolio so, in Chapter 17, I discuss the factors and techniques that appear to be related to superior stock returns. Although I consider a large number of things, the fact remains that there are few superior managers. Either what I discuss doesn't work when applied to real portfolios, or fund managers don't consistently use these things. I think the latter is the case, but that is not the same as saying you will outperform if you read Chapter 17, or that it's even worth making the effort.

Much of what I discuss in Chapter 17 involves following mechanical rules and setting your judgement to one side. It also has a strong element of buying "value" instead of "glamour". Too many managers seem too confident in their skills to follow simple rules. Maybe you can do better. Nonetheless, I still think you should buy a fund, partly because of what I've discussed, and partly because as you'll see from Chapter 17, active management involves hard work. Also, when I argue that, for example, high-yielding shares outperform, I'm not saying every high-yielding stock does. The argument is that if you buy them all, you will outperform over a period of years. Maybe 55% will outperform and 45% underperform, and on average you will come out ahead. To implement the insights of Chapter 17 requires broad diversification, which will be very costly for all but the largest of portfolios. Chapter 18 covers market timing and international investment strategy, both things I recommend that you don't try.

Private client investment managers should read Chapters 17 and 18. The wise private investor will skip over both.

In Chapter 19, I discuss bonds. Bonds are usually seen as less risky than shares, and therefore should have come after cash-based investments and before equities. But most people find bonds rather boring, and equities more interesting, so I have covered equities first.

In Chapter 20, I discuss PEPs, a tax-efficient way of investing in equities and certain types of bonds.

Some people know that equities have produced high returns over the years but are put off by their risky nature. In Chapter 21 I discuss how you can reduce your investment risks. I concentrate on equities, but the analysis applies to all assets. Chapter 21 is one of the most important chapters in the book.

You don't need to use a stockbroker to put together a portfolio of pooled funds, as I explain in Chapter 16, but you can use one if you wish. If you decide to buy individual shares, you will need a stockbroker. Selecting a stockbroker is discussed in Chapter 22.

16

Building a Portfolio of Equity Funds

Nothing astonishes men so much as common sense and plain dealing.
Ralph Waldo Emerson

This chapter looks at how you might form a portfolio of trusts, whether investment trusts or unit trusts. I will look at how you can buy trusts, whether you should have investment trusts or unit trusts, whether your portfolio should have a tilt, how international your portfolio should be, and which trusts you should buy. Don't skip to the end of the chapter for "The Answer". There isn't a single answer—what is best will depend on your circumstances and needs, your view of how markets work, and your attitude to risk.

HOW TO BUY AND SELL AN INVESTMENT TRUST

You can buy investment trusts in four ways and sell them by three:

● Through the manager

● Through a stockbroker

● Through a financial adviser

● As a new issue by prospectus (buy only)

Investment trust managers

With a regular savings plan the minimum sum you have to invest may be as little as £25 per month. With a lump-sum scheme the minimum may be as little as £250, i.e., you invest £250 and you have no further commitment. One scheme allows subsequent lump-sums to be as little as £30. The charges for these schemes vary, but are generally modest. The purchase charge may be anywhere from no commission up to 1%, but sales are usually slightly more expensive. There may be a minimum charge (of perhaps £10), or commission might be charged at 1.5%. The only catch with these schemes is that your order will not be executed when it is received. Orders are aggregated and dealt on a particular day of the month, or weekly, or perhaps daily for sums over £5000.

For a regular savings plan it's not really a catch that your money isn't invested at a specific moment you determined. The idea of a savings plan is to feed your money into the stockmarket on a regular basis, taking the rough with the smooth, but ensuring you don't put all your money into the market at the top. However, you may feel that it is a catch that you can't sell on a day you choose.

To get details of investment trust regular savings or lump-sum schemes contact the Association of Investment Trust Companies for a copy of the *Monthly Information Service* which contains the basic details for all companies, and then contact the companies that interest you—see READ ⬜ WRITE ⬛ RING ☎.

Stockbrokers

I discuss dealing through a stockbroker in Chapter 22. This is the best way to deal if you want to make a lump-sum investment of perhaps £10 000 or more, or to sell immediately. All stockbrokers will be expensive for deals of, say, £1000, and many will be expensive even for deals several times larger.

Financial advisers

You can get your adviser to arrange your investment trust deals for you but he or she will only go on to the manager or a stockbroker. The adviser will want remuneration. You will either pay a flat fee or pay commission on each deal. If you use an adviser, you will pay more. This is not usually the case with a unit trust, as I discuss later.

New issues

Finally, you can buy a new fund by completing a prospectus form. While that sounds a bit grand and mysterious, it's no more than many people have done for privatization issues. An advert—but an incredibly unexciting one, because it is a legal document—appears in some of the newspapers (especially the *Financial Times* and *Daily Telegraph*) and you fill in the coupon. Some financial advisers will send to you, often unsolicited, a prospectus.

In my view it never makes sense to buy an investment trust this way. The problem basically is that new trusts are sold at more than their asset value—some of your subscription disappears in fees, the amount varying with the trust—and it is likely the trust will move to a discount in the months following issue. You therefore suffer two blows. There can also be more subtle disadvantages, which I'll illustrate with a recent new issue.

The Gartmore Micro Index Trust was offered at 100p per share plus warrants on a one for five basis. The estimated net asset value was 97.25p. That's a loss, but not too bad if you allow for the fact that you are not paying any commission and you would suffer a bid/offer spread if you were buying in the market. However, with a new trust you are effectively buying cash—the trust still has to invest in shares when it has received your cash. This trust pointed out that it would take some time for it to be fully invested in shares, that the transaction costs of buying the shares would reduce its net asset value, and there would be a big impact from the bid/offer spread of small shares. As the prospectus explained: "When acquiring securities the Manager may well pay the offer price. These shares will then be valued in the portfolio at the average of their bid and offer prices, the mid price. The differences between mid and offer prices are relatively large for smaller companies due to their illiquidity and may have a greater impact on the portfolio's net asset value than they would for a portfolio comprising shares of larger companies."

Some investors get hooked on the idea that a particular market, or sector, or whatever, is about to soar and they had better jump in immediately, even if it means buying a new fund, because the rising market will easily absorb any costs and problems with a discount developing. All one can say is maybe, maybe not. Take the case of Old Mutual South Africa Trust (OMSAT). This was launched on 8 July 1994 at 100p and its assets rose by approximately 34% by the year end 31 August 1995. But, after costs, the initial assets were only 95.7p. per share, so the 34% rise only took the assets to 128.6p. Unfortunately OMSAT had slipped to a 21% discount by the year end, so the shares were priced at 102p. In this case, spectacular performance was almost fully offset by the issue costs and the subsequent move to a discount to NAV.

HOW TO BUY AND SELL UNIT TRUSTS

You can buy or sell unit trusts in three ways:

- From the unit trust manager

- Through your stockbroker or financial adviser

- Through a unit trust discounter

Unit trust managers

Dealing through the manager is straightforward. I'll assume initially that you want to buy. If you know which trust you want to buy, you find the unit trust prices section of your newspaper and look up the management company. For example, if you want to buy the Barclays Unicorn General Fund discussed in Chapter 13, you look up Barclays Unicorn, and you'll see its telephone number. You then call and say you want to buy either 1000 units, say, or invest £3000. The Barclays salesperson will then tell you what documents you will get from Barclays, when you have to send your cheque, and so on. You might ask for a discount—you can see in the *Financial Times* that the "Init Charge ", i.e., initial charge is 5.25%. If you are buying £100 000 of units, the manager might cut its fee for you, but if you are buying £3000 you will be met with a polite refusal. (I don't know Barclays policy—this is a general comment.) You do your deal (or not), receive a contract note, send off your cheque and eventually receive a certificate.

When it's time to sell, you can phone the manager, get a price, do your deal, and then sign the back of your certificate and post it off. A few days later you will get a cheque. You could sign the certificate and send it in without a phone call. You will have sold your units when the unit trust company receives your certificate instead of when you telephoned.

Each unit trust sets a minimum sum that you may invest. A sum of £1000 would be typical, although subsequent purchases of perhaps £250 may be permitted. Very small sums are expensive to administer. For many people, £1000 will be too large a sum to invest in one go. The answer is a regular savings plan.

Many unit trusts encourage regular savings. Many will allow you to invest as little as £50 per month. Some have an even lower minimum. Savings plans can usually be cancelled at any time, but the manager may require you to sell your units if you stop before you reach the normal minimum single purchase sum. The idea is to stop you circumventing the minimum by setting up a savings plan and then cancelling when you have £50 invested. Savings plan purchases will be made at the full buying price.

To get details of all unit trust groups' regular savings schemes contact AUTIF. Then contact the unit trust groups that interest you—see READ 📖 WRITE 🖻 RING ☎.

Stockbrokers and financial advisers

If you use a broker or financial adviser, he or she will do the paperwork for you. But you will still have to make a decision, get in touch with your adviser and write a cheque. If you can select, buy and pay for beans at Tesco, you can handle unit trust paperwork yourself. It's no more complicated. If your adviser buys for you, he or she will usually be rewarded by 3% commission which the unit trust company will pay from its initial charge. You won't pay extra. However, if you are buying from a low front-end load firm such as Murray Johnstone, there is not much to rebate to a broker or adviser. For some products, e.g., cash funds, gilt funds, and index funds, many unit trust companies either don't levy an initial charge or levy a reduced charge so there is nothing, or very little, to rebate to your adviser. In that case your adviser may ask you to pay an additional commission on top of the reduced or nil commission he or she receives.

Clearly, there is no particular reason to have an IFA execute your purchase if you make your own decisions. However, if you get advice, you should pay the adviser in some way. To pay via rebated commission is attractive as it costs you nothing extra. In effect you get free advice. Indeed it's actually cheaper than paying a fee. For example, if the adviser gave you extra units to the value of his rebated commission, but then charged you a 3% fee, the fee would be subject to VAT, so you would pay 0.525% extra. Of course, if you go the commission as opposed to the fee route, your adviser will not have an incentive to recommend trusts that don't pay commission, so to get truly unbiased advice, you should be willing to pay commission out of your pocket on those products.

You should make sure you understand whether your adviser expects to execute unit trust sales (as well as purchases) on your behalf. Unit trust companies do not make a charge on sales, so there is no commission to rebate on a sale. Will your adviser expect you to pay commission to him for a sale? Or will he be content to let you make the sale? You may or may not find this easy to do. Stockbrokers love registering everything in their nominee company's name. (I discuss nominee accounts in Chapter 22.) If your broker has done that, you won't be able to sell the unit trusts, only your broker will, something you will pay commission for. You can get round this by asking for your unit trust deals to be registered in your name although the broker may refuse to do this if your other assets are registered in its nominee name.

Unit trust discounters

Unit trust discounters include some of the discount stockbrokers, e.g. Fidelity, and others that are better known for other activities, e.g., Skipton Building Society, or specialists in discounted financial products, e.g., Chelsea Financial Services. Discounters will buy and sell any unit trust group's units for you.

The basis of charging by these companies varies, and you should make sure that you are using the cheapest for each particular deal. For example, Skipton, in November 1995, was charging a joining life membership fee of £5, 1% commission on each sale and purchase up to £5000 (minimum commission £15) and 0.1% commission on the excess over £5000. In turn, it would rebate the commission it received from the unit trust managers, typically 3%. So, if you bought £10 000 of units through Skipton, you would save 2.45%—in fact you would not get cash, but extra units to that value. If you don't need advice, this would be a much better way of buying units than going to the unit trust group direct, or through an adviser. Skipton registers the certificate in your name.

But there is a catch. On trusts with a low or zero initial charge, you could end up paying more with Skipton. You should make sure that the discount offered exceeds Skipton's commission. You could sell through Skipton too, but it will charge you for what you can do for free by dealing direct with the unit trust managers, and with less paperwork! Some specialist discounters (such as Chelsea Financial Services) basically split the commission with you. Which discounter you use is up to you, but it seems silly to buy any other way if you don't need advice.

Now you may wonder whether you need to go to all this trouble over pennies. Perhaps you'd rather give the order to your broker and pay up. Yet most people will happily wait all year for a return of 10%. A return—in the form of a cost saving—of 1-2% for a few minutes' thought must be one of the great investments. Think of how that will aid your compounding over the years—remember Table 3.1?

INVESTMENT TRUSTS VERSUS UNIT TRUSTS

Now you know how to deal, which type of trust should you be buying? There is no simple answer.

Over the years investment trusts have given superior returns, but that does not mean investment trusts are automatically the best buy. The superior returns may have partly come from genuinely superior management. That, however, seems unlikely. First, it is not clear that superior management exists, as I discussed in Chapter 14. Second, there is a large overlap in the management groups providing investment trusts and unit trust management. Why would the same company manage one type of fund better than another? In reality, most of the outperformance by investment trusts will have come from capital gains resulting from the discount narrowing over the last decade, from the effect of the discount increasing the income received by investors, from lower management charges, and the modest gearing of investment trusts. These sources of advantage may not last.

If you buy investment trusts on a narrow discount, you are less likely to make gains from the discount continuing to narrow. You may even lose by the discount widening.

Whatever happens, you can be sure that the discount will fluctuate in size. You may feel that this uncertainty, or risk, requires that you be rewarded with extra return. In other words, part of the better performance of investment trusts would disappear if we looked at matters on a risk-adjusted basis. As to charges, annual management charges on recently launched investment trusts have tended to be close to the level on unit trusts. Also, it is now possible to pay a reduced front-end load on most unit trusts by dealing through a discounter. So it is less certain that there will be a cost advantage in favour of investment trusts in general, although some remain exceptionally cheap. Finally, gearing can be a two-edged sword. In a prolonged bear market, investment trust returns would suffer from being geared.

It is difficult to claim that one type of pooled fund is superior to another, although I favour investment trusts because of the opportunity to buy funds at a discount and many have a low annual management charge. But there are a few points worth stating:

1. If you can buy a large general investment trust on a 10–20% discount you will probably outperform a unit trust with similar objectives. The discount will increase your income, the annual charge plus VAT will probably be lower (by up to nearly 1½%), and the odds favour the discount narrowing rather than widening. But only time will tell if this last statement is true. In fact, if you have a long holding period, movements in the discount are not too important because the higher income will offset quite a large increase in the discount.
2. Purchasing a new issue investment trust is hard to justify. You will be paying more than net asset value, and most trusts eventually trade at a discount. You are likely to do better by buying an existing investment trust with a similar record trading at a discount, if one exists, or a unit trust. Investment trusts in "hot" investment areas (typically those with good historic performance or a new concept, plus lots of new fund launches) may all be priced at NAV or selling on a premium. Hot areas come and go, and discounts may appear. If you want to invest in such an area, a unit trust seems a less risky course.
3. Illiquid markets or areas are best bought in the form of an investment trust. Unit trusts are open-ended and, if a market turns sour, the investors can sell their units back to the manager. The manager is then forced to sell the underlying investments. In an out-of-favour area, the spreads on the underlying investments may be wide. Of course, while an investment trust doesn't have to sell the underlying investments, the trust itself may suffer a widening discount when the market falls, so shareholders may be no better off. However, if investors are willing to hold such investments over a complete market cycle, or can buy investment trusts that have wide discounts, the investment trust route seems better.
4. If you don't need advice, it makes no sense to buy a unit trust from the manager when a number of specialist firms will share the front-end commission with you.

SHOULD YOU GIVE YOUR FUND A TILT?

You may decide that the returns from the stockmarket have been so good over the years that you would like a piece of the action. Nothing fancy, a plain vanilla fund that will get you in the game. That's a perfectly sensible view and you would be best served by a general fund.

You might decide that you need an income tilt to your portfolio because you have a need for income. In that case you should be looking to a fund with a high yield. But don't buy a bond fund. Either buy a high-yield equity fund or, if you want an even higher yield, buy a gilt through National Savings (see Chapter 19).

If you believe any of the material discussed in Chapter 17, you might want to buy a fund that has a tilt towards a factor that has been related to superior performance. To save you reading the chapter, the evidence seems to point away from shares that promise fast growth to those that are simply cheap in terms of having a high yield, or a low price–earnings ratio. This sort of approach is described as value-orientated. Small shares have also performed well. While there are some funds that take a value orientation, there are none that simply buy, for example, low price–earnings ratio shares. The two tilts that are related to superior performance, and which you can buy, are smaller shares and high yield. Had you bought the average performing fund in the four unit trust categories of general, growth, smaller companies and income ten years ago, the total return to 29 September 1995 per £1000 invested would have been £3184, £3112, £3022 and £3496 respectively (source: HSW in *Money Management*, November 1995). In other words, the income emphasis would have worked, but not the smaller companies emphasis. However, as I show further on, you get a different picture if you look at a five-year record. It's up to you whether you go for a vanilla fund or one with some kind of tilt.

HOW INTERNATIONAL SHOULD YOUR FUND BE?

There are two ways of approaching this. The first asks what is ideal, the second asks how much income you can afford to give up. The point here is that international markets generally have a lower yield than the UK market. Thus if you have a yield requirement for your portfolio as a whole, you will not be able to have much of an international exposure.

If you are not constrained by an income requirement, remember that British firms are very internationally orientated. Partly this is a result of the colonial tradition, partly a belief that growth prospects are better abroad. About half of all British stockmarket profits are earned from either exports or from owning firms overseas. You could argue that if you have a general British portfolio you don't really need to have foreign shares. (A British investment trust investing only in Japanese shares is technically a British share. For my purposes here, I'd count it as a foreign share.) There is an argument about diversification, however, that suggests you should hold some foreign shares. British shares with big overseas exposure tend to move more with the British market than with the overseas markets. By holding some foreign shares that don't move in step with the British market, your total portfolio will show less price variability, i.e., it will be less risky. On the other hand, the greater your overseas exposure, the greater your asset/liability mismatch—your assets will be in foreign currencies and your expenditure will be mainly in sterling. About 30% of what you consume is imported.

What is the ideal solution? I'm not sure there is one. I think you probably should have 10–30% invested in foreign shares, but if you have all British ones, I wouldn't worry. I would worry if you have predominantly foreign shares. Who knows what will happen to the pound versus other currencies? If you will be living in the UK, it seems sensible to keep most of your money in sterling and not bet on a foreign currency.

If you decide to have international exposure, you can do it in three basic ways. You can buy individual international shares, buy general international trusts, or buy specialized international trusts. Buying individual international shares is a non-starter. You face all the problems of selecting shares, but now on a world-wide scale. You will also face steep commissions and safe-custody charges (i.e., you will be charged by a foreign bank for holding your shares in the country of origin). Buying a pooled fund is the only sensible approach.

A general international fund invests abroad but the exact country weightings are changed from time to time by the fund manager. Such funds can range all the way from funds which never invest in the UK, funds which do include the UK but at around 10–20% (reflecting the size of the UK market as a percentage of world markets), and funds which invest in the UK anywhere from 50 to 80% of the fund and invest the rest internationally. Some of the biggest pooled funds in the UK adopt this approach, for example, Alliance Investment Trust, Foreign and Colonial Investment Trust, Scottish Mortgage Investment Trust and Witan Investment Trust. Say you want 20% invested abroad and one of these big funds has 40% abroad. All you need do is buy a pure UK fund and the general fund in equal amounts and you have your 20% international weighting.

Alternatively you could buy a UK fund or funds with 80% of your money and put, say, 5% in a specialist US fund, 5% in Japan, 5% in Europe and 5% in emerging markets. This way you aim to get best of the best, the best US fund, the best Japanese fund and so forth. The problem is that it's not clear that you or your adviser will be able to pick the best, and also you will have to decide your international asset allocation. If you want to change it, you will incur costs. The general trusts will make asset changes more cheaply than you can, but the problem with the general trust is that you have no say over the weighting of the USA versus Japan, etc.

I prefer the general trust route, but that's just my view. Here's how I reason. Say you want 20% in the international markets. Unless you wish to go nap on some smaller area such as New Zealand (and I wouldn't recommend you go nap on any area), you will probably want some money in each area. The general funds will do that. Since we are talking about 20% of your money, it would be surprising if you got more than 5% more than you wanted in an area (say 10% in the USA, instead of the 5% you want). In the end, 5% isn't much. Imagine the area performs 20% worse than others. You'll have lost 1% ($5\% \times 0.2$) as a result of not being able to control your asset allocation. That's not the end of the world—anyway, the manager may be right and you wrong, and in that case you'll make money. If you do want a lot more in any area, you can easily add a specialist fund in just that area.

Emerging markets

There has been increasing interest in "emerging markets" and while they are just part of international investing, it is worth saying a little about them. They are either developing economies or markets that have only recently opened to outside investors and may still have significant restrictions. They include, for example, Argentina,

Brazil, Chile, Colombia, Mexico, Venezuela, South Korea, Philippines, China, Taiwan, India, Indonesia, Malaysia, Pakistan, Thailand, Greece, Jordan, Nigeria, Portugal, Turkey, Russia, Zimbabwe, Botswana and South Africa.

The current size of these markets is not necessarily a good guide to the size of the underlying national economy. Depending on how you do the sums, India may have a larger economy than four of the G7 Group of industrial nations, i.e., France, Italy, the UK and Canada. Brazil and Mexico also have larger economies than Canada. China may well be the second largest economy in the world. The emerging markets will be very important in the long term, but they already have interesting characteristics for investors.

Emerging markets are very risky, they have offered high returns, and they have low correlation of returns with each other and also with more developed markets. Individually, the emerging market countries are very risky indeed. But taken as a group the risk is greatly reduced—although still high. The reason risk falls so much by taking all the markets together is that their returns have a very low correlation with each other. (I discuss correlation of returns in detail in Chapter 21.) The emerging markets are quite different from one another.

There are many ways of looking at these differences: size, political stability, growth rates and so forth. Jordan is a small country while Indonesia, with a population of 180 million, is one of the largest in the world. Zimbabwe has a tiny stockmarket, while the value of Taiwan's stockmarket is about the same as that of Austria, Denmark, Finland, Ireland and Norway combined. Emerging market growth rates are on average higher than developed countries', but the spread of rates is much wider amongst emerging markets than amongst developed countries. There are few trade ties between the various emerging markets although there are, of course, some ties between countries in the same geographical area. And, from a strictly stockmarket viewpoint, the restrictions on investment that have existed, or still exist, tend to isolate the markets from each other.

Making certain assumptions about risk and return, some American consultants have shown that if investors are happy with the risk level of the major world equity markets, they should be at least 30%–40% invested in emerging markets for a significantly enhanced return at no extra risk. Beyond that point, extra return comes at the cost of extra risk. This is a result of the low correlation of returns. At a commonsense level these weightings seem excessively high, and they are very sensitive to the assumptions made about the correlations and excess returns earned by the emerging markets. But exposure to emerging markets does seem warranted.

Many managers claim to be able to pick the best shares and markets. But you should be aware that the political and economic issues they will have to deal with in emerging markets are not the usual ones. Researchers Ibbotson and Brinson, discussing a different age, point out the dangers: "Eighteenth- or nineteenth-century investors who bet on the United States, Canada or Britain would have been prodigious forecasters of the world economy. In 1900, an international investor might well have bought Austro-Hungarian, Russian, and German stocks instead of US and British issues. The Austro-Hungarian equities would have lost all their value by the end of World War I. The Russian equities would have been rendered worthless by the communist government, which nationalized firms not long after the Russian Revolution of 1917. And German equity claims were wiped out by World War II."

To avoid these sort of risks an investor should buy a fund that is well diversified by country.

Most managers will run a general international fund with regard to market capitalizations, i.e., they will tend to have large weightings in big markets. Because the emerging markets, even as a group, have a small market capitalization, a general fund will not give you much exposure to emerging markets. If you want to get more, you may have to hold a small weighting in a specialist fund as well. But don't be seduced by the name. Emerging markets sound as though they are a sure-fire winner: you could rename emerging markets as "markets that haven't made it yet, and may never". Emerging markets really are risky.

ACTIVE FUNDS VERSUS INDEX FUNDS

I argued in earlier chapters that there were theoretical arguments for doubting that fund managers would display consistently good performance. I claimed that the record of UK pension fund managers was consistent with chance. And the US mutual fund evidence suggests that buying past winners is not a sure way to superior returns. What's the evidence for UK pooled funds? It's generally consistent with what I've said.

Which? looked at picking investment trust winners on the basis of past performance. Unfortunately, the statistical details weren't published, so it's impossible to judge how careful the study was. For what it's worth, it concluded: "Our analysis shows that past performance figures don't guarantee future performance. In fact, in most cases they don't even give you a guide. It doesn't mean that past performance information is useless: some of our tests showed that by considering past performance you may do better than you would expect by chance" (August 1993, p. 55).

With regard to unit trusts there are a number of popular notions of the best way to pick a unit trust. Here are some of the notions, and what *Which?* researchers found (for details see READ 📖 WRITE 🖃 RING ☎):

- *Small trusts (in terms of asset size) are best.* Not true.

- *Past performance is the best guide.* Unreliable guide.

- *A good fund management group is the key.* Little supporting evidence.

- *Newly launched trusts are the best.* True to a degree, but new funds don't remain new for long, so expensive switches would need to be made to follow this strategy, and that would kill it. Also, while new trusts do a bit better than old trusts investing in the same area, a different type of trust may well do even better.

- *Trusts investing in small companies are best.* Has been true over long periods.

- *Go for income and growth will follow.* Income trusts have outperformed other trusts over the long term, but it is not true that the highest yielding of the income trusts have been the best income trusts.

I take this to mean that your chances of picking the best pooled funds in each category are low. (In a more recent article, *Which?* seems to have had a change of heart, because it provided a list of good performing funds and management groups. But it didn't address the issue of whether good recent performance would be maintained.) If you are sceptical about the chances of picking funds that will perform well in the future, you should consider index funds.

Whatever the theoretical merits of index funds, it has to be noted that they have not been very popular amongst investors or financial advisers. Part of the dislike is almost certainly the fact that most people find it hard to believe that there are not good fund managers. The racy investor will want to be in the latest hot area or with a top-performing fund manager (on an historical basis). The staid investor will probably find equities in general too racy and so will not be drawn to an index fund either. Financial advisers claim to offer a service by picking the best fund managers. If they said there was no such thing, their clients might wonder why they needed the adviser. A better argument against index funds is that the experience of index funds has been somewhat mixed, and which index fund to buy is not a simple decision.

There are three ways for the private investor to index, via unit trusts (both onshore and offshore), investment trusts, and bonds whose payments are related to an index. I'll begin with unit trusts, discussing only onshore trusts.

There are more than 40 unit trusts that attempt to match an index. Some of the funds have very large minimum investments, but most investors will be able to find a trust they can invest in which tracks each of the UK market, the USA, Japan, Europe (with or without the UK) and the world ex-UK. The problem begins when we look at the index being tracked. Some indices are quite broad such as the FT-SE-A All-Share (for the UK) or the S&P 500 (for the USA), but others are more limited and track large companies (FT-SE 100) or very small companies (Gartmore MicroCap Index), or something in-between (FT-SE-A Mid 250). Some indices will not mean much at all to most investors—who knows the significance of the differences between the Nikkei Dow Jones 225 and the FTA World Japan Index, both indices of the Japanese market?

Now the problem is that these arcane issues matter. There can be significant differences between the performance of the two Japanese indices for example, both of which are supposed to measure the Japanese market as a whole. So it matters which index you track. And it clearly matters if you decide to track the total market, but smaller companies outperform.

In general, unit trust managers probably tend to invest in smaller size foreign stocks on average than those comprising the total market indices, so an index fund for a foreign market probably can't be fairly compared against the active funds. For what it's worth, the foreign market index funds don't have a compelling record.

Where one can clearly compare like with like, the index funds do well. In the UK General category, the index funds which track the All-Share index show up as good performers. All the funds in the General category have a broadly similar benchmark: funds with a smaller companies bias are shown in a separate unit trust category. The fund that stands out here is Gartmore UK Index. Its ranking, and that of some other good performers, is shown in Table 16.1. The periods are to 29 September 1995. The first number shows the value of a £1000 investment, and the second its ranking during each period. Below the funds is the value of £1000 invested in the average fund in a number of categories. The index funds perform better than the average fund in each category except for smaller company funds where only the top three index funds do better over five years. Part of the generally good performance of index funds comes

Table 16.1 Index Unit Trusts Performance
(periods to 29/9/95)

	£1000, buy to sell, net income reinvested and ranking							
	1 year		2 years		3 years		5 years	
Gartmore UK Index	1177	2	1210	4	1554	16	2010	9
Morgan Grenfell UK Index	1103	48	1125	36	1434	44	1928	21
Norwich UK Index	1120	22	1146	17	1463	17	1948	16
Royal Life UK Index	1092	63	1135	25	1438	43	1929	20
Schroder UK Index	1133	11	1146	16	1467	34	1910	25
Number of Funds		99		97		92		85

	£1000, buy to sell, net income reinvested			
	1 year	2 years	3 years	5 years
Average UK General Unit Trust	1096	1111	1452	1837
Average UK Growth Unit Trust	1098	1121	1520	1863
Average UK Smaller Companies Unit Trust	1069	1142	1720	1928
Average UK Income Unit Trust	1074	1082	1515	1827

Source: HSW in *Money Management* November, 1995

from their lower charges. The bid/offer spread varies from about 1.6% to 6.5% and the annual charge from 0.22% to 0.75%. Not surprisingly, the funds with the lowest costs tend to perform best.

Turning to investment trusts, there are a number that attempt to match indices. Malvern attempts to match the FT-SE-A All-Share Index, Abtrust European Index attempts to match the FT-SE Eurotrack Index, and there are several which aim to match smaller company indices. The Malvern fund is an alternative to the unit trust UK index funds that track the total market. It trades at close to net asset value, and a large discount is unlikely to appear because professional traders would arbitrage away the discount by buying the fund and selling other assets. Also it can be wound up each year (i.e., investors can vote for it to be liquidated and the cash returned). The Abtrust fund has sold at discount of 10% or more. It tracks the FT-SE Eurotrack 100, a large company index, which is not especially interesting.

The third way of indexing is more exotic. A number of investment trusts (e.g., Scottish American, British Assets and Broadgate) have issued loan stocks that are linked to the FT-SE-A All-Share Index. Technically these issues are bonds, but their returns are linked to the stockmarket. In general the idea is that the bonds are issued at, say, £100, and the redemption (or repayment) value is the £100 increased (or decreased) by exactly the same percentage change as the FT-SE-A All-Share Index has enjoyed or suffered. Interest is paid by reference to the gross yield on the All-Share Index.

Although these stocks can trade at a discount or premium to net asset value, they have tended to trade at close to net asset value. This seems likely to continue to be the case, at least for a large issue such as British Assets Equities Index Unsecured Loan Stock 2005, because if it trades at a significant premium or discount, professionals would use it in arbitrage activities and this would drive it back to asset value. How do you know whether this stock is cheap or dear? First, find the value of the FT-SE-A All-Share Index which is shown in the *Financial Times* in line 89 of the "FT-SE Actuaries Share Indices: The UK Series" and also in "Indices and Ratios" in the

"Market Report". Then shift the decimal point one point to the left. That is the fair value of the stock. For example, if the index is 1,597.23, the fair value of the stock is 159.723p, i.e., 160p.

These loan stocks are unsecured loans—i.e., they are not guaranteed by specific assets—so investors are taking some risk in indexing by this method. However, in general, the loans are only about one-third of each trust's assets, so there is negligible risk for the loan stock holders.

If you are willing to take the risk of an unsecured loan, these stocks should give the best return of the various ways of indexing, especially if bought at a modest discount to theoretical asset value, and through a discount broker. It is often possible to buy, after all costs, at slightly less than the asset value. Since there is no annual management charge, you will get the full index income. In effect, there are no costs at all.

To sum up, there is a reasonably good case for arguing that a UK index fund would be a very sensible investment decision, but the case for non-UK index funds is not compelling for a private investor.

BRINGING IT ALL TOGETHER

There is no perfect way of constructing a portfolio. Perhaps I can best give the flavour of how it might be done by "thinking aloud". I could do this for a hypothetical person, and derive, say, Peter's portfolio, but I'll do it as though it were my own. That will make the discussion seem more real. What I'll come up with isn't my actual portfolio, but it's a plausible portfolio for the assumptions I make. You should not assume that anything I say is a recommendation. I'll just think aloud in a rational way consistent with the discussion in this book. I'll use real products, but I'm not making recommendations. I'll assume that I've no particular yield requirement, so I can invest in whatever I want.

Beginning with my international allocation, I'm not sure what to think about the international weighting I should have. I'm going to go for 20%, partly because I'm going to put 10% in one particular area and that only leaves 10% to be spread round the world. I'm not going for 30% because I'm mindful that UK companies are big international investors themselves.

I find the evidence on index funds persuasive for the UK, but I note that index funds in other markets haven't always beaten the average manager, probably because they are investing against slightly different benchmarks. I'm often abroad, indeed I'm writing this in the gardens of a beach hotel in Goa. I can do without having to worry about what my investment managers are up to in my absence. I'm going to put 50% into UK index funds: when I see on satellite television that the market is up so much or down so much, that will be more or less what I've done. I won't come back to find my star stock has imploded and left a black hole in my portfolio. I doubt that my index funds will be the best performers, but I will be disappointed if my funds aren't in the top third of all funds over a five-year period, and the top quarter over ten years.

I like the idea of the effectively cost-free loan stocks that track the market. But I note they are unsecured. I'll buy the cheapest on the day, but only put a third of my index money into it. I'll also buy the Gartmore UK index unit trust (based on its small price spread, modest annual charge, and Table 16.1) and Malvern UK Index investment trust (which also has a good record). Having three index funds is less risky than having one (someone may steal the assets at one, have cash with bank that goes bust, or whatever—unlikely, but possible) and this way I'll get dividends more often. Since I'm doing all the thinking, I'm not going to pay for advice, so I'll buy the investment trust and loan stock through a discount stockbroker (see Chapter 22), and I'll buy the unit trust directly from the manager since there is no initial charge to recoup through a unit trust discounter.

I think UK smaller companies may do well, but I doubt fund managers can spot the winners. I'll put 5% into small companies and 5% into really small companies. I'll go the index route, and select the Hoare Govett Smaller Companies Investment Trust and the Gartmore Micro Investment Trust, but only if they are not selling at a premium.

I think the emerging markets are very risky, but could give spectacular returns. I'll invest 5% into each of two of the most broadly diversified funds I can find. I don't know which area is best, so I don't want more than about 10% of each fund in any country. At the time of writing there are investment trusts meeting this specification on substantial discounts. I'll buy two of them. Were they around net asset value, I'd buy unit trusts. A 10% weighting in emerging markets is aggressive. However, I can bear risk, I don't need income, and I have lots of non-stockmarket assets.

I've now invested 60% of my money in the UK and 10% overseas. To get another 10% overseas I'll invest the remaining 35% in three actively managed general funds that overall give me about a 30% exposure to foreign markets and 70% to the UK. I'm therefore picking up about 10% international exposure this way (i.e., 30% × 35% = 10.5%). I prefer investment trusts because of the low fees and the extra income because of the discount. I'll start there and look at the past performance record. I'll eliminate the worst performers, but I won't necessarily buy the best performers. For example, if a good performer is on a narrow discount, I'll probably ignore it. I'll also favour funds with low annual charges. I'll read each fund's objective. I want vanilla funds, rather than those with a tilt. I'll use the sort of data that appeared in Tables 12.3 and 12.4. If I can't find three I like, I'll look at unit trusts.

I could have turned to an IFA or the press for advice on who are the best managers. But basically they tell you who was best in the past. You can find the same information yourself in *Money Management* and *Planned Savings* and other professional publications, or Micropal's Star Ratings™ (based on processing historical performance data). But, as I discussed in Chapter 14, the past isn't necessarily prologue. So I prefer the approach of the previous paragraph.

Isn't it irrational to have active UK investment in the general investment trusts given I've gone the index route earlier? Possibly, but I can live with it. It's only a quarter of my portfolio, I will be paying very low annual charges, I will get some gearing, I won't have to continually make decisions, and the discount will increase my income. And my orientation in picking the trusts has been value rather than a star manager.

Let's say I've built my portfolio as I've outlined. I'm now 60% indexed, with 50% indexed via three funds to the FT-SE-A All-Share, and a further 10% indexed via two funds to two small company indexes. I've got five active funds, two specializing in emerging markets and three covering the whole world but with a UK bias. So I've got nine funds, with about 17% in an unsecured loan stock (but performing like UK equities),

17% in a unit trust, and the rest in investment trusts. Had the investment trust discounts been less attractive, I'd have more in unit trusts and less in investment trusts.

In this example, the asset allocation discount is the total portfolio allocation. But if you hold PEPs (discussed in Chapter 20), the portfolio construction should be juggled to take account of those holdings. For example, the non-PEP portfolio might have a bigger weighting in emerging markets than 10%, if the PEPs have none, and the goal is 10% of all equities to be in emerging markets.

Will the portfolio discussed be the best performing? Definitely not. It's not concentrated enough for that: you have to bet everything in one area to be best – or worst. Unfortunately I don't know which the best portfolio will be. My portfolio won't be bad, and it meets my hypothetical needs as specified earlier. Could you construct a portfolio to meet your needs? I think so, if you take it step by step, diversify, and don't delude yourself about your skills.

When will I change my portfolio? I'm not sure why I'd want to change the main UK index funds. I guess if I anticipated a really awful recession I'd sell the smaller company funds. If the emerging market funds doubled in a year I might get out. But I doubt that they will. I'm not sure why I'd sell the general funds. Maybe if I read in the Annual Report of one of them that a new go-go manager had been appointed and he is going to gear the fund to the hilt. Otherwise I can't see what action will be needed. A snooze on the beach seems in order. Should you have the portfolio I've constructed? No, it's just an example of how anybody who is willing to think about constructing a portfolio might reason and I am not recommending the products mentioned. You may well reason differently, and have different circumstances, resources, goals, attitudes to risk, and so on.

READ 📖 WRITE 🖅 RING ☎

♦ For details of investment trust savings plans, see *Monthly Information Service*, from the Association of Investment Trust Companies, Durrant House, 8–13 Chiswell Street, London, EC1Y 4YY. Tel: 0171 588 5347. Fax: 0171 638 1803.

♦ For details of unit trust savings plans, contact The Association of Unit Trusts and Investment Funds (AUTIF), and ask for *Monthly Savings* and *Unit Trusts: The Directory*. AUTIF, 65 Kingsway, London, WC2B 6TD. Tel: 0181 207 1361.

♦ The *Which?* study of investment trusts and performance mentioned in the text is: "Are Investment Trusts For You?", *Which?* August 1993, 52–57.

♦ The *Which?* study of unit trusts and performance persistence is "Which Unit Trust?", *Which?* July 1990, 384–389. The more recent study which selects "best buys" is: "Are You Trust Worthy?", *Which?*, September 1995, 30–37.

♦ The study by the American consultants mentioned in the text is: A. B. Divecha, J. Drach and D. Stefek, "Emerging Markets: A Quantitative Perspective", *Journal of Portfolio Management*, 19, Fall 1992, 41–50. It is reprinted in Stephen Lofthouse, *Readings in Investments*. Chichester: Wiley, 1994.

♦ The Ibbotson and Brinson quote is from: R. G. Ibbotson and G. P. Brinson, *Investment Markets*. New York: McGraw-Hill, 1987.

17

Selecting Shares

Don't gamble; take all your savings and buy some good stock, and hold it till it goes up,
then sell it. If it don't go up, don't buy it.

Will Rogers

I recommend that you don't select individual shares, but stick to investment trusts or unit trusts. That said, many investors insist on picking shares, so in this chapter I give a guide for stock pickers. However, this chapter is geared to the needs of experienced investors and investment professionals. Readers new to investment should skip it.

There are a number of ways to select stocks, but many of them require information that will not usually be available to the private investor. I will indicate when a style can be put into effect by a private investor. I sometimes advise that the necessary information will be available in a public library. You may see that as unhelpful advice, as you aren't going to waste time in a library. However, if you are not willing to make at least some of the effort the professionals do, you should be buying investment trusts or unit trusts, even if you are an experienced investor. OK, you've been warned: now for the advanced course.

EARNINGS-BASED APPROACHES

Expectations about earnings (i.e., profits) lie at the heart of much investment analysis. Theoretical models of share appraisal usually require earnings estimates and investment analysts spend a great deal of time forecasting earnings. There are four main ways of utilizing earnings estimates:

- The first assumes that fast earnings growth is always attractive.

- The second assumes that shares are correctly priced, based on consensus earnings (i.e., the average of stockbrokers' forecasts of profits), and the investor buys or sells depending on whether he or she thinks the consensus is too low or too high. This approach relies on the investor having superior earnings forecasting skills.

- The third approach is a variant of this approach and relies on other investors reacting slowly to earnings surprises (i.e., results that turn out different from brokers' expectations) and to earnings revisions (i.e., brokers changing their forecasts) while reacting quickly oneself.

- The fourth approach involves calculating the price a share should be selling at by looking either at the anticipated dividend stream (this approach is usually described as the dividend discount model) or calculating a justifiable price–earnings ratio. I'll briefly discuss all four approaches, although I will omit the justifiable price–earnings approach, as I will discuss a variant later.

Forecasting profits

The simplest approach to selecting shares is to assume that earnings are self-evidently "a good thing" and that investors should buy shares with the highest consensus earnings growth. This equates to the ordinary person's "It's a good company making lots of money". If many investors take this view, however, it is likely that shares will be priced to reflect consensus earnings estimates: as a result there may be no relationship between returns and consensus estimates.

A slightly more complex approach would be to assume that shares are correctly priced based on consensus forecasts and to try to make a more accurate forecast than the consensus. Investors with forecasting skills might assume that if their forecast is, say, 10% higher than the market's, then the share price should be 10% higher than it currently is.

In a famous American study it was shown that good forecasting skill is highly desirable. Stocks with the highest *actual* profits growth produced the highest returns. But investors don't know actual earnings, they have to make do with forecasts, which are often wide of the mark. Unfortunately investors were unable to achieve excess returns by buying the stocks with the highest consensus *forecast* growth of earnings. It seems consensus expected earnings are reflected in stock prices. This suggests that so-called growth stock managers are wasting their time, and your money.

You will only pick winners if your forecasts are better than the market's. There is no evidence that some professional forecasters are consistently superior. Can you forecast more accurately than the professionals, and do you know what the market consensus is? You need to know both that the market expects ABC Ltd's profits to rise by 37%, say, and that it will really be 52%. I doubt you can make money this way.

Reacting to surprises and revisions

Stocks that produce favourable earnings surprises perform well, and stocks that produce unfavourable surprises perform poorly. By surprise, I mean surprise in relation to the consensus forecast. The good performance both precedes and follows the earnings announcement. It is possible to outperform by reacting quickly to surprises. Further, analysts periodically revise their earnings forecasts. They tend to be too cautious, and often keep revising in the same direction. You can beat the market by responding to these revisions and to trends in earnings revisions.

The market is inefficient in its response to earnings surprises and revisions and it is possible to base a share selection strategy on these findings. Unfortunately, most private investors will not be able to follow stockbrokers' analysts' forecasts and their revisions (although they are available, albeit a bit late, in the publications *The Estimate Directory* and *Company REFS*). However, you often see that a stock has slumped when the results are announced. The press comments may explain it as "below analysts' expectations". That's a negative surprise. If you have held a stock that has suffered an adverse earnings surprise and watched the price slump you may have found it hard to admit you had goofed and then rationalized no action by saying that the fall in earnings was now in the price, the earnings disappointment was a one-off, and so forth. You would probably improve your performance if you sold immediately after such a disappointment. Despite the chance to earn a commission, your broker, if he put you into the stock, is unlikely to recommend a sale. His ego over-rules his pocket. Press comment on share price moves is usually contained in a market report section (e.g., on the back page of the Companies and Markets section of the *Financial Times*; the "Stockmarket" feature in *The Times*: the "Market Report" feature in *The Independent*; "The Market" in *The Daily Telegraph*).

Dividend discount model

This is the favourite approach of the textbooks. In the same way that you can assess the value of a bond on the basis of the interest payments it makes, you can assess the value of a share on the basis of all the dividends it pays. Of course, this means forecasting dividends from here to eternity, no small task. The usual approach is to simplify the task by forecasting actual dividends for a few years, and then assume some rate of growth for the next so many years, and finally assume that the dividend growth rate will approximate to that of the whole stockmarket. You would buy the shares that look cheap on the basis of their anticipated dividend stream. In America, some firms use this approach, but in the UK it is not widely used. Private investors will not be able to make the forecasts, so I will ignore this approach.

STOCKBROKER AND PRESS RECOMMENDATIONS

Many investors buy shares on the basis of other people's recommendations, especially those of stockbrokers and the press. The evidence is that it may be worth following these recommendations, but the benefit is small.

The major academic studies of brokers' research do not assess the typical broker's buy, hold and sell recommendations. The bias of brokers' research to buy and hold recommendations would probably produce poor results if the recommendations were slavishly followed. The major studies have assessed forecasts of specific returns, or looked at the value of changes in analysts' recommendations. In the latter case, a "buy" recommendation would not be especially interesting, but a change from "hold" to "buy" would be. Usually private clients will not have access to this information.

Private clients who do not have access to brokers' research need not despair, they are not missing something that is especially useful. The size of outperformance achievable by following brokers' views is modest in relation to some of the outperformance offered by other strategies mentioned in this chapter. Indeed, since analysts' recommendations will be partly based on their profit forecasts and changes, it is reasonable to ask whether their recommendations have any value over and above that contained in their profits forecasts. Since strategies based on earnings surprises and revisions seem to lead to higher returns than following recommendations, one might argue that analysts' views are actually something to avoid if one is already looking at their forecasts!

Press recommendations may have some value, but it would be very surprising if you could get rich from following newspaper tips. If the tips were really good, the market makers would change share prices as soon as the market opened, and before you could deal.

FACTORS

A factor-based approach to share selection is one that selects shares that are high on a factor that has been found to be related to superior returns. Some of these factors are: low price–earnings ratio; low price-to-sales ratio; low price; small size; high yield; neglect; high book-to-market value; net current assets less than price and other accounting attributes; new issues.

Low price–earnings ratio

The price–earnings ratio, abbreviated to PER or P/E, is the price of a share divided by the earnings (i.e., profits) per share. It tells you the number of years of constant profits it would take to equal the share price. A share expected to grow rapidly should have a high price-earnings ratio, whereas one with poor prospects should have a low price–earnings ratio. There should not be a systematic relationship between returns and price–earnings ratios. But in fact numerous studies have shown that there is—low price–earnings ratio stocks offer higher returns. In other words the cheap, or "value" stocks, outperform the expensive or "glamour" stocks. This has been true over long periods, although not necessarily over short periods.

In Figure 17.1, I show the findings of one UK study. Stocks have been divided into five groups, or quintiles, on the basis of their price–earnings ratio. The lowest fifth of PERs go into one quintile, the next lowest fifth into the next, and so on. Excess returns are measured as the return from a particular quintile less the return from the

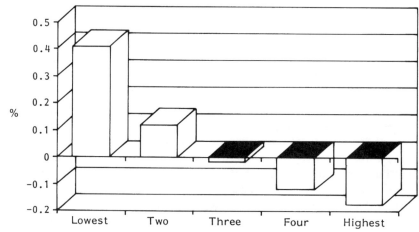

Figure 17.1 UK 1961–85 Monthly Excess Returns: PER Quintiles. Source: Drawn from data in Levis (1989, p. 687)

market as a whole. As you can see, picking the low PER stocks would have enabled an investor to beat the market. Specifically, low PER stocks earned about 0.4% per month, or 4.8% per year, more than the market.

There have been many explanations put forward for these findings. The one I find most plausible is that price–earnings ratios do not reflect prospects but history. I think investors give companies glamour ratings on the basis of their past performance and not their prospects. However, sometimes in the short run, certainly in the long run, the growth rates of glamour and value stocks converge or overshoot. A recent major US study supports this view.

Additionally, low PER stocks have often experienced problems in the recent past. Both institutional managers and fund trustees prefer to act "prudently" and not make mistakes. There is less criticism when a fund holds a glamour stock that underperforms than when a problem stock is held and it underperforms. Managers and trustees are less likely to be replaced for being wrong with the crowd than if they act alone.

Can you buy low PER stocks? Indeed you can. Many newspapers publish the relevant data. For example, the *Financial Times* gives the market's PER in its table "FT-SE Actuaries Share Indices: The UK Series". In the "London Share Service" section of the paper you will find the PER of each share. It is easy to find shares selling well below the market's (i.e., the average) PER. Sometimes, some large sectors (discussed later) of the market sell on above market PERs. For those sectors you should buy shares that are cheap relative to their sector. PERs are also given in *Company REFS*.

Low price-to-sales ratio stocks

Buying stocks with a low price-to-sales ratio (PSR) is sometimes recommended in the USA as a worthwhile investment strategy but is seldom discussed in the UK. The approach may work, but it is probably inferior to a low PER approach. You would need the sales of each firm to implement this strategy. Since that information is not readily available (although it is included in *Company REFS*), I will not discuss this approach further.

Small capitalization stocks

The size of a firm may be measured by the market value, or capitalization, of its ordinary shares, i.e., the price of a share times the number of shares in issue. Over long periods of time, and in many countries, small companies have produced higher returns than large companies. Sometimes there have been a few years of underperformance, but this has, in the past, been quickly reversed.

Figure 17.2 is similar to Figure 17.1, having been derived from the same study. As you can see, the smaller the stock, the greater the return.

Why have smaller companies generally outperformed larger companies? There is no good answer. Smaller companies have generated faster earnings growth than larger companies. However, one would expect faster growth to be anticipated by the investors and reflected in the share price, so that smaller stocks should not keep on outperforming. Perhaps smaller stocks are simply riskier: certainly they are more

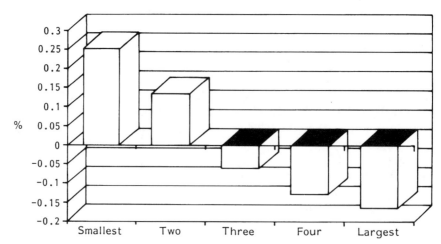

Figure 17.2 UK 1961–85 Monthly Excess Returns: Size Quintiles. Source: Drawn from data in Levis (1989, p. 686)

vulnerable to recessions. Also they are more illiquid and difficult to deal in. And the spread between the buying and selling price is wider than for large stocks, making part of the outperformance illusory. There is less information available on small stocks and it is disproportionately expensive to collect information. Some investors will expect higher returns to offset this. Another possibility is that smaller firms have been neglected, an issue which is discussed below.

You can easily select a portfolio of low capitalization stocks. The *Financial Times* "London Share Service" feature contains market capitalizations. However, I would not recommend this approach. The cost of dealing in small stocks for a private investor is too high—private investors can't usually get inside the wide buying and selling price spread, whereas an institutional investor often can. Remember, costs kill returns. You would be much better off buying a small firm fund.

Low-price stocks

Very low-price or "penny" stocks seem to have attractions for many private investors. Perhaps this is because they can buy a lot of shares for a given sum of money; or perhaps it is thought that a low price has more scope to rise than a high price. Many sophisticated investors scoff at such "reasons", and they are probably right, yet low-price stocks have been studied for more than 50 years and most studies have concluded that low-price stocks outperform. For one piece of evidence, see Figure 17.3.

While it is easy to find low-priced stocks, I would not recommend this as a share selection strategy. Stocks with a low price inevitably overlap with small capitalization stocks (because: capitalization = price × number of shares), and it is hard to know whether the excess returns are for low price or small size. Costs of dealing in low-price stocks are high, and there are no low-price stock funds. The sensible strategy is therefore to buy the small stock funds instead—you will be getting low-price stocks anyway, and won't suffer the high spreads.

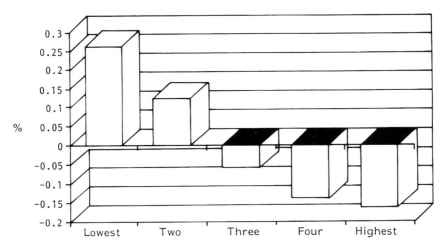

Figure 17.3 UK 1961–85 Monthly Excess Returns: Price Quintiles. Source: Drawn from data in Levis (1989, p. 687)

High yield

Whether high-yielding stocks offer higher returns has been a subject of debate for a long time. In many countries income has been taxed at a higher rate than capital gains. Even when the tax rates have been the same, capital gains tax has not been paid until gains were realized and thus the tax could be postponed in a way that income tax could not. If investors are interested in after-tax income they will presumably only purchase high-yielding stocks if they offer the same after-tax income as low-yielding stocks, i.e., if they offer higher returns than low-yielding assets on a pre-tax basis. Another argument suggesting high-yielding stocks will offer higher returns is the belief that investors demand a high yield in compensation for poor growth prospects. If investors are poor at assessing growth prospects—see the arguments in the section on low price–earnings ratio stocks—high yield may be related to high return. This is my preferred argument.

On the other hand, some private investors may require high income and may therefore prefer high-yielding stocks. Both tax-paying and tax-exempt investors might prefer high-yielding stocks on the grounds that a dividend today is more certain than a capital gain in the future.

So what is the evidence? In both the USA and the UK, high-yield stocks have outperformed. Some evidence for the UK is shown in Figure 17.4. Of the four factors shown in Figures 17.1–17.4, high yield offers the highest returns. It should come as no surprise that over long periods income unit trusts have provided a higher total return than growth unit trusts.

Neglected stocks

There is evidence that neglected stocks in the USA market outperform. Neglect is defined in terms of little or no brokerage research on a stock, and few institutional investors holding the stock. In the USA, there are publications which identify

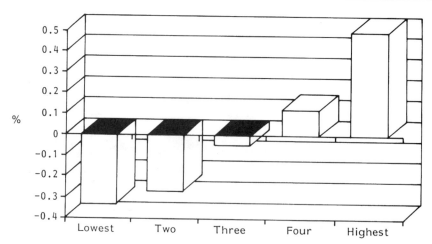

Figure 17.4 UK 1961–85 Monthly Excess Returns: Yield Quintiles. Source: Drawn from data in Levis (1989, p. 686)

neglected stocks. There are no similar publications in the UK, and there is no comparable research on neglected stocks. Neglected stocks will often be small, so anybody who buys small stocks will, to some extent, be investing in neglected stocks.

Asset values

Investors who consider asset values to be important calculate the net asset value (ordinary shareholders' funds divided by number of ordinary shares in issue) and relate it to the price per share. This can be done either by calculating a premium or discount to net asset value, or the ratio of price to net asset value, or net asset value to price. In the USA the equivalent concept is the book-to-market ratio.

Various studies have found that high net asset to market price stocks have provided superior performance. This finding has been reported for the UK, the USA, France, Germany, Switzerland and Japan. Net asset value figures are included on Extel cards, which are available in many public reference libraries. Price-to-book value and price-to-tangible book value statistics are given in *Company REFS*. Investors with an accounting background can calculate the statistics themselves from various books which give key financial data for the larger companies. Alternatively, Annual Reports and Accounts can be obtained for many companies by writing to the *Financial Times*—see READ 📖 WRITE 🖃 RING ☎.

Accounting ratios

A number of studies have shown that accounting ratios can be useful in selecting shares, but this will involve skills that few readers will possess, so I will not cover this here.

Avoiding firms that go bust

A firm that goes bust ruins your investment returns. You should always be aware that a cheap-looking stock may really be expensive because it might go bust. Technical accounting skills are required to assess the likelihood of this happening. Judging by the number of times institutional investors get caught, either these skills are not infallible or many of the biggest investors aren't able, or don't bother, to make the necessary appraisal.

What should you do? There is a short-cut. Many of the famous problem stocks of recent years had long been subjected to adverse comments about their accounts, e.g., Polly Peck, Trafalgar House, Coloroll, MCC (Maxwell) and Burton. One must admit some stocks have been criticized and subsequently the shares have performed well, while others haven't been criticized and still gone bust. However, I think it would be worth while to factor in adverse comments on a firm's accounts. Anybody selecting their own stocks should be reading the financial press and be aware of such comments, but the sensible thing to do would be to read McCarthy Cards on any stocks you consider buying, and eliminate those with adverse comments. McCarthy Cards is a press cutting service which reprints all articles about all quoted (and many unquoted) companies. It is available in many public reference libraries in either print or CD-ROM format.

Quality of management

One might expect excellently managed companies to perform well and investment analysts often write about the quality of the management of the company they are appraising. They expect the shares to have a higher rating when they perceive high-quality management. Private investors are often keen to buy well-managed firms.

Studies relating measures of quality of management to share returns suggest there is no relationship. This is not really surprising. Not only will the market tend to discount any obvious factors, it should always be borne in mind that economic forces tend to eliminate both good and bad margins: new firms enter attractive areas and some firms exit from unattractive areas. Also, there is a large random element in economic life—e.g., think how UK insurance firms are adversely affected by hurricanes in the USA. Finally, it is doubtful that most people can assess good management. Most people just assume that good past results imply good management. Bottom line: don't assess management.

Chartist analysis

There is no substantial evidence supporting the notion that you can select superior stocks on the basis of analysis of charts of past price behaviour. Save your money, don't buy books of charts.

Directors' trading

Following the trades of directors in their own companies appears to make sense. But directors buy and sell for a variety of reasons related to their own financial circumstances as well as on the basis of their expert knowledge. And this expert knowledge relates to their companies and not to how the stockmarket will react to news. Moreover, many directors will feel inhibited about dealing in advance of major news affecting their company.

In broad terms, following directors is a successful strategy, but it is not necessarily worth adopting. The point is that directors' deals are concentrated in small stocks and, in the USA, where most work on this has been done, stocks with low PERs. We know both types of stock have outperformed. If you are following these strategies, there will be no added value from following directors' deals. You would do better investing in small stocks or low PER stocks than subscribing to a service that monitors directors' deals.

Contrary thinking

Going against the crowd is often described as contrary thinking or contrarian investment strategy. Going against the crowd just for the sake of it does not seem sensible, but when emotions run strongly and one can see how the crowd could be wrong, a contrarian bet may be warranted. Buying low PER stocks could be seen as a contrarian strategy. However, often what people mean by contrary thinking is just a good dose of healthy scepticism.

Anyone who has read the investment columns for a period will have seen articles with titles such as "how to tell if it's the top" or "how to spot a company going bust". These articles consist of lists of serious and jokey points and usually most investors would agree there is some sense in the lists. The lists are then forgotten. Since there are some sound observations in the lists, I'll give one here. Signs of possibly overvalued stocks include:

- Reliance on creative accounting—Polly Peck, Parkfield, Coloroll, British and Commonwealth

- Resignation of directors

- Changing financial advisers

- Chairman or managing directors with bow ties, gold bracelets, toupees and sun tans. All these are signs of vain management—e.g., Roger Levitt, the disgraced financial salesman and Peter Goldie, of British and Commonwealth, both wore bow ties

- Moves to new headquarters or sumptuous headquarters buildings—e.g., Saatchi and Saatchi. Before atriums were common in the UK, this point was often expressed as "company with atrium"

- Bullies holding the position of chairman and chief executive—Maxwell and Ashcroft at Coloroll—Ashcroft asked an analyst who had criticized the company to leave a meeting

- Changing the year end—Maxwell—or the company name—Systems Reliability

- Bear squeezes and profits warnings. Bear squeezes often do have some basis in reality—Lonrho—and one company profit downgrade is frequently followed by another

- Substantial director share sales—Yellowhammer, Hodgson, Shandwick

Most investors will recognize some truth in this list and it provides a useful reminder that many investment disasters could be avoided if investors showed a bit of common sense and scepticism. Contrary thinking inevitably appeals to anybody who believes that markets overreact. The problem is the subjective nature of the approach rules out tests to show whether it is helpful or not. For anyone drawn to value stocks, combining a bit of contrary thinking with some more rigorous techniques will have attraction.

SECTOR VALUATIONS

If you look at the list of share prices in any newspaper, you will see they are listed under various headings, or sectors. Professional investors use the FT-SE-A All-Share Index classification. This is shown in Table 20.4 (Chapter 20). Investors have to decide how much of their portfolio to invest in each sector. Sector weights can be approached in several ways. One is to look solely at company valuations and then derive sector weights as a result of stock decisions. Thus, if an investor selects shares with low price–earnings ratios, sectors that possess many such shares will be heavily weighted automatically.

A different approach is to make sector decisions separately, and adjust the quantity of shares purchased to be consistent with the sector weights. Some investors select sector weights on the basis of the stage of the economic cycle. There is, unfortunately, no mechanical formula that has been demonstrated to work. A different approach is to buy sectors that are cheap in relation to their own past history on some valuation measure, e.g., one might buy sectors trading at a price–earnings ratio discount to their historical average, or sectors with a dividend yield above their historical average. There is some weak evidence that these approaches may be useful.

A different approach is to set sector weights equal to those of an index. I think that this is the best strategy for most private investors. It is easy, it ensures good diversification, and will ensure you beat the market if your stock selection is any good. Notice in Table 20.4 that sectors are brought together in various groups. You should aim to get close to each group weighting and also the weighting for some of the larger sectors. It is not necessary to exactly match all 38 sectors.

CONSTRUCTING A PORTFOLIO

Having discussed a number of techniques for valuing stocks and various findings which relate factors to returns, I now turn to constructing a portfolio. As I noted above, it is sensible to divide the UK market into sectors and ensure a broad representation of the sectors. It is also sensible to specify some additional constraints such as the number of stocks to be purchased. About 30 are necessary to ensure broad sector diversification, 20 at a pinch. I think you need at least £100 000 in your portfolio for this not to be very uneconomic in terms of transaction costs—and more if you don't use a discount broker. (Remember, even £250 will buy you a well-diversified investment trust at minimal cost through an investment trust savings plan.) The maximum size of a holding should also be specified (typically 5–7½% of the fund) and sometimes a minimum size too (perhaps 2%).

Which shares should you buy for your portfolio? You can either buy the "best" shares in each sector based on a single share selection method—which can be a subjective one based on your knowledge and experience, or one of the factors listed above such as high yield—or you can use a combination of factors. In general, a combination method is to be preferred. Share selection methods have limited power, and if different methods are measuring different aspects of high-performance stocks, combining methods will improve your selection skills. Experience shows that about four factors are as many as you need. Beyond that you will not improve your performance: indeed, your criteria may be so demanding that you find it hard to find 30 acceptable stocks. The combination can be made intuitively, or more formally by a weighting method or by screening.

In broad terms the weighting approach gives a stock points for the possession of desirable factors: the more of a factor possessed, the greater the number of points and the more points the better. The screening approach is all or nothing: it's more like a hurdle race—a stock has to clear the hurdle or it's out. If high yields are deemed to be desirable, all stocks with yields less than say, 5%, might be eliminated from further consideration. (At the time of writing, the market yield is 3.9%.) Surviving stocks go on to another screen. After passing through all the screens, the survivors are the pool of stocks from which you can construct your portfolio.

The two methods will select some shares in common, but there will be differences. The weighting method allows a poor score on one factor to be offset by good scores on other factors. The screening approach does not—in the case just mentioned, if a stock has a low yield, it will not be selected, irrespective of the fact that it may score highly on every other factor. Because the screening approach imposes a series of hurdles, each one of which will eliminate stocks, setting many hurdles, or high hurdles (e.g., setting a hurdle at 150% of the market yield), soon diminishes the population of eligible stocks to a very small number. To avoid this, you have to limit the number of screens, and adjust the hurdle height, to allow enough stocks to survive to permit a diversified portfolio to be constructed.

The screening approach is the one that appeals to most people who are interested in formal approaches, and who are not mathematicians. If you want to use this approach, I suggest you read a discussion by Arbel which is referred to in READ 📖 WRITE 🖹 RING ☎.

In the weighted composite approach you specify your selection factors. You then have to weight them. If you think some factors are more important, give them more weight. Otherwise weight them all equally. The highest scoring stocks are the ones you consider for inclusion in your portfolio.

For both approaches I have said you end up with a pool of eligible stocks from which you construct your portfolio. The reason that it is not your portfolio is that it may have far too many stocks or far too few stocks in one sector. You don't want to buy six food stocks, for example. You should leave some out. Conversely, if you have decided to have a stock in all major sectors, you may find that you have not got a major integrated oil stock in your pool of potential stocks. In that case, you will need to review the stocks in this sector and find the one least inconsistent with your criteria.

FINALLY

Well, that about does it. I haven't covered everything you need to know, but anybody who has read this far will probably be able to work out what to do when faced with a problem. But I have a question. Do you really want to do all this? Wouldn't it be easier to buy an investment trust or unit trust and wouldn't your time be spent more productively or pleasurably doing something else?

READ 📖 WRITE ✉ RING ☎

♦ The attributes of shares that have beaten the market are discussed in more detail in Stephen Lofthouse, *Equity Investment Management*. Chichester: Wiley, 1994. *Equity Investment Management* is written at a more technical level than this book.
♦ If you want to use several attributes in your share selection I suggest you read the clear discussion by Avner Arbel which is reprinted in Stephen Lofthouse, *Readings in Investments*. Chichester: Wiley, 1994.
♦ The figures in this chapter were drawn from data which is reprinted from *Journal of Banking and Finance*, 13, Mario Lewis, "Stock Market Anomalies: A Re-assessment Based on UK Evidence", 675–696, 1989, with kind permission of Elsevier Science-NL, Sara Burgerhartstraat 25, 1055 KV Amsterdam, the Netherlands.
♦ *Company REFS*, a monthly publication, provides many of the statistics discussed in this chapter. At £795 per annum, most readers will prefer to look at a library copy rather than subscribe, although not many libraries will be able to afford it. For earnings estimates, there is *The Estimate Directory*. This has wide coverage of brokers and companies, but many of the estimates shown are quite old, and the publication is only quarterly. It costs £105 per annum, but is available in major public business libraries.
♦ Annual Reports and Accounts can be obtained for many companies by writing to the *Financial Times*. Details of this free service are given in the bottom right-hand corner of the second page of the "London Share Service" feature.

18

Market Timing and International Shares

Buy when everyone else is selling, and hold until everyone else is buying. This is more than just a catchy slogan. It is the very essence of successful investment.

J. Paul Getty

Professional investors distinguish between strategic and tactical asset allocation and most private investors would benefit if they did the same. A definition of the two activities is:

- Strategic asset allocation—the allocation between asset classes that is thought appropriate for a portfolio over the long-term; and

- Tactical asset allocation—the short-term deviations from the strategic allocation based on a view of short-term risk and return prospects.

Everybody should do strategic asset allocation. It's just the fancy way of saying you match your assets with your objectives. It's the sort of stuff I talk about in various parts of this book. Your strategic asset allocation will change over the years as your family increases and decreases in size, or as you get older, or if your financial circumstances dramatically change. Tactical asset allocation, a fancy way of saying market timing, is where you decide that shares, say, look very expensive, so you are not going to invest in any, even though your strategic plan says you should be investing in equities. You plan to keep your money in cash until you get a better buying opportunity. You can engage in market timing in buying and selling any assets, but most people who engage in market timing do so with regard to their holdings of equities, gilts and cash. Within their equity holdings, they may vary the split between UK and overseas equities.

Many investors like to try to time the market and buy when it's cheap, and sell when it's dear. Most people actually do the opposite: buy dear when greed is high, and sell cheap when fear takes over. Most people would be better off not timing, but since some investors will try to time, I'll say a few words on this. I think you should not be active in international markets, but I'll also say a little on that too.

As for the previous chapter, my recommendation is that only experienced investors or investment professionals should read this one. Novice investors simply don't need to know this complex material. Even experienced investors may find they have neither the time nor interest to benefit from it. Most investors should simply determine their strategic allocation and stick with it.

IS MARKET TIMING IMPORTANT?

Since the financial markets are supposed to be efficient, you may wonder why any-body would want to engage in market timing. The answer is that the market level is less likely to be efficiently priced than are individual shares. It is easy to buy one share and sell another when you think you see mispricing. And there isn't too much risk since you are still invested in the market. I don't think that you should be doing this, but the professionals will be. But for the market as a whole, it is harder to trade on mispricing. Of course, if the market seems too expensive, an investor can sell the market and hold cash—and vice versa—but this is not a risk-free trade. There is a large role for judgement, and the timing is more difficult than with individual shares. A market judgement may take years to come right, if it ever does, adding to the risk. Moreover, professional fund managers, who have the funds to effect the trades, are generally measured on a short time horizon. It would seem reasonable to assume that the market as a whole is more likely to deviate substantially from fair value than are individual stocks relative to each other.

This view is reinforced if one examines the way many investors behave. Many act as though "the trend is your friend", and they are likely to believe that a trend, once started, will continue for ever. Indeed, some professionals, such as chartists, publish stock advice which has a strong element of trend following. Finally, there is psycho-logical evidence which suggests that people pay too much attention to recent vivid news (the market is going up) and too little to general background information (there is always a cyclical downturn). If investors find psychological comfort in doing what other investors are doing, it would not be surprising if equity markets deviated from fair value and were buffeted by changing sentiment.

One might expect rational professionals to bet against the trend followers. But how can they be sure that they are witnessing a short-lived trend? They do not know what the future holds, and even professionals have emotions and may act just like everyone else. Indeed, going with the trend may be a rational strategy even if it is self-evident that the trend will be eventually reversed. To be wrong with the crowd will not lead to a loss of clients, whereas to be wrong alone will.

It seems the market is influenced by fundamentals, but there is more to the market than that. Investors watch each other and the market as a whole; some investors chase trends. The market is too volatile—trends persist for too long, but they then reverse. This suggests that a pure value and contrarian approach to market timing will eventually work because trends do reverse. But it may be a painful approach for an investor if short-term results matter as well as the final outcome. Many investors in the 1980s felt the Japanese market was over-valued for a very long time before it cor-rected. They missed a lot of good performance before they were proved right. A pure trend-following approach will work too, right up to the point it does not. Combining some measure of sentiment or momentum and some measure of value may be a sensible way of approaching market timing.

While it is possible to make money with market timing, it is much overrated. There are two reasons why this is so. First, whatever is theoretically possible, it is difficult in practice to market time successfully and, second, the gains are unlikely to be large anyway. I'll deal with the first point at some length in this chapter, but on the second point all that need be noted is that while there are huge differences in the returns from various asset classes such as gilts and equities, and from one international market to another, if you don't make big bets, none of these differences will affect you. And most professionals don't make big bets, and neither should you.

For example, if you had £100 000 in UK equities because you were saving for the long-term, it would be madness to suddenly move the whole lot into gilts because you thought gilts would do better over the next six months. What if you are wrong? Will you cut your loss and go back into the asset you thought you should be in for the long term, or will you hang on, hoping things will turn out right? Perhaps you have £90 000 in equities and you have just got your bonus of £10 000. Should you market time with that? Let's say you do, and equities fall 10% and gilts rise 10%. If you put your £10 000 into equities, your £100 000 total would fall to £90 000. If you put the £10 000 into gilts, your £100 000 would fall to £92 000 (i.e., (£90 000 × 0.9) + (£10 000 × 1.1)). This modest degree of tactical asset allocation, which is what most people will do in practice, has only resulted in a gain of 2% despite a 20% difference in the performance of the markets. Now we shouldn't dismiss 2%, but it's not much when you remember the big difference in market returns I've assumed, and that you could have got it wrong. And if your long-term position is in equities, you still have to buy your way back into equities. If you mistime the move, you could lose your gain.

I'll now discuss some of the ways of making market timing decisions. You'll soon realize that there is as much art as science involved.

MARKET TIMING METHODS

Market timing techniques fall into five types: business cycle anticipation, valuation measures, liquidity approaches, technical analysis and bottom-up stock-driven approaches. It is sensible to combine several approaches, providing they contribute new information and do not just duplicate each other. The combination used will depend on an investor's knowledge and skills: for example, some will be drawn to methods that involve economic forecasting, whereas others will avoid such methods.

The most widely used methods are business cycle anticipation and various valuation methods, and that's what I'll discuss here.

BUSINESS CYCLE ANTICIPATION

The stockmarket is intimately linked to the economy. Changes in gross national product (GNP)—the nation's income—impact firms' sales and prices which in turn affect revenues, costs and profits. This, in turn, feeds through to dividends and retained earnings. Changes in GNP affect the general price level and interest rates. Dividends, growth and interest rates are all factors in determining share prices. Understanding and forecasting changes in the economy might be expected to be important for anyone wishing to forecast the stockmarket.

Many people try to forecast the markets by forecasting the economy, but this is not as useful an approach as it might seem. There are two reasons for this. First, we should not expect an exact one-to-one correspondence between changes in the economy and changes in the stockmarket, if only because other investors will be trying to anticipate the economy's moves and the effect on the market. Thus, one has to forecast both the course of the economy, and how much has been discounted by investors. Second, economic forecasting skills might be so poor that, in practice, there is no added value from forecasting.

I'll start with economic forecasts but not go into any detail here: it is sufficient to note that there are numerous forecasts produced by the UK Treasury, UK stockbrokers, and various other commercial organizations. The important question is: whose forecast is best? The general finding is that there is no consistently best buy amongst forecasters. Combining forecasts leads to increased accuracy and simple averaging of forecasts is useful. This sort of information is published periodically in the *Financial Times* and other papers, and is available in more detail on subscription from organizations such as *Consensus Economics*.

Having forecast the course of the economy, the next stage is to use the information. The problem is that the economy and markets do not move in perfect unison, in fact the markets tend to anticipate the course of the economic cycle. However, if there is some regular pattern to economic fluctuations (the business cycle), and if the markets respond in some regular way to the business cycle, business cycle anticipation becomes a viable method of market timing.

Here is a stylized story of what a business and stockmarket cycle might look like:

(a) The story begins in recession with the stockmarket anticipating, by about five months, the end of recession. At this time interest rates are likely to be low, reflecting low demand for credit, falling inflation and monetary easing.

(b) Once the economy starts to pick up, bond yields will begin to rise, on average eight months after the trough of the recession. Credit demands increase and bond purchasers will anticipate future inflation and expect higher nominal returns. The authorities will stop easing monetary policy and there will be expectations that the next move in short interest rates will be up.

(c) Rising interest rates at first do not hurt the stockmarket. Investors will be focusing on large profit gains and equities will look attractive, especially against rising bond yields (i.e., falling bond prices and declining capital values). As time passes, rising credit demands, increasing inflation and tighter monetary policy will force up interest rates further, and this will start to slow the economy. The equity market will begin to focus on the competition from higher yields on bonds and cash. Prospects for profits will deteriorate as costs rise and margins can no longer be pushed up. Investment in plant and machinery may slow as a result of inadequate prospective returns caused by poorer profit prospects and a higher investment discount rate, resulting from higher interest rates. The stockmarket will peak.

(d) The pressure from the authorities to slow the economy, and the natural slowdown resulting from reduced business investment, will cause the economic cycle to turn down. The stockmarket will fall.

(e) The pressures pushing bond yields up when the economy was growing now operate in reverse and bond yields will start to fall.

(f) The move into recession will continue, the authorities will start easing policy, inflationary pressures begin to dissipate and, after a period, the stockmarket will trough.

The big problem with business cycle anticipation as a timing strategy is that what has been described are averages within wide ranges: for example, in the USA, where these matters are more intensely studied, bond yield troughs have led US stock price peaks on average by 13 months, but the range is 1 to 31 months. In other words you could be a year too early or too late if you play the averages.

Business cycle anticipation is not the be-all and end-all of market timing.

VALUATION MEASURES

Two of the most widely used market valuation measures are the market price–earnings ratio and the market yield. These may be considered on their own or in relation to other variables.

Absolute price–earnings ratio

If you believe that the market swings about too much around some notion of fair value then, if you examine a measure of value, you might expect that when the market has moved away from the average level of the measure, it will move back towards it. The simplest valuation measure that can be derived from the market's price-earnings ratio is the absolute level of the ratio. Figure 18.1 shows the UK price–earnings ratio from 1965 to 1994.

The obvious decision rule is to sell at high price–earnings ratio levels and buy at low. But how useful would this approach really be? What exactly would the decision rule be? Say you decided to buy at PERs under five. That would have worked, but you would only have bought in a few months of the 30-year period. You might like to try different numbers and see what the implications would have been. Try also putting your hand over the graph so you can see only part of the data. You'll find your rule changes with the amount of data you can see. For example, devise a rule when you know only the history up to July 1972, and then again when you know the history up to January 1975. And, of course, we can't simply look at price–earnings

Figure 18.1   UK Equity Market Price–earnings Ratio, 1965–94. Source: Datastream

ratios, we have to take into account what is happening to profits before we can tell what is happening to the market.

What we find is that in broad terms it makes sense to sell on high price–earnings ratios and buy on low price–earnings ratios, but that misvaluation can last for long periods and that the valuation standards can change. You won't make as much as you might hope from this method. However, if you want to track the market yourself, the market price–earnings ratio is shown in the *Financial Times* in line 89 of the "FT-SE Actuaries Share Indices: The UK Series".

Absolute yield

The simplest market yield valuation measure is the absolute value of the yield. Figure 18.2 shows the UK dividend yield since 1919. The yield has shown remarkable stability around an average of 5.1%, seldom exceeding 6% or falling below 4%. The US market, incidentally, has shown nothing like the same stability, with low-yield periods in the mid-1950s through to the mid-1970s, and again in the last few years.

Does the simple strategy of buying the market on high yields and selling on low yields work? It does. Even in the USA, where the yield has been much more unstable, one study found that over nine- or ten-year holding periods, returns increase continuously as dividend yield in the prior year increases. Nonetheless, for short holding periods, especially at around average yield levels, the dividend yield will be less useful as a guide. If you want to track the market yourself, the market dividend yield is shown in the *Financial Times* in the "Indices and Ratios" section of the "Market Report" or line 89 of the "FT-SE Actuaries Share Indices: The UK Series".

Equity yields relative to bond yields

The previous approach looks at equities in isolation. Many investors relate equity yields to bond yields. This can be done as either a difference or a ratio. In recent years

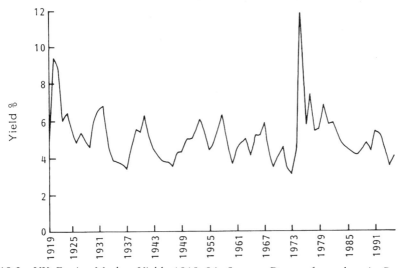

Figure 18.2 UK Equity Market Yield: 1919–94. Source: Drawn from data in Barclays de Zoete Wedd (1995, pp. 48–49)

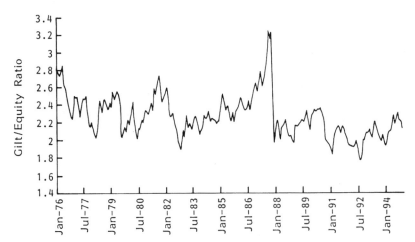

Figure 18.3   UK Bond/Equity Yield Ratio: 1976–94. Source: Datastream

the ratio has been the more useful measure and is shown in Figure 18.3. For a DIY approach use the equity yield you used earlier and the yield on UK gilts over 15 years, shown in the *Financial Times* under "FT-Actuaries Fixed Interest Indices" in the "UK Gilts Prices" section.

Based on consideration of diagrams such as Figure 18.3, various rules of thumb have been developed, such as investors should buy equities on yield ratios of less than 2 and sell on ratios of more than 2.6. But it is not clear that this is a useful guide.

Look at the longer history in Figure 18.4. You can see equities used to yield more than gilts (to compensate for business risk) and then in the late 1950s gilts started to yield more than equities (because investors focused on the fact that equity yields grow over time but conventional gilt yields do not). So, does Figure 18.3 hold some long-term truth, or does it just happen to describe what has happened in the last few years without holding any useful message?

A different way of looking at equities is in relation to index-linked gilts, as shown in Figure 18.5. Because index-linked are relatively new, the history is short. This short history does appear to show that equities are overvalued if the real yield from index-linked is close to the dividend yield on equities. To find the real yield on index-linked, turn to the *Financial Times'* "FT-Actuaries Fixed Interest Indices" table and look under the heading "inflation 5%".

The equity risk premium approach

Because equities are riskier than gilts, we expect them to offer a higher return. The size of that extra return is the equity risk premium. The equity risk premium approach calculates the size of the equity risk premium and if it is sufficiently high, equities are favoured, but if it is low, gilts are favoured. This is not an approach most private investors will be comfortable with because it is difficult to make a sensible forecast of long-term dividend growth which adequately reflects near-term expectations as well as long. But many quantitatively orientated professional investors use this approach, so I'll briefly outline it. If you want to try to use it, I suggest you use a

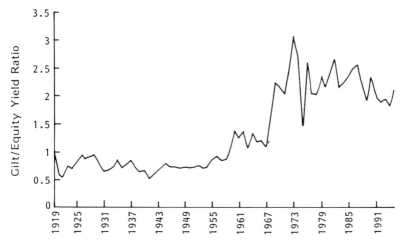

Figure 18.4 UK Gilt/Equity Yield Ratio: 1919–94. Source: Drawn from computations made on data in Barclays de Zoete Wedd (1995, pp. 48–51)

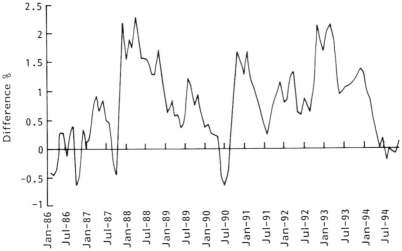

Figure 18.5 UK Equity Yield and Index-Linked Gilt Real Yield Difference, 1983–94. Source: Datastream

long-term real dividend growth rate of 2½% as a starting point, and add on your forecast of long-term inflation.

It can be shown (by means of the dividend discount model, details of which I'll omit) that:

equity market expected return = dividend yield + dividend growth rate

When gilts and equities are both "correctly" priced, we would expect the returns from equities to equal the return from bonds (i.e., the redemption yield) plus an equity risk premium to compensate for the greater risk of equities, i.e.:

dividend + dividend growth rate = bond yield + equity risk premium

By swapping terms around, as you did in school algebra, you can see that:

equity risk premium = dividend yield + dividend growth rate – bond yield

How could you use this? Say you think the equity risk premium should be 5% (which is lower than its long-term average—see Chapter 4). Assume also that the dividend yield is 4%, you expect dividends to grow at 7%, and the long-dated gilt redemption yield is 8%. The premium is therefore 3% (i.e., 4%+7%–8%=3%). Since this is less than the required premium of 5%, either gilts are cheap, or equities dear. Either way, investors should prefer gilts.

SHOULD YOU MARKET TIME?

As we have seen, there are a number of ways of assessing whether markets are cheap or dear. What must always be remembered is that there are two calls to be made. You have to know when to get out, but you also have to know when to get back in. Most people don't seem to be very good at making both calls. Moreover, you do have to make enough profit to cover your round-trip costs of dealing, including price spreads.

It may seem obvious when markets are at extremes of valuations. But even here you won't necessarily do well. For example, the crash of 1987 is fixed in many investors' minds. What is often forgotten is that the total return from equities in that year was plus 8.4%. If you had sold in early October and bought in late October 1987 you would have done very much better. But if you sold early in the year and bought back later in the year, you would not necessarily have done better than someone who rode the market roller-coaster all year. Most investors who are not investing all their money at one time but doing so over a period, possibly of decades, would be well advised to just keep putting their money into the markets and not to attempt market timing. Do you really want to become a junior economist and follow market valuations, and even if you do, will it really benefit your portfolio?

INTERNATIONAL ASSET ALLOCATION

In Chapter 16, I discussed why you might want to invest abroad. The question here is whether you should try to actively make country selection bets or just hand your money over to an internationally diversified pooled fund. My inclination is to do the latter. There is no fool-proof method of international allocation, and most private investors will find it too difficult to follow a large number of markets. I recommend that you skip the rest of this section because you shouldn't need it.

Still reading? Oh, well, there are a variety of approaches that might be used to determine the most attractive international markets. Some investors:

- Ignore countries and simply buy the cheapest stocks in the world, deriving their country allocation as a residual

- Compare markets as though they are simply different stocks within a market

- Treat each market separately and rate it cheap or expensive relative to its own history

- Forecast total returns

- Use international business cycle anticipation

- Use differences in international liquidity

- Use chartist techniques

I shall comment on the first four approaches. I shall ignore the last three as I have little to add to the earlier business cycle analysis and there is no evidence that the last two are useful.

Buying the cheapest stocks

Simply selecting the cheapest stocks in the world and ignoring international asset allocation appeals to many investors who believe they have stock selection skills. This approach could take the form of buying, say, the forty cheapest stocks in the world and, if they are all telephone companies, so be it. Usually, however, investors construct portfolios that are diversified by sector and they try to buy the cheapest oil company in the world, the cheapest chemical company, and so on. Whether it is a sensible approach depends on whether a stock's return is more correlated with its global industry's return or that of its national market. The evidence is that the national factor predominates. While picking cheap stocks may be a viable strategy, the evidence points to country factors as being the most rewarding starting point for international asset allocation.

Of course, if you are investing internationally via pooled funds, you won't be using this method. But some funds you might invest in may claim to use this method.

Selecting markets as though they are stocks

Presumably, whatever the reason for low price–earnings stocks or small stocks performing well within a market (see Chapter 17) should carry across to entire markets too. If investors concentrate too much on the past and reward past success, and that accounts for low price–earnings stocks tending to outperform, that should apply to markets too. And if poor liquidity is the explanation for small stocks performing, that should probably affect markets too. On this tack you should look for low price–earnings ratios, high yields, high book value, and so forth.

What does the evidence show? Two of the most basic stock attributes are the price-earnings ratio and dividend yield, and international data is readily available. These seem to be a good starting point for analysis. Some investors, however, argue for replacing the price–earnings ratio with a price-to-cash flow measure because of international accounting differences with regard to depreciation policies. Germany and Japan, for example, over-depreciate relative to the USA. Some investors argue that focusing on cash, i.e., profits plus depreciation, levels the playing field.

One published study used these two selection criteria and was successful in ranking portfolios by return, whether measured in local currency or a common currency. High-yield countries and low price-to-cash flow countries produced the highest returns. Based on this evidence, it would seem that treating countries as though they were stocks and using standard share selection screens has some value.

Getting information on attributes such as yield, price–earnings ratio, price-to-book, etc., for international markets is not easy for private investors. Publications that produce this data are prohibitively expensive. You either have to forego this approach, or persuade a full service stockbroker to provide you with the data.

Selecting stocks by local standards

The case for assessing markets on the basis of local standards is that despite the above evidence, there is room for doubting that markets are directly comparable and, moreover, within each market the local investors are the dominant force. If local investors everywhere relate their own equity market more to local bonds and local cash than to other equity markets, then the sensible approach might seem to be to go native. International valuation then becomes a process of assessing markets on the basis of relative cheapness and dearness of each market based on its domestic valuation standard. These valuation standards may be based on simple measures such as the price–earnings ratio in relation to its historical range and average, or more complex standards such as an equity risk premium comparison with local bonds.

There is surprisingly little published evidence on selection by local valuations, but most international investors probably do make comparisons based on various local bond/equity measures, although most of these are unsophisticated and will simply take the form of noting that UK equities are, say, cheap against UK gilts whereas US equities are, say, dear against US bonds.

Some investors use different valuation measures for different markets. For example, the book-to-price ratio might be thought to be especially relevant for Japan, or the gap between the earnings yield and long bond yield. The stability of the dividend yield in the UK might indicate that the dividend yield would be more relevant in the UK than in other markets. The point is clear: there are some market idiosyncrasies so that different measures may be important in different markets.

This may suggest a chalk and cheese problem: how can the cheapness/dearness of the UK on a yield basis be related to the cheapness or dearness of Japan on a book value basis? One solution would be to measure each market's value in terms of how far it is from its average. Then, if the UK is way above its average dividend yield, and Japan is only a little above its average book-to-price ratio, the UK would be cheaper. This approach seems beyond the skills of most private investors.

Forecasting total returns

Some investors make total return forecasts, e.g., by using price–earnings ratios. For a UK investor investing abroad four forecasts would be required for each market:

- Expected change in market price–earnings ratio
- Expected change in profits
- Yield
- Change in foreign currency relative to sterling

If £10 000 were invested in a market in which it was thought that in the next year the price–earnings ratio would rise from 10 to 12, that profits would rise by 20%, that the yield would be 5% and the currency would appreciate by 10%, then the annual total return in sterling would be:

$$((\pounds 10\,000 \times 1.2 \times 1.2) + (\pounds 10\,000 \times 0.05)) \times 1.1 = \pounds 16\,390 \text{—a total return of 64\%.}$$

Total returns can be produced in this, or other ways for all countries, and the returns compared. But could you do it?

SHOULD YOU MAKE INTERNATIONAL BETS?

When you have mastered the techniques that I've discussed, there is still no guarantee that you will be much good at selecting international markets. I ended Chapter 17 with some questions which are just as relevant here. Do you really want to do all this? Wouldn't it be easier to buy a pooled fund and wouldn't your time be spent more productively or pleasurably doing something else?

READ 📖 WRITE ✉ RING ☎

♦ In the text I refer to some studies or evidence without providing details. This may be found in Chapters 23–29 of Stephen Lofthouse, *Equity Investment Management*. Chichester: Wiley, 1994.
♦ Data on international price–earnings ratios, price-to-book, dividend yield, and price-to-cash flow for both developed and emerging markets appears in the monthly *World Equity*, subscription £395 per annum, details from 0171 369 7536. Data on emerging markets appears in the monthly *Emerging Markets Investor*, subscription details from 0171 487 5326. PER and yield data on the UK, USA, Japan, Hong Kong, France, and Germany appears in the "Investment" sub-section of the "Statistics" section of the *Investors Chronicle*.

19

Bonds: Fixed Interest Stocks

Gentlemen prefer bonds.
Andrew Mellon

The word bond is used in many different senses and is often a source of confusion for private investors (and some advisers). In its most general sense the word bond refers to an IOU issued by a borrower, usually a government or company. The purchaser usually receives a set sum of interest, typically twice a year, and repayment—or redemption—of the principal at a specific date. Bonds in this sense are also described as fixed-interest or fixed-income investments.

Bonds issued by companies are called corporate bonds, those issued by the UK government are known as gilts (or gilt-edged), those by the US government are called Treasury bonds. There are some other types that you'll encounter, which I'll discuss later. There are some special forms of bonds, such as zero-coupon bonds and index-linked gilts, which I will also discuss.

Unfortunately, numerous quite dissimilar financial products have been described by their promoters as bonds, e.g., broker bonds, single premium bonds, etc. These are not bonds in the sense discussed above. They may or may not pay a fixed rate of interest and may or may not be particularly safe. When you read press reports that talk of falling or rising bond prices affecting the equity market, they are referring to the IOUs I have described in the first paragraph. It is these bonds that this chapter is about.

Many people find shares quite sexy, albeit risky. They may not understand all the details, but they get the idea that shares are a way of owning part of a company and sharing in its success or failure. Many people—probably incorrectly—think they can spot a good company. Bonds, by comparison, are boring. Bonds are just IOUs which are affected by broad macroeconomic forces, and to assess their value requires a certain amount of arithmetic. Most personal finance books skip the details of bonds. That's wise from the writer's point of view: the book is more readable. But I think it's irresponsible. Bonds are sold as a relatively safe investment, but that need not be true. If you don't understand some basic bond arithmetic, you don't understand bonds, and I don't think you should invest in anything you don't understand. So, at the risk of reducing readability, I'm going to explain enough about bonds for you to be able to decide whether you should invest in them.

BOND BASICS

When governments or companies spend more than they take in either tax or profits, they have to cover the difference. Companies can borrow from a bank, issue more shares or issue debt instruments, i.e., bonds. Governments can print more money (which may cause inflation), borrow short-term (via Treasury bills), or borrow long-term by issuing bonds. The rate of interest that has to be paid on a bond will vary with the level of interest rates in general, and the creditworthiness of the borrower.

The British government can borrow at a lower rate of interest than British companies, because it has never defaulted and it is assumed that it won't, i.e., it will not be unable to pay interest or repay the original sum borrowed. This seems a safe assumption because the government can always tax, and should therefore always be able to meet its debts. Since some foreign governments have defaulted, perhaps I should say that this seems a safe assumption for the time being. Companies cannot tax and therefore generally must have a greater credit risk. But for the best companies the risk will not be great. A top quality company might borrow at 1% above the rate the government can. For the extra risk of default, investors demand extra return. For companies with poor financial standing, investors will demand a large premium over both government bonds and high-grade corporate bonds. Bonds issued by very high risk companies are called junk bonds. To keep the discussion simple, I use gilts to illustrate my discussion of bonds for the rest of this section and discuss other types of bonds later. There are two main types of gilts, conventional gilts and index-linked. I discuss conventional gilts first.

Gilt essentials

Gilts, or British government IOUs, are issued with a name (which generally has no significance), a nominal value, a coupon rate of interest, and a repayment date. For example, the Bank of England might issue a bond for the government with a nominal value of £100, a 10% coupon or rate of interest and a repayment date of 30 November 2000. Most recent issues of gilts have been called either "Treasury" or "Exchequer", so this bond might be called Treasury 10% 2000. If you hold the bond on 30 November 2000, you will get the nominal value of £100 repaid to you. Every year you will get interest of £10 (£100 × 10%). You can buy a gilt from the Bank of England when it is first issued, or you can buy it second-hand later on in the stockmarket.

The repayment date of a new bond might be a few years in the future or 30 or more years ahead. However, with the passage of time, all bonds become shorter, i.e., there is a shorter period till they mature, or are redeemed. Thus you can find bonds that have only a few months to run till redemption although they may originally have had a thirty-year life. Bonds with a remaining life of less than five years are called "shorts", those with five to fifteen years are called "mediums", and those with more than fifteen years are called "longs".

There are a few gilts that are "undated" or "irredeemables". For example, Consols 2½% has a redemption date of "1923 or after". Nobody expects these bonds to be redeemed because the interest rate is so low. If the government redeemed these bonds and issued new bonds to replace them, the new bonds might have a coupon of around 8%, the current rate of interest (November 1995). Why would the government want to pay 8%, when it can pay 2½%? Unless interest rates fall to below 2½%, Consols 2½% will not be redeemed.

The value of a second-hand gilt will depend on the general level of interest rates and the maturity of the bond. I explain this in the next section. It is important that anybody investing in bonds understands the following section. If you find it too hard to understand, you should not buy bonds. Consider a high interest deposit account instead.

What drives bond prices?

I'll begin with a gilt that has a nominal value of £100 and a coupon of 5%. Anybody who bought this would get £5 of interest per annum. Now assume that interest rates rise in the rest of the world and UK interest rates are forced to follow them up, perhaps to support the value of sterling on the foreign exchange markets. The government wants to borrow more money and issues bonds, but is now forced to pay a rate of 10%. New bonds will be priced at £100 with a 10% coupon, paying £10 interest per annum.

Second-hand bonds, traded in the stockmarket, now look distinctly unattractive. New bonds pay £10 interest and old bonds pay £5. Nobody would want to hold the old bonds. There would be a desire to sell old bonds and buy the new. But who would be daft enough to buy the old bonds? What has to happen is that price of the old bonds must change so that all bonds are equally attractive. Say the price of old bonds fell to £50. The £5 interest—calculated at 5% on the original nominal value of £100—would give a current yield (also known as an interest yield, flat yield, or running yield) of 10% (i.e., £5/£50 × 100%). At this price both the old bonds and the new bonds would be equally attractive. Notice that the coupon yield (5%) and current yield (10%) can be different: indeed, they usually are.

This example illustrates the important point: *when interest rates rise, bond prices fall*. A similar argument would show that *when interest rates fall, bond prices rise*. Think of bond prices and interest rates as opposite ends of a see-saw. When one rises, the other goes down. North Americans call see-saws teeter-totters. That name appeals to me, especially in this context. If interest rates doubled and your bond's price fell from £100 to £50, I think you would totter—you would have made a huge capital loss.

My example holds only if we are looking at irredeemables, the ultimate in long-dated bonds. If you have a bond with a shorter maturity date, prices will not change as much as I have indicated when interest rates change. Imagine that my example was for a bond with a life of one year. The price would not fall from £100 to £50. You can see this by imagining that it did. At the end of the year the return would be £5 of interest and a £50 capital gain when the nominal value is repaid (i.e., you get £100 from the Bank of England, but you paid £50). That would give a return of 110% (i.e., £55/£50 × 100%), and would be so attractive that everybody would buy the bonds, immediately forcing up their price.

Instead, we should expect the price to fall to about £95.45. That way the £5 of interest plus £4.55 of capital gain (i.e., £100 – £95.45) divided by £95.45 would equal 10%, the yield on the new bonds (I've slightly simplified here). The total return of capital gain and interest from the old bonds would be the same as the total return from the new.

What this shows is that although bond prices always move in the opposite direction to interest rates, the size of the move is related to the maturity of the bond. Bonds with long maturities move much more than bonds with short maturities. *Long-dated bonds are more volatile, or riskier, than short-dated bonds.*

I could play around with numerical examples to demonstrate another point, but instead I'll just assert it. ***Bonds with low coupons are more volatile than bonds with high coupons.*** So:

- Bond prices and interest rates move in opposite directions, like the two ends of a see-saw or teeter-totter.

- Bonds with long maturities have bigger price changes in response to interest rate changes than do short-maturity bonds.

- Bonds with low coupon rates have bigger price changes in response to interest rate changes than do high coupon bonds.

I have mentioned coupon yield and current yield. In the last numerical example I introduced a third yield concept, that of the redemption yield or yield-to-maturity. That takes into account both the interest you receive from a bond and any capital gain or loss when the bond is redeemed. The computation of the redemption yield is a little tricky unless you have a computer and can understand the manual, or you have an 11-year-old child. Fortunately, redemption yields are shown in many newspapers.

The redemption yield is an important concept. It is a measure of the total return from a bond if held to redemption. It combines both interest and capital gains or losses. You are guaranteed this return if you hold a bond to redemption (there is a minor mathematical complication I explain later), but not otherwise. Once you have bought a bond, no matter what happens to interest rates in general, or to the price of your bond, you are guaranteed your interest payments and repayment of the nominal value on the redemption date. All this is, of course, subject to the bond issuer not defaulting. If you sell before the redemption date, you may make more or less than the redemption yield. If you buy a bond with a 5% redemption yield, but you sell it one year later after prices have risen by 10%, you will have made far more than 5% total return. And vice versa if prices slump.

Some examples

I have invented the examples above. What happens in the real world? If you looked in your newspaper at the end of 1994—the most recent complete calendar year at the time of writing— you might have found the information shown in Table 19.1.

The first thing you might notice is that the table has both decimals and fractions.

Table 19.1   Gilt Prices and Yields

| Year | | Stock | Price £ | +/− | Int. Yld % | Red Yld% |
High	Low					
107 9/32	101 15/32	Treas 12% 1995	100 15/32xd	...	11.94	5.88
128 7/32	111 25/32	Exch 12¼% 1999	112 1/16	+1/16	10.93	8.75
159½	126 3/16	Exch 12% 2013-17	129 15/16	+¼	9.24	8.73
54 13/32	39 21/32	War Loan 3½%	41 11/32	− 5/32	8.47	...

When the UK went decimal, the gilt market was exempted and continues to quote prices in fractions. The stocks shown have all had their names abbreviated. "Treas" is short for Treasury and "Exch" is short for Exchequer. Each name also includes the coupon the stock was issued at. All but War Loan show a redemption date. The Exchequer 12% shows two dates (known as double-dated): it will be redeemed between those dates at the issuer's option.

The high and low columns show the highest and lowest prices the stocks have traded at in 1994. The range increases with maturity. For the short-dated stock the range is about 6%, for War Loan the range is 37%. That 37% move is worth reflecting on. Many people think bond prices don't vary much. Some bond prices, in some years, move a lot. 1994 was quite a volatile year. If you look in your newspaper, you'll see how much bond prices have varied so far in the year you are reading this. The price column in Table 19.1 shows the closing price the day before the newspaper was published. The "+/–" column, sometimes shown as "chg", shows the price change from the previous day. The symbol "..." or "unch" means the price was unchanged. All the price columns are for £100 of nominal stock. The prices shown are "middle prices": if you want to buy, you'll pay a bit more, and if you want to sell, you'll get a bit less. The difference provides the income of the firms that make a market in bonds.

There are two yield columns. The first shows what I called the current yield. It's the interest yield you will get if you bought at the price shown, given the coupon. For our first stock, the coupon is 12%, but the purchase price is not the nominal £100, but £100 15/32. Since this is more than the nominal price, the current yield is less than 12%. The same is true of the next two stocks. War Loan costs much less than the nominal £100, so the current yield is much more than the 3½% coupon.

The second yield column gives the redemption yield. The redemption yield for the first bond may seem too low. It isn't, it's to do with the bond being redeemed in January 1995, less than a month from the date of the table, but I'm going to skip the maths. The redemption yield on this short-dated bond is about the yield available at the time on high-interest deposit accounts.

The medium and long dated bonds offer higher redemption yields. Note that they will suffer large capital losses on redemption, (i.e., each bond price exceeds the redemption value of £100) but this does not affect the returns too much, because the losses are spread over a long period. No redemption yield is shown for the undated stock. This is because it is assumed that the stock will not be redeemed, so there will not be a repayment of the nominal value. Accordingly, only a current yield can be calculated.

The yield columns show gross returns: if you pay tax, your returns will be lower. There is no capital gains tax on gilts (or on qualifying corporate bonds—which are most normal commercial sterling loan issues and which you acquired after 13 March 1984), but interest payments are subject to income tax. (See Appendix 1.)

Tax on interest is, in general, deducted at source at the lower rate of tax. There are four exceptions:

- If you buy gilts through National Savings (which I discuss later), lower rate tax is not deducted at source, and so if you are a non-taxpayer you do not have to reclaim the tax. If you are a taxpayer, you will be liable to 20% or 40% income tax.

- Interest is always paid gross on 3½% War Loan, however you buy it.

- Interest is paid gross on any gilt if the gross interest does not exceed £5 per annum.

- Overseas investors who can establish that they are not ordinarily resident in the UK may apply to receive interest gross from certain gilts (see READ 📖 WRITE ✑ RING ☎).

Finally, as with equities, because newspapers publish Friday's prices on Saturday and the markets close at the weekend, come Monday, the papers can either publish the same information again, or change it in some way. Many make some changes, and I'll use the *Financial Times* as an example. Tuesday to Saturday it reports the information shown in Table 19.1. On Monday it reports for each gilt its price, the percentage change in price over the past week, the size of the issue, the day and month interest payments are made, and the last date the share went xd—which I discuss in the next section.

Accrued interest

With equities, you are either entitled to the next dividend or you are not. With bonds the position on interest is more complex, but you don't have to master the rules, as the broker does all the sums for you. It is worth having a rough idea though.

Bond interest is usually paid twice a year, four times in a few cases, but it is assumed that interest accrues to the stock on a daily basis. Bonds are quoted cum dividend and ex-dividend. In the case of gilts, they usually go ex-dividend 37 days before an interest payment. When a price includes accrued interest it is called a dirty price, and when it excludes accrued interest it is a clean price. Buyers of a cum dividend gilt pay the clean price plus the accrued interest up to the settlement date. They receive the full interest on the payment date, but they have already paid part of it away to the seller. Once a gilt goes ex-dividend, the buyer doesn't get the next interest payment. Since the buyer is holding the gilt for a period without getting interest, the accrued interest is actually negative. So, if you buy a gilt when it has gone ex-dividend, you will pay less than the clean price because of negative accrued interest—this is called rebate interest.

SOME OTHER BONDS

Local authority debt

As well as the central government, local authorities also have need to borrow from time to time. You can make loans direct to a local authority or buy local authority bonds on the stockmarket. Most people can ignore local authority debt.

Corporate bonds

My discussion of bond basics was quite general, although I emphasized gilts. The same basic notions apply to corporate bonds, although these do have a few distinguishing features. For example, they come with a variety of descriptions such as debentures, unsecured loan stock and so forth. These different types reflect the sort of security attached to the bonds—e.g., a bond may be guaranteed in some way by being attached to specific assets of the issuing company, or just by a general charge against the company.

Corporate issues are typically smaller than government issues and so less marketable. You will be able to deal in the usual size that private clients deal in, but the spread between the buying and selling price is likely to be wider than for a gilt. Commission costs may be higher, and you will have to deal through a stockbroker. You will find it harder to discover the price of your corporate bond than that of a gilt, since most don't appear in a newspaper. And you will have to assess the credit quality of the issuer. For all this you will be rewarded with a higher redemption yield.

It's worth saying a little more about credit quality. Surely if you hold a famous name, you'll not be taking a risk? Probably not, but big companies such as MCC (Maxwell), Polly Peck and Queens Moat collapsed. Some companies are restructured but the bond holders may still lose their money. So while most corporate bonds won't go bust, some will. Now this applies to equities just as much as to bonds. The secret is to diversify. The problem is that it is costly to diversify except through a fund, and while you should buy an equity fund, I don't think you should buy a bond fund except, perhaps, in a PEP (see Chapter 20). I explain why later in this chapter.

Eurobonds

Bonds may be issued in a domestic market or in the international markets. International issues are called Eurobonds. Bonds may be issued in any of the major currencies. Were ICI to issue a bond denominated in sterling in the international markets, it would be called a Eurosterling bond. These bonds will become more familiar to many private investors in the coming years as they have been permitted investments within PEPs since the 1995–6 tax year. This is discussed in Chapter 20.

Permanent interest bearing shares—PIBS

PIBS were introduced in 1991 and have been pushed aggressively by some financial advisers, either as individual shares or in a fund. PIBS are building society shares which are listed on the Stock Exchange. However, they are best thought of as irredeemable bonds. You will need to use a stockbroker if you wish to buy or sell them.

PIBS pay interest twice a year at a fixed rate. They have no redemption date and will be repaid only on the winding up of the society that issued them, subject to the prior rights of other creditors, including depositors. If paying the interest on the PIBS would drive a society into loss, it need not make the payment, and this unpaid interest is non-cumulative, i.e., it would not have to be made good if the society's financial health improved.

PIBS pay a higher rate of interest than gilts, with the smaller societies paying a larger premium than the bigger. The yield in November 1995 on War Loan was 8.05%, while that on a Halifax Building Society PIBS was about 9.9% and on Newcastle Building Society PIBS 10.4%.

PIBS offer a known fixed rate of interest, higher than that from gilts, but with higher risks. Because they are irredeemable, the price varies dramatically in response to interest rate changes (see the earlier discussion showing that long dated bonds are the most volatile). Investors may make large capital gains or losses if they trade them. Interest is paid net of lower rate tax, and can be reclaimed by non-taxpayers. PIBS are treated as qualifying corporate bonds, so there is no liability to capital gains tax for individual investors; capital losses cannot be used to offset capital gains on other assets.

A list of some PIBS and their yields may be found in the "Weekend Money" section of the Saturday issue of *The Financial Times* and in *Moneyfacts*.

ZERO COUPON BONDS

Most people think of bonds as a way of getting a regular income payment. But zero coupon bonds are bonds that do not pay interest. Instead, they are issued at a large discount to their nominal value, so that the return comes entirely in the form of capital gain. Accordingly, there is no coupon yield or current yield, only a redemption yield.

Many financial advisers get quite excited about "zeros", but the market is rather small (though this will change, probably in 1997—see the following section). There is also a market in zero coupon preference shares (see Chapter 32), but these are shares and not bonds.

Zeros might be attractive to anyone who has to pay a specific bill at some time in the future, but does not need income in the meantime. You might have to pay £35 now to receive £100 in 13 years' time on redemption, just in time to pay for a child's university education. Zeroes might also be attractive to someone who intended to hold the bond to maturity, but thought that interest rates were going to fall. The reason has to do with the way redemption yields are calculated, but only people who like maths should read the rest of this paragraph. The redemption yield calculation assumes that the interest payments that are made during the life of the bond can be reinvested at the redemption yield. If yields fall during the life of the bond, the coupons will be reinvested at less than the assumed rate, so the redemption yield actually obtained will be lower than that calculated when the bond was purchased. Thus, if you were buying a bond during a period of very high interest rates which you did not expect to last, you might prefer a zero to a conventional bond. Because there is no interest to reinvest with a zero, you are bound to get the redemption yield you calculate at the time of purchase. All conventional bonds will return rather less than their redemption yield in these circumstances. This assumption about the reinvestment rate is the "minor mathematical complication" I mentioned a few pages ago.

Despite their attractions, zeros have been very risky:

- The British government has not issued zeros, so if you wanted one, you were forced to buy a higher risk corporate bond—but see the following section.

- If a conventional bond defaults, the blow will be softened by the interest you will have received. With a zero, you will not have received any interest.

- I noted earlier that if interest rates change, low coupon bonds' prices change by more than high coupon bonds' prices. Zeros are the ultimate in low coupon bonds.

If interest rates fall, you will make a spectacular short-run profit by selling your bond. But you will also make a spectacular loss if rates rise and you are forced to sell.

EVERYONE CAN BE A STRIPPER

Stripping is the process of separating a normal bond into its component parts and trading each part individually. It's normal to think of a bond—by those rare people who do think about bonds—as a series of interest payments and a final repayment of the principal. But another way of thinking of, say, a 10-year bond, is as 20 separate interest payments (one every six months) and one principal payment. Each of these 21 payments, or strips, could be traded separately.

For example, a £1 000 000 gilt might have a 10% coupon, and pay interest every six months. So, there might be an interest payment of £50 000 on, say, 1 February 1997, 1 August 1997, 1 February 1998, etc., with the principal (£1 000 000) repaid on 1 August 2006. You might not be interested in the whole gilt, but you might be interested in the buying the 1 August 2002 interest payment, a month or so before your daughter goes to independent school. If this interest strip were separately traded, you would be willing to pay, say, £33 000 in late 1996, to receive £50 000 in five years' time. In effect, you would be buying a zero-coupon bond.

The Bank of England is currently working on a plan to have an official gilt strips facility, in which coupon and principal strips would be direct obligations of the government. This facility is unlikely to be available before early 1997.

The first strips were introduced in the USA in 1985—the term strips is derived from Separate Trading of Registered Interest and Principal of Securities —and the strips market has been very successful. Similar success seems likely in the UK.

Should you become a stripper? Well, it depends. Having a gilt zero would be much less risky than having a corporate zero, because there would be no risk of default. But you would still have a zero, with all the peculiar risks and rewards I noted in the previous section. However, if you insist on buying a zero, a gilt zero would seem the best choice. Because zero gilts will be less risky, they will be less rewarding. But for the sort of investor that wants a set sum at a set date, a little less return for less risk seems appropriate.

INDEX-LINKED GILTS

If you want to lock in a guaranteed return for a period of years, bonds, especially gilts, are great. Whether you should want to do that is another matter. For example, if inflation turned out to be 10% per annum, your bond with a redemption yield of 8.75% would not look so good. You would be losing money in real terms, i.e., 8.75% − 10% = −1.25%, and that is without taking into account the fact you would be paying tax on your annual interest.

Faced with high inflation in the 1970s, some investors wanted an instrument to give guaranteed real returns. At the start of the 1980s, inflation was still very high. The government said it would fall to low levels, but investors were sceptical. They thought inflation would fall, but not to levels as low as the government thought. As a result, investors would only buy bonds on yields that the government thought were too high. For example, if the government thought inflation would fall to 3%, it would think that bonds with a coupon of, say, 6%—or a real yield of 3%— might be fair. But if investors thought inflation would average 7% over the life of a bond, they might want a coupon of 10%, so they would get an expected real yield of 3%. On the government's view this would be a 7% real yield.

In 1981 the government issued the first index-linked gilt. The government was offering a guaranteed real return, instead of a guaranteed money (or nominal) return. Investors who wanted a real return got it, and the government was issuing debt that would have a lower interest rate cost if its view of future inflation was correct. At first, index-linked were restricted to pension funds, but in the 1982 budget this restriction was removed. Since 1982, many index-linked gilts have been issued, and at the time of writing there are 14, with redemption dates ranging from 1996 to 2030. The gilts that existed before index-linked were issued, and with a guaranteed money return, are what I discussed earlier as "conventional gilts".

So what exactly is an index-linked gilt? It is one whose interest payments and principal are indexed to the Retail Prices Index. A simple example is probably more useful than a long-winded explanation. Interest payments are made twice a year but to simplify matters I am going to assume one payment, and a gilt with a life of two years. I'll assume a coupon of 3½%, a nominal value of £100 and inflation of 10% in year one and 5% in year two:

- Year one interest will be: £100 × 0.035 × 1.1 = £3.85 (i.e., 3½% interest increased by 10% to match inflation)

- Year two interest will be £3.85 × 1.05 = £4.04 (i.e., the last dividend increased by 5% to match inflation)

- The value of the principal on redemption will be: £100 × 1.1 × 1.05 = £115.50 (i.e., the principal increased by each year's inflation)

The effect of these adjustments is that the investor will have achieved a real return of exactly 3½%. Had inflation turned out to be something different, say 2% in each year, the investor would still have made a real return of 3½%, but received different sums of money.

Of course, if the gilt was bought by an investor at an initial price of more than £100, a real return less than 3½% would be achieved, and vice versa for prices lower than £100. After one year, if it were to offer a real yield of 3½%, the bond would trade at £110 (i.e., £100 increased by 10% inflation). But it could trade at another price, in which case the coupon would not indicate the real redemption yield. To find the redemption yield of an index-linked gilt you should look in your newspaper. Unfortunately, newspapers will often show two redemption yields. The reason is complex, and you can either just average the two, and skip the next two paragraphs, or you can read on.

I explained above that the bond market operates on the basis of accrued interest. To be able to do this, the market must know the money value of the next interest payment. That is easy enough for conventional bonds, because the value is always the same. For index-linked, we would need to know the rate of inflation over the next six months. Since we don't, indexed bonds are linked to historic inflation, which we do know. The obvious thing to do is to use the last six months' rate. However, the RPI is not published immediately so it takes a while to know the historic rate of inflation. As a result, indexation of interest and principal is linked not to current inflation, but to the RPI eight months earlier.

Because of this indexing lag, index-linked gilts do not totally guarantee a specific real return. If inflation were a million per cent in the last eight months, you would not be protected because your indexing would have stopped eight months earlier. On more reasonable assumptions, say inflation jumping by 5%, there will not be much effect, but there will be some. Because of this, the redemption rate will be partly dependent on the rate of inflation. Strictly, you should calculate the redemption rate using your assumed rate of inflation. The newspapers don't know what you are assuming so they generally use a rate of 5% and a rate of 10%. You should assume the redemption rate to be the one shown for the inflation rate nearest your forecast. If you don't have a forecast you can average the two rates, or take the rate closest to current inflation.

Some examples

In Table 19.2, I show the data you might have seen in your newspaper at the end of 1994.

You read Table 19.2 in a similar way to Table 19.1. However, the yields shown are real redemption yields. The column listed (1) assumes inflation at 10%, while (2) assumes 5%. As with the conventional gilts, notice the much larger movements there have been in prices over the year for the longer dated stock than for the shorter.

Table 19.2 Index-Linked Gilt Prices and Yields

Year		Stock	Price £	+/−	Yield %	
High	Low				(1)	(2)
113 9/32	106 3/16	Treas IL 4 5/8% 1998	106¾	...	2.95	3.82
129 1/16	106 3/8	Treas IL 2½% 2024	111 1/16xd	...	3.69	3.82

Corporate index-linked

As well as government issued indexed-linked stocks, there are a few corporate issues. For example, there are issues by Severn River Crossing, Anglian Water, Nationwide Building Society, Shires Investment Trust and Dartmoor Investment Trust. These all offer higher real returns than the government issues of anywhere from about 0.3% to 1%. In addition to the higher risk, these issues are less marketable and the dealing costs are higher. They might make a sensible alternative to an index-linked gilt for somebody investing about £10 000 and willing to hold the stock to redemption.

HOW TO BUY BONDS

You can construct a bond portfolio by:

• Buying individual bonds

- Buying bond funds

- Having a fund managed for you

Unlike my advice for equities, where I recommend buying funds, I recommend that you buy individual gilts and that you don't buy funds. I doubt that most private investors really need a personal managed bond fund.

I'm going to focus on gilts. There are three ways of buying individual gilts:

- From the Bank of England

- Through a stockbroker (or a bank or other agent, which will use a stockbroker)

- Through National Savings by post or via the Post Office

When the government issues a new gilt, it advertises it in the major papers and anyone can apply. Most of us don't, however, and I'll relegate the details to Appendix 2 of this chapter. You can buy gilts through a stockbroker. The issues that apply to buying shares apply to buying gilts—I discuss stockbrokers in Chapter 22. The only thing worth adding is that gilts normally have to be paid for the day after purchase, although a broker can deal for longer settlement.

You can buy gilts cheaply through the National Savings Stock Register. You get a booklet called *Government Stock* which explains what gilts are, lists the gilts you can buy and contains an application form and envelope. You get the booklet from almost any Post Office or National Savings (see READ 📖 WRITE ✑ RING ☎). You fill out the form, attach your cheque and send it off. Next day, your stock will be purchased. You have no control over the price paid, so if the market moves between the time you post off your form and the deal being struck, you will get a better or worse price than you expected. However, gilt prices don't usually move much over 24 hours—less than 1% typically—and you won't know whether they are about to go up or down, so this doesn't really matter. The dealing charges are shown in Table 19.3.

The most you can invest in one gilt on one day through National Savings is £25 000, but you can invest in as many gilts as you like on one day. If you buy gilts through National Savings, you generally have to sell them through National Savings.

I don't think you should buy a gilt or bond unit trust (there are no gilt or bond investment trusts). You may find this strange given the emphasis I put on diversification elsewhere in the book, but there are sound reasons for this view.

When you buy an individual equity you run a risk that the underlying business will turn sour or that the company is poorly financed. Either way you could lose all or part of your investment. But you don't run these risks with a gilt. What you have done is make a loan to the government. You don't really run a risk of the British

Table 19.3 National Savings Gilt Commission

Cost of purchase transaction or proceeds from sale	Rate of commission
Up to £5000	0.7%, subject to a minimum commission of £12.50 for purchases (no minimum for sales)
over £5000	£35 plus 0.375% of the amount in excess of £5000

government defaulting since it can just raise taxes to pay you back your loan. If you insist that there must be a default risk, no matter how small, you will probably agree that it applies to all gilts equally, so diversification does not help.

Of course, gilts are not identical. They have different coupon rates and different maturities. But let's ask why you want to hold gilts. I discuss this in more detail in the next section and you'll see that in general a gilt fund would offer no advantages over a single gilt. However, in some cases there would be disadvantages, e.g., if you want gilt exposure to reduce risk in some way or be sure you have a specific sum available on a specific date. A fund will have gilts of varying maturities, and the manager will change the maturities depending on his or her view of the market. As time goes by, the holdings will gradually have less time to maturity and, if the manager does nothing, they will all get redeemed. The manager will stop this happening by continually adjusting the fund so that bonds with a long time to maturity are bought to replace those close to redemption. If you want a gilt to match a specific event, a single bond which is redeemed on the appropriate date is much less risky than a gilt fund, which never redeems. Even for general risk reduction, a single gilt is likely to be better.

A gilt unit trust will suffer a price spread, an annual management charge and the costs of the manager continually readjusting the portfolio. A single gilt is cheap to buy, need never be sold (it gets repaid to you automatically) and if you buy through the Post Office you will get the income without deduction of income tax. If your income is high enough, you will have to pay tax, but you will pay it late, thereby getting an interest-free loan.

As well as pure gilt funds there are more general bond funds, i.e., funds which invest in corporate bonds as well as gilts. Corporate bonds yield more than gilts and may seem attractive. Unfortunately corporate bonds do run a default risk, so diversification is required, and purchase of a fund is appropriate. But that still doesn't make such funds worth buying. The point is that corporate bonds are riskier than gilts. During a recession, corporate bond yields tend to increase to allow for the greater default risk. Just when your equities might be falling in value, so too might your corporate bonds. If you are buying gilts to reduce risk, is it worth adding riskier corporate bonds for the extra return? Moreover, because of the costs of a fund, you may not earn any more than you could get from a gilt bought at the Post Office—the manager's annual charges may consume the extra yield corporate bonds offer compared to gilts.

There is a final reason not to buy a gilt or bond fund. Gilts are free from capital gains tax (for individuals and trusts), whereas you pay CGT on gains made by a unit trust investing in gilts.

In short, you should not buy a gilt or bond fund rather than a gilt because:

- The cost is higher
- The risk is higher
- The tax position is unfavourable.

WHY OWN BONDS?

Now that I've covered most of the details necessary to understand bonds, the question "Why own bonds?" has to be considered. This question has to be split into two. Why hold conventional bonds? Why hold index-linked? They may both be bonds, but they have little in common.

Conventional bonds

People hold conventional bonds for a variety of reasons. Five important reasons are:

- For a high income
- For a fixed sum on a specific date
- To reduce risk
- To diversify
- To make an interest rate bet

High income The average yield on the equity market is about 4%, that on gilts about 8%. Cash yields anywhere from about 1% up to 6% on saving accounts that impose neither especially onerous conditions nor require huge deposits. It is possible to get higher rates of interest on some deposit accounts and on some insurance products. In short, bonds offer a high income relative to most assets, although not all. But the rate is fixed, so if inflation is high, the real value of the interest will be less and less. The yield on cash is likely to rise as inflation increases. It may or may not keep pace, but it will offer some protection.

One way of hedging your bets with bonds is by a strategy known as laddering. You buy a number of gilts with different maturity dates. One might mature in a year or two, another in five years or so, another in 10 years, and so on. When your first bond matures you can reinvest it at the current rate of interest. If rates have risen, you can at least lock in part of your money at that rate. Of course, your long-dated bonds offer no protection against rising rates. If, on the other hand, rates fall, you'll do worse when you reinvest the proceeds of your short-dated gilt, but your long-dated bonds will offer some protection. If you had put all your money in cash, and cash rates fell, you would have no protection against a falling income.

Equities offer lower starting yields but your income is likely to grow. If dividends grow at 5% per annum, it will take 15 years for them to reach the current gilt yield and a further 15 years to double again. If you retire at 50, you may prefer to forego the higher immediate income of gilts for the growth of equities. You might also be able to dip into any growth of your equity capital.

Obtain a fixed sum Bonds can be used to produce a fixed sum on a specific date. The sum, however, is fixed in money terms and most gilts offer little growth of the capital invested. If you look in the newspaper at a list of gilts you will find only a few trading at prices significantly under £100, the price they will be redeemed at. (The undated stocks are trading at significantly less than £100, but they have no guaranteed redemption date.) Corporate zero coupon bonds do produce capital growth (and no income) but you are taking a credit risk, and you could lose a lot of money if you have to sell before the redemption date.

Reduce risk   Bonds are sometimes held because they are less risky than equities. But it depends on what you mean by risk. If you use the uncertainty of the return you will get as your risk measure, bonds are less risky than equities. Yet if you look back to Figure 4.1, you will see that while gilts returns have been less volatile than equity returns, they have actually produced more years of negative returns than equities have. And bonds are completely exposed to the inflation risk. However, unlike equities, gilts are not exposed to credit risk, although corporate bonds are.

Diversify risks   Bonds, clearly, are not risk-free assets. But their risks are different from those of equities. If you put bonds and equities together you get a diversifying effect. The problem here is that bond returns are more closely correlated with equity returns than are cash and equity returns. In other words, if you put cash and equities together, you get better diversification. And cash over long periods has offered a higher return than gilts. Now this may not be the case in the future, but cash is in many ways less risky than gilts. So if you want to diversify an equity portfolio, you could easily argue that the sensible thing is to keep some of your resources in cash and not buy bonds.

Interest rate bets   As I explained, when interest rates fall, bond prices rise. The effect is greatest on irredeemables and zeros. If you think you can call interest rate movements, you might use bonds to make short-term bets. You can buy bonds when you think rates will fall, and hope to sell the bonds soon after for a capital gain. You'll have to get your bet right, and act before the professionals. Is this investing or speculating?

Are conventional bonds for you?   Whether conventional bonds are right for you, will depend on your objectives. But, as I've just shown, the common assertion that bonds are the automatic choice for high income at low risk is too simple. You have to think carefully before you buy bonds, just as you have to think carefully before buying equities.

Index-linked bonds

Index-linked bonds don't offer a high yield or a guaranteed money return. But they do offer a guaranteed real return if held to redemption. Index-linked bond returns are less volatile than equity returns and they can be used for diversification purposes, although the record is too short to see just how useful they might be in this regard. The great attraction is the guaranteed real return, of which the capital component is not subject to tax for individual investors and trusts.

Should you buy an index-linked gilt? There is a natural tendency to see the word "gilts" in "index-linked gilts" and compare them to conventional gilts. That's fair enough, because all assets can be compared to all others, but index-linked gilts are more like equities than conventional gilts. They have a low initial income but they offer both income and capital growth. I'm going to make three comparisons: professionals and experienced investors should read the next three sub-sections, but novice investors may prefer to skip them.

Index-linked versus conventional gilts   With a conventional gilt you get fixed payments of interest and repayment of principal. The value of both types of payment is known in advance. With an index-linked gilt, the money value of the interest pay-ments and the repayment of principal will depend on the rate of inflation. So, to decide which will give the higher return, a conventional or index-linked gilt, you have to make an assumption about the rate of inflation. The two types of gilts will be priced to reflect the average investor's view of the likely rate of inflation. At that rate of inflation, the two types of gilts should offer roughly equal returns.

Clearly you receive more cash with an index-linked gilt the higher the rate of in-flation so, if inflation turns out higher than expected, index-linked gilts will be the better value, and if inflation turns out to be lower than expected, conventional gilts will be the better buy. This is the key to assessing which type of gilt offers the better value.

How do you know what the market is assuming the rate of inflation will be? One way of finding out is to assume a whole range of inflation rates, and see what the nominal return from an index-linked gilt would be for each of these rates. You can then compare the various returns to the returns from a conventional gilt with the same maturity. The inflation rate at which the index-linked gilt gives the same return as the conventional one must be the rate of inflation the market is assuming. It is called the break-even inflation rate—it's the rate which makes the two returns break even.

While you won't want to do these sums, gilts brokers do them all the time. A full-service stockbroker can tell you break-even inflation rates for various index-linked gilts. If you don't use a stockbroker, *Moneyfacts* (under the heading "Index-linked Gilts" in its "Fixed Rates" section), and the *Financial Times* (every Saturday in the "Weekend Money" section), publish the information. Before I give you an example, I have to introduce one further complication.

The return you are interested in is the total after-tax return of interest plus or minus capital gain or loss. For individuals and trusts, neither type of gilt is subject to capital gains tax, but both are subject to income tax. For certain types of tax-exempt institutional investors such as pension funds, both income and capital gains are tax-free. Now the current yield on conventional gilts is generally greater than for index-linked gilts. More of the return comes from interest, thus more of the return from a conventional gilt is taxed. Clearly the greater your tax rate, the higher must be the pre-tax return from a conventional gilt to give a post-tax return equal to that from an index-linked gilt. Strictly speaking then, there is not one break-even inflation rate but one for each income tax rate.

In Table 19.4, the index-linked stock maturing in 2013 is compared—using prices of Autumn 1995—to a conventional gilt maturing in the same year. If you pay no income tax, the index-linked stock will give the better return if inflation is greater than 4.48%, and the conventional stock if inflation is lower. If you pay tax at 40%, and if inflation exceeds 2.28%, the index-linked stock will pay the better return. This inflation rate is not for this year or next year, but the average rate of inflation over the life of the stock, or over about 17 years in the case of the gilts in this example.

Table 19.4   An Index-linked Gilt versus a Conventional Gilt

Index Linked Stock	Price in 32nds	Comparison Stock	Break-even Inflation Rate	
			Tax 0%	Tax 40%
2½% IL 2013	£136'30	Treas 8% 2013	4.48%	2.28%

If you pay tax at 40%, and think inflation will be, say, 4%, does this mean you should prefer index-linked? Not necessarily—many people buy conventional gilts for their high current yield, i.e., high income. Index-linked don't offer that—much of their return comes in the form of capital gains. But for after-tax total return, index-linked would look the better buy.

The worst outcome approach   A second way of assessing an index-linked gilt is to concentrate on the worst outcome. If you think of Consols 2½%, you can see the dangers of conventional gilts. If inflation soars, your capital will be decimated and your income will be very low. Anybody who bought Consols 2½% at £100 when they were issued now has an investment worth about £31, and yielding to that investor 2½% on the original investment, while market rates are currently much higher. An investor in index-linked, on the other hand, is protected against inflation.

What if there is no inflation, indeed prices fall? You would be better off holding cash or conventional bonds. With index-linked, you could get less than your original investment back. How bad would that be? Not too bad. The point is that you would still get a real return. If you bought the gilt on a 3% real return, you would get a 3% real return even if you got less than your original investment back. For example—and let's just focus on the principal—if you bought at £100, and prices fell by 6% in one year, and the bond is redeemed after a year, you would get £97 back (i.e., £100 + £3 − £6). You would only need £94 at the redemption date to buy the goods and services that would have cost you £100 at your investment date. Thus you could spend £94 to buy what would have cost £100, and you would still have £3 left, your 3% real return. This all seems very odd, but only because we are not used to falling prices.

I interpret the last two paragraphs in this way. If inflation soars, conventional gilts will not only be a poor investment in relative terms, but also in absolute terms. Index-linked gilts will give your 3% real in absolute terms and will probably be excellent in relative terms. If prices fall, conventional gilts will be an excellent investment. Index-linked will be a poor investment in relative terms, but in absolute terms, your purchasing power will have been increased by 3%. You will have come out ahead. So index-linked gilts will be a fine investment in absolute terms, but by no means the best. I think this analysis makes index-linked an attractive investment for part of anybody's long-term funds. Heads you win, tails you don't lose. Of course, if you *know* inflation is dead, you might wish to ignore index-linked. But nobody really knows.

Index-linked versus equities   A third way of assessing index-linked is in relation to equities. Equities are a growth investment. Over the long term, we expect equities to grow with the economy and both our capital and income to grow. We expect to make a real return from equities. Index-linked gilts are also a growth investment, with growing income and capital, and a real return. Of course, if there is no inflation, index-linked gilts will not be a growth investment, although they will still offer a real return. But remember that part of the growth of profits comes just from keeping pace with inflation, so equity dividend growth would be much more modest in money terms if inflation were to be permanently low.

The real return from equities has been about 8% since 1919. The real return from index-linked gilts bought today (November 1995) is about 3.7%. Index-linked gilts look inferior from a rate of return viewpoint. However, let's think about that. If you buy an index-linked gilt from the Post Office, it will cost you 0.7% in commission, so for every £100 you invest, £99.30 will be working for you. There will be no annual charges. In other words, ignoring tax for the moment, you will get pretty much the real rate that the papers show. If you buy equities, you might buy through a unit trust. If you invested for 10 years, and equities produced a real return of 8%, and the investments in your fund matched that, you might get a real return of only 5½% after all charges. This is more than the return from index-linked, but few people think that equities will always give an 8% real return. Some experts think 5% would be a better long-term bet. I'll split the difference and suggest 6½%. This would imply a 4% real return from equities, after charges.

I could play around with these numbers but, when all is said and done, you might expect to earn more from equities, although not as much as the historical market averages might suggest. And you should take into account risk. I don't know what will happen to the economy over the next 20 years, and neither does anyone else. For all I know, equities may have a lousy period; maybe not all of the period, but certainly for enough of the period to produce poor returns overall. Don't forget, we expect a high return from equities but we may not get it. Remember the stockmarket crash of 1987? Returns were great to the start of October, and less than great at the end. Quite a shock if you retired at the end of the month and wanted to cash in your shares.

Index-linked aren't as risky. Sure, they slump when interest rates rise, but on redemption day you will get the real return you expected when you bought them. As redemption day approaches, the price of the stock will reflect the redemption value much more than current market conditions. If you will retire in the year 2013, you can buy an index-linked stock with that redemption date. You are guaranteed your real return over that period on redemption day. Up to redemption, your investment could look pretty sick, but on the day it will be just fine. There is no such guarantee with equities. If you retired the day after the 1987 crash—tough.

Index-linked gilts: a guaranteed real return Since index-linked are less risky than equities, we should expect them to offer a smaller return. In my view, index-gilts are a very attractive investment for the private client and should form part of many portfolios:

● Index-linked gilts offer a guaranteed real return if held to redemption.

● Although the real return on offer is less than equities have achieved over long periods, the difference narrows once a private investor's costs are allowed for.

● Index-linked gilts are much less risky than equities.

If index-linked gilts are so attractive, why are they not widely recommended? I don't know, but it's not in most advisers' interests to recommend them: you can buy them at the Post Office, and you then just hold them until redemption. There are no fat fees, and you don't have to switch around, as your broker will recommend that you do with your shares. Also, in the decade or so that index-linked gilts have existed, they have given much lower returns than the quite exceptional returns from cash, conventional gilts, and equities. Most people make their decisions for the future on what has happened in the recent past.

APPENDIX I: BOND TAXATION

You may have seen many press articles in the last year or so about changes in bond taxation. First one set of changes were proposed, then in July 1995 some rather different rules were announced, then the Chancellor scrapped all the proposed new rules for individuals and trusts in his November 1995 Budget. So, for individuals and trusts, bonds are taxed as they have been for many years. Specifically, for gilts and qualifying corporate bonds (basically all corporate bonds denominated in sterling and repayable in sterling), individuals and trusts are taxed on interest received, but not on any capital gain. Any capital loss cannot be used to offset a capital gain on another asset. Since 1 April 1996, new rules have applied to companies, but these rules lie outside the scope of this book.

APPENDIX II : BUYING GILTS FROM THE BANK

In most parts of this book I stress the advantage of dealing at a cheap rate. Low commissions boost your returns. As a result, I feel obliged to say a little more about buying stock directly from the Bank of England, because such deals are commission free, but I haven't recommended them. There are three reasons for not buying from the Bank: you might not want the stock, you may not understand what you are doing, and you may want to buy less than the Bank's minimum of £1000 worth of stock. I'll comment on the first two points.

The Bank sells only new issues, so you will only be able to buy what it happens to be selling. If your needs are for a stock with five years to maturity, but the Bank is issuing a stock with a life of twenty years, it makes no sense to buy that just to save commission. You can always buy exactly what you need through the Post Office at very little cost, so there is no point waiting for a new issue that might not meet your needs.

The second problem is the method of issue. Most recent sales have been by auction. Here you won't know in advance what you are paying, and the pricing method is complicated.

With an auction, if you invest £500 000 or more (and I doubt many readers will be doing that) you may make a competitive bid for stock, i.e., you say what you are willing to pay. The Bank supplies stock to the highest bidder, then to the next highest, and so on till the stock has all been sold. If you are investing less than £500 000 you can make a non-competitive bid. You will get stock at the weighted average price of the price paid by the large investors who make successful bids.

Some new issues have been made by tender. Here the Bank sets a reserve price that it won't sell below. Investors can bid at or above the reserve price. If the issue is oversubscribed the Bank sells the whole issue at the price that balances supply and demand. For example, say the total issue is £1 000 000 and the reserve price is £1. Imagine that it gets three bids only at £1.02, £1.01 and £1, and each is for £500 000 nominal stock. It can sell the full £1 000 000 at £1.01 and both the highest and second highest bidder will get stock, and *both* at £1.01. If the issue is undersubscribed, i.e., the Bank can't sell all of it at the reserve price, it will sell what it can at that price and keep the rest.

READ 📖 WRITE ✉ RING ☎

♦ A very clear and simple guide to the gilts market is the Bank of England's booklet *Investing in Gilts: A Guide for the Small Investor*. A more detailed guide by the Bank is *British Government Securities: The Market in Gilt-Edged Securities*. Copies may be obtained from: The Bank of England, Threadneedle Street, London, EC2R 8AH. Tel: 0171 601 4540. Or from: Bank of England, Registrar's Department, Southgate House, Southgate Street, Gloucester, GL1 1UW. Tel: 01452 398000.

♦ To buy new gilt issues from the Bank of England, you need an application form. You will find one in some newspapers, or you can contact the Bank of England for one, or can get your name added to the Bank Registrar's Department's mailing list for interested investors—addresses above.

♦ For information about buying and selling gilts through National Savings, look for details in a Post Office, or contact National Savings, Blackpool, FY3 9YP. Tel: 01253 697333.

♦ Overseas residents wishing to receive interest gross on certain gilts should contact: Inspector of Foreign Dividends, Inland Revenue, Lynwood Road, Thames Ditton, Surrey, KT7 ODP.

20

Personal Equity Plans (PEPs)

The avoidance of taxes is the only pursuit that still carries any reward.
John Maynard Keynes

PEPs were introduced in 1986, but only became popular when the rules were changed to increase the amount that could be invested and to allow investment in investment trusts and unit trusts. Now the weekend would not be the weekend without having to plough through endless articles on PEPs in the newspapers. This has probably more to do with the rich source of associated advertising revenue than investor interest. Although you would never know it from the amount of press coverage, TESSAs are much more popular than PEPs. There is about 50% more money invested in TESSAs than PEPs, despite having been in existence half as long, and the cumulative sum you have been permitted to invest in TESSAs being much smaller.

THE BASICS

PEPs are available to anyone aged 18 or over who is resident in the UK. You can invest up to £9000 each year in PEPs, with up to £6000 in a General PEP and up to £3000 in a Single Company PEP. You can take out only one of each type of PEP each year (although you can switch your PEPs to another PEP provider) but, unlike TESSAs, you can take out new PEPs each year, and leave your money in your PEPs as long as you wish.

The amount you can invest in a PEP has changed over the years. Had you invested the full amount every year since 1987, you could have invested a total of £73 200. The amount allowed each year is shown in Table 20.1. If you don't use a particular year's allowance in that year, it is lost.

PEPs are tax-free; there is usually neither income tax nor capital gains tax to pay. You can draw out your income and your capital at any time. Once you have drawn out money, you can't reinvest it into that PEP. But you can invest it, or any other money, into a new PEP in the following year. Interest (but not dividends) that exceeds £180 per annum is taxed.

You can't usually directly transfer shares you hold into your PEP. If you own ICI shares and want to switch them into a PEP, you must sell the shares, and buy them again in the PEP. This is costly in transaction charges, and could trigger a capital gains tax charge. There are two exceptions to this rule. First, you can transfer new

Table 20.1   Annual PEP Investment Limits

Year to	General (£)	Single Company (£)
31/12/87	2400	
31/12/88	3000	
31/12/89	3000	
5/4/90*	4800	
5/4/91	6000	
5/4/92	6000	3000**
5/4/93	6000	3000
5/4/94	6000	3000
5/4/95	6000	3000
5/4/96	6000	3000
5/4/97	6000	3000

* 1/1/90–5/4/90
** 1/1/92–5/4/92

issues (including privatization issues) into a PEP within 42 days of the issue. Second, company employees who have acquired shares under approved employee profit-sharing schemes can make a direct transfer of the shares.

There are additional specific rules for General PEPs and Single Company PEPs. The rules for General PEPs are that the PEP must be invested in UK and EC shares, and in sterling convertibles, preference shares and corporate bonds with more than five years left to run, and authorized unit and investment trusts. If you invest more than £1500 in a trust, it must be a "qualifying trust". This means that it will keep at least 50% of its portfolio in UK or EC quoted shares, sterling convertibles, preference shares and corporate bonds with more than five years left to run. You can invest up to £1500 in a non-qualifying unit or investment trust, which is one that fails the above test but has at least half its assets in shares or listed on any recognized stock exchange in the world other than in the UK or EU. But you don't have to worry about the definitions, product providers of investment trusts and unit trusts always tell you the status of their products. You can mix qualifying and non-qualifying trusts: e.g., you can have, say, £3000 in a qualifying trust and £1500 in a non-qualifying trust. You keep cash in your PEP as long as you wish, providing your intention is to eventually invest it in shares, bonds, etc.

A Single Company PEP must be invested in the shares of one UK or EU company. You can switch the company as often as you wish, but you can have only one company at a time. If you have Single Company PEPs for different years, you can hold different companies in each. Although investment trusts are companies, you cannot invest in one in your Single Company PEP. You cannot keep cash in a Single Company PEP for more than 42 days. You can transfer shares from an approved company profit-sharing or savings related scheme directly into a Single Company PEP provided you do so within 90 days of receipt from the scheme trustees.

Those are the rules, but how do you manage your PEP money? For a General PEP, there are four types of PEP management structure:

• Choice or self-select

• Managed

- Investment trust/unit trust

- Corporate

In *choice PEPs*, investors make their own selection of shares, bonds or investment and unit trusts, sometimes from a restricted list drawn up by the product provider. In *managed PEPs*, the plan manager makes the investment choice, and provides discretionary management. *Investment and unit trust PEPs* are investments in either type of trust within a PEP wrapper. *Corporate PEPs* are PEPs that a quoted company is sponsoring. The company wants you to invest in its shares (and only its shares), and may levy low charges to encourage you to do so. You can invest your General PEP in the shares of a single company, and it remains a £6000 General PEP. From all that I have said in earlier chapters, it hardly needs saying that I think you should invest your General PEP in an investment trust or unit trust, and not select shares.

For a Single Company PEP, the same management structures are available as those listed above, with the exception of the investment trust and unit trusts.

If you have a PEP and subsequently want to switch to a new PEP manager, you can. But you must be aware of two things. First, **don't** close your PEP, get cash and send it to the new manager. When you close your PEP, you lose the right to have a PEP for the year you opened that PEP in. You must make a transfer: let the PEP manager you plan to switch to handle the transfer. The second point is that there will be charges for making a transfer. You may be able to transfer shares, but the manager losing the PEP will usually make a charge for the re-registration of the shares out of his nominee name into the new manager's. If you hold a unit trust and are switching to another manager's unit trust, the sale will take place at the selling price, and the purchase at the buying price, perhaps reduced by a commission rebate. Nonetheless, the total cost you will suffer will be significant.

SHOULD YOU HAVE A PEP?

Originally this amounted to asking whether you should hold equities in the form of a PEP. Now the question is broader because of the changes made in the 1994 Budget to include various types of bonds. The problem is that you can't set up your own PEP, and many PEP providers levy fees, so you have to offset the fees against the tax savings.

Most interest has been shown in General PEPs. That's partly because unit trust and investment trust companies have actively sold the General PEPs, but have no interest in the Single Company PEPs. Moreover, it's rational for investors to begin with the PEP that gives greatest diversification potential (but can also be invested in a single company). Thus, although it's possible to invest £9000 a year in PEPs, most investors do not exceed £6000. There are about seven times as many General PEPs as Single Company PEPs opened each year.

I'll begin by looking at all-equity PEPs. With regards to capital gains tax, you may or may not make a saving by having a PEP. Everyone can realize gains of £6300 per annum without suffering CGT, and this £6300 is after indexation allowance has been applied. Only about 90 000 investors in the UK pay CGT each year, so it is unlikely that most investors will actually save CGT by having a PEP. Against this, it is usually argued that if you open a PEP each year, you will soon build a substantial portfolio, and anyway investors with large portfolios of stocks will immediately benefit. Let's look at these arguments.

Since you can invest £9000 a year, if you invest every year, over the years, your PEP pool will grow (recall Table 20.1). This is true, but most people don't invest £9000 a year. Second, many people will use PEPs to meet medium-term targets such as school fees, and so will only build a modest PEP pool which they will then spend. Third, a Labour Government may end the PEP tax-break. However, let's assume that PEPs continue for a few more years and that you have built up a PEP pool of £100 000. Say the market rises by 10%, and inflation was 5%. Would you have paid CGT if you had invested outside a PEP? Your gain after indexation would fall below your annual exemption (i.e., £10 000 – £5000 = £5000, which is below the current £6300 exemption). Even if it exceeded it, the tax is only charged on realized gains so you could postpone paying the tax. And you could bed and breakfast part of the gain.

Some advertisements point out that a married couple can invest up to £18 000 in PEPs and imply that this gives an additional CGT advantage. It doesn't. Each partner is only investing up to £9000 and, because of individual taxation, each will have a £6300 CGT exemption. Even if both invest the full £9000 the same argument that I made above about CGT applies. Of course, there will be potential for CGT savings if originally all £18 000 was held by one partner, and the money is split equally and put into PEPs. But there would be a potential for CGT saving if the money was split and not placed in PEPs, since there would be two CGT exemptions to be enjoyed instead of one.

To sum up. Most people don't pay CGT, so they don't make a CGT savings by having a PEP. They should make their decision on the basis of income tax savings, which I discuss below. Of course, if you are rich, have a large share portfolio and do pay CGT, you should be investing in PEPs.

There was a tremendous amount of hype from unit trust marketing departments preceding the introduction of corporate bond PEPs. But corporate bonds are normally exempt from CGT. In other words, there is no CGT advantage from holding bonds in a PEP. Indeed, by doing so, you force out equities which might benefit from escaping CGT. Of course, if you had held bonds in a unit trust, any capital gain would have been liable to CGT. So in that regard a bond unit trust PEP will offer a tax saving compared to a non-PEP bond fund. But from the viewpoint of CGT, either approach is distinctly inferior to simply buying a gilt through the Post Office. The gilt would be less risky, and also exempt from CGT. The case for a bond PEP has to be made on the basis of income tax savings.

How worth while is the advantage of escaping income tax on dividends and bond interest in a PEP? Well, you avoid income tax in a PEP, but you pay a fee, so you have to do a cost/benefit sum. Annual charges, whether for managing a PEP or a unit trust annual charge, are subject to VAT. This means that the true charge is somewhat higher than is usually claimed. You may recall my discussion of tax credits in Chapter 8. When you receive your savings income, it has suffered tax at 20%. If you pay income tax at 20% or 25%, there is nothing further to pay. A 40% taxpayer has to pay a further 20%. Now, when we do things in reverse, and the PEP provider claims back tax, 20% is credited. This means that the break even yield for a 20% or 25% taxpayer will be yield that when multiplied by 0.2 equals the annual charge plus VAT. For the 40% taxpayer the same calculation must be made but using 0.4 instead of 0.2. Table 20.2 shows the results for various charges.

Table 20.2   Yield Required to Cover PEP Charges at Two Tax Rates

Stated % Charge	+ Vat	= True Charge	Required Break-even Yield	
			20% Taxpayer	40% Taxpayer
0.25	0.04	0.29	1.47	0.73
0.50	0.09	0.59	2.94	1.47
0.75	0.13	0.88	4.41	2.20
1.00	0.18	1.18	5.88	2.94
1.25	0.22	1.47	7.34	3.67
1.50	0.26	1.76	8.81	4.41
1.75	0.31	2.06	10.28	5.14
2.00	0.35	2.35	11.75	5.88

As you can see, if you pay 20% tax on your savings, you have to have either very low annual charges or a very high yield for your PEP to generate a tax saving for you which exceeds the charges. For example, if the PEP charge is 1% plus VAT, your fund must yield at least 5.88% for you to benefit. For a 40% taxpayer a PEP yields an income tax-break at lower yields and higher charges. Still, with the equity market yielding less than 4%, you have to be careful to make sure you benefit from your PEP. Bond funds are likely to provide an income tax shelter for 40% taxpayers, but may not for 20% taxpayers, especially if the bonds are held in a high charge unit trust.

You may recall that in Chapter 19, I argued that you should never hold a gilt unit trust. The same argument does not necessarily apply to a bond unit trust held in a PEP because, if you hold bonds you will be holding corporate bonds as you can't hold gilt unit trusts in PEPs (although up to 49% of your fund can be invested in gilts). Unlike gilts, it is necessary to diversify corporate bonds to reduce risk. Holding a single corporate bond is riskier than holding a diversified fund in terms of default risk, i.e., your bond could go bust. Holding a diversified portfolio of corporate bonds with no redemption date is, however, likely to be riskier than holding a single gilt with a redemption date. Corporate bonds are riskier *per se* than gilts and even more so if they do not have a redemption date. For a 20% taxpayer, there will be at best a marginal income advantage from holding a corporate bond unit trust. Given the higher risk, it is hard to justify a bond fund PEP over a single non-PEP gilt. For 40% taxpayers, the income tax savings *may* tip the balance in favour of the PEP route.

TO PEP OR NOT TO PEP?

Is the gist of all this that most people should ignore PEPs? No.

- If you normally pay CGT you should have a PEP.
- Most people who own unit trusts should have a PEP. The unit trust industry has been very keen to get its hands on PEP money and has generally offered a PEP wrapper for its funds for free. So, if you would have held a unit trust anyway, it makes sense to hold it in a PEP. Indeed, some unit trust PEPs have cut their front-end charges to encourage you to buy them. That is a bargain—if you want those particular unit trusts.

- Investment trusts typically have a PEP charge, and often a set-up fee plus annual charge. (Alliance Investment Trust, however, has a no fee PEP that allows investment in Alliance and any qualifying investment trust.) For most investment trust PEPs you do have to do the sums in Table 20.2 to see if an investment trust is worth while. This is especially true if you do not invest the full £6000, and the fees are set in money terms and not percentage terms. Does this mean that unit trusts PEPs are better value than investment trust PEPs? Not necessarily. Don't forget that while there are no extra costs for a unit trust PEP you are still paying around 1.5% annual management charge. A large general investment trust such as Witan levies an annual PEP charge of £30, or 0.5% for a £6,000 PEP. Witan's annual charge is about 0.25% so, despite the extra PEP charges, total PEP and management charges are much lower than those for most unit trust PEPs. For small investment trusts, the annual charges will be higher.

- If you go the route of a managed, self-select, or corporate PEP, you will be charged for the PEP wrapper. You should check your position against Table 20.2 and also decide whether you would pay CGT if you invested outside of a PEP. Be sure to look at cheap providers such as discount brokers before you abandon the idea of a PEP.

- Finally, if you don't like the risk associated with equities and corporate bonds, don't invest in a PEP just for the tax-break. If you sell every time the markets fall, you'll incur costs and never be invested when the markets rise. You'll never have the gains necessary to benefit from the tax-break.

PICKING A PEP

If you decide to have a PEP you should approach selecting one much as you would any other equity or bond investment. If you like index funds, go that route, if you believe in star managers, invest with one, if you think you can pick the best shares, do that.

If you have gone the pooled fund route in your investments in general, you may be baffled by having to pick a Single Company, as you must do with a Single Company PEP. On £3000, the tax-break after charges is not enormous, even for a 40% tax-payer, so you could just pass up the opportunity. Otherwise, especially if you are half of a couple and together you can buy two shares a year, you might just take a long-term view and build up a portfolio of big stocks. For example, if the two of you steadily bought the biggest companies, in five years you would have 10 companies between you which might represent about 20% of the market's capitalization. You would not be running too many risks over a period of years by adopting this strategy, although the results might be erratic in the early years. The biggest stocks by capitalization are shown in Table 20.3. (The largest 100 are shown in many of the Sunday newspapers.) If you start at the top and work down it would be sensible to skip a share that is in the same sector as one you have already bought. That way you will build a more diversified portfolio. Since you are tax sheltering income, you might prefer the higher yielding stock of any two that are closely ranked and in the same sector, e.g., you might prefer Shell to BP.

As well as looking at big shares you might look at sector weights. For example, one

Table 20.3   25 Largest Shares (November 1995)

Share	Value £bn	Yield %	Sector
Glaxo Wellcome	30.8	4.3	Pharmaceuticals
BP	28.2	3.5	Oils, Integrated
Shell	26.4	4.5	Oils, Integrated
HSBC	24.7	3.7	Banks, Retail
BT	22.7	6.3	Telecommunications
SmithKline Beecham	18.4	2.4	Pharmaceuticals
BAT	17.5	5.0	Tobacco
Barclays	13.0	3.5	Banks, Retail
Marks and Spencer	12.7	2.9	Retailers, General
BTR	12.4	5.3	Diversified
Zeneca	12.2	2.7	Pharmaceuticals
NatWest Bank	11.9	4.2	Banks, Retail
Lloyds Bank	11.2	3.9	Banks, Retail
British Gas	10.4	7.6	Gas
Reuters	10.4	1.7	Media
RTZ	10.1	3.3	Extractive
Cable and Wireless	10.0	2.6	Telecommunications
Unilever	10.0	2.8	Food Producers
Hanson	9.9	7.9	Diversified
Guinness	9.3	3.8	Alcoholic Beverages
Grand Metropolitan	9.0	4.2	Alcoholic Beverages
GEC	8.8	4.5	Electronics
Prudential	8.4	4.2	Life Assurance
Abbey National	8.0	4.0	Banks, Retail
Sainsbury, J.	6.9	4.0	Retailers, food

of the biggest companies is BAT. Now you might prefer to exclude it on moral grounds, as I would. But if you don't take this view, you might look at Table 20.4 and see that the tobacco sector is only 2.0% of the market. You might feel that if you skipped down Table 20.3 to the diversified sector stocks you would be getting closer to buying the UK market if you bought one of them, because Table 20.4 shows that the diversified sector is 4.3% of the UK market. What I am suggesting is a very crude form of indexing. But you may prefer to take a more aggressive share selection approach.

PEPS AS PART OF YOUR PORTFOLIO

If you have PEPs, they are part of your total equity and bond portfolio. You should make sure that the asset allocation of all your bonds, equities and PEPs together meets your requirements and not consider each asset on its own. It's OK to be invested solely in pooled funds investing abroad in your non-PEP share portfolio if all your PEPs are invested exclusively in UK equities and together your PEP and non-PEP portfolios give you the asset allocation you want. And if you follow the big company bias I outlined for your Single Company PEPs, you might give your General PEP a bit more of a small company tilt.

Table 20.4   FT-SE-A All-Share Index (January 1996)

GROUP OR SECTOR	% OF ALL-SHARE INDEX
Mineral Extraction	**9.1**
Extractive Industries	1.4
Oil, Integrated	7.0
Oil Exploration and Production	0.7
General Manufacturers	**18.2**
Building and Construction	0.8
Building Materials and Merchants	2.4
Chemicals	2.2
Diversified Industrials	4.3
Electronic and Electronic Equipment	2.3
Engineering	3.9
Engineering, Vehicles	0.8
Paper and Packaging, and Printing	1.3
Textiles and Apparel	0.5
Consumer Goods	**17.5**
Alcoholic Beverages	3.1
Food Producers	3.5
Household Goods	0.5
Health Care	0.7
Pharmaceuticals	7.7
Tobacco	2.0
Services	**22.8**
Distributors	0.9
Leisure and Hotels	1.9
Media	5.6
Retailers, Food	2.8
Retailers, General	5.5
Breweries, Pubs & Restaurants	2.3
Support Services	1.6
Transport	2.2
Utilities	**11.2**
Electricity	3.3
Gas Distribution	1.3
Telecommunications	4.9
Water	1.7
Total Non-Financials	**78.7**
Financials	**17.6**
Banks, Retail	10.4
Banks, Merchant	0.5
Insurance	2.1
Life Assurance	1.8
Other Financial	1.2
Property	1.7
Investment Trusts	**3.6**

Source: Datastream

READ 📖 WRITE 🖹 RING ☎

♦ The major newspapers, investment magazines, and the professional magazines all periodically review PEP charges and performance.

21

How to Reduce Investment Risks

Don't put all your eggs in one basket.
Proverb

Now that I've discussed equities and bonds, it's time to discuss risk again. Many people see equities and bonds as just too risky for them: on the other hand, some people take what I would consider to be too many risks. There are ways of reducing investment risk, and that's the topic of this chapter—it should offer something for both the cautious and the foolhardy. The two most important ways of reducing investment risks are by knowing your objectives and by diversifying. This is one of the most important chapters in the book. Along with Chapter 4, it is perhaps the most important. I discuss diversifying first.

DIVERSIFICATION IS DIVINE

Diversification is a sure-fire way to reduce risk. There are four forms of diversification:

- Diversification within asset classes

- Diversification over time

- Diversification over purchase periods

- Diversification across assets

DIVERSIFICATION WITHIN ASSET CLASSES

I'm going to talk about companies and shares in this section, but what I say can be applied more generally.

If you've decided to hold some shares, you have to decide which ones. Most shares don't go bust. But some do. If you hold just one share, it is quite possible that you will hold one that goes bust, and you will lose all of your money. If you hold two shares it is less likely that you will lose all of your money. Diversification into two shares has reduced your risks. This is an example of diversification within an asset class.

Diversification will reduce risk in a more subtle way too. When you combine risky

Table 21.1 Profits and Losses for Two Companies

Economic Cycle	Advertising Agency	Insolvency Practice	Total
Growth	+100	−50	+50
Recession	−50	+100	+50

assets, you will usually find that the whole is less risky than the sum of the parts. To understand this, imagine two companies, one an accountancy partnership specializing in insolvency and the other an advertising agency. The insolvency partnership will do well in recessions and, let us assume, will do badly in good times. And vice versa for the advertising agency. Let us assume that good and bad times occur with equal frequency. If we assume some profit and loss figures, we might have the situation shown in Table 21.1.

Although both companies deliver profits over an entire economic cycle, profits are very variable. Each company is risky. An investor owning either company would have variable profits, but if both companies were owned in equal amounts, profits would be stable. Diversification would eliminate the risk of profit variability because the returns from the two companies are negatively related. When one goes up, the other goes down. Diversification achieved by combining two advertising agencies would not be so effective—both companies are likely to do well and badly at the same time.

Constructing a plausible example of perfect diversification is quite difficult—when the economy does badly, most companies and their stocks do badly. And vice versa when the economy does well. However, companies' profits do not move exactly in tandem, and selecting a basket of stocks at random will reduce risk. In my simple two-company example I chose companies whose returns moved in opposite directions. When one did well, the other did badly. By holding both assets in a 50/50 ratio, the risk was totally eliminated. Because most assets move together to some extent, diversification will only reduce risk and not eliminate it.

In short, the risk of a portfolio is a function not only of the risk of each of the assets comprising the portfolio, but also of the extent to which the risks affect the assets at the same time. Professionals talk of this in terms of correlation, a statistical measure that tells us how much two assets move together. If assets are highly correlated, bringing them together in one portfolio will reduce risk less than if they were not correlated. I'll talk about that some more in the next but one section. When constructing a share portfolio, you will reduce your risks if you select lots of shares whose returns are not highly correlated. How will you know that? You won't, but a little common sense will go a long way.

Which of the following do you think would be the least risky? One bank share or two? Two bank shares or a bank and a food manufacturer? What about three bank shares or a bank, a food manufacturer and a oil share? The answer is the wider the selection of shares, both in terms of numbers and types of industry, the lower the risk. You should hold a well-diversified portfolio. For most people, the easiest and cheapest way of reducing the risk of individual shares is to buy a ready-made well-diversified fund, such as an investment trust or a unit trust.

More generally, diversify within any asset class. If you own property, for example, don't own one building, own several, in different parts of the country, and mix offices with warehouses and so on. Unless you are fabulously rich, this again will mean buying some form of pooled investment. The only exception to diversification might be gilt funds, for the reasons given in Chapter 19.

DIVERSIFICATION OVER TIME

One of the best ways of reducing risk is to diversify over time. While it's clear that equities are pretty risky if held for one year, what happens if you hold them for longer periods? What I've done is to make a mass of calculations. I've looked at the returns for every 1, 3, 5, 10, 15 and 20 year holding period in the last 49 years. For example, I looked at the three year holding period 1946–8, then 1947–9, and so on. For the five year period I look at 1946–50, then 1947–51, and so on. To go back to the first of the three periods 1946–8, what I have calculated is the average annual return (in the form of a geometric mean) you would have got if you had sold out at the end of 1948. I've charted that return at year 1948. Because it makes the charts a bit easier to read, I've put periods of 1 and 3 years on Figure 21.1, 5 and 10 years on Figure 21.2, and 15 and 20 years on Figure 21.3.

When you look at the figures you have to be careful. The lines in two figures may look to jump about as much as each other, but that will be misleading if the scales are different. Here's an easy way to understand the three figures. Begin by looking at the vertical scale. My computer chose the scale so the data charted would fit in. As you can see the scale is very wide in Figure 21.1, less wide in Figure 21.2, and much less wide in Figure 21.3. Indeed, in Figure 21.3, there are no negative numbers. This basically tells you the full story. In any year equity returns could be just about anything,

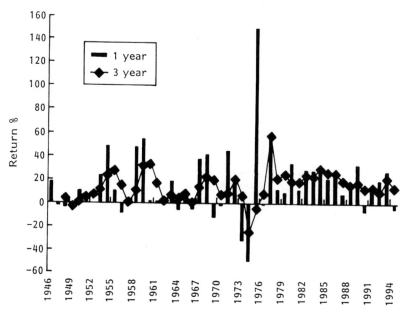

Figure 21.1 Annual Average Returns for Holding Periods of 1 and 3 Years. Source: Drawn from computations made on data in Barclays de Zoete Wedd (1995, p. 54)

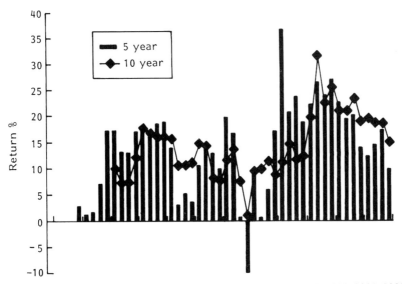

Figure 21.2 Annual Average Returns for Holding Periods of 5 and 10 Years. Source: Drawn from computations made on data in Barclays de Zoete Wedd (1995, p. 54)

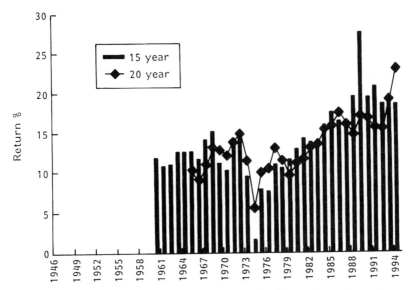

Figure 21.3 Annual Average Returns for Holding Periods of 15 and 20 Years. Source: Drawn from computations made on data in Barclays de Zoete Wedd (1995, p. 54)

and will often be negative. If you hold equities for only three years, the returns are much less extreme and the chances of making a loss are much reduced, and this is even more so at five and ten years. For 15- and 20-year holding periods, there were no negative returns in the years charted.

I've used nominal returns in these figures because I think most people who distrust equities think more in terms of nominal than real returns. Rightly or wrongly, Figures 21.1–21.3 give a clear indication of what those people perceive as risk.

The figures are not as compelling as they may seem. There are not a huge number of observations for the 15- and 20-year holding periods—the first 15-year period doesn't end until 1960. And notice that the next period uses 14 of the same years as the preceding period, so it's not surprising that the return is not dissimilar. The number of truly unrelated returns presented in the charts is quite small. Still, the historical record is that the longer you have held equities, the lower has been your risk.

DIVERSIFICATION OVER PURCHASE PERIODS

One risk that concerns many investors is buying at the top of the market. The obvious way to reduce this risk is not to try and put all your money into the stockmarket (or into any asset) all in one go. If you put it in over a period, you are diversifying over purchase periods. The ultimate in this type of diversification is a monthly savings plan, ideally one set up through a Direct Debit. That way you can't cheat and hold back money when you don't like the markets—when the market is scary, it's probably cheap, a time when you should be buying.

Some books discuss this sort of diversification in terms of pound cost averaging. Sometimes you get the impression that it's the secret of the universe. It's not, but it is worth thinking about.

Say you save £30 a month for three months and you buy a share that rises from £1 to £2 to £3. The average price is £2. You will buy 30 shares in the first month, 15 in the second and 10 in the third. You will have a total of 55 shares which will have cost £90, so your average purchase cost is £1.64. Because you buy more shares at the low price than at the high price, your average purchase cost is below the average price the shares traded at (i.e., £2). Another way of looking at this is to imagine that when you come to sell the price falls back to the average market price of £2. You might expect to break-even. However, because you have 55 shares your proceeds are £110 against your purchase cost of £90.

Can pound cost averaging be a bad thing? Of course. You might be buying more and more of a share going bust. Pound cost averaging works best with investment trusts and unit trusts because when their prices fall, it's nearly always a result of the market falling—and the market as a whole usually bounces back, even if some individual shares don't.

DIVERSIFICATION ACROSS ASSETS

I have shown that if you add companies whose profits or share price movements are not perfectly correlated, you reduce risk. The same thing applies to asset classes such as equities, gilts, cash, property and so on. Many people who find equities a little too risky decide to have none and buy a fancy product which dilutes the risk of equities in some way and also reduces their returns, both because of the lower risk and the product provider's profits. But you can always reduce risk yourself by holding another asset in addition to equities. In the UK, it has been better to hold cash with equities

Table 21.2   Risk, Return and Asset Diversification

Equities/cash split	Average return	Worst year	Best year
100% equities/ 0% cash	13.1%	−49.4%	149.9%
90% equities/ 10% cash	12.5	−43.2	136.0
80% equities/ 20% cash	11.9	−37.0	122.1
70% equities/ 30% cash	11.3	−30.8	108.2
60% equities/ 40% cash	10.7	−24.6	94.3
50% equities/ 50% cash	10.1	−18.4	80.4
40% equities/ 60% cash	9.5	−12.2	66.4
30% equities/ 70% cash	8.9	−6.0	52.5
20% equities/ 80% cash	8.3	0.2	38.6
10% equities/ 90% cash	7.7	6.4	24.7
0% equities/ 100% cash	7.1	12.6	10.8

than to hold gilts with equities. The reason is that gilts have been riskier than cash, their returns have been more highly correlated with equities than have those of cash, and gilts have not offered a high return.

If you find equities too volatile, you can reduce some of this risk by holding some cash. How much cash should you hold? That depends on how much return you wish to give up for risk reduction. This is a complex area, but I have an illustration in Table 21.2. The table requires some explanation.

I calculated the average annual return (geometric mean) for the entire period from 1946–94 for both equities and cash. The average return was 13.1% for equities and 7.1% for cash. This is what you would have got without any adjustments for inflation. So, if you held equities for a very long period, you would have been well rewarded relative to cash.

But you might have had a few scares along the way. We've seen how equity returns vary dramatically from year to year. In fact, in the worst year of the period, 1974, you would have lost nearly half your money—49.4% to be precise—if you held equities. I'll focus on that. During that year the return from cash was higher than normal at 12.6%. The best year for equities was 1975, when equities produced a return of 149.9%. Cash returned 10.8%.

OK, that's the background to Table 21.2, now let's look at the nitty-gritty. In the first row of the table I assume you are invested 100% in equities. If you had hung in there for 49 years, you would have averaged 13.1% per annum. The best year was awesome, but the worst was pretty scary. In fact, some people would have cut and run in that awful year, and missed out on the following year, which was the best. If you missed the best year, you would not have achieved the 13.1% average. Does the idea of your shares halving in value in a year scare you? If it does, you shouldn't be 100% invested in equities. But note I said not 100%, I didn't say you shouldn't have any equities.

If we move to the second row, I've assumed that you are invested 90% in equities and 10% in cash. Your return is now a mix of the return on equities and cash. Had you held that mix for 49 years your return would be lower at 12.5%, and the worst year was still really scary. As we work down the table, I keep reducing the amount of equities and increasing the amount of cash. Finally there are no equities, and just cash. Note that my table headings "worst" and "best" refer to equities. I haven't shown the worst and best returns from cash, but the return from cash in the years that were worst and best for equities.

What should you conclude from Table 21.2? Well, it's clear that the best returns have come from equities and if you diluted them with cash you lowered the return. On that basis you want a high equity weighting. But it's also clear that an all-equities position can produce some pretty scary years. By mixing in some cash, the scare factor is reduced. In fact, if you had a 20%/80% equity/cash split, even in the worst year for equities since the Second World War you would not have lost money. If you can't face losing money in any year, perhaps you should have a 20%/80% split. But if around a 10% loss in a year doesn't faze you, perhaps you could go to 40%/60%.

You might ask why you should fiddle around with any equities. The answer is that if you look at the all-cash weighting, the long-term return was 7.1%. By going to 40%/60%, the return goes up to 9.5%. Nearly 2½% extra return each year is very important over a long holding period.

On the other hand, as economists love to say, you might to tempted to dismiss Table 21.2 as too cautious. You might be able to remember why equities did so badly in 1974—and those problems won't occur again. Maybe, maybe not. But just think of all the things that have happened in the last few years that few people would have predicted: the fall of the Soviet Union, the USA and Coalition going to war against Iraq, Britain going to war against Argentina, the explosion at Chernobyl, and so on. None of these brought a collapse in world markets, but you would have to agree that the world is an unpredictable place. Surely it is possible to imagine that the equity market could fall by at least 50% in a year.

But Table 21.2 really is too cautious in some ways. Many investors have some of their equity exposure in foreign stockmarkets. To the extent that these are not perfectly in sync with the UK stockmarket, the risk of an internationally diversified high equity exposure will be somewhat less than Table 21.2 implies.

Let me recap on this section. What I've shown is that if you combine different assets, you reduce the risks you bear. I've concentrated on equities and shown how adding some cash reduces risk. Even if you think equities are risky, you may think it worth having some. The reward, if history is a guide, will be a higher return over the long term.

Now I'm going to combine the ideas of this section with those of the last but one section. In that section we saw that the longer the holding period, the less the return variability. What happens if we do the same analysis as above, but with a five-year holding period? I've chosen five years because it's commonly said that unless you are willing to take a five-year horizon, you shouldn't invest in equities. And Figure 21.2 shows only one five-year period produced a loss.

It may come as no surprise that the worst five years include 1974. You can see that for yourself in Figure 21.2. And in 1973 you would have lost nearly a third of your money. However, in 1970 the market was roughly flat but in 1971 and 1972 you would have made 45.2% and 21.7% respectively. Your annual return (geometric mean) over the five years would have been minus 9.9%. The average return from cash over that period was 8.1%. In Table 21.3, I repeat the calculations made in Table 21.2, but this time using the five-year figures. I've omitted the best returns column and added an extra row. Look what happens now. If you are willing to take a five-year view, and you didn't want a negative return year you could go as high as 45% in equities. If losing 10% doesn't faze you, you could go as high as 100% in equities.

Table 21.3   Risk, Return, Time and Asset Diversification

Equities/cash split	Average return %	Worst 5-year period %
100% equities/ 0% cash	13.1	−9.9
90% equities/ 10% cash	12.5	−8.1
80% equities/ 20% cash	11.9	−6.3
70% equities/ 30% cash	11.3	−4.5
60% equities/ 40% cash	10.7	−2.7
50% equities/ 50% cash	10.1	−0.9
45% equities/ 55% cash	9.8	0.0
40% equities/ 60% cash	9.5	0.9
30% equities/ 70% cash	8.9	2.7
20% equities/ 80% cash	8.3	4.5
10% equities/ 90% cash	7.7	6.3
0% equities/ 100% cash	7.1	8.1

Now you might think that the above argument is a little odd. Why would you be willing to consider no return after five years? Well, it's not what you would want. Your long-term expectation from a 45%/55% equity/cash split would be a return of 9.8% as shown in the second column of Table 21.3. That's higher than the expected return of 7.1% from an all-cash portfolio. But in any period it's unlikely you'll get exactly 9.8%. You could get more and you could get less—as you can see from Figure 21.2. If you want the prospect of earning an extra 2.7%, you have to take a risk. Table 21.3 tells you that the worst pain you would have had to bear in any five-year period in the last 49 years would have been receiving no return at all.

Notice that as we have lengthened our investment horizon, the equity weighting that gives no loss has increased from 20% of the portfolio to 45%. Alternatively, if you had stuck with the 20% equity weighting from before, and you were invested for the very worst five years for equities since the Second World War, you would still have made 4.5% per annum. In any other five-year period you would have done much better.

What should you conclude from the above? You should ignore the exact numbers. If somebody does this exercise using a different time period, the specific numbers will change. And there is no guarantee that the future will be the same as the past. What does seem a reasonable bet is that equities will give the highest return over long periods, but with the greatest risk. If you hold equities and another asset, you will reduce both the risk and the return from an all-equity portfolio. There is no magic formula for the correct asset mix. It depends on your attitude to risk, and your time horizon. If you are 20 years of age you can afford to have lots of equities. Time is on your side, and if things don't work out, well, if the worst comes to the worst, you can save some more. If you are 75 years of age, time is not on your side and you can't go out to work again. You should be well diversified to reduce your risks, and have a lower equity weighting than a young person.

DIVERSIFY

To get high returns, you have to bear risks. But risks can be reduced by diversification. Diversify within any asset class (e.g., own many shares instead of one), diversify across asset classes (e.g., own shares—domestic and foreign, cash, bonds, etc., rather than just one type of asset), diversify over time (the longer you can hold a volatile investment, the better your chance of getting close to your expected return), and diversify over purchase periods (to make sure you don't buy only at the market peak). Diversification rules, OK.

KNOW YOUR OBJECTIVES, YOUR INVESTMENTS AND YOURSELF

Many people refuse to draw up realistic objectives, learn about the investments they are buying, and take account of their own personality. Equities are not especially risky if held for long time periods (at least five years), but very risky if held on a short-term basis. However, if a fall in the stockmarket makes you panic out of equities, even if you have a long investment horizon, they are not for you. Your personality will make equities riskier than they really are. You and your investments should be compatible.

Many investors simply buy investment products that are sold to them. That's very risky. Your strategy is dictated by product launches and salespeople's commissions and not by your needs and attitude to risk. To reduce risk, take responsibility for your finances, do some homework, and only buy products you understand. And diversify.

READ 📖 WRITE ✉ RING ☎

♦ The figures in this chapter are based on data in Barclays De Zoete Wedd, *BZW Equity-Gilt Study 1995*. London: Barclays De Zoete Wedd Securities Limited, 1995.
♦ Professional investment managers with a statistics background who want to study time diversification at a more advanced level should read: Paul A. Samuelson, "The Long-Term Case For Equities: And How It Can Be Oversold", *Journal of Portfolio Management*, Fall 1994, 15–24 and Mark Kritzman, "What Practitioners Need to Know ... About Time Diversification", *Financial Analysts Journal*, January–February, 1994, 14–18.

22

Selecting a Stockbroker

With an evening coat and a white tie, even a stockbroker can gain a reputation for being civilized.

Oscar Wilde

If you adopt the approach I recommend, you could become a millionaire and own lots of stocks without ever having spoken to a stockbroker. Stockbrokers will buy stocks for you and manage your money if you want but, as I have already argued (in Chapter 15), it is not obvious why you would want one to manage your money, and it is not necessary for you to deal with a broker to buy pooled funds. You can buy unit trusts directly from the managers, or from unit trust discounters, as explained in Chapter 16, and many investment trusts can be bought through the investment trust company, also explained in Chapter 16. Not all investment trusts can be bought in this way, however, and sometimes you may want to deal immediately. In that case you need a stockbroker, as you will if you ignore my advice and deal in individual shares. Stockbrokers also deal in bonds, although you can buy gilts through National Savings.

TYPES OF STOCKBROKER

There are a number of ways of classifying stockbrokers, e.g.:

- Execution-only, advisory and discretionary services
- Discount and full service

An *execution-only* or *deal-only broker* simply does the deal. You ask the price of, say, Murray Ventures Investment Trust, the broker tells you, and you decide whether to deal or not. If you say, "Do you think Murray Ventures is any good?" or "Do you think I could get it cheaper in a few days?" the broker will answer that he or she is not allowed to give advice. For this bare-bones service, the broker usually deals at a low commission rate. *Discount brokers* are always execution-only.

Full service brokers may offer execution-only, but they will also offer dealing with advice, and advisory and discretionary broking. If you *deal with advice*, the broker gives you advice. He will answer your questions and may make his own suggestions. Murray Ventures is a trust specializing in unquoted shares, so the broker might say, "If you are interested in a fund that invests in unquoted companies, are you aware that Electra is currently selling on a bigger discount?" You might even be told that following poor balance of payments figures the market is falling sharply and be asked whether you would like the broker to place your order later in the day. It is still up to you what you do.

As well as buying and selling shares, a full service broker will offer a portfolio management service, which can be either a *discretionary service* or an *advisory service*. In a discretionary service, you agree your objectives with the broker and then he can deal on your account without reference to you. Why anyone would allow a stranger to hold their wallet is beyond me, but people do it all the time. (You could argue that this applies to pooled funds too since you hand your money over, but there you can more easily see the sort of shares the fund holds, what it has done in the past, get a legal record in a standard form, and so on. You may also be investing alongside institutional investors, especially in investment trusts, who you might expect to look after their interests, and thereby, your interests.) With an advisory service the broker knows your objectives, but cannot deal at his discretion. He must contact you with his idea, and you have to agree that he can deal. If you turn him down too often, he will lose interest in talking to you and you may get the worst of all worlds. You think he is looking after your interests and do nothing, he thinks you are a waste of his time because you don't follow his advice and generate commission for him, so he also does nothing.

Dealing with advice is not the same as advisory portfolio management, but can be very similar. The difference between the two is that in the first case you initiate the deal, but in the second, the broker does. However, even that distinction may be blurred. If you deal a lot, the broker will see you as a good client (i.e., a good source of commission) and may call you up with an idea, even if you are not a portfolio client. The idea may be good or bad, and he is not your friend. He just hopes you will deal.

Although stockbrokers buy and sell shares, many have a section that gives a comprehensive financial planning service, advising on pensions, life insurance, school fees etc. Stockbrokers which are part of financial conglomerates may call on specialists in a group company to provide this advice. Thus, some stockbroking firms are just specialists in stockmarket investments, while others can offer more extensive financial advice.

You should remember that while a full service broker may have a huge research department supplying advice, it may have minimal research staff. Indeed, even at a major research firm, the broker you deal with may still give advice as much on the basis of his reading of the press as on the basis of the firm's research. Full service doesn't necessarily mean the broker is well informed, although he may be.

If you do not have much money, the big full service London brokers may not be interested in your account. Dealing in your £200 holding of a privatisation stock won't pay their overheads. In my view that is not a problem. You should be dealing with a discount broker. You don't need advice, so you don't need to pay fancy fees.

Costs

Which are the cheapest brokers? The answer depends on how fast you want to deal and whether you are selling a small amount of a privatization issue or a larger amount of a non-privatization issue. And there will be different fee structures for gilts and equities. In general, however, amongst the cheapest are Killick and Co.'s postal execution-only service, Yorkshare, Sharemarket and City Deal Services. Amongst the largest of the discount brokers, with a wide range of services, is Fidelity. Fidelity has two charging structures, one for people who deal frequently (at least 25 times a year) and another for less frequent traders. I'll discuss the fees for the less active traders. On these, Fidelity charges about twice as much as the cheapest discount broker on a small deal of, say, £1000, and about half as much as a full service broker. For a deal of £25 000, Fidelity is about twice as expensive as the cheapest discounters, and about a third of the cost of the average full service broker (see READ 📖 WRITE 🖳 RING ☎).You can trade international shares at a discount commission through Fidelity, although I think you should only buy international exposure through a fund.

Since Fidelity is well known, and neither the cheapest nor dearest broker, I have chosen its equity commission rates as an example. In Table 22.1, I show the commission Fidelity would charge on deals of various values as at November 1995. Very small deals are very expensive because of a minimum charge. Because Fidelity charges on the basis of a specific sum of money for considerations that fall within a range, the fee as a percentage of consideration will jump if a deal moves from the top end of one range into the bottom end of the next. Fidelity charges £25 for deals between £0 and £2500, and £35 between £2501 and £5000. As you can see from Table 22.1, commission is 1% for a £2500 deal and 1.17% for a £3000 deal. In general, however, the commission percentage falls as the size of the deal increases.

Even using a discount broker, you won't be able to deal as cheaply as institutional investors. They deal at between zero and 0.2%.

If you want to set up an account with a broker, be sure to ask:

● What is your commission scale?

● Are there any other fees that bump up the effective commission cost, such as a joining fee, or a per contract administration charge (often passed off as a "compliance charge")?

● Do you deal at the best price on the SEAQ screen, or do you attempt to improve on it?

● Do you deal when the order is placed, or are orders aggregated and dealt at set times?

Table 22.1 Example of Brokerage Charges: Discount Broker

Consideration	Commission as % of consideration
£200	12.50
£1000	2.50
£2000	1.25
£2500	1.00
£3000	1.17
£4000	1.25
£5000	1.00
£10 000	0.70
£25 000	0.34

- What is your policy on nominee accounts (discussed below) and are there any charges?

- What is your annual management fee?—if you want management.

In my experience there is little relationship between commission rates and quality of service. For example, discounter Fidelity charges no joining fee, makes no compliance charges, normally attempts to improve on the best screen price, offers a Free-phone number, does deals while you are on the phone, makes no nominee charges, and forwards all company correspondence. If you mainly deal as an execution-only client with a full service broker, you may pay a lot more, and not get as much service.

Nominee accounts

Shares may be registered in the name of the owner or a nominee. Brokers often act as nominees, holding and collecting income on behalf of the beneficial owner shares. (Strictly speaking, brokers set up a separate company which functions solely as a nominee company). Brokers like nominee accounts because when you come to sell, they can check their records to see whether you do own the stock you are selling. They also know they will be able to deliver it to the market on the settlement date. You also don't have to worry that you will lose the share certificate. If the broker holds your stock in a nominee account, the company will send your shares to the broker, and usually all correspondence (Annual Reports, dividends, etc.) will go to the broker. The broker will pass on your dividends, but not always immediately, and may not send you the Annual Report, etc. You should expect to receive all information sent by the company and all dividends, and at no extra cost. (You don't have to read the information, but I think you should.) If the broker makes charges, or does not pass on all information, go to another broker.

Nominee accounts can be pooled or separately designated. In a pooled account all ICI shares bought by the broker (Big Time Broker) will be registered in the name of "Big Time Broker Nominees", and in the nominee company's records it will show that you are the beneficial owner of 1000 shares, John Smith the owner of 2000 shares, and so on. In a designated nominee account, if your account number is 12345, the stock will be registered as "Big Time Broker Nominees A/C 12345". John Smith's holding might appear as "Big Time Broker Nominees A/C 12349". Most institutional investors insist on having their stock separately designated in this way. You may wish to choose a broker that does this.

Some investors are being subjected to pressure to have a nominee account because of changes in settlement procedures that have recently taken place. For two hundred years, UK shares were settled on an account basis which resulted in relatively leisurely settlement. In July 1994, 10-day rolling settlement was adopted. You had to pay for shares you had bought, or deliver shares you had sold, 10 business days after the transaction was made. In June 1995, five-day rolling settlement was adopted. This is a short period for private investors to settle their deals. Not only must both you and your broker act immediately, but the post has to be on time, and your cheque has to clear promptly. For many investors the solution will be to use a nominee account and perhaps a broker cash management account (i.e., a deposit account). But if you don't want to use a nominee account, there are alternatives.

Some brokers will allow you to pay for your purchases by using your debit card. You just read your number over the phone when you do the deal. Again, market makers are not currently charging for extended settlement (up to 10 days). This may change, but for the time being, you can ask your broker to deal for extended settlement. If market makers do begin to charge, you should compare their charges and those your broker will make if you simply pay late. Some brokers charge 10% above base rate, or a total of 16.75% currently. Although that sounds horrific, it is 0.046% a day. So, if you settled five days late, it would cost you less than an extra ¼%. If you dealt through a cheap discount broker and paid this extra interest, your total cost would still be well below the commission charged by many full service brokers who hold your stock in their nominees. You really don't need to go into nominees if you don't want to.

The true cost of dealing

The commission charge is only part of the cost of dealing. In addition there are hidden charges such as contract note administration charges, compliance charges, and so on, but you would be foolish to use a broker which makes such charges (they just improve the broker's standard of living at the expense of yours). On purchases, but not sales, there is stamp duty—a tax—of 0.5% of the consideration. Finally, and something not considered by many novices, there is the spread. This can be the biggest cost of all.

The price of a share you see quoted in a newspaper is a middle price. It is half-way between the price you could buy at and the price you could sell at. The difference provides the market makers with their living. If you trade in a very large share, the buying and selling prices might be 101p and 99p. If you bought the share and then sold it, you would immediately lose 2% of your money on the spread, plus the cost of stamp duty and commission. Some of the smaller shares in the market may have a spread of 10%. If you trade in and out of them, you will get killed by the costs. Further, many of the small shares can only be dealt in small quantities. If you can only buy £2000 worth of the share, you will pay a high percentage commission. With a full service broker with a high minimum fee, the cost will be prohibitive.

While it is important to minimize commission costs, the costs that really kill your returns are those of frequent trading. Even low commission costs mount up if incurred often enough, but the spreads on share prices are always significant, and they can be penal on small stocks.

READ 📖 WRITE ✉ RING ☎

♦ The *Investors Chronicle* carries a list of brokers and their charges from time to time. At the time of writing, the most recent long list was a supplement "Stockbroker Survey", in the issue of 30 June 1995.
♦ A useful brochure to help you select a broker can be obtained free from APCIMS, 112 Middlesex Street, London E1 7HY. It only includes its members, however, and does not fully specify costs.

23

Life Insurance

For almost seventy years the life insurance industry has been a smug sacred cow feeding the public a steady line of sacred bull.

Ralph Nader (on the US insurance industry)

Life insurance is probably the most mis-sold financial product. Many people have bought life insurance believing they were getting a tax-break when they weren't; many people who have bought it probably didn't need it in the form they bought it; and many people who need it haven't bought it because they thought it to be too expensive because they weren't told about term insurance. In this chapter I provide a guide through the life insurance maze.

I begin with a few words of warning. The Inland Revenue is reviewing the way life insurance is taxed. Currently, life insurance funds suffer tax, and in many cases the receipts are tax-free in the hands of the policy holder. Many commentators think this approach will be changed to taxing insurance policies in the hands of the policy holder instead, and not taxing the funds. The rule that allows 5% income to be taken from non-qualifying policies (which I discuss later) may also disappear. The position described in this chapter is that as at November 1995, with allowance made for the changes announced in the 1995 Budget.

LIFE INSURANCE BASICS

When you are young, you have lots of bills. The mortgage, the car, the kids, and so on. And then the breadwinner dies. Disaster. The problem is that the typical family will have no resources to fall back on. How does the surviving spouse cope? You may be lucky and benefit from a pension for the surviving spouse, or the deceased's company may have paid for life insurance. But in many cases the family's standard of living will plummet unless it has taken out life insurance.

What is life insurance? It is a contract between you and an insurance company which covers a specified period (the term) during which you pay so much per month or year (premiums) to the company and, when you die, it pays out a lump sum (the sum assured—or, sum insured as most people refer to it). There are three main types of life insurance:

- Term insurance: this is a temporary insurance policy—you pay premiums for a specified term and the sum insured is paid only if you die during that term

- Whole-life (or whole-of-life): you pay premiums until your death or a specified age, and the sum assured is paid on your death, whenever that is

- Endowment: premiums are paid for a specified term and the sum assured is paid at the end of the term or on earlier death

Before I get into the details, notice that there are significant differences between these forms of life insurance. Term insurance is a bit like contents insurance. When you insure your home contents you don't know if you will be burgled. You might not, so you might never get a payout (and you should be grateful). Term insurance is much the same. If you die during the term, there is a payout, but if you don't, there isn't. Are the premiums wasted if you don't die? No, because you get insurance—you are not making an investment, you are seeking protection, just as with contents insurance.

With whole-life insurance there will be a payout, because you will die. You are therefore buying both protection and an investment, unlike term insurance which is pure protection. But term and whole-life insurance do have something in common. *You* won't get the sum assured, because *you* will be dead when it's paid. Your estate, or somebody else, will benefit. What this means is that if you have no dependants, there is little point in taking out these forms of insurance. Of course, if you want to have the largest possible estate so you can leave money to your favourite charity or whatever, you can do so, but if the idea of life insurance is to save your family from being thrown out on to the streets if you die when you are young, don't get life insurance if you don't have a family.

Endowment insurance will pay out whether you live or die, so *you* might collect the payout. The investment element is at its highest with endowment insurance. You can buy an endowment policy as a free-standing protection plus investment package, but most people who have an endowment policy do so in conjunction with a mortgage.

Only term insurance is pure protection. Whole-life is both protection and investment. Endowment is mainly investment. Before I look at these three types of life policies, I'll explain insurable interest, and how much protection you need.

Insurable interest

All life policies pay out to the people that the policy is designed to protect. These people must have insurable interest, the legal right to insure, which will exist if they will lose financially if the insured person dies. Naturally this includes family members, but it may also include a divorced spouse who receives payments from the person whose life is insured, or it may include a business that has made a loan to the insured life.

How much life insurance do you need?

For most people the answer is simple: lots, although it is not simple to calculate the specific amount. The answer will depend on your circumstances and needs, and also if the survivors are willing to cut back if the breadwinner dies. The way you should work it is as follows.

Decide what income you think the family will need. That can be your current income or something different. (For single people with no dependants it is zero.) Take

Table 23.1 Lump Sum Per £1000 Income Required:
Assumed After-Tax Return of 7% and Yearly Income
Indexed At 5%

Number of Years	Lump Sum Required
5	£4727
10	£9028
15	£12941
20	£16503
25	£19744
30	£22693
35	£25376
40	£27818
45	£30040

off any income that the family will get, for example pensions, State benefits, income from investments and income from the surviving spouse working (less child care if needed). Now you know what is needed each year, or the shortfall. Next you need to work out for how many years the money is needed (say, up to the surviving spouse's retirement). The number of years times the shortfall gives you the sum you will spend over the period. You should adjust this number upwards to allow for the expected rate of inflation. Now it is a simple matter (for folks who like maths) to calculate the sum you will need today to generate that total, assuming some specific rate of return on investment. You've guessed it—most people don't do the sums.

If you are young, with a couple of kids, reckon on a minimum sum assured of about ten times your required income as a rule of thumb. (But don't forget any insurance you get from your employer.) Twenty times your required income would be better. If you are a couple nearing retirement, you don't need nearly as much. An example of a more exact calculation is shown in Table 23.1, where I have assumed that it is possible to invest for an after-tax return of 7%, and the beneficiaries would like their income to grow at 5% per annum. Table 23.1 shows for every £1000 of income required, and for various periods, what lump sum is required. Thus, if after allowing for all sources of income, you want your family to have an extra £10000 per annum, growing at 5% per annum, and lasting for 25 years, you will need a sum assured of £197440 (i.e., 10 × £19744, the sum shown against 25 years). This lump sum, if invested to produce a return of 7% after-tax, would produce the required income for 25 years. As you can see, the rule of thumb of "lots" is not a bad guide.

I now consider the major types of insurance in more detail.

TERM INSURANCE

Term insurance is the simplest, cheapest and, for many people, the best form of life insurance. If you die during the term there is a payout, if you don't there is no payout. The insurance term may last as long as desired. For example, a professional couple may intend to have children and the wife to stay at home for perhaps 10 years. Thereafter, she will return to work. This couple may decide that they only need term insurance for 10 years. Another couple might plan for the wife to stay at home permanently. They might feel they need term insurance for 25 years so that they cover the period the kids are their responsibility. After that, savings might be expected to provide sufficient income for the wife should the wage-earner die.

Since term insurance is pure protection, there is no point in insuring a non-waged spouse. If that spouse dies, there will be no loss of income to make up. And there is no point in the term running into retirement age unless the surviving spouse would not have enough income from savings, pensions, etc. While single people don't need term insurance for their spouse (because they don't have one) they may need it for a dependent partner, or if they have a child, or if they have an elderly parent who depends on them.

Some people argue that even a non-waged spouse should be insured if the couple have children. If the non-waged spouse died, there would be costs incurred in looking after the children. This is true, although there would of course be some savings too (two can't live as cheaply as one), and the extra costs of caring for the children would only apply while they were young, the surviving spouse might remarry, and so on. There is also the point that most people simply can't insure against every eventuality. If there is a case for non-waged spouse insurance it is for a smallish sum, for perhaps ten years at most.

Because term insurance is so much cheaper than other forms of insurance, there is a much greater likelihood that you will be able to afford to get the proper amount of cover than with other forms of insurance. In my view (and that's all it is), you should never buy other forms of insurance in preference to term insurance for basic protection if the higher cost will mean that you cannot get the full amount of cover that you think you need.

There are a number of different types of term insurance, and they can be used for more than simply protecting your family. The main types are outlined below:

- **Level term.** The sum assured remains unchanged throughout the term. This might be used to repay a fixed value loan on the death of the policy holder.

- **Decreasing term.** Here the sum assured declines throughout the period. This can be used to match a declining debt. It is used with a repayment mortgage where the sum owed declines over time as the mortgage is repaid (see Chapter 24).

- **Convertible term.** This gives the policy holder the right to convert the term policy to whole-life or endowment. This option does not give favourable rates for the conversion, but the option can be exercised whatever the policy holder's state of health. Many advisers argue that anybody taking out term insurance should take convertible term as the extra cost is low (perhaps 10%). However, because of AIDS, many companies restrict the length of the term of convertible term insurance.

- **Renewable term.** This gives the option to take out a new term insurance policy when the existing one matures. The option does not give favourable rates, but it guarantees that a policy can be taken out whatever the policy holder's state of health.

- **Family income benefit.** In this policy, the benefit is payable from death until the end of the term. The benefit takes the form of an income paid monthly (or less frequently). The income is not taxed.

Table 23.2   Examples of Cost of Term Insurance

Type	Sum Assured: £50 000, male, aged 30, non-smoker
Level term: 10-year term	£4.57 per month
Convertible term: 10-year term	£7.20 per month
Decreasing term: 25-year term	£5.69 per month

How much does term insurance cost? This varies with the terms of the policy, the age and sex of the person taking out the policy, and so on. However, Table 23.2 gives some illustrations (as at Autumn 1995) using one of the cheapest providers in each case: AIDS and related illnesses may be excluded.

In general, term insurance policies are qualifying policies, and no income or capital gains tax will be due on payment of policy benefits. Qualifying and non-qualifying policies are explained later in this chapter. The payment may lift the deceased's estate into the inheritance tax bands. To avoid this the policy may be written in trust (see Chapters 34 and 35).

You will probably need the help of an IFA in choosing the best type of term insurance for you, and to find the best terms.

WHOLE-LIFE INSURANCE

With term insurance the policy benefit is only payable on death if that occurs in a specified term, whereas with whole-life insurance the benefit is payable on death whenever it occurs. Since death is inevitable, the policy must pay out and is therefore more expensive than term insurance. Whole-life insurance is part protection and part investment. If the policy is surrendered (i.e., terminated) or made paid-up, i.e., no further premiums are paid, the policy will have a value because of the investment component of the policy. But the surrender value or paid-up value may not be very good, and there may be no value at all in the first few years. Surrender values are discussed in more detail later in this chapter. Early surrender may also lead to higher rate tax being paid. Policies should always be maintained if possible. If you are not going to stay the course, whole-life insurance will be a poor way of investing.

There are various types of whole-life policies. They include:

- Without profits

- With-profits

- Unit-linked

- Universal

- Low cost

- **Without profit policies.** These policies pay a fixed sum at death and offer no protection against inflation. They are not marketed nowadays, although older readers may have one.

- **With-profits.** These policies are more expensive, but give both a guaranteed sum and a share of the investment returns of the insurance company's life fund. The objective of the fund is to be able to pay the guaranteed benefits and to be able to pay good bonuses or profits—hence the name with-profits. However, the guaranteed benefits are the prime consideration. As a result, although the fund will be invested in a number of asset types, there will be a heavy weighting in gilts because of their guaranteed returns on specific dates. I showed in Chapter 4 that over the years gilts have given a lower return than equities, so we should not expect with-profit life funds to be star performers. In addition, actuaries tend to value funds very cautiously. Sums are set aside to reserves, but the annual valuations still produce surpluses and these form the basis of the bonuses. There are two important bonuses, the annual reversionary bonuses and the terminal bonus.

  Once a *reversionary bonus* is declared, you cannot lose it. As a result, these bonuses tend to be somewhat lower than fund performance justifies. Moreover, the full declared value of reversionary bonuses is only available at the time of death. At the end of the plan, a *terminal bonus* will reflect overall investment performance. The terminal bonus may be up to half the total bonus. Both terminal and reversionary bonus rates may be reduced in some years (compared to previous years' levels). In particular, many companies have been cutting these rates in the last few years.

  An example may be useful. In return for agreeing to pay a certain premium per month, you may be guaranteed £10000 at the end of 25 years. I'll assume that at the end of Year 1, you get a reversionary bonus of 5%. This will raise your guaranteed sum to £10500, i.e., an increase of 5%. If you get another reversionary bonus of 5% in Year 2, the sum will be £11025. If this happens for 25 years, the guaranteed sum will rise to nearly £34000. At the end of the 25 years you will get a terminal bonus, which is usually quite large, so you might get a total of, say, £60000.

  Usually these policies make two kinds of charge, a regular policy fee and a deduction from the life fund.

- **Unit-linked.** In a unit-linked plan you are, in effect, buying life company unit trusts (see Chapter 13 on unit trusts). There is a guaranteed sum assured, but the death benefit will be the higher of that sum and the value of the units at the time of death. You can usually invest in cash, fixed interest stocks, equities, property and a managed fund—which will invest in all of these asset types. The return you get will be a function of the funds you select. Their performance will depend on the performance of the underlying markets and the manager's performance.

  With this sort of policy the premiums are used to buy units. The charges are the usual unit trust bid–offer spread, an annual management charge plus life insurance charges. These consist of a benefit charge, policy fee and front-end charge. The benefit charge pays for the life insurance cover and usually is taken by cashing units each month. The policy charge is usually about £1 or £2 per month, and the front-end charge pays for the selling costs (commission) and setting up costs. It may be charged in a number of ways, but will consume a large part of the first two years' premiums.

  Most unit-linked policies are flexible, and allow a choice as to the amount of insurance cover. The lower the cover, the higher the investment content of the policy. Unit-linked policies have regular reviews, often after every five years, when the benefits and investment reserve are assessed. If the reserve is too low, the benefit will be reduced, or the premium increased.

Unit-linked policies are riskier than with-profits policies. Your reversionary bonuses can't be withdrawn, even if the stockmarket collapses in the last year of your policy, whereas the value of your units will collapse with the market—you will, however, get the sum assured if this is more than the value of your units.

- **Universal policies.** These are similar to flexible unit-linked policies but offer a wide range of benefits such as permanent health benefit, critical illness cover and so on. These benefits are paid for by encashment of units each month.

- **Low-cost policies.** These policies are a low-cost version of with-profits policies. Decreasing term insurance is combined with a with-profits policy. Low-cost policies are common with endowment insurance and I explain low-cost policies in the section "Regular Premium Endowments", on p. 219.

Is whole-life insurance a good deal? Before answering that, I have to explain the difference between qualifying and non-qualifying policies, and how policies are taxed.

QUALIFYING AND NON-QUALIFYING POLICIES

Life insurance sales have been encouraged by two tax reliefs on qualifying policies:

- Life assurance premium relief (LAPR) was available on policies taken out before 14 March 1984. LAPR has been abolished for new policies, but it remains in force for premiums on old policies which have not had the benefits increased or the term extended. Currently the rate is 12½% of the gross premium. The insurance company reclaims the tax relief from the Inland Revenue.

- The excess of proceeds over premiums is free of tax.

LAPR is of no interest to young or new investors, but is of interest to many others as there are probably more policies benefiting from the relief than not. This relief is limited to the greater of premiums of £1500 or one-sixth of your income.

With regard to tax payable on gains, it is important to understand the distinction between qualifying and non-qualifying policies. The rules are exceedingly complex: the important thing is to make sure you know into which category a policy falls, and the insurance company will always tell you. In the broadest of terms, most regular premium products (where, e.g., you make a monthly payment for a number of years) with terms of at least 10 years (except for term insurance) and with a genuine insurance component—i.e., products which are not simply regular savings schemes in disguise—will be qualifying policies. Non-qualifying products include single premium products, i.e., policies for which you make only one payment.

The proceeds of a qualifying policy that has not been surrendered, or made paid-up in its first 10 years or first-three quarters of its term, are tax-free. Tax is levied on the proceeds of non-qualifying policies, but such policies can be used to generate a tax-efficient income for higher rate taxpayers by means of top-slicing. I discuss this later.

Tax pluses and minuses: qualifying policies

Insurance companies and salespeople often stress the tax advantages of insurance. But you have to be careful. Insurance company fund taxation is complex but, broadly speaking, the funds are taxed at a rate of 20% on income and 25% on capital gains. (Fund manager Ivory & Sime's research found that 90% of investors who own insurance-linked investments are not aware that they are taxed in this way.) Non-taxpayers cannot reclaim the tax paid by the insurance company. This means that non-taxpayers will suffer more in tax in an insurance product than they would in a similar investment outside of an insurance wrapper, such as an equally performing investment trust or unit trust. Lower and basic rate investors who have unused capital gains tax exemption will also suffer more tax in an insurance product than they would outside of it.

For a higher rate taxpayer there may be a tax advantage. Such taxpayers save 20% income tax (i.e., 40% − 20%), but if they would not have paid capital gains tax on alternative investments, they are suffering unnecessary CGT at 25%. For higher rate tax payers who do pay CGT on their non-insurance investments, the tax treatment will be favourable, compared to an investment trust or unit trust. But relative to tax-free PEPs and TESSAs, insurance products are tax-inefficient for all investors. This doesn't matter for a pure protection product such as term insurance—because PEPs and TESSAs don't give you protection—but it does matter for insurance products that combine protection and investment such as whole-life insurance.

In Table 23.3, I set out the tax treatment of a regular premium unitized qualifying insurance product, a regular savings plan for a unit trust, and a unit trust PEP. I have chosen a unitized insurance product as this provides the clearest comparison.

Table 23.3   Tax Treatment of Three Savings Products

	Unit-linked Insurance	Regular Savings Unit Trust	Unit Trust PEP
Income Tax	Paid by insurance company at 20%. Cannot be reclaimed by non-taxpayer.	Taxed at 20%. Can be reclaimed by non-taxpayer. Higher rate taxpayer must pay 20% more.	PEP manager claims back the 20% tax paid by the unit trust. No PEP holder suffers tax.
Capital Gains Tax	Paid by insurance company at 25%. Cannot be reclaimed.	None paid by unit trust.	None paid by unit trust.
End of Plan	No tax payable on qualifying policy proceeds.	Unit holder pays CGT according to personal liability after indexation and £6300 exemption. Tax due on realization only.	PEP holders are exempt from CGT.
Early Surrender	If cashed in before 10 years, or ¾ of the policy term, whichever is less, higher rate taxpayers may pay a further 16% income tax on any gain.	N/A: no pre-determined holding period.	N/A: no pre-determined holding period.

TERM INSURANCE VERSUS WHOLE-LIFE

Should you have term insurance or whole-life? In my view you should always choose term. Whole-life bundles together investments and protection. Term gives you protection at lower cost and you can invest the money you save. Protection and investment become two separate activities.

Saving via insurance is likely to be a bad deal. There are a number of reasons for this: tax, costs, surrender values, and investment performance.

Although the proceeds of qualifying policies are tax-free, the investments have already been taxed in the hands of the insurance company. As I discussed in the previous section, in most cases insurance products are tax-inefficient.

Insurance contracts are expensive, with high commission and administration costs. Investment trusts and unit trusts offer a better deal. Moreover the surrender values of insurance products in the early years are simply penal. If you surrender your policy, i.e., don't continue with the contract, in the first few years you will not get back what you paid, let alone make a return on your payments. Given the large number of whole-life policies that are surrendered, whole-life is simply an inappropriate investment for most people. (I discuss surrender values in more detail later in this chapter.)

Criticism of investment performance is common, but less compelling. With-profit investments have been criticised because the large gilt component will lead to under-performance against a more equity-based product. That point is fair, but policy holders do have the option of unit-linked policies which can be 100% equity if the policy holder wants.

Many young parents can't afford to get all the protection they need with whole-life. It seems much more important to get all the protection you need for your family today, and worry about saving later, when the burdens of a young family have eased. Because term insurance is cheaper than whole-life, you should get the protection you need with term.

Despite my generally negative tone on whole-life, if you already have it, you will probably be better off sticking with it, especially if you get LAPR, because you have already suffered the high initial costs and you will get a poor surrender value.

LIFE INSURANCE AS AN INVESTMENT

So far I have discussed life insurance which was mainly, but not exclusively, for protection. I noted that whole-life insurance mixed protection with investment. The types of policy I discuss below also mix protection with investment, but here the protection is minimal, and the investment aspect is the key feature.

There are many types of insurance that could be discussed as investments, but I'm going to focus on the following:

- Regular premium endowments

- Maximum investment plans

- Friendly society bonds

- Investment bonds

- Guaranteed income and growth bonds (guaranteed equity bonds are covered in Chapter 31)

None of the products which include the word "bonds" are bonds in the sense of Chapter 19.

REGULAR PREMIUM ENDOWMENTS

The most common form of endowment insurance consists of regular premium qualifying policies. Premiums are paid for a specified period and the sum assured is paid at the end of the term or on earlier death: unlike term or whole-life insurance, *you* might collect the benefit.

Endowment policies, like whole-life policies, may take the form of without profit, with-profits, low-cost and unit-linked and an additional low-cost, low-start policy. As with whole-life, without profits policies are rare.

With-profits endowment policies offer a guaranteed sum assured. If the policy holder dies on the first day, he will get that sum, but if he dies some years into the policy, or lives the entire term he will get the assured sum plus reversionary and terminal bonuses. These bonuses were discussed earlier in with-profits whole-life insurance.

Low-cost endowment policies are just what the name describes. They achieve the low cost by combining decreasing term insurance and with-profits endowment and, instead of paying a large guaranteed sum and bonuses on top of that, they offer a lower with-profits guaranteed sum and add bonuses to that. An example will make things clearer.

Say you want a sum of £100000. A with-profits policy will assure you that sum, but you will get more because of bonuses. A low-cost policy also assures you a sum of £100000, but with, say, £60000 from a with-profits endowment, and £40000 from a decreasing term insurance. So, if you die tomorrow, or indeed any day during the term, the sum assured will be £100000. However, over time your with-profits policy will start to acquire bonuses. If the bonuses are worth £10000, the term insurance can be decreased to £30000. This process will continue over the years. Note carefully though that this policy only guarantees £100000 *on death*. If the bonuses are lower than expected, the value of the policy at the end of term will only be the assured £60000 and the bonuses, which may not produce £100000. You won't get anything from the term insurance, because you didn't die. If a low-cost policy had been used for an endowment mortgage, and it looked as though the £100000 would not be achieved, the annual premiums would have to be increased to ensure the mortgage could be repaid.

Low-cost low-start endowments are low-cost endowments but start with an especially low premium (to make them even more affordable) which then rises for perhaps the next five years.

Unit-linked endowments are linked to unit funds in the same way as was described earlier for whole-life unit-linked. Investment performance will be evaluated periodically and, if it is poor, either the benefits will be reduced or the contributions increased.

Criticisms of endowments

Like whole-life policies (where I discussed the following points), endowments have been criticized for staid investment performance of with-profits funds, high costs for all types of fund, high penalties for early surrender, and tax inefficiency. Other packaged products exist which do not bear the high insurance, selling and administrative costs. Most investments have better surrender values. Many are more tax efficient. For general savings purposes endowments do not seem to be an attractive option.

There may be a role for using endowments when saving for a specific purpose, where you want your savings goal met whether you live or die, e.g., paying school fees, or repaying a mortgage. But this only makes sense if the policy holder can be sure that early surrender can be avoided. I discuss endowments in the context of mortgages, and the problem of selecting a policy provider, in Chapter 24.

SURRENDER VALUES

Surrender values have been mentioned a number of times. If you don't want to continue with your policy you will be able to surrender all endowments, and most whole-life, and receive a sum of money. The problem is that with a 25 years with-profits endowment you might not get as much as you put in during the first five years: in the first year, or even first two years, you might get nothing back. Many of the charges are borne in the first few years. Even after 20 years you will be short-changed if you surrender. These poor surrender values make life products totally unsuitable as short-term investments and are one of the strongest arguments for separating savings from insurance. The simple fact is that most people don't know if they will be able to maintain a long-term contract. In broad terms, short-term endowments have better surrender values than long-term endowments, and unit-linked have better surrender values than with-profits policies, and with-profits better than low-cost.

Most policies do not last the full term and if you don't want to continue a policy on its original terms, there are four alternatives to surrender:

- Partial surrender

- Borrowing

- Becoming paid-up

- Selling the policy

Which option is best will depend partly on whether you want to raise cash or simply can't pay the premiums.

A partial surrender will require your insurance company's agreement. For a with-profits endowment or whole-life, you cash in the reversionary bonuses that have been earned. You get a cash sum and continue to pay the premiums. This means bonuses will again be earned, but these will not be based on the earlier bonuses, so you'll lose the compounding effect.

Another option for with-profits policies is to borrow from the insurance company using your policy as collateral. The money can be used for anything, including paying premiums. The interest rate is usually attractive, and this is a particularly sensible option in the final years of a policy when the rate of return from maintaining the policy is especially high.

You can make your policy paid-up, which means you pay no more premiums. The original term will remain unchanged, but the value of the sum assured will be reduced to reflect the premiums that have been paid.

You might be able to sell your policy. For an endowment, even after selling costs, you are likely to make at least 10% more than the surrender value, and perhaps a lot more. For details, see the discussion of traded endowment policies in Chapter 31.

MAXIMUM INVESTMENT PLANS

Maximum investment plans are unit-linked life assurance policies with a term of 10 years. They are qualifying policies. The proceeds can be withdrawn free of tax after 7½ years, although most people remain invested for 10 years. A full range of insurance company unit trusts are available, and a plan may be invested in a number of the funds, including a managed fund which will mix equities, gilts, cash and perhaps property. The insurance element is the lowest possible which allows the plan to be a qualifying policy. Essentially these are investment vehicles structured to take advantage of the tax treatment of qualifying insurance products. The minimum life cover permitted would normally be 75% of total contributions over the ten year term, i.e., with annual premiums of £2000, the life cover would be £2000 × 10 × 0.75 = £15 000. If death occurs during the 10-year term, the payout will be the greater of the guaranteed life cover, or the value of the units.

The fund units are bought and sold with, usually, a 5% spread and suffer a 1% annual management charge. Switching between funds is permitted, typically at low-cost, and without any tax consequences.

These plans were devised when LAPR existed. Now, however, LAPR has been abolished for new plans, and the plans are not especially appealing. You are paying for life insurance (which may mean a medical examination), but your intention is really investment, your proceeds are tax-free but the fund will have already borne some tax—see the earlier section "Tax Pluses and Minuses"—and you may suffer higher rate tax on early surrender. These plans can, nonetheless, be advantageous to fund an inheritance tax liability which may arise on the death of the policy holder, or as a way of giving money to minor children in order to mitigate inheritance tax. In both cases the policy would have to be written in trust (see Chapters 34 and 35). There may also be a role in school fee planning (see Chapter 29).

FRIENDLY SOCIETY BONDS

A number of Friendly Societies actively market their bonds. You can often get a free pen for requesting information, and luggage and other goods you probably don't want by taking out a policy. These are signs of fat margins. For these bonds you have to trade off charges against tax advantages.

Friendly Societies offer bonds which have a small element of life insurance, but are essentially saving vehicles. They are qualifying policies which provide a lump sum on maturity or on earlier death. Friendly Societies' products are entirely free of tax, unlike insurance company products. This is because investment returns bear no tax in the hands of the society and no tax is payable on the sum you receive on maturity. You can invest £25 per month or £270 per year and you must invest for 10 years. You can stop paying at any time before 10 years and make the bond "paid-up". If you wish to withdraw your money before the 10-year period is completed you will get the current value of the bond (which, because of charges, will be minimal in the first two years). If you die before the bond matures, your estate will receive a modest guaranteed sum or the value of your bond, whichever is the larger. Most bonds are linked to building society deposits or equity unit trusts.

While the tax shelter is attractive, this has to be offset against the small sum you can invest (over the *entire* 10 years you can invest less than half the value of *one* year's general PEP), the long time period of the policy and the charging structure. Charging structures vary, but it is common for half to all the first year's payments (depending on your age) to be consumed by charges. Some bonds make a further charge of £5 per year or 50p per month, every year (about 2% on £270). There is at least a 5% initial charge for units when they are allocated, a 1% annual management charge by the unit manager, and perhaps a further 0.15% management charge by the Friendly Society.

What are the effects of the charges? To take one example, the Tunbridge Wells Equitable Friendly Society's charges are such that even on the assumption of 9% investment returns per annum, you would receive only 4.4% after charges (excluding the value of the death benefit). It is hard to believe that most small investors would not be better off with a National Savings product where the returns are guaranteed, the lock-in period is shorter, and the penalty for early surrender less harsh. This remains true even if you have to buy your own luggage.

TAXATION OF NON-QUALIFYING POLICIES

Single-premium products are non-qualifying policies so, before I discuss some single-premium products, I'll outline the taxation of non-qualifying policies. There are two issues here—tax on income, and tax on encashment.

Up to 5% per annum of the premium on a cumulative basis may be taken as "income" for 20 years. For example, with a single premium bond costing £100 000, income of £5000 could be taken each year with no tax charged. If no income is taken in a year, it may be carried forward. For example, if no income is taken for four years, then in the fifth, income of £25 000 (i.e., £5000 × 5) could be taken. The income may be generated by genuine income from your investments, or it may be a return of part of your capital. If the income withdrawals exceed 5% per annum, there is no tax liability for a lower or basic rate taxpayer, but higher rate taxpayers will have to pay a further 16% tax on the excess income over 5%.

On encashment of the policy, there is no liability to CGT, but gains are subject to income tax. When calculating the gain, any income taken is included in the calculation. So, if in the previous example the policy was encashed for £95 000, the gain would be £20 000 (i.e., £95 000 + £25 000 − £100 000 = £20 000).

Gains are not liable to lower or basic rate tax, so only higher rate taxpayers will pay tax on any gain, and this will be at a rate of 16%. If you fall into the higher rate tax bracket, top-slicing relief should be claimed. Here's how top-slicing would work with my example in the previous paragraph, and on the assumption the policy had been in force for five years:

1. Divide the chargeable gain by the number of complete years the policy was in force to calculate the "top-slice" (i.e., £20 000 ÷ 5 = £4000)
2. Add this slice to the income of the year in which the policy was surrendered or matured
3. Calculate any higher rate tax (less basic rate tax) due on the top-slice of income (say all £4000 falls into this category, then £4000 × 16% = £640)
4. Multiply this number by the complete number of years of the policy to find the total tax assessed (i.e., £640 × 5 = £3200)

If the slice does not attract higher rate tax, the gain is free of tax. This tax treatment can be attractive for higher rate taxpayers as it means that tax can be deferred for 20 years on income that is taken, or the income can be left to roll within the fund after bearing a tax rate of only 20%. There will also be a tax gain if the policy is cashed when the policy holder has become a basic rate taxpayer.

INVESTMENT BONDS

Investment bonds are single-premium whole-life policies. There are a large number of such products with a variety of names which reflect their particular emphasis. However, they are all basically unit-linked bonds with very low life insurance cover. They are non-qualifying policies.

The funds to which the bonds are linked are internal insurance company funds which can only be invested in through unit-linked policies. The charges on the funds are similar to those of unit-linked whole-life described earlier. The funds cover the usual spectrum found amongst unit trust groups. In addition, some insurance companies offer unitized with-profits funds, and all offer a managed fund which invests in cash, gilts, equities and property. Policy holders are allowed to invest in a number of the funds, and may make switches between the funds for a small charge. The bond may be split into a number of identical segments which may be surrendered at different times to suit tax planning.

Investment bonds can be used to provide a tax-efficient income for higher rate taxpayers, to provide school fees, and for inheritance tax mitigation—but they are not as tax efficient as PEPs or TESSAs. If you don't pay higher rate tax, even a non-PEP investment trust or unit trust would be better.

GUARANTEED INCOME AND GROWTH BONDS

Guaranteed income and growth bonds (GIBs) offer a fixed rate of return, paid either as income (monthly or yearly) or left to accumulate for the life of the product. They are often recommended for investors who want a high income. The bonds available for purchase are constantly changing. To find the best rates on current bonds you should consult the latest issues of *Money Management, Planned Savings* or *Money-facts*, or ask an independent financial adviser. The bonds may be issued for periods ranging from one to ten years. For example, a bond might have a five and a half years' life, paying 7.5% monthly income or 7.75% annual income, or 50.76% capital growth. Each of these rates is free of basic rate tax. There are no separate charges or commissions made—these have been taken into account in the quoted rates.

GIBs are constructed in a variety of ways. Growth bonds are often constructed by means of a non-qualifying single-premium endowment policy whereas the income bonds might consist either of a non-qualifying single-premium endowment policy which is part surrendered to produce income, or a series of such policies which are surrendered over the life of the bond. In the latter case, the bonds that are surrendered in the early years will have a value equal to the stated income, while the final policy to be surrendered will have a value equal to the principal and the final income payment.

The insurance company pays tax on its funds, and because of this the bonds do not suffer lower rate tax in the hands of the investor. However, non-taxpayers cannot reclaim the tax paid by the insurance company. Higher rate taxpayers will have to pay further tax of 16%. The tax position is somewhat complex, and depends on the specific structure of a bond. If you pay higher rate tax, you should not buy a GIB unless you understand how you will be taxed on that specific bond.

GIBs are fixed return investments, and while early surrender is usually possible, you may not get your original investment back. When comparing the return with that available on other products, bear in mind that you are effectively locked in, perhaps for a substantial period. Despite the word "growth" in the growth version of the bond, this is a fixed return product, and if inflation rises the returns may be very unattractive. There is also a potential tax problem for older people who get age-related tax allowances. If they cash in their bond, their "total income" is increased in that year and they may lose their age-related allowances.

Although GIBs are described as guaranteed, this is only as sound a guarantee as the company making the guarantee. In addition, there is no guarantee if you surrender early, and there will usually be a small print get-out clause. One such clause states that the issuer: "reserves the right to alter the terms of the policy and benefits payable, in such a manner as it considers appropriate should legislation on the basis, incidence, rate, or level of taxation change—or should any relevant levy or charge be imposed...". Translation: "This product does not really carry a guarantee."

READ 📖 WRITE 🖹 RING ☎

♦ For a list of companies offering term insurance, see Catherine Williams, "Keeping on Good Terms", *Planned Savings*, June 1995, 53–65.
♦ For whole-life insurance providers, see Catherine Williams, "Back to Basics", *Planned Savings*, December 1995, 51–61.
♦ For details of unit-linked fund performance, see Stephanie Spicer, "Insurance Company Winners", *Money Management*, March 1995, 28–3
♦ A fax list of all Guaranteed Income Bonds is available from *Moneyfacts* Fax Service: calls are charged at 39p per minute cheap rate and 49p per minute at other times. Tel: 0336 400240.

24

Buying a Home

They live in a beautiful little apartment overlooking the mortgage.
Anon

In the UK, owning one's own home is a common goal. There is something special and reassuring about owning your home: it gives a sense of freedom and independence. Well, that's one view. It also saddles you with debt, you run the risk of buying a property in an area that suddenly declines in popularity and you can't easily move out of, you have to find the cash to make repairs to a leaking roof, and so on. The old view was that homes were, well, as safe as houses, now people are not so sure. Should a home be your first major investment? Yes.

ARE HOMES STILL A GOOD INVESTMENT?

Some people think that while homes were once a good investment, they haven't been since 1988 and won't be in the future. I think that houses will be a sound investment in the future, maybe not the best investment, but a sound one. But you must make your own decision.

There are a lot of myths about house prices. You'll often see press reports of how home prices have fallen about a third since their peak in the late 1980s. This is true for some parts of England, but omits to point out that in large parts of the UK—Scotland, Northern Ireland and the north of England—prices are substantially higher than they were in 1988. It's just not true that there has been an across-the-board slump in home prices. Even within regions there have been wide ranges in price movements, e.g., in London, prices are down about 43% in the Isle of Dogs and up about 27% in Barnes. Prices across the UK are down about 12%.

Whatever the exact number, many people seem to feel that any fall in home prices is just not supposed to happen. Home prices are supposed only to go up. But that doesn't fit the historical facts, especially if we look at matters in terms of real prices, i.e., prices that take account of general inflation. Part of the problem is that the UK has suffered from high inflation for part of the post-Second World War period, and many people have confused the money return from owning a home with the real return. Home prices have generally gone up, but so too have all prices. While home prices have outpaced inflation, the amount has been by less than most people probably imagine. In the last 50 years, home prices have increased by about 2.7% per annum in real terms—i.e., on average home prices have risen about 2.7% more than other prices. That's way lower than the real return from shares, and less than the real return currently available from indexed gilts. However, because of various tax-breaks, and the ability to gear up with a home by putting down only a small deposit, the attraction of owning a home for most people would have been much greater than these figures might seem to imply.

Since the third quarter of 1989 and the start of 1995, home prices have fallen in money terms by 12% and in real terms by 35%. Although most people don't believe it, there have been periods in the past in which home prices have slumped in real terms. For example, between the third quarter of 1973 and the second quarter of 1978, home prices rose by 43% in money terms but, because of very rapid inflation, fell by 35% in real terms. And home prices in the past have also fallen in money terms as well as real, e.g., the first half of the 1950s.

In the last 50 years, home prices have fallen in real terms in about 40% of the years. If this percentage were to hold in the future, and if inflation in general were to be low, then we should expect home prices to fall in money terms in many years, even if the historical 2.7% per annum real increase were to hold. You may find all this confusing, but that's just because most of us aren't used to thinking in both money and real terms.

In sum, it seems to me that while the fall in home prices has not been fun, especially for the nearly 900 000 homeowners in the UK who have negative equity, i.e., whose home is worth less than their mortgage, it is far from clear that we have witnessed anything that is historically abnormal. But we might feel more confident about this if we can explain why the price boom and slump took place when they did.

The boom in home prices in the 1980s can probably be explained by the strong growth in average income for much of the period, greater competition amongst mortgage lenders who relaxed their lending standards, a big increase in the number of people in the 20 to 29 age group (the key age for first-time buyers), and a change in August 1988 of the mortgage interest tax relief rules which led to a rush to buy by people wanting to beat the change. At the end of the 1980s, interest rates rose, making mortgages more expensive and adversely affecting demand. The economy moved into recession and unemployment rose. This too reduced demand for homes. Many people with negative equity were unable to move home, and this reduction in transactions tended to reinforce the downward pressure on prices. Finally, some demand that might otherwise existed had been pushed forward by the August 1988 tax relief change. The general belief that homes were a sound investment began to evaporate.

Many of the adverse factors will work themselves out naturally. The economy is currently growing, unemployment has fallen, and interest rates have fallen. Negative equity remains a problem, but there are now schemes that enable many people with negative equity to move. The relaxed lending standards of the 1980s have mainly gone, but homes were a good investment before the standards were relaxed, and can be again. Many people feel burnt by the housing market, and vow "never again", but investors in the stockmarket say that every time the market slumps, but it has no lasting effect.

There are three negative factors worth noting. First, the key home buying age group will decline in the 1990s. However, the decline is modest, and part of the effect has been felt. Second, if the ordinary person believes that inflation will be lower in the coming decades than it was in the past, and if buying a home was one of the few inflation hedges available to the ordinary person, there might be less demand for homes. Finally, mortgage interest relief is being phased out, but the impact of this is unlikely to be significant, especially compared to the phasing out that has occurred.

My guess is that over long periods homes will continue to appreciate in value at least as fast as inflation, although perhaps by less in real terms than in the past. There may also be more years in which house prices fall in money terms. If this is the case, owning your own home is unlikely to be the way to instant riches, but there are bound to be periods when home prices offer better value than at other times. This may be one of them. The ratio of average home prices to average income is about as low in 1995 as it has ever been in the last 45 years. And, contrary to the tales of those who focus just on declining mortgage interest tax relief, the fall in interest rates in recent years has resulted in the average married couple only paying about 15% of their combined take-home pay to service the average mortgage at the start of 1995, compared to 36% at the peak of servicing cost in 1990. Even if there isn't a boom, home prices currently probably offer good value and the payments are affordable.

You can assess all these factors as you wish, but there is an air of unreality in any discussion about buying a home in the UK. If you don't buy a home, what is your alternative? In some countries the answer is to rent, but the UK has the smallest private rental sector in Europe. You can get a home to rent, but the choice is not great except, perhaps, in London. To some extent you are forced to buy. This small rental sector may well be a major cause of the periodic housing booms in the UK.

If you believe home prices are going to decline a lot, you should not buy a home. Nor should you buy if you are likely to move in the next two years, since you bear a lot of costs in buying and selling, e.g., legal, survey and estate agent fees, stamp duty, the costs of new furniture, and so on. If you think a boom is around the corner, you should buy. And if you think home prices will be OK over the long term, neither boom nor bust, but up a bit? You should buy, because of the various tax and other breaks you get.

TAX AND OTHER BENEFITS

You get three tax-breaks when you buy a home, and you may get an additional benefit from your employer:

- Any increase in the value of your principal private residence—for most of us the only home we have—is exempt from capital gains tax

- The interest on the first £30 000 of your mortgage qualifies for income tax relief at 15%

- You are not taxed on the rental value of your home

- Some employers will subsidize all or part of your mortgage by paying you the difference between your actual mortgage rate and, say, 5%

Most people understand the first two benefits, but few think of the tax-break on rental value. It's an odd notion, but it is valuable. It is a benefit-in-kind, but is not taxed. This is not how benefits-in-kind from your employment are treated. For example, if you get a company car, you are receiving a benefit-in-kind. That benefit is taxed. When you buy a home and live in it you are also getting a benefit-in-kind, but it is not taxed. Well of course not, it's your home, not your employer's. But if you put your money in a bank, there is tax to pay on the benefit you get, in this case interest. So really you are getting a tax-break by owning your home.

Think of it this way. If you deposit £150 000 in a bank and get £10 000 interest and you rent a £150 000 home at a rent of £10 000 per annum, you would pay tax on your bank interest of perhaps £4000, so you would be paying out £10 000 in rent while receiving £6000 in interest after tax. You are worse off by £4000. If you withdrew your deposit, and bought the home and lived in it, you would have no cash flow at all. An instant gain of £4000—that's the benefit from not being taxed on rental value.

As to the fourth benefit, not every firm subsidizes mortgages. And the benefit is taxed. Nonetheless, for those who get this benefit, this is another reason for buying a home.

Because of the three tax-breaks (and the employer subsidy for some people), owning a home is likely to make a good investment and generate a valuable capital gain. Many people deny this. They say you have to live somewhere, so any capital gains are notional—you can't realize them. Well, you can't while you need a family home, but once you are old, you do have the option of trading down and realizing some capital.

There is another benefit from buying a home, although I hesitate to mention it. Buying a home is a geared investment. You put down a small deposit, but all the change in value belongs to you. Of course, to all the people who have been unable to keep up their repayments and whose home has fallen in value, this gearing has worked in the wrong direction. But many of these people probably borrowed too much and put down too small a deposit.

BORROWING TO BUY

Most of us have to borrow to be able to buy a home. Borrowing to buy a home is one of the few cases where borrowing makes good financial sense. However, it is still easy to borrow badly. You need to get two decisions right: how much you borrow and the form of the borrowing.

How much should you borrow?

Many people borrow as much as they can. If buying a home makes sense, surely gearing up as much as possible, and buying as big a home as possible makes sense? Well, not necessarily, because you do have to meet the repayments, and these could rise with rising interest rates. Moreover, your income may decline, either because of unemployment, demotion, or, in the case of a married couple, the wife leaving the job market. The last thing you want to be is a forced seller in a poor housing market.

The old rules of thumb for borrowing by a traditional married couple were:

- A maximum of two-and-a-half times the husband's salary, plus the wife's salary

- Home-related payments (mortgage, insurance, rates, etc.) of less than one quarter of total income

In calculating income, bonuses were treated with some scepticism unless it could be shown that they were guaranteed.

In the 1980s, the mortgage market became much more competitive and banks, both domestic and foreign, and insurance companies, muscled into what had been the building societies' patch. To grab market share, lenders started taking a more liberal view as to how much debt the borrowers could manage. As a result, the traditional standards went out of the window. The consequence was bigger loans, but it has also led many borrowers into difficulties. This sometimes results in the borrowers losing their home and, nearly as bad, meeting the mortgage payments has become a constant worry for some borrowers.

So, how much should you borrow? It depends on your attitude to risk, your view of your prospects, your view of the prospects for the housing market and how important it is for you to have a grander home than your friends (or maybe just the same type of home). Since your home is likely to be your biggest single investment, my own preference is to err on the side of caution. I can cope with the notion of passing up the chance of making as much in the housing market as other people might, for the security of knowing I'll be able to meet the payments come what may. But that's my view: you have to do what's right for you.

At the time of writing (November 1995), many lenders were offering:

- Three times one salary plus one times a second salary; or

- Two and a half times the joint salaries

If you are cautious like me, you will bear in mind that the old standard for a mortgage was time-tested, and you may wish to borrow less than the current norm, even if your lender encourages you to borrow more. If you think I'm over-cautious, you should borrow more. If you really want to gamble, there are plenty of lenders who will offer enhanced multiples (e.g., three times one salary plus one and a half times the second, or even three times the joint salary).

As well as the money sum you wish to borrow, you should consider the percentage of the cost of the home you wish to borrow. The old standard required you to make a deposit, but a few years ago, deposits were optional. I think you should make a deposit. If you make a deposit of 10%, you could still sell your home after a 10% price fall and not have a debt to repay. You would have lost your money, but you would not be trapped. If you don't put a deposit down, and have no savings, you may be trapped for years if home prices fall, as you will not get as much from sale proceeds as you owe the lender. If you are a first-time buyer, you may argue that you don't want to wait to raise a deposit. That's OK providing you realize that you are making a bet that either home prices will rise immediately, or that you will live in the same home for years to come. People moving up the housing ladder who don't put 10–20% down are being greedy, foolish, or making a clever speculation. Take your pick.

Methods of borrowing

There are two basic types of mortgage:

- Repayment mortgages
- Interest-only mortgages

With the repayment mortgage you pay monthly interest and repay part of what you borrowed. With an interest-only mortgage you pay monthly interest and make separate arrangements to generate enough money to repay the sum borrowed at the end of the loan period. These two basic types can be further subdivided. Repayment mortgages come in two forms, and interest-only mortgages can be endowment, pension and PEP mortgages, with endowment mortgages coming in several versions:

- Repayment mortgages
  - Constant net repayment
  - Gross profile

- Endowment mortgages
  - With-profits
  - Low-cost
  - Low-start, low-cost
  - Non-profit
  - Unit-linked

- Pension mortgages

- PEP mortgages

For each type of mortgage there are a number of ways that interest rates and the currency of the loan may be set:

- Interest payments
  - Variable rate
  - Fixed rate
  - Cap and collar

- Currency
  - Sterling
  - Foreign

Finally, there are three mortgage products you may come across, depending on your type of mortgage and its size—mortgage indemnity policies, mortgage protection policies and payment protection policies.

All-in-all, an off-putting list of things to think about. But it's not too bad if taken step by step. I'll begin by looking at the items in the previous paragraph, then I'll give the basic information on each method of borrowing and follow that with an evaluation of the methods.

Three mortgage protection policies

The institutions which lend you money are keen that they get their money back. So keen in fact, that they usually force you to take insurance at your expense (on which they probably earn commission) so that they can be sure you will pay them back. If you borrow over 75–80% of your home's value, you may be required to take out **mortgage indemnity insurance**. This covers the lender if it has to repossess your home and it is not worth what you owe to the lender. It does not usually cover you for any shortfall, and the insurer may be entitled to sue you for any loss it has suffered. In other words, although you pay the premium to the insurer, it is entirely for the benefit of the lender, and this insurance does absolutely nothing for you, and may leave you liable for any shortfall.

With some forms of mortgage repayment methods, a **mortgage protection policy** may be taken out. This is life insurance which repays the mortgage if you die before it is repaid. Technically, mortgage protection policies are term insurance policies, with the sum insured decreasing during the life of the mortgage. It is common with repayment mortgages, but unnecessary for traditional endowment mortgages where life insurance is automatically included. Shop around for this insurance—the big lenders such as the Abbey National and Halifax charge much more than companies such as Canada Life and Zurich Life. For a couple in their early 40s, with a £60 000 repayment mortgage over 20 years, the monthly premium will be around £30 from one of the cheaper insurers.

Payment protection insurance covers your repayments if you are ill or made redundant (see Chapter 7). With the recent changes in Income Support rules, everybody will get less State assistance with their mortgages if their income is reduced for whatever reason, and there is pressure on borrowers to take out this type of insurance. Expect to pay about £7 per £100 of monthly interest repayment.

REPAYMENT MORTGAGES

Repayment mortgages are the easiest mortgages to understand. You borrow money and repay it over the period of the loan. Each month you repay part of the loan and interest on the balance outstanding. In the first period you pay interest and repay a small part of the loan. In the next period, there is less loan outstanding, so there will be less interest due. So, if you make the same payment every month, at first you will mainly pay interest, but towards the end of your loan period you will be paying less and less interest and repaying more and more loan.

Table 24.1—which is easy to understand despite all the numbers—is drawn up under the assumption of a loan of £100 000, a 15% interest rate, a repayment period of 25 years and monthly payments. I've ignored insurance and any tax benefits. What I show is the first five months of payments and the last five. The monthly payment is £1280.83: don't ask me how that number was determined—my computer cranked it out. But you can see that it seems to be right since in the last row the balance ends up at zero.

You can work out in your head that 15% of £100 000 is £15 000. That's the first year's interest bill. If you pay monthly it will be £15 000 divided by 12 or £1250. So that would be the interest due in month 1. The computer has asked for £1280.83 per month, so in the first month there is an extra £30.83 that can go to repaying the sum borrowed.

In month 2, the loan outstanding has been cut by the £30.83 to £99 969.17. The interest on this will be a bit less than month 1's, but I can't do that sum in my head. My machine says it is £1249.61, so if you still pay £1280.83 per month, you can repay another, and bigger, bit of the loan. And so it goes, month after month. Come the last few months, you can see from Table 24.1 that very little interest is being paid, but a lot of the loan is being repaid. Finally, in the last month the loan is fully repaid.

Table 24.1 Illustrative Repayment Mortgage: Interest Rate 15%

Payment Number	Date	Beginning Loan	Interest	Repayment of Loan	Loan Outstanding	Cumulative Interest
1	01/1995	100 000.00	1250.00	30.83	99 969.17	1250.00
2	02/1995	99 969.17	1249.61	31.22	99 937.95	2499.61
3	03/1995	99 937.95	1249.22	31.61	99 906.35	3748.84
4	04/1995	99 906.35	1248.83	32.00	99 874.35	4997.67
5	05/1995	99 874.35	1248.43	32.40	99 841.94	6246.10
296	08/2019	6170.83	77.14	1203.70	4967.14	284 093.00
297	09/2019	4967.14	62.09	1218.74	3748.39	284 155.09
298	10/2019	3748.39	46.85	1233.98	2514.42	284 201.94
299	11/2019	2514.42	31.43	1249.40	1265.02	284 233.37
300	12/2019	1265.02	15.81	1265.02	0.00	284 249.18

The last column of Table 24.1 is included just to depress you—the loan of £100 000 incurred total interest of £284 249.18.

In Table 24.2, I've repeated the exercise using an interest rate of 5%. The monthly repayments in this case are only £584.59 and, right from the start, more of the loan is repaid each month. Total interest comes to £75 377.01.

There are two main types of repayment mortgage. My tables illustrate a **gross profile mortgage**. With this mortgage, on the assumption of constant interest rates, constant gross payments are made. However, as I have discussed above, more interest is repaid in the early years than in the later years. Accordingly, the after-tax payments will be slightly lower at the start of the repayment period, and higher at the end. This type of repayment mortgage may be attractive for a first-time buyer, because of the lower initial after-tax payments. But remember that you may be getting this advantage when you are a two-income, two-person family and you may start to pay more when you are a one-income, three-person family.

With **constant net repayments**, providing tax rates and interest rates don't change, you pay back a constant amount net of basic rate tax. You pay the same after-tax amount in your first month as you do in your last. Of course, tax rates and interest rates change. The lender therefore recalculates what you have to pay on the assumption that the new rates will be unchanged. While payments will change, the intention with constant net repayments is that you pay the same net amount in your first month as you do in your last. It is the method used by most building societies.

For either type of repayment mortgage it is usual to take out a mortgage protection policy to repay the mortgage in the event of death.

If you ran into financial difficulties, perhaps because you lost your job, you could probably arrange some kind of deal with the lender. For example, the amount you pay each month will depend on, amongst other things, the length of the loan. It might be possible to extend your loan and thereby reduce the monthly payments. Or it might be possible to switch to paying on an interest-only basis for a period, with none of the loan being repaid. If you look at Tables 24.1 and 24.2, you can see that if, for example, only interest is repaid, the impact will be much greater if this happens late in the life of the loan rather than early (compare month 1 interest with month 296 inter-

Table 24.2   Illustrative Repayment Mortgage: Interest Rate 5%

Payment Number	Date	Beginning Loan	Interest	Repayment of Loan	Loan Outstanding	Cumulative Interest
1	01/1995	100 000.00	416.67	167.92	99 832.08	416.67
2	02/1995	99 832.08	415.97	168.62	99 663.45	832.63
3	03/1995	99 663.45	415.26	169.33	99 494.13	1247.90
4	04/1995	99 494.13	414.56	170.03	99 324.10	1662.46
5	05/1995	99 324.10	413.85	170.74	99 153.36	2076.31
296	08/2019	2886.77	12.03	572.56	2314.20	75 352.86
297	09/2019	2314.20	9.64	574.95	1739.26	75 362.50
298	10/2019	1739.26	7.25	577.34	1161.91	75 369.75
299	11/2019	1161.91	4.84	579.75	582.16	75 374.59
300	12/2019	582.16	2.43	582.16	0.00	75 377.01

est in either table), or if interest rates are low (compare month 1 interest in Table 24.1 with month 1 interest in Table 24.2).

ENDOWMENT MORTGAGES

The best way of understanding an endowment mortgage is by contrasting it with a repayment mortgage. During the life of a repayment mortgage there are three types of payment being made:

- Payment of interest

- Repayment of the loan

- A small term insurance premium

For a **with-profits endowment,** only two types of payment are made:

- Payment of interest

- Life insurance premiums

No repayment of capital is made. The idea is that the endowment policy being purchased will be worth sufficient at the end of the mortgage period to repay the loan and to leave something over for you. If you die during the mortgage period, the life insurance policy will pay the assured sum, which will have been set equal to the size of the loan, plus any bonuses. In effect there are two things happening here:

- A mortgage is being repaid

- An investment is being made

I can use Tables 24.1 and 24.2 to illustrate what is happening with an endowment mortgage. All we have to do is focus on the first line. Since the loan isn't repaid until the end of loan period, the interest each month will be the same as that shown in month 1. If you pay the same total each month as for the repayment mortgage, then you can see in Table 24.1 that there will be £30.83 to invest every month, while in Table 24.2 there is £167.92.

Will an investment of £30.83 every month for 25 years grow to £100 000? No, not unless you assume some extraordinary investment returns. Will a monthly investment of £167.92 grow to £100 000 over 25 years? Well, if we assume an investment return of 10% per annum, the investments would grow to more than £200 000. In short, if interest rates are low, and investment returns good, an endowment will pay off the mortgage at the same monthly cost as a repayment mortgage and, in addition, provide an extra capital sum which you can spend on whatever you want. If interest rates are high, however, the endowment will not generate enough to repay the loan unless you pay more each month for the endowment mortgage than for the repayment.

While many commission-earning advisers stress the investment aspects of an endowment mortgage, many home buyers have to focus on cash flow. They just want a cheap mortgage. Clearly, if interest rates are very low, endowments require low monthly payments, but if they are high, they will require high payments. This has led to a modification of endowment mortgages whereby the investment element is reduced. These **low-cost endowment policies** have three elements:

- Payment of interest

- (Smaller) life insurance premiums

- Decreasing term insurance

The way this works is that part of the insurance cover is provided by cheap term insurance, and the reduced life insurance premiums produce a smaller sum at the end of the mortgage period. But remember what I noted in Chapter 23. While the death benefit will be sufficient to repay your mortgage, there is no guarantee that the sum available at maturity will be sufficient to repay your mortgage. If bonuses are poor, you may find that you will have to increase your payments to ensure that you repay your mortgage.

A **low-cost, low-start policy** is a low-cost policy but the premiums are lower initially and rise for say, the first five years, and then remain the same at a level somewhat higher than those for a low-cost policy. What I said earlier for gross profile repayment mortgages applies here. This type of mortgage may be attractive for a first-time buyer, because of the lower initial payments. But remember that you may be getting this advantage when you are a two-income, two-person family and you may start to pay more when you are a one-income, three-person family. Again, these policies do not guarantee to repay your mortgage.

A fourth type of endowment policy is the **non-profit** or guaranteed policy. Here the policy pays off the mortgage but there is no surplus. This type of policy should be avoided.

Finally, **unit-linked policies** are policies that invest in unit-linked funds, effectively unit trusts, and you will experience more volatility in the value of your investment than with an insurance company's with-profits policy. Once again, these policies do not guarantee to repay your mortgage. The chance of making a large surplus above the value of your mortgage exists, but if there are poor investment results during the mortgage period, the possibility of having to increase the monthly payments exists.

For any type of endowment it is worth noting that the interest bill will be larger than for a repayment mortgage because the loan is not being reduced each month, so the amount of interest repaid doesn't fall each year as it does with a repayment mortgage. This means that tax relief will be greater for an endowment. When tax relief applied to the full interest bill at your marginal rate, this was a big plus for endowments. However, with relief restricted to 15% on the first £30 000 of interest, this is no longer so important.

Because the loan is not reduced each month with an endowment mortgage, if interest rates rise, this will have more impact on the monthly payments than for a repayment mortgage. Moreover, extending the repayment term will not reduce monthly payments as it will with a repayment mortgage. By extending the loan period, the monthly repayment of principal is reduced for a repayment mortgage. With an endowment, there is no monthly repayment of principal, and extending the loan will not reduce the monthly interest payment, so the monthly payment will not fall. Lenders may waive capital repayments for a repayment mortgage for a period, especially if the State or an insurance company is meeting the interest payments. With an endowment mortgage, there is usually only a short time that missed premiums will be permitted. It is more likely, therefore, that you will run into difficulties with an endowment mortgage than a repayment mortgage.

Pension Mortgages

These are akin to endowment mortgages but are very tax efficient. Three payments are made:

- Payment of interest

- Payment into a pension plan which will pay off the mortgage at the end of its term from the tax-free lump sum, and pay a pension

- Level term insurance

These mortgages are available to the self-employed who have their own pension scheme, or to employees with personal pension plans. The tax advantages accrue from payments into a pension plan getting tax relief (subject to various limits, see Chapters 27 and 28) and the income and capital gains within the fund accumulating tax-free. For higher rate taxpayers, pension mortgages will be cheaper than endowment or repayment mortgages.

The draw-backs are worth noting. There are limits on the amount of earnings which qualify for pension contracts (the "earnings cap", see Chapters 27 and 28), and this will affect the value of the pension fund that can be built up, and the size of the cash lump sum that can be taken on retirement and used to repay the loan. If a large part of the lump sum is used, the size of your pension will be reduced. It is not usually possible to receive a pension before age 50, so a mortgage cannot be paid off before that age. Finally if you change your employment (e.g., ceasing self-employment or moving to an employer with an occupational pension scheme), you will not be able to pay into your existing personal pension scheme and you will need to find another way of paying off your mortgage.

PEP MORTGAGES

PEP mortgages are akin to endowment mortgages but are much more tax efficient. Once again, the payments consist of three elements:

- Payment of interest

- Payment into a PEPs saving plan which will pay off the mortgage at the end of its term

- Level term insurance

A PEP savings plan, which offers tax-free returns, is more tax efficient than life insurance where the insurance funds suffer income and capital gains tax (see Chapter 23), so the sum your savings generate to pay off your mortgage and provide a surplus for you should be greater with a PEP mortgage. However, while we might expect the PEP to be the better performer, a with-profits life policy will repay the mortgage with greater certainty. You will lose much of the value of your PEP if there is a stockmarket crash, but declared reversionary bonuses cannot be withdrawn. With the recent inclusion of corporate bonds in PEPs, however, you should now be able to reduce the risk level of a PEP.

PEP plans can be packaged or unpackaged, i.e., after finding a mortgage lender which accepts PEP mortgages, you can get the PEP and insurance in a package from one institution, or you can put the two together yourself (or with an IFA's help). Each taxpayer can invest up to £6000 per year into a General PEP (i.e., £12 000 per couple) and this will be sufficient to repay most mortgages. (You will need to use another method in addition if you plan to buy a home worth more than about £400 000.)

PEP mortgages are more flexible than endowment mortgages because the terms can be more easily changed. If you have good investment performance, it is easy to pay back some, or all, of the mortgage early. You can also switch managers easily. However, you should be aware that some of the flexibility of a PEP mortgage may be lost in the packaged version.

You should be very careful about the charges you pay for a PEP mortgage. Some unit trust groups appear to have high charges and to bias their charges to the early years so that if you cash in early, you will be hit by the same sort of poor cash-in values that you suffer with endowments.

INTEREST AND CURRENCY VARIATIONS

I've now covered the main types of mortgage, but there remain a couple of variations that should be mentioned, relating to interest rates and currency. If you would naturally go for a variable interest rate sterling loan, skip this section.

Interest rates

It is usual in the UK for mortgage interest rates to be variable. If interest rates in general go up, so will most mortgage rates, and both will tend to fall together. That makes good sense for the lenders. They are matching their assets and liabilities in as much as they mainly pay variable interest rates on the deposits they receive, and charge variable rates on their loans. In the USA, fixed rates have been more usual. The mortgage rate is set for its duration when the loan is taken out.

While the usual British approach makes good sense for the lenders, does it make good sense for the borrowers? The problem is that you may borrow an amount you can comfortably repay at the current interest rate, but if it then rises, you may find yourself in difficulties. I would argue that this just means you have borrowed too much. If you follow the traditional rules of thumb for how much you can borrow, you won't encounter problems because they allow for the possibility that rates may rise. You may also have the opportunity (with a repayment mortgage) of extending your loan period instead of paying more each month.

You may wish to have a fixed rate mortgage for a different reason. You may feel that interest rates will be higher over the life of your mortgage than they are currently, so you wish to have a fixed rate to take an interest rate bet. Now over the long haul, homes have been a good investment. Do you really want to add a bet on interest rates? Rates may go up, but they could fall too. Many people worry about investing a few thousand pounds. If you are one, why would you want to make an interest rate bet with many thousands of pounds, i.e., the value of your mortgage? What is your track record as an interest rate forecaster? Most people should probably opt for a variable rate mortgage. But maybe that's just my British bias to the traditional British product: in America, where fixed rates have been the norm, most financial advisers recommend fixed rate mortgages.

Cap and collar mortgages have variable interest rates but only between a maximum rate (cap) and a minimum rate (collar). These reflect the ingenuity of marketing people more than any obvious product virtue.

Currency of loan

It is possible to have a mortgage in a currency other than sterling. For anyone buying a home in the UK, but earning a non-sterling salary, a non-sterling mortgage may make good sense. But sometimes non-sterling mortgages are recommended either as a currency play or as a means of reducing the interest rate paid (because Swiss interest rates, say, are lower than British). Analogous points to those raised in the last subsection have to be faced. Many people torment themselves as to whether they should change their holiday currency when they book their holiday or wait till just before they go. When will they get the best rate on a few hundred pounds? If you are such a person, why would you want to make a currency bet with the value of your mortgage? What is your track record as a currency forecaster?

Choosing a foreign currency mortgage because, say, Swiss interest rates are lower than UK rates may seem straightforward. But it's not. Usually low interest rate currencies are expected to appreciate against high interest rate currencies. In other words you may pay a lower interest rate, but you may have to pay far more pounds than you expected, because the pound has depreciated against the Swiss franc. If you don't understand this you, should you not be gambling with a foreign currency mortgage. Most people should opt for a sterling mortgage.

WHICH TYPE OF MORTGAGE IS BEST?

This is easy to answer, but the answer is not helpful ... it all depends. The point is that the best mortgage is affected by your current and future circumstances, your attitude to risk, the level of future interest rates and investment returns, future tax policy, and so on. What does seem likely is that too many people have taken out endowment mortgages. In 1994, 60% of the mortgage market was taken by endowment mortgages, and 27% by repayment mortgages.

Repayment mortgages simply repay a loan. Interest-only mortgages are, in effect, borrowing to invest. If you refer back to Tables 24.1 and 24.2 you may recall that for Table 24.1, I argued that the endowment mortgage would not be a very good deal, whereas for Table 24.2, it probably would. In broad terms endowments will be a good deal if investment returns exceed mortgage interest rates. You will recall that equity returns have exceeded cash returns over long periods. That might suggest that borrowing to invest will be a good deal. Unfortunately, matters are not that simple.

When you borrow, you have to pay more than you get when you lend money to banks, building societies or the government. You are not such a good credit risk as they are. And the return you get from an endowment investment will depend upon exactly which assets it is invested in (probably lots of gilts), the charges, penalties for cashing in early, tax factors and so on.

A reasonable guess, according to the Office of Fair Trading, based on the last 30 years or so, is that investment returns after charges might exceed the mortgage borrowing rate by 1.63% per annum. If that applies to the future, then an endowment will be a profitable way of paying for a mortgage relative to a repayment mortgage. However, once other factors are considered, this conclusion may not hold.

In Chapter 23, I discussed the severe penalties for early surrender of insurance products. If you surrender your policy in the early years, you will not get much back and are likely to be worse off than if you had taken a repayment mortgage. This may not apply to the endowments with the best surrender terms, but it will be true for the majority of endowments. Probably 30% of endowments are surrendered in the first five years. Will you surrender an endowment early? It is hard to know. The odds of surrender are greater if you have borrowed too much and are vulnerable to rising interest rates, have little savings to draw on, and have a greater than average chance of being sacked or made redundant. And don't forget how common divorce is. If you get divorced, you may be forced to sell your home.

One estimate is that only about 20% of endowments are held to maturity. A lot of people will therefore surrender their endowment after year five, but before maturity. In this situation the case for an endowment is stronger than if surrendered in the first five years, but in many cases a repayment mortgage would still be a better bet. Other factors need to be considered too. For example, there is a wide range in the charges made by insurance companies and the 1.63% differential assumed above is an average. Endowment mortgages from high-charging companies will be less attractive than a repayment mortgage. Many people with an endowment mortgage struggle to meet the repayments and often have to borrow short-term, for example by running up credit card debt, to meet their payments. The cost of borrowing for these people is far higher than the average mortgage interest rate. For them a repayment mortgage would be a better bet. And the advantage for all endowments would be reduced if the 15% tax-break on mortgage interest were removed.

Of course, endowments will look more attractive if the differential between borrowing rates and investment rates is greater than the 1.63% per annum assumed (as it was during 1983–93) and worse if it is lower (as it was during 1973–83, when there was a negative return).

In short, if the future is like the past, it will make sense to have an endowment mortgage *providing* you are sure you will be able to see it through to maturity, you have a low or average cost insurer, and you don't have to borrow at more than the normal mortgage rate. If you are not sure about any of these factors—and who is—you should probably go for a repayment mortgage.

PEP mortgages have not been very popular, but have tax advantages over endowments. Providing you choose a low-cost PEP manager, a PEP mortgage should be better value than an endowment mortgage. It is also more flexible as you may be able to stop making payments for a period if necessary. And if the PEP performs well, you can pay off your mortgage early. Being tied to the markets, a PEP is volatile. But it is no more volatile than a unit-linked endowment. Its volatility can be reduced if corporate bonds are held as well as equities, and if some funds are shifted out of the PEP and into cash-based investments as the repayment period draws to a close. If you meet the criteria for contemplating an endowment mortgage you should definitely consider a PEP mortgage.

Pension mortgages are very specialized and I am not going to add to my earlier comments here. They will probably not be suitable for most people, and anybody considering one should seek specialist advice.

For most people, buying a home is such a major decision that I think a little repetition will not go amiss. I end this section with a quote from the Office of Fair Trading on what it thought were the key messages for anybody choosing between the various ways of repaying a mortgage.

> *"Weigh up certainty and risk*
> Keeping up a straight repayment mortgage will mean that your loan is paid off.
> Using an investment vehicle like an endowment or a PEP unit trust will involve more risk, with the possibility of either a shortfall in meeting your loan or an increase in premiums, or, on the other hand, a welcome surplus.
> With-profits endowments (including unitized with-profits) offer a safety net against stockmarket year-by-year fluctuations, while unit-linked endowments and PEP unit trusts are more volatile.
> *Take account of the effects of charges and surrender penalties of endowments*
> You can never tell whether you might have to surrender an endowment early; if you do, the overall costs would generally be higher than if you had used straight repayment.
> Charges on individual endowments vary considerably, and the level of charges may well determine whether a particular endowment will involve more or less overall cost than straight repayment.
> *Look at the tax advantages*
> The tax advantages of PEP unit trusts will generally mean that they will be less costly overall than straight repayment and endowments both on early surrender and at maturity, though a high charge PEP unit trust could be more costly overall than a very low charge endowment. Do not forget that tax laws may change over time.
> *Consider your capability to keep up monthly outgoings*
> Endowments often involve slightly higher monthly outgoings than straight repayments and PEP unit trusts; if you have difficulty in meeting these extra outgoings (and you have

to borrow occasionally through an overdraft or other costly means), then over the mortgage period the extra costs involved could be significant.

And when you move home

Whatever your repayment method, adjust or increase your existing arrangements but keep to the original term if possible.

Above all, avoid being 'churned', that is being persuaded to surrender an existing endowment to take out another, as the costs involved can be very substantial."

© Crown copyright 1995

NEGATIVE EQUITY

Your equity in your home is the difference between the value of the home and what you owe on it. Thus, if you owe £45 000, but your home is worth £50 000, you have equity of £5000. If, however, your home is worth £45 000, and you owe £50 000, you have negative equity of £5000. If you don't have any other assets, you appear to be stuck in your current home because if you sold it you would need to find £5000 to pay off the lender. And if you wanted to buy another home, you might need to find a deposit as well.

If you are in this position you should be aware that most mortgage lenders now offer schemes that get you out of the trap. You will, however, be stuck with your existing lender. In broad terms, the typical scheme will cover negative equity of up to £25 000 and will give you a maximum loan of 125% of the value of the new property. You will either not have to make a deposit, or it will be 5%. The maximum repayment period for the negative equity portion of the loan is usually between 10 and 20 years, while the rest of the loan will have a normal repayment period.

Very few people have made use of these schemes. Should you take one? If you want to move, and you can service your current mortgage, probably you should. You may feel that taking on more debt will just make you worse off, but that's not necessarily so.

It's clear that if you have negative equity, you will have made a capital loss. But that's happened, and there is nothing you can do about it. In Chapter 2's terms, your net worth will have fallen. But if you can meet your mortgage payments, you don't have a cash flow problem. If you want to move, you may have to use a negative equity scheme. At the extreme, you could just buy a home worth what your existing home is worth. Thus if you have a mortgage for £50 000 but your home is worth £45 000, you could buy another £45 000 home. You would be servicing a mortgage worth £50 000, but that's exactly the same situation as now. You would not be taking on more debt.

Of course, you might wish to take on more debt by buying a more expensive home. If you bought your home in 1988, your salary might now be 50% higher, so you could easily afford the payments on a higher mortgage, and you may be tempted to buy a more expensive property. Is that wise? It will be if home prices rise, and it won't be if they fall. What will happen? You'll have to make your own mind up on that.

EARLY REPAYMENT

If you have the money, should you pay off your mortgage early? It depends. It does not make sense to terminate an endowment policy. The investment value mainly comes from the later years. But you can still keep the endowment payments going and repay all or part of your loan. Then the maths is similar to that for a repayment mortgage.

If you have high-cost debt, such as credit card debt, you should pay that off before you consider paying off relatively cheap mortgage debt. Then you should compare the cost of your loan (after-tax) versus what you could earn if you invested the money elsewhere. However, you should bear in mind that if you pay off all or part of your mortgage, the money has gone for ever. If you invest the money, it will be available if you need it for any reason.

In Table 24.3, I give an example of how you might compare mortgage debt and investments. If you have spare cash you can pay off all or part of your mortgage early. Your return from doing that is the interest you save. Interest on the first £30 000 of your mortgage attracts tax relief at 15%. So, with an 8.5% mortgage interest rate, the after-tax cost to you is only 7.2% on the first £30 000 of loan (i.e., 8.5% × 0.85 = 7.2%), but 8.5% thereafter. The tax relief is 15% irrespective of your marginal tax rate. Your return from paying off your mortgage is therefore either 7.2% or 8.5%.

If you don't pay off the mortgage but make an investment instead, I'll assume you pay tax on the return. Now your tax rate matters. In Table 24.3, I've done the sums for the two rates on savings. If you are getting tax relief at 15% on your mortgage and you pay 20% tax on savings, you will need to earn at least 9% or more pre-tax on your investments to be better off by keeping on the mortgage and investing rather than paying off the mortgage (i.e., 9% × 0.8 = 7.2%). The required rate is higher on the portion of your mortgage that doesn't get tax relief and even higher for a 40% taxpayer, as Table 24.3 shows. Investment returns as high as those shown in Table 24.3 are quite demanding, and if you can't get at least these returns, paying off the mortgage may be a sensible strategy. Of course, if your investments escape tax, the case for paying off a mortgage is reduced.

Before you make early repayments you should make sure you know how your lender will treat them. Some charge an interest rate penalty for early repayment—you should build that into your sums. And find out when your repayment will be credited. Some lenders credit once a year, and don't adjust the interest due until that date. For such a lender, wait until just before that date.

Another thing you should think about if you pay off your mortgage early, is what you will do with the deeds. You may have to pay £25 per annum, or more, for your bank to hold them. This might make it worth reducing your mortgage but not quite paying it off. Or you could just buy a safe and keep your deeds in that, along with all

Table 24.3 Mortgage Debt at 8.5% and Required Investment Return

Your Tax Rate	First £30 000		Thereafter	
	After-tax Mortgage Cost	Required Pre-tax Investment Return	After-tax Mortgage Cost	Required Pre-tax Investment Return
20%	7.2%	9.0%	8.5%	10.6%
40%	7.2%	12.0%	8.5%	14.2%

your important papers. A fire-proof safe with alarms and a bolt for securing it to a floor or shelf costs about £200.

Finally, you may prefer to pay off your mortgage simply because it will give you a buzz. Providing you can pay the Council Tax, you've got a place to live. How do you value that?

WHICH IS THE BEST MORTGAGE LENDER?

This is impossible to answer. You will be borrowing for a period of perhaps 25 years. While you can look at who has been the best, for a repayment mortgage you are trying to find the cheapest lender over the *next* 25 years. For other types of mortgages you are looking for both the cheapest lender, and the best investment returns over the *next* 25 years. Remember that most big lenders are tied to one insurance company. You can, however, usually select a different insurance company for your endowment if you go that route, although the lender may not tell you this unless you ask. So while it is sensible to find a low-cost lender (if you can), you should not stop there. You also want a good investment product provider. I have more faith in getting good investment returns where I can control the investments. So I would be more inclined towards a PEP, where I could use index funds, than an endowment investment. But that's just my view, and only makes sense if a PEP mortgage is suitable for you. I discussed selecting funds in general in Chapter 16, but I will discuss endowments specifically after saying a few words on lenders.

With regard to low-cost lenders, *Which?* reported that on the basis of historical analysis over six years, none of the largest 16 lenders stood out as especially cheap or dear. You could try selecting amongst the largest by putting their names into a hat. However, *Which?* found the Buckinghamshire, Chesham, Newcastle and Principality Building Societies had all been significantly cheaper than other lenders. All are small-ish societies, so they might be taken over by somebody with a different fee structure which would affect you if you had a variable rate mortgage, but not if you had a fixed rate. A more recent study by *Which?* reported that over a nine-year period the historical best buys were from the Chesham, Chorley and District, Penrith and Stafford Railway building societies. You'll notice that only one society is in both lists, and that's the Chesham, but unfortunately it only lends to people who live in the Home Counties. So even choosing on the basis of past performance isn't easy.

A list of lenders, their terms, special offers, providers of enhanced multiple loans and so forth may be found in *Moneyfacts*. You can get a specialist advisers to assist you, but while this will be comforting, and you may avoid the worst pitfalls, I don't know how they will be able to solve the problems mentioned in the first paragraph of this section.

Selecting an endowment provider

You would be wise to get independent advice when you select an endowment mortgage provider. As a minimum you have to consider:

- Which type of endowment

- Product features

- The charges

- The surrender values

- The investment performance

- The level of premium

I have discussed the various types of endowment such as with-profits and unit-linked. You will have to choose which type suits you, given your attitude to risk.

Product features are important too. There are a number of issues here such as simplified acceptance for life insurance, free life insurance between exchange of contracts and completion, guaranteed insurability options and so forth. You will need to get a specialist to talk you through these features and decide how much they are worth. One rather unromantic feature that you should seek is the ability to transfer from joint to single ownership. With the high divorce rate, and frequent split-ups of cohabiting couples, it is desirable that your policy will not be cancelled if you have to transfer the ownership of the home and endowment from joint to single ownership. The potentially high cost of early surrender is discussed later.

You should then look at the charges you will suffer—the higher the charges, the less that is being invested for you. These charges will take the form of cost of advice, administration costs, and life insurance costs.

Product providers assume an illustrative growth for your investment, but use their actual charges. Thus for an assumed premium of £75 per month over 25 years for a with-profits endowment mortgage, it is possible to see what this would grow to at, say, 7.5% per annum and what the actual money charges would be. Alternatively one can work out what the rate of growth to the policy holder would be after allowing for charges. For example, an investment return of 7.5% might be reduced to 6% after charges have been borne. In a survey of some of the major providers by the *Financial Times*, the growth after charges on a 7.5% pre-charges assumption varied between 7% and 4.6%. There is no obvious reason why anyone should buy a high charge fund.

An additional way of looking at charges is to ask what surrender value you would get if you surrendered your endowment at various dates. Again the range is wide. For example, with a premium of £75 per month over 25 years and assuming 9% growth, the *Financial Times* survey found that Equitable Life would have given surrender values after 1, 3 and 10 years of £866, £2790 and £12 100 respectively, while Royal Insurance would have given values of £0, £406 and £5554 for the same periods.

If you believe my discussion about investment performance (Chapter 14), you will pay little attention to past performance and concentrate more on other factors. Low charges give a head start in the performance stakes. I would select a low-cost provider who has been in the top half of the performance ratings over five years, rather than one that has done well but has high costs. Performance comes and goes, but high costs undermine performance consistently. You may, however, prefer to find a "star" investment manager.

You will naturally look at how much per month each product provider will expect you to pay. Be careful with this comparison. With similar investment performance, a low-cost provider can set the monthly payment lower than a high-cost provider. In this case cheap is good. But simply by assuming a high investment return, any provider can set a low monthly payment. For example, in the *Financial Times* survey, providers were asked what the monthly premium would be to pay a £50000 mortgage off over 25 years. For unit-linked endowments, Abbey Life asked for £67.98 while Standard Life asked for £82. Unfortunately, Abbey Life assumed investment returns of 9.25% per annum whereas Standard Life assumed 7%. It doesn't matter whose assumption turns out to be right, comparing the two premiums is comparing chalk and cheese.

Say the return is actually 7.5% per annum, then the premium Standard Life asked for would pay off the mortgage and leave a surplus of £3912. Abbey Life's premium, however, would not pay off the mortgage, in fact you would be £11500 short. This wouldn't happen of course. At some stage you would be asked to pay more each month to ensure you could repay your mortgage. Is a high premium always safe? Not necessarily. London and Manchester would have asked for £86 per month and you would still be £100 short with a return of 7.5% per annum. You would do much better to look at the size of costs than the level of the premium. With an assumed growth of 7.5% per annum, and using actual charges, the growth after charges for London and Manchester, Abbey Life and Standard Life were 5.2%, 5.29% and 5.98%.

As I said at the beginning of this section, you would be wise to get an IFA to help you select an endowment provider.

HOW TO REALIZE THE VALUE IN YOUR HOME

The largest asset many people have is their home. Half of all people aged 65 and over own their home, and the average home is worth about £42000 in Northern Ireland, the cheapest region, through to about £80000 in Greater London, the dearest region. The trick is to find a way of realizing some of this value to make your retirement more comfortable. The best position to be in, is not to need the money. In that case, if you like your home, just enjoy it. You may find, however, that a home that was the right size for a family is too big when there are just two of you, and even more so when there is just one. So you may wish to move for non-financial reasons.

If you do need extra income, you may wish to realize some of the value in the home. There are three obvious ways:

- Move to a smaller home or to a cheaper area

- Sell your home and rent another

- Rent out part of your home

None of these options may appeal. In the first case you have to go to all the bother of buying and selling property, and may mean moving away from friends. The second option poses many of the same problems. Renting out part of your home may or may not involve a lodger. If you have a flat, it probably will, but in a house, a self-contained flat might be constructed. That does mean you get to stay with your friends, and perhaps keep your garden, but it may not be easy to arrange, or cheap, and you may not like the idea.

What most people would prefer is to be able to stay in their own home and yet be able to get their hands on some of the money locked up in it. There are three ways of doing this:

- Home-income plans
- Home-reversion plans
- Interest roll-up mortgages

Home-income plans combine a mortgage and an annuity. The mortgage is given on your home and at least 90% must be used to buy an annuity, which is like a reverse insurance policy. Instead of paying money each year to get a lump sum at the end, you pay over a lump sum for the right to an income for, usually, as long as you live. (Annuities are explained in more detail in Chapter 28.) So, with a home income plan you pay interest on the mortgage and the principal is repaid out of your estate when you die. Your home remains yours. Tax relief at the basic rate is granted on the mortgage interest if you are aged 65 or over. The income from the annuity is taxable, but part of the payment you receive is deemed to be repayment of capital and is not taxable. The income in this type of plan comes from the annuity income exceeding the interest payments you make.

Mortgage loans are limited to the lower of 80% of the value of your property or £30 000. In general, these plans are not worth taking out unless you are in your 70s and in good health. The costs are relatively high and the £30 000 limit obviously does not unlock much of the value of many homes in the South East. If you die immediately after taking out the loan and annuity, the loan must be repaid, but the annuity terminates, so your capital falls. It is possible to take out insurance to cover this. Because the annuity gives you an income, you may lose some means-tested State benefits. You should check the rules for any benefits you get before you take out a plan.

Home-reversion plans involve the home being sold to a financial institution, but at a substantial discount to current market value. In return you become a sitting tenant. You are responsible for maintaining the home, but you will pay only a peppercorn rent. You do not need to sell all your home, but usually you have to sell at least 50%. These plans are sold to people from about age 65. The major problem with these plans is that you lose any capital growth that occurs in your home, although some versions do allow you to share in any growth. The great advantage of these plans is that there is no £30 000 limit, so large sums of money can be raised. Don't forget that an injection of capital could affect your State benefits.

Interest roll-up mortgages are loans on which no repayment is made until death. Prior to that interest rolls up. If interest rates rise sharply and property prices fall or remain constant, the property may have to be sold during your lifetime to repay the loan.

While you should seek independent advice on any of the three plans discussed, it is essential that you get very detailed advice on interest roll-up plans. The safest advice is not to consider them. For details of the income available for various sets of circumstances, and for a list of product providers, see the appropriate article listed in READ 📖 WRITE 🖹 RING ☎.

BUYING PART OF A HOME: SHARED OWNERSHIP

If you find the cost of buying a home too much, you might consider shared housing. If this isn't your thing, but you have an elderly parent with a home which is a financial drain, you might still find it worth reading this section.

Shared ownership is intended to help people who cannot afford to buy a home because they cannot afford the deposit or mortgage payments. Through shared ownership with a housing association, you buy a share of the house or flat and pay rent on the remainder. You can buy the rest of the property if you can afford to, at a later date. If you want to sell, you can, but if you own only, say, 50% of the home, you will only get 50% of the proceeds.

Housing associations are non-profit making organizations that provide and manage homes for rent or enter shared ownership schemes. While some housing associations use money from private sources such as charities, most finance is provided by local authorities or The Housing Corporation. This is a body set up by Parliament to help fund housing associations and to ensure that they spend their money properly.

Shared ownership homes may be new or renovated, flats or houses. The scheme is intended for people who cannot buy a property in any other way. Priority is given to first-time buyers, local authority and housing association tenants, those on waiting lists, and owner-occupiers moving to high-cost areas. The basic scheme is for homes developed by the housing association, but there is a Do It Yourself scheme where a home on the open market (in England only) may be purchased.

For elderly people who have some savings, or a house that is too big or expensive to maintain, there are leasehold for the elderly schemes. A housing association will build a group of homes, which may be flats or bungalows, which will have a resident warden and some communal facilities. The homes may be purchased by people aged 55 or over, and on a 99-year lease. Usually shares of 25%, 50% or 75% may be purchased, with rent payable in the case of the 25% or 50% shares, but not for the 75% share. In the general schemes, the home can eventually be wholly owned. In the scheme for the elderly, the maximum that can be purchased is a 75% share.

To get further information on shared ownership see READ 📖 WRITE 📧 RING ☎.

BUYING A SECOND HOME (INCLUDING TIMESHARE)

If buying a home is a good idea, how about a second one? It may be a good idea, but it must be a less good idea than buying a first home because the tax advantages in terms of capital gains and mortgage interest relief only apply to the first home. Additionally, insurance, maintenance, Council Tax, etc., have to be paid in full. For most people a second home will not be a good financial decision, although there is no reason why non-financial considerations should not dominate the decision.

Many people plan to let their second home to cover part of the expense. That is OK, and providing it is available for commercial letting for long enough, there may be tax reliefs (for details consult your accountant or a book on tax). However, if your intention is to have your second home as a home at the seaside or in the country, somewhere comfy for you to go, you have to realize that you are beginning to move from that towards running a business. If you move to your second home some of your favourite old furniture, such as the battered sofa that has dips where you have lumps, you may find the home is not of a suitable standard for letting. You start having to decorate and furnish in a style that ensures lets, rather than your comfort. And you can't go there any time you please, because your home may be let. You will probably have to find, and pay, a letting agent. Moreover, you may enjoy your property in the summer, but will anyone want to rent it in the winter? Of course if you are buying a property abroad, the letting season may be longer, but the complications of buying abroad, and managing a property from a distance, are greater. Why not invest your money in shares, and use the dividends to buy a few days, whenever you want, in a decent (or even indecent) hotel?

Timeshare often seems a good compromise to many people. Here you don't buy a whole house or flat, but the right to live in one for a specific week or weeks of the year, for ever. You can also buy abroad more easily, with less hassle about deeds, and not have to worry about whether you are joined to the water supply. However, if you multiply the cost of your week by 52, you will find you are paying a lot more than 1/52nd of the value of the property. You may not feel this matters:

- You get access to a nice property in an area you like

- You get to meet the same people each year, so you may make some holiday friends (although you could hate them too)

- You can swap your week for another timeshare somewhere else in the world

But:

- You have bought the same holiday for the rest of your life, which seems to me like a prison sentence, although the possibility of swapping does allow time-off for good behaviour

- You will pay a fee to arrange a swap, and you will pay maintenance charges whether or not you use your time

- You will find it hard to sell your timeshare

The last point is especially important. Timeshares are usually sold rather than bought. Most people don't plan to buy a timeshare: it's probably not on your list of financial goals. You are on holiday, relaxed, in the sun, had a few drinks and surrounded by beautiful bronzed bodies. Your financial defences are down, and somebody sells you a timeshare. Fine, but when you want out, you may find it hard to get rid of your timeshare because you are not selling aggressively, and there are few natural buyers.

Still interested in timeshares? There are two sensible strategies. First, consider renting a week in a timeshare. You may get a nice property for less than the cost of an equivalent standard hotel. Second, if you must buy, don't buy from the developer, buy from an individual trying to sell. The price may be a bargain.

READ 📖 WRITE 🖹 RING ☎

♦ Many of the numbers at the start of this chapter were taken from, Joanne Cutler, "The Housing Market and the Economy", *Bank of England Quarterly Bulletin*, August 1995, 260–269.

♦ A fax list of residential mortgages products and rates is available from *Moneyfacts* Fax Service: calls are charged at 39p per minute cheap rate and 49p per minute at other times. Tel: 0336 400239.

♦ The *Which?* reports mentioned are "Pick the Right Mortgage", *Which?* June 1995, 20–25, and "Choosing the Right Mortgage", *Which?* June 1993, 29–33.

♦ For data on the best performing with-profits endowments over the last decade see Stephanie Spicer, "With Profits: A Decade of Results", *Money Management*, April 1995, 59–72.

♦ The *Financial Times* survey of endowment costs and returns mentioned in the text is by Debbie Harrison and reported on pages 15–18 of *FT Quarterly Review of Personal Finance*, April 28 & 29, 1995.

♦ For details of some PEP and pension mortgage providers see: Catherine Williams, "Taking Alternative Measures", *Planned Savings*, October 1995, 50–54.

♦ For a list of home-income and reversion plan providers and some examples of the income available, see: Robert Budden, "Home Sweet Home", *Money Management*, August 1995, 56–60.

♦ The Housing Corporation will provide information on shared housing: The Housing Corporation, 149 Tottenham Court Road, London, W1P 0BN. Tel: 0171 393 2000.

♦ Professionals should read: Office of Fair Trading, *Mortgage Repayment Methods*. London, April 1995. Available free from the OFT on 0181 398 3405. The extensive quote I made from the OFT came from pages 45–6 of this report.

25

The Facts of Life . . . and Death

The more you think of dying the better you will live.
Italian proverb

I guess if you are reading this book, you already know *those* facts of life. But there are some other facts of living and dying that you will know about, whose implications you may not have fully thought through. The key facts are simple enough, the population is ageing, we are living longer on average, but we will all die. These facts should affect a large part of your financial planning.

The ageing demographic profile of the country will mean that there will be a constant debate as to how much we can expect from the State, and how much we will have to fend for ourselves. If we have to fend for ourselves, the lesson from compounding is that the sooner we start planning for our future, the better. A second aspect about old age is that much financial retirement advice is wrong: in particular the view that you should immediately move away from growth-orientated investments as you approach retirement. Finally, despite people living longer on average, you may die before you expect to, and this may warrant buying life insurance. I discuss the first two issues in this chapter, and the third was discussed in Chapter 23.

THE POLITICAL ECONOMY OF OLD AGE

All round the world, State pension schemes have been running into problems. To see why, I'll first discuss private pensions. It is usual for private pension schemes to be fully funded. What this means is that there has to be a pot of money set aside which can pay any pensions that have been promised. The accounting is a bit tricky, but that's the general idea. This doesn't apply in all countries, but it's common. Since companies can go bust, we want to know that there is a separate pension pot that will survive, irrespective of our employer's or insurance company's fate. State pensions are different. Since the State is ongoing, and since it has the power to tax, it should always be able to pay its bills. As a result, State schemes usually aren't fully funded, but are, instead, "pay as you go"—that's to say, current pensions are paid out of current taxation. In short, current workers pay past workers' pensions.

The problem is this. The industrialized world's population is ageing, so there are increasing numbers of old people (pensioners) and fewer young people (workers). This ageing of the population is caused by today's middle-aged parents having had

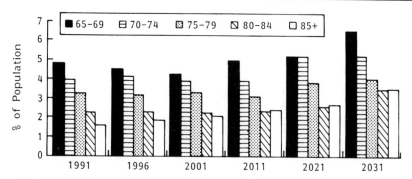

Figure 25.1 Percentage of UK Population in Various Age Groups. Source: Graph computed from data in the *Annual Abstract of Statistics 1994*

fewer children than their parents, and by people living longer. In Figure 25.1, I show the percentage of the UK population in various age groups as a percentage of the total population, at various dates. Notice the rapid growth of the percentage of older people in the next century, especially those aged 80 and over.

This move towards an older population is much greater in some countries than in others, and Britain is by no means the extreme case. But there is a problem nonetheless. With fewer workers supporting more pensioners, something has to give. Either taxes have to rise, or State pensions have to decline in value as a percentage of national income, or both. Now this is very unattractive for today's workers. They may have to pay more tax now to pay for existing pension commitments, while knowing that by the time they draw their pensions, they will be much less attractive in real terms. That means they should save more for their own future, as well as paying tax for past generations.

While it might seem unthinkable that the State will reduce pensions, it has been doing just that, albeit in a sly way. State Basic Pension used to be tied to average earnings. Now it is tied to prices, which rise more slowly than earnings. While State Basic Pension has gone up in money terms, as a share of national wealth it has been declining. And, as I discuss in Chapter 27, the State has been backing away from tying your State pension to your own earnings.

The latest estimates by the Government Actuary suggest that because of these changes, the State can pay pension entitlements without raising taxes, but the money is being found at the expense of the poorest pensioners. Anyone who expects to depend on the State for a large percentage of their retirement income should be looking at ways of arranging additional income. And society may not accept that the poorest pensioners should get ever poorer in relative terms. In that case one comes back to the possibility of higher taxes.

If you have a good company pension scheme you may well feel protected from some of these problems. But higher taxes might affect you. Since raising taxes is not popular, the obvious approach is to try to raise taxes in a way people don't notice, and one way might be to reduce the tax exemption enjoyed by pension schemes. Dividends and interest received by schemes, currently not taxed, might be, as might capital gains. This might lead companies to offer less generous pension schemes in the future—the most likely way of this happening is for firms to move from final salary (defined benefit) schemes to money purchase (defined contribution) schemes. These schemes are discussed in Chapters 27 and 28, but basically such a shift would mean that employers would not guarantee you a pension tied to your pre-retirement salary, but you would get whatever the pension investments, after tax, generated. Another option might be for the government to prohibit the tax-free lump sum payments that many schemes allow.

The only advice one can give is that you shouldn't rely too much on a State pension, and perhaps you should build up as much private pension entitlements as possible while pension schemes get the generous tax-breaks discussed in Chapters 27 and 28.

Pensions are one problem for an ageing population. A second is that old people have greater health care needs than younger people. Many illnesses are closely related to age. For example, about 6.5% of the population aged 65 plus suffer from dementia; about 10% of those aged 75 plus; and 18.5% of those aged 80 plus. You should allow for the possibility that you will spend part of your life in some form of care—about one in seven of us will. Women live longer than men, and are therefore especially likely to need care.

These problems again lead the State to back away from providing care from the cradle to the grave. The State doesn't want you in the NHS: if the NHS can't cure you—and there is no cure for dementia—it will kick you out of hospital into a nursing home. Nursing homes cost around £300 per week (and often much more). Once again, the State will want to avoid having to pay some of these costs.

Here we encounter some interesting problems. As I detail in Chapter 26, many State benefits are means-tested, either in terms of income or capital. The key figures for means-testing by capital are £8000 and £3000. Before April 1996, for nursing home care, above £8000 you paid everything, below £3000 you paid nothing, and in-between you paid part of the costs. Now for the really rich it made sense to provide for themselves as well as they were able. But for many people, capital of £25 000 say, was a fortune. But if you ended up in a nursing home, it would have taken about a year to reduce your capital from £25 000 to £8000. To have £25 000 to have a few luxuries in your final years seems desirable, but if the State might demand the money from you simply for being old and having been prudent, there may not be much incentive to be prudent. Indeed, the situation was worse. If you had a home, that counted as part of your assets. If you didn't have a spouse or partner living in it, it could be sold to pay your bills if you went into a nursing or residential home. Your children saw their inheritance being consumed by the State.

In November 1995, a number of changes were made. First, from April 1996, the lower capital limit was raised to £10 000, and the upper was raised to £16 000. Second, insurance benefits for long-term care were made tax-free (see Chapter 7). Third, the Chancellor announced that he was consulting on how occupational pension schemes could enable pensioners to defer some income early in retirement to help with the cost of long-term care. Fourth, consultation began on partnership schemes. These would mean that in return for insuring a certain amount of your long-term care costs, you would be allowed to keep a similar amount of your assets on top of the new capital limits. This bundle of changes shows how seriously the problem of long-term care is being taken. But the measures are far from a solution.

By increasing the capital limits, the beneficiaries of your estate are being subsidized by the taxpayer. But the amount of help being given is not sufficient to stop most of a modest estate being rapidly consumed, or to stop homes having to be sold. Making long-term care insurance benefits tax-free is of limited value—benefits paid directly to a home were already tax-free. As to deferring pensions, most experts seem to think that most people do not have sufficient pension benefits to be able to draw a reason-able pension and also leave sufficient money to provide for long-term care. Finally, the partnership schemes may be of some value, but only to people with some assets that might be fully consumed by long-term care costs, say, assets around £100 000, and who might be willing to insure for three years' care in return for a higher upper capital limit. People with £25 000 might still see it as rational to spend it all.

One way out for the State is to ensure that everybody has more income in their old age so that they can pay more of their nursing costs out of their income. Since the State won't want to provide this income, it is a small step to demanding compulsory private pensions or compulsory social insurance, where, say, 10% of all salaries must be paid into a private pension or insurance scheme. We are some way from this, but it is done in some countries.

So what exactly should you do based on what I've said? I don't know, since social policy is rapidly changing in this area. But, if you think you will need more money for your old age, the only sure way to build up a decent sum is to start early—recall the story of Harry and Sally in Chapter 3.

YOU WILL DIE, BUT IT MAY BE A WHILE YET

Now that I've suggested you may need to save more money than you might have expected, I want to relate living longer to investment strategy. I have shown in Chap-ter 4 that equities have, in the past, been the best way of ensuring that your invest-ments have grown. I have also discussed how a short investment horizon is the major contra-indication for investing in equities. Many advisers tell you to rush off to bonds as you approach retirement. I think that is bad advice, and here I am talking about your investments, not your personal pension plan if you have one. You really have to think hard about your investment horizon, and not get hooked on stereotypes.

The advisers' equation is all too obvious: retired = old = die = short time horizon. But should you have a short horizon? You know you will die, but do you know when? Take a look at Table 25.1. It shows how many years more life a man or a woman of a certain age can expect.

Table 25.1   Additional Life Expectancy at Various Ages

Present Age	Male	Female
50	26	30
55	22	26
60	18	22
65	14	18
70	11	14
75	8	11
80	6	8
85	5	6

Source: *Annual Abstract of Statistics 1994*. Numbers have been rounded.

A 60-year-old man has, on average, a life expectancy of about 18 years, which is not a short time. His wife will, on average, be two years younger, and have a life expectancy of about 24 years. When you plan for your retirement, think carefully about how long your investment horizon really is. Of course, if you have some known illness, you may have only a short life expectancy, but most people will convince themselves that they are going to live longer than the average, say five additional years. Super-optimists might like to note that in 1951, 300 people reached 100 years of age. In 1991, there were 4390, of which only 500 were men. Ah, to be a centenarian bachelor, fighting off the girls.

When the average man is 60, his wife, if she is an optimist and adds on five years to the average life expectancy for a woman, might expect to live for another 29 years. It seems sensible to structure your investments to allow for this possibility rather than act on an adviser's stereotypes. Don't scoot out of equities at the first sign of a grey hair (or when your head grows through your hair).

FIN

The message is stark. You will finally run out of steam, but it may take longer than you think. You will need a pension, or investments, for longer than you might have thought, and you may well spend your final years being cared for. The odds are that the State will be even less generous than it has been in the past. You may well want to invest in growth investments as soon as possible, and for longer than conventional advice dictates.

In Chapter 26, I look at many of the benefits you can expect from the State, and in Chapter 27 I outline the State pension system before considering private pensions, which I further discuss in Chapter 28.

READ 📖 WRITE 📖 RING ☎

The source for Figure 25.1 and Table 25.1 is: *Annual Abstract of Statistics 1994*. Central Statistical Office. Crown Copyright, 1994. Reproduced by the permission of the Controller of HMSO and the Central Statistical Office.

26

Social Security Benefits

If a free society cannot help the many who are poor, it cannot save the few who are rich.
John F. Kennedy

Social Security is a system of cash benefits that are paid in specific circumstances. These include being unemployed, being on a low income, being retired, being sick, and so forth.

Social security benefits are often neglected when people make their financial plans. That's a pity, because having paid tax and National Insurance Contributions (NICs), it makes sense to see what benefits are available. To do otherwise would be a bit like buying a share and not bothering to find out what the dividend is worth, or not bothering to collect it. For some people benefits will comprise a large part of their income. Further, some benefits depend on NICs, and some people may have to decide whether it is worth making voluntary payments to establish a good contribution record.

You may feel that people who read books like this won't fall into the benefits category. But we all will, if only because of the State pension, and most people also get married and have children, so they will get Child Benefit. And, nowadays, even high-flyers may find themselves unemployed and "signing on". Further, other members of your family such as your children or your parents may be eligible for benefits, and your parents especially may need help to make a claim. You should have a look at social security benefits to make sure your family is not missing out on something you are entitled to. It's thought that 10% of the value of benefits available are not claimed.

Many people feel that if things went wrong, they could fall back on the State. If you read this chapter, you will see that the amount of support you will get is minimal. I think that's worth knowing, and it should affect how you provide for yourself. For example, the benefits relating to long-term illness are so low that you will probably decide you need to make your own provisions by means of savings or insurance. If you are unemployed, you will get some benefits. How large they are in relation to your current income will affect your decision as to how large your emergency cash fund should be. In other cases, e.g., Child Benefit, a well-off family might treat this as a bonus and decide to invest it on behalf of the child.

You may think that if you get benefits, they will be tax-free. Some are, but by no means all, so to work out your cash flow you will need to know not only the benefits you are entitled to but, in addition, whether they are taxable. Some benefits are means-tested, either by income or by capital.

Having argued that you should be aware of what's on offer doesn't by itself help you to find out. And it's not an easy task. The Benefits Agency's introductory booklet *Which Benefit?* runs to more than 70 pages, and it in turn refers to numerous publications setting out matters in more detail. For example, the section on retirement in *Which Benefit?* refers to a number of publications including *A Guide to Retirement Pensions* which in turn runs to more than 80 pages. This chapter inevitably gives only the barest outline of State benefits but, even so, it's a chapter for skimming rather than reading. A mass of rules and regulations doesn't make for an easy read. You will need to get more information on any benefit you think you are entitled to, or will be, and which you should include in your financial planning. For a guide to getting more information, see READ 📖 WRITE ✑ RING ☎.

KEY FEATURES OF SOME MAJOR STATE BENEFITS

Table 26.1 provides an overview of Social Security. It shows some of the major benefits (including pensions which are discussed in Chapter 27), and whether the benefit is subject to a NIC requirement, is taxable, and is means-tested, either with regard to income or capital.

Table 26.1 Key Features of Some Major State Benefits

Benefit	NICs required	Taxable	Means-tested on capital	Means-tested on income
Unemployment	✓	✓	✗	✗
Redundancy	✗	✗	✗	✗
Income Support	✗	✓	✓	✓
Family Credit	✗	✗	✓	✓
Maternity Pay	✓	✓	✗	✗
Child	✗	✗	✗	✗
One Parent	✗	✗	✗	✗
Sick Pay	✓	✓	✗	✗
Incapacity	✓	✓ *	✗	✗
Severe Disablement	✗	✗	✗	✗
Basic Pension	✓	✓	✗	✗
SERPS	✓	✓	✗	✗

Key: ✓ = yes; ✗ = no; * from week 28.

NATIONAL INSURANCE AND BENEFITS

Most working people, but not all, pay NICs. The four classes were given in Chapter 8. NICs help you to qualify for certain benefits which you can get only if you (or your husband, in some cases) have paid enough of the right class of contributions at the right time. These benefits are:

- Retirement Pension

- Unemployment Benefit

- Sickness Benefit

- Incapacity Benefit

- Maternity Allowance

- Widows' benefits

The rules on what NICs are required are absurdly complicated. The rest of this sub-section will give you an idea of some of the issues involved. My intention is just to give a few pointers to the sort of things that matter, and not a definitive statement.

Most people will pay Class 1 NICs as employees. Self-employed people will usually pay Class 2 NICs and perhaps Class 4 as well—those with very low earnings don't have to pay at all, but they may elect to pay Class 3 voluntary contributions. These can help protect rights to the State Retirement Pension and, for a married man, they can protect his wife's rights to Widow's benefits. But they do not count for Unemployment Benefit or any other NIC benefit. Instead of paying Class 3 contributions, it may be better to volunteer to pay Class 2 NICs as these only cost 10p a week more than Class 3. They give everything Class 3 contributions do plus Incapacity and Maternity benefits. Class 2 contributions can be paid if you work abroad either for an employer or yourself, or if you are self-employed in the UK and have a small earnings exception.

Some people will get NIC credits e.g., if you are unemployed (but you must be signing on at a Jobcentre), off work sick, if you get benefits such as Invalid Care Allowance, and if you're 18 or over and taking a full-time training course to help you get a job. If you look after someone at home and you cannot work as a result, you may qualify for Home Responsibilities Protection. These credits help you qualify for NI benefits, but you do need to have made some NICs as well.

While some benefits require NICs, not all do. Those that don't include:

- Income Support

- Family Credit

- Housing Benefit

- Council Tax Benefit

- Social Fund Benefits

- Child Benefit

- One Parent Benefit

I discuss some of the main benefits in the following sections. The rates are for 1996–7.

UNEMPLOYMENT BENEFITS

Benefits for unemployed people include:

- Unemployment Benefit

- Redundancy payments

Unemployment Benefit is payable to people who normally work for an employer, but are out of work. It lasts for a year if you were unemployed before 8 April 1996, and for six months if your unemployment began on or after 8 April 1996. To qualify, you must be actively seeking work and have paid a specified number of NICs. Unemployment Benefit is a taxable benefit. It is paid at a flat rate of £48.25 (or £61.15 if you are over pensionable age) but may be affected by anything you earn, although this won't apply to most people. It is not affected by any savings that you may have. There is an additional payment if you have a dependent partner, but you won't get it if the partner earns more than the amount of the addition.

Don't be bashful about signing on for Unemployment Benefit. On the first day you are unemployed, sign on, as the benefit is not usually back-dated. *It is necessary to sign on to get NIC credits which are useful to help ensure that you get a full State pension.*

Redundancy payments are made to people meeting certain criteria who are made redundant. If you are sacked for doing your job badly, you will be unemployed, but not redundant. You are redundant when your job disappears. This may be because your firm hasn't been making a profit and everybody is made redundant or it may be quite specific to you, because new working practices have made your particular job unnecessary. If you are made redundant, make sure you really are redundant, and you haven't been unfairly dismissed. For helpful leaflets on this, and other redundancy issues, see READ 📖 WRITE 🖃 RING ☎.

To qualify for redundancy payments, you must have worked for your employer for at least two years, and be age 18 or more and under 65. You will be paid a sum based on your age and salary, but only up to a maximum of £210 per week. The age rules are:

- 18–21-year-old: half a week's pay per complete year worked

- 22–41-year-old: one week's pay per complete year worked

- 41–65-year-old: one and a half week's pay per complete year worked with a maximum of 20 years' service.

Your employer may pay more than the legal minimum, especially if it is seeking voluntary redundancies. You do not pay tax on statutory redundancy payment.

LOW INCOME SUPPORT

Benefits for people on low incomes include:

- Income Support

- Family Credit

- Housing Benefit

- Council Tax Benefit

- Social Fund benefits

These benefits do not depend on NICs.

Income Support is paid to those aged 18 and over, who are not working 16 hours a week or more (nor is their partner), and whose income falls below certain levels. It can be paid to the unemployed, and those with part-time jobs. You must be attempting to get work, unless you fall into certain categories such as sick, aged 60 or over, or in certain stages of pregnancy. Benefit will be reduced if you and your partner have savings between £3000 and £8000, and you won't qualify at all if your savings exceed £8000. Any benefit you get is taxable at your marginal rate.

How much you get depends on a number of factors such as your age, whether you have a partner or children, whether you are disabled and so forth. Your benefit may be made up of a personal allowance, a premium for special needs, and help with mortgage interest and certain other housing costs.

There has been substantial press discussion recently about mortgage interest where the rules have been changed. If your mortgage is worth more than £100 000, you will only get help with payments on the first £100 000. If you had a mortgage before 1 October 1 1995, you will receive no help for the first two months you are not earning. Half your mortgage interest payments will be paid for the next four months, then the full amount. For mortgages taken out after 1 October 1995, you will receive no help for the first nine months, half your mortgage interest will be paid for the next four months, and the whole amount thereafter. This change is part of a strategy to encourage people to cover life's risks by self-insurance rather than relying on the State. Unfortunately, the people most likely to need the insurance are those least likely to be able to afford it, and least likely to be able to get it (see Chapter 7).

Family Credit is a tax-free benefit, paid for 26 weeks. It is paid to people (or their partner) working more than 16 hours a week, and responsible for at least one child under age 16, or under 19 if in full-time education up to A-level standard. Benefit will be reduced if you and your partner have savings between £3000 and £8000, and you won't qualify at all if your savings exceed £8000.

The amount you get depends on your income, your partner's income and the number and ages of your children. The income level below which your family will qualify for benefit is shown on the second page of your Child Benefit book.

Housing Benefit is a tax-free benefit paid to those who need help in paying their rent. It is not paid to help with the costs of mortgage interest payments. You and your partner must not have more than £16 000 in savings and you will get reduced benefit if you have savings of between £3000 and £16 000. The amount you will get depends on your circumstances, including the amount of rent you have to pay.

Council Tax Benefit. Council Tax is the new version of the "Poll Tax". The benefit rules are much the same as for Housing Benefit.

Social Fund Benefits are unlikely to be applicable to most readers of this book. The benefits are to help people with expenses that are difficult to meet out of regular income. The benefits include funeral payment, crisis loans and so forth.

MATERNITY BENEFITS

Benefits during pregnancy and when the baby is born include:

- Statutory Maternity Pay
- Maternity Allowance

Statutory Maternity Pay (SMP). If you are pregnant and working for an employer, whether or not you intend to work after the birth, you may be able to get this benefit from your employer. To qualify, two conditions relating to continuous employment and earnings must be met.

SMP is paid at a higher or lower rate. The higher rate is 90% of average earnings for 6 weeks (subject to a minimum of £54.55) then £54.55 for 12 weeks. The lower rate is £54.55 for 18 weeks. SMP is treated as earnings, and so may be subject to tax and NICs. It is not means-tested.

Maternity Allowance. Some women will not qualify for SMP. They may qualify for Maternity Allowance providing they have been employed, or self-employed and paid standard rate NICs for at least 26 weeks in the 66-week period ending with the week before the week the baby is due.

Non-employed or self-employed women get £47.35 for 18 weeks: employed women get £54.55 for 18 weeks.

CHILD SUPPORT

Benefits for people bringing up children include:

- Child Benefit

- One Parent Benefit

- Guardian's Allowance

Child Benefit is tax-free and is not subject to means-testing. Almost anyone responsible for a child living with them is eligible. Child Benefit applies to children under 16 years, or up to 18 if studying full-time for a qualification up to A-level standard. The benefit is £10.80 per week for the eldest child and £8.80 for each other child.

One-Parent Benefit is tax-free and is not subject to means-testing. It can be claimed only by lone parents, i.e., those bringing up a child on their own. It is £6.30 a week for the eldest dependent child only.

Guardian's Allowance is a tax-free payment in addition to Child Benefit, payable to the guardian of an orphaned child. Usually both parents must be dead, but there are exceptions. The weekly rate is £9.90 for a child for whom the higher rate of Child Benefit is payable, and £11.15 for children for whom the lower rate of Child Benefit is payable.

HOSPITAL/RESIDENTIAL CARE/NURSING HOME

People going into hospital, residential care, or a nursing home may get new benefits or find some are stopped. Call Freeline Social Security for details—see READ 📖 WRITE ✎ RING ☎.

The Community Care Act, which came into effect on 1 April 1993, made residential care the responsibility of Local Authorities. This means care for the elderly or the incapacitated now comes from two sources—your local authority and the DSS. I'm going to discuss only residential care here.

If you have to go into a residential home (if you are mobile and reasonably able) or nursing home (if you need qualified nursing care) you can apply to your Local Authority for financial assistance. You will be assessed for your medical and social needs and your financial resources. You will not get assistance if your capital exceeds £16 000. Below £10 000 you will have your fees met, and if you have capital between £16 000 and £10 000 you will get some help.

Whatever you think of the rights or wrongs of this, most people are shocked when they realize how the rules are applied. The value of your house will count as part of your capital, and unless your spouse is living in it you will be forced to sell it (the rules are a bit more complex than this and may change, so check). If you try to give capital away, the Local Authority may claim it back. So, while you can give your money away to beat Inheritance Tax, you can't do the same to beat the Local Authority. If you are a married man with an occupational pension, and you end up in a nursing home, your wife will be able to stay in your marital home, but half of the pension will be taken to pay the nursing home fees.

FOR THE SICK, INJURED AND DISABLED

Benefits for people who are sick, injured, or disabled include:

- Statutory Sick Pay

- Incapacity Benefit

- Severe Disablement Allowance

- Attendance Allowance

- Disability Living Allowance

- Disability Working Allowance

- Invalid Care Allowance

Statutory Sick Pay (SSP) is given to most people who work for an employer and are sick for four or more consecutive days. SSP is paid by the employer for a maximum of 28 weeks in any spell of illness or any linked spells. If you are still sick after 28 weeks you will normally get Incapacity Benefit automatically. The amount of SSP you get depends on your pre-illness earnings. It is nil if your earnings were less than £61 per week, and £54.55 if they were £61 or more.

Incapacity Benefit replaced Sickness Benefit and Invalidity Benefit in April 1995. It is a benefit for people under State pensionable age who are unable to work because of illness or disability and have paid enough NICs. Incapacity Benefit is not means-tested. It is paid at three basic rates to people under State Pension age. For the first 28 weeks of sickness it is paid at the short-term lower rate (£46.15 per week); from weeks 29 to 52 at the short-term higher rate (£54.55); and after one year at the long-term rate (£61.15). You can get short-term Incapacity Benefit for up to a year after you reach State Pension age providing you were incapacitated before reaching State Pension age. The rate is £58.65 per week. Extra benefits may be paid for dependant adults and children. Incapacity Benefit from the 28th week is taxable.

From 13 April 1995 there have been two tests of incapacity: "own occupation test" and "all work test". The first applies for the first 28 weeks of your incapacity and is carried out by your doctor. The test aims to determine if you can do your normal work. The "all work test" is carried out after 28 weeks and aims to determine if you can do any type of work (it is also applied from week one if you don't have a work history). This test may involve a medical examination by a Department of Social Security doctor.

If you are capable of working under the "all work test", you will not be able to get Incapacity Benefit, or the disability premium with Income Support, Housing Benefit or Council Tax Benefit because of incapacity for work. If you sign on at a Jobcentre, you may get Unemployment Benefit and/or Income Support, Housing Benefit and Council Tax Benefit.

Severe Disablement Allowance (SDA) is a tax-free benefit for those who have been unable to work for 28 weeks but, because of insufficient NICs, cannot get Incapacity Benefit. The rate depends on your age when incapacity began: the basic rate is £36.95 per week. The "all work test" for incapacity (see above) will normally be used for SDA.

Attendance Allowance is a tax-free benefit for people aged 65 or over who need help with their personal care because of illness or disability. There are two rates. For people needing care by day or night it is £32.40 and for those who need it all the time it is £48.50.

Disability Living Allowance (DLA) is a two-component tax-free benefit for people under 65 who need help with their personal care (care component) or getting around (mobility component). To be eligible for DLA you must usually have needed help for three months and expect to need it for a further six months. There are three rates for the care component, £48.40, £32.40 and £12.90 and two rates for the mobility component, £33.90 and £12.90. Which rate is paid depends on how much help is needed.

Disability Working Allowance (DWA) is a tax-free means-tested benefit for people 16 or over who are working at least 16 hours per week and whose earning ability is limited by illness or disability. In addition you must be receiving one of a number of specified illness-related benefits. If you, or you and your partner, have more than £16 000 in savings, you are not eligible for DWA; savings between £3000 and £16 000 will reduce your benefit. How much you get will depend on whether you have a partner and children, and how much you earn.

Invalid Care Allowance (ICA) is a taxable weekly benefit of £36.60 paid to those spending at least 35 hours a week looking after a severely disabled person and meeting certain criteria.

READ 📖 WRITE 🖃 RING ☎

♦ The Benefits Agency's booklets *A Guide to Benefits* and *Which Benefit?* are a good starting point to learn about benefits. They will guide you to other material. To get copies: visit your local Social Security office (address in the phone book under Social Security or Benefits Agency); some Post Offices and your local public library may have copies; write to BA Distribution and Storage Centre, Manchester Road, Heywood, Lancashire, OL10 2PZ and request leaflets MG 1 and FB 2; or call the Freeline Social Security number: 0800 666 555. This is also the number to call for general advice.

♦ There are leaflets for each type of benefit. Some benefits and the appropriate leaflet codes are:

Benefits	Leaflets
Attendance Allowance	DS 702; HB 5
Child Benefit	CH 1; NI 17A
Council Tax Benefit	CTB 1; RR 2
Disability Living Allowance	DS 704; HB 5
Disability Working Allowance	DWA 1; DS 703
Family Credit	FC 1; NI 261
Guardian's Allowance	NI 14
Housing Benefit	RR 1; RR 2
Incapacity Benefit	SSP 1; SC 1; IB 202
Income Support	IS 1; IS 26; IS 20
Industrial Injuries Disablement Benefit	NI 6
Invalid Care Allowance	DS 700; FB 31; HB 5
Maternity Allowance	FB 8; NI 17A; PL 958; MA 1
One Parent Benefit	CH 11
Residential care and nursing homes	IS 50
Severe Disablement Allowance	SDA 1; NI 252; NB 5
Social Fund Maternity Payment	FB 8; SB 16; SF 100
Statutory Maternity Pay	FB 8; NI 17A; PL 958
Statutory Sick Pay	NI 244 SSP
Unemployment Benefit	FB 9; NI 12
Widowed Mother's Allowance	BW 1; NP 45; D 49
Widow's Payment	BW 1; NP 45; D 49
Widow's Pension	BW 1; NP 45; D 49

♦ For helpful leaflets on redundancy go to your local Jobcentre, or write to: Customer Service Unit, The Redundancy Payments Office, 7th Floor, Hagley House, 83–85 Hagley House, Birmingham B16 8QG. Or call the Helpline on 0800 848489. Ask for leaflets PL 718, PL 833, PL 703, PL 699 and PL 808.

27

Pensions: Part 1

You can be young without money but you can't be old without it.
Tennessee Williams

You need to think seriously about pensions because you will probably spend a large part of your life depending on your pension(s). And you should think about pension provision as soon as possible because providing for a pension is a tax-efficient form of saving, and also because the sooner you start, the sooner compounding will work for you.

You may get a pension from three sources:

- The State: "the old age pension"
- Your employer: an occupational pension
- A personal pension scheme

You may qualify for only the State scheme, but many people will also qualify for a pension from their firm. Some people will qualify for all three: this may be a result of having spent a period working for an employer and a period of self-employment.

There can be little doubt that while pension provision is an important subject, most people avoid thinking about it. Pension jargon has a mind-numbing quality, and few young people can conceive of themselves at age 60 or 65. When I was young, it was fashionable not to trust anybody over 30, and I certainly could not conceive of myself after 30. Most young people simply ignore pensions. Middle-aged people think about them, but they may still be responsible for children who are draining their financial resources. By the time most people get round to both thinking about pension provision and being able to do something about it, they don't have much time left for their payments to compound to full effect.

But the picture need not be as bad as I have painted it. While most people will have limited options, a little thought can stop them doing positively silly things, some people will have the ability to make suitable provisions, and anybody who saves should think about whether saving through a pension plan would make sense. I've split my treatment of pensions into two chapters: many sections won't apply to you, and I point out where you should skip sections. So, grit your teeth and read on.

STATE PENSIONS

State pension benefits for retired people include Retirement Pension and additional pension benefits. I'm only going to discuss pensions here, but State benefits such as

Income Support don't stop when you reach retirement age. If your pension is inadequate, or if you don't qualify for a pension, you may still get State benefits (see Chapter 26).

You can get a State Retirement Pension if:

- You have reached pensionable age **and**

- You have enough National Insurance Contributions (NICs)

Pensionable age is currently 65 for a man and 60 for a woman. The two will be brought into line by gradually increasing the retirement age for women from 60 to 65 between the years 2010 and 2020. In other words, women born before 6 April 1950 will not be affected, those born between 6 April 1950 and 5 April 1955 will have a State pension age between 60 and 65, and women born on or after 6 April 1955 will get their pension when they reach 65.

If you are a man, and you retire before 65, you have to wait until age 65 to get your State pension. If you are a woman, the same rules apply but at age 60 (currently). If you are a married woman and you are claiming a pension on the basis of your husband's contributions, you will have to wait until he is age 65 before you can get a pension.

If you work past your retirement age, you won't get your pension until you retire, unless you are age 65 or more (for a woman) or 70 or more (for a man). At those ages you can get your pension and still work. If you postpone your retirement for all or part of the five years after the normal retirement age, you will get extra pension when you do retire. You will earn one-seventh of a penny for every pound of pension you postpone for a week, which works out at about a 7½% increase in your pension for every year you put off receiving it.

To get enough NICs you must either have made them yourself, or have them by virtue of another person's contributions. You can qualify in the second way if you are a married woman, a widow or a widower on the contribution record of your husband, late husband or late wife, respectively.

If you have led anything other than the simplest of lives, it is not easy to work out if you have enough NIC contributions to qualify for a full pension. Fortunately you don't have to work out your entitlement as the Benefit Agency will do it for you if you complete form BR19. For details, see READ 📖 WRITE 🖃 RING ☎. As a rule of thumb, you will qualify for a full pension if you have worked about 90% of a normal working life.

State Retirement Pension is made up of two parts plus other additions, if applicable. The two parts are:

- Basic Pension

- Additional Pension

The other additions are:

- Graduated Retirement Benefit

- Age Addition

Note also:

- Over 80 Pension

Basic Pension

If you qualify for a full Basic Pension on the basis of your own contributions it is currently worth £61.15 per week for a man or a woman. A wife who is not entitled to a pension on the basis of her contributions will be entitled to a maximum pension of £36.60 per week on the basis of her husband's contributions. This will give a married couple's pension of £97.75 per week. If the wife has earned a full pension on the basis of her contributions, the couple's pension will be £122.30 per week.

Additional Pension (SERPS)

The Additional Pension is an earnings-related supplement to the Basic Pension. It is generally known as SERPS, short for State Earnings-Related Pension Scheme. You get Additional Pension if in any year since April 1978 you have paid standard-rate Class 1 NICs as an employee and had earnings between the upper and lower band. These bands increase each year: in 1996–7 the weekly bonds are £61 and £455. (NICs are discussed in Chapter 8.) The maximum Additional Pension is currently about £5000 p.a.

When SERPS was devised, it was intended that you would get 25% of your middle band earnings (i.e., earnings between the two bands) as an additional pension. Specifically, you would get 1.25% times your best 20 years' earnings, and your earnings would not be your actual earnings, but your earnings revalued upwards in line with the annual increase in average national earnings (to take account of inflation over the period).

Not long after introducing SERPS, the Government became concerned about pension costs and changed the scheme. Now the scheme aims to deliver 20% of the band earnings and it is based on the average of revalued earnings over your entire working life (not the best 20 years). This obviously penalizes anybody who stops work for a period. The full effect of the new scheme will be felt in the year 2010. Between the years 2000 and 2010 there will be a transition from the old scheme to the new.

You should note that while having an occupational or company pension will not affect your Basic Pension, it may affect your Additional Pension. Employees and employers have the right to contract-out of SERPS. If you are contracted-out, your Additional Pension for that job will be reduced by a contracted-out deduction. Contracting out is discussed in the next chapter.

If you have found this general discussion hard to relate to your own position, don't worry, if you complete form BR19, the sums will be done for you.

Graduated Retirement Benefit

This benefit is based on the amount of graduated NICs you paid when the scheme existed between April 1961 and April 1975. Even if you are eligible, you will only qualify for a few pounds per week. Complete BR19 for details of your entitlement.

Age Addition

You will automatically get an increase in your Retirement Pension when you reach 80. In 1996–7 the addition is 25p, and no, that's not a typo.

Over 80 Pension

If you are aged 80 or over, and your State Retirement Pension is less than the amount payable on a spouse's contributions, you can, subject to certain conditions, get an Over 80 Pension of £36.60.

Your State pension forecast

I've mentioned form BR19 on a number of occasions. If you complete it you will get your State pension forecast. Even that is not an easy read—it will run to five or six pages. Since the State pension is a large part of the income of many older people, it is worth discussing the forecast letter. To make the discussion real, I'll use mine and then a divorced friend's (both forecasts were obviously obtained before 1996–7, so the forecasts aren't based on current pension rates).

My forecast begins by telling me:

- If I were getting a State Retirement Pension now, I would be entitled to £56.86 week based on my present National Insurance Contributions record

- By the time I am 65, I am likely to be entitled to a State Retirement Pension that would be £76.87 a week if I were getting it now

What the first bit means is that if I dropped out of the labour force now, my pension would be based solely on my past record. On that basis I would get £56.86, using the rates that apply today (i.e., when I completed BR19). I don't have the option of getting my State pension today because I'm not 65. Of course, if there is inflation between now and when I'm 65, and if the State pension rises with inflation, I'll get more.

If I continue working, I can improve my pension. The second statement is the Benefits Agency's stab at what I might get. Again, it uses the rates currently in force. They will be different when I'm 65.

How were the forecasts arrived at? We have to look at my Basic Pension, Additional Pension (SERPS), and Graduated Retirement Benefit.

For my Basic Pension, I've only paid enough NICs to get 66% of the full amount. That's not surprising as there are quite a few years to go before I'm 65, and I've lived abroad. Still, if I stop paying NICs, I'm stuck with my record to date, and that will get me 66% of the full pension, or £38.84. However, the letter tells me that if I go on working till 65, and pay full contributions, I could get a full pension of £58.85. The letter then points out that I might get credits in certain circumstances, and there is a page of discussion. Then my letter tells me that I didn't pay enough contributions in 1993–4 for that year to qualify, and how much it would cost to pay the missing contributions.

Moving on to Additional Pension, it seems I'm entitled to £48.77 per week. However, there will be a contracted-out deduction of £35.41, leaving £13.36, which is what the State will pay me. The deduction is because I belonged to two contracted-out schemes and I'll get at least as much as the contracted-out deduction from my two employers' schemes. So, I'll get £13.36 from the State, and at least £35.41 from private sector pensions. If I remain self-employed until age 65, I won't qualify for more Additional Pension (unlike my Basic Pension, which I can improve).

Finally, I'm entitled to £4.66 from Graduated Retirement Benefit. That's not much, mainly because nobody gets much, and because I was at school and university for part of the period to which it applies.

So, my total State pension is either:

- £38.84 + £13.36 + £4.66 = £56.86, at today's rates if I stop work now

- £58.85 + £13.36 + £4.66 = £76.87, at today's rates if I work to 65 and pay NICs

With either pension, it's going to be lentil bake rather than caviar.

My divorced friend has a somewhat different forecast. She is told that her forecast assumes that she got her decree absolute on a certain date and that she won't remarry before she is 60. If she does, she should ask for another forecast.

Her Basic Pension rights are calculated taking her former husband's contributions into account. Because of her date of birth, her State retirement age is 60. Currently she has qualified for more of her Basic Pension than I have, and it is worth more. But, if she keeps working to 60, and qualifies for a full Basic Pension, it will be worth the full current rate.

Her forecast contains some general information on NICs. In the past, many women paid reduced-rate NICs (the "small stamp"), and relied on their husbands' contributions to collect a pension. This option ceased in April 1977, but many women will still have the right to pay reduced-rate NICs. This right can be lost in certain circumstances, and in the case of my friend, she is told that she lost the right on 5 April 1980. (A woman still paying reduced-rate contributions needs to consider whether she should switch to the full rate. There may be some benefits from doing so if she will retire before her husband, he has a broken NICs record, or she might want to claim unemployment and other benefits. If you fall into any of these categories, call Social Security Freeline—see READ ⬜ WRITE ✎ RING ☎.)

My friend's Additional Pension statement is more complicated than mine. She is already entitled to a total Additional Pension of £24.48, of which £6.65 is a contracted-out deduction, so the State will pay her £17.83. Unlike me (unless I work for an employer), she can increase her Additional Pension. The estimate of its value if she goes on working to 60 has been calculated in two ways, but I'll spare you the details.

Now you know how my friend and I are placed, you should find out your position.

NON-STATE PENSIONS

There are two types of non-State pensions, occupational or employer pensions and personal pensions. I will discuss occupational pensions in this chapter, and personal pensions in the next. There are three issues that affect both types of pension, and I will discuss them first.

Tax savings

In calculating your income tax bill, your pension contributions are deducted from your income, and the bill worked out on the remainder. This tax-break is very attractive. Imagine that your marginal rate of income tax is 40%. On your last £100 of income you will pay £40 in tax and keep £60. You could invest that £60 if you wanted. However, if you put £100 into pension contributions, it is deducted from your pay before calculating your tax. You would therefore escape tax on the entire

£100. In effect, you invest £60, and the Inland Revenue invests £40 for you. Capital and income growth within the pension scheme is also free of tax. Go for it!

Inland Revenue limits

Making pension contributions is tax efficient, so it might be tempting to get your employer (if you have one) to pay you a low salary and make huge pension contributions for you, and for you to pay the maximum pension contribution you can. To stop this, the Inland Revenue has various limits that must be adhered to. These limits take a number of forms and have changed from time to time. I discuss some of the issues below, and give an overview for employer schemes and personal pension plans in the appendices to this chapter and the next.

The Inland Revenue limits are just that, limits. How much you will actually get is also dependent on the rules of your scheme, and how many years you have been in the scheme. One Inland Revenue limit is that you can't get a pension of more than two-thirds of your final salary, but most people don't get that much. There is a further limit for people who have joined a scheme on or after 1 June 1989, or joined an occupational scheme set up since 14 March 1989, and this is the "earnings cap". The earnings cap is usually increased each year in line with inflation. In 1996–7, the cap is £82 200. This is the maximum amount of earnings on which a pension may be calculated. Combined with the two-thirds final salary limit, the maximum pension would be £54 800. But you won't hit that limit if you don't earn as much as £82 200.

Lump sum

Although pension schemes are often seen as a way of completely escaping tax, that is not quite correct. You do escape tax when you put your money into a pension scheme, and the capital and income grows free of tax, but you will pay income tax on the pension when you receive it. Your pension is taxed as though it were earned income. Most schemes, as well as paying a pension, give the option of taking a tax-free cash lump sum on retirement. The exact amount varies with the type of scheme, and when you joined it, and details are given in the appendices to this and the next chapter. For example, with an employer scheme you might get a lump sum of 1½ times your final pay. On the lump sum, you really do escape tax totally. When you take a lump sum, you give up some of your monthly pension payment—because part of your pension pot has been given to you in cash rather than used to generate an income for you—but it is sensible to take the tax-free payment, especially as you can tax shelter it in TESSAs, PEPs, and National Savings products. You should remember that if you qualify for, say, a two-thirds final salary pension, you will receive less than that if you take a lump sum. In other words you can't qualify for both the maximum pension and maximum lump sum: if you take a lump sum it reduces your pension.

OCCUPATIONAL OR EMPLOYER PENSION SCHEMES

With an occupational or employer pension scheme, your employer makes contributions into the scheme on your behalf. These contributions don't count as a benefit-in-kind, and so you don't pay income tax on their value. You can contribute up to 15% of your earnings (including the value of most benefits-in-kind) and get tax relief. You will usually be required to make a contribution to an employer scheme, typically between 5% to 8% of your pay. In some schemes—non-contributory schemes—you won't have to make a contribution.

If you do not have, and have never had an occupational pension, you should move on to the next chapter.

Types of scheme

There are two main types of employer pension scheme:

- Final salary, or defined benefits schemes

- Money purchase, or defined contributions schemes

The vast majority of members in occupational pensions schemes are in *final salary schemes*. What this means is that your pension is based on your salary near to retirement. Because of inflation, most people will earn a higher salary in the final years of their working life than in the early years. You might also hope to get a higher salary because of promotions. Clearly, you want your pension based on your earnings at the end of your working life rather than at some other stage. Final salary schemes do this, although the details vary. Some use the average of your last three years, some use the best three consecutive years in the last 13 years, and there are other formulas. As well as your final salary, however defined, your pension will depend on the number of years you have been in the scheme.

What I have discussed determines your pension in the year of your retirement. If you were still working, you would expect to get pay rises every year. The average pay increase is about 2% above inflation. Pensioners are not so lucky. The best you can reasonably hope for is to have your pension fully indexed to the inflation rate, perhaps with some additional increases. Most pensions outside the public sector are not indexed, and in the past any increases that were paid were entirely at the discretion of the trustees. Many people started off reasonably well provided for, but were driven into poverty if inflation was rapid and they got no increase.

There are a large number of *money purchase employers' schemes*, although there are fewer members of these schemes than there are of final salary schemes. In money purchase employers' schemes the combined employer/employee contributions are invested. When you retire, the value of the investments is used to buy an annuity to pay you a pension. An annuity is like a reverse insurance policy. Instead of paying money each year to get a lump sum at the end, you pay over a lump sum for the right to an income for as long as you live. Annuities are discussed at length in the next chapter.

In a money purchase scheme, what your pension is worth will depend on how much was invested, how well the investments performed, and what interest rates were when your annuity was bought. You might get a bigger pension from a money purchase pension than from a final salary scheme, or you might get less. What is certain is that it will be hard to forecast your pension.

If you dislike risk, a money purchase scheme will be inferior to a final salary scheme. With a final salary scheme, the employer will be investing the contributions to provide a pension for you. If the investments do poorly, the employer will have to top up the pension pot. In a final salary scheme, the employer bears the risk of bad investment performance. In a money purchase scheme, you bear that risk. But if investment performance is good, you get the reward in a money purchase scheme. Unfortunately, you will have little choice as to whether you have a money purchase or final salary scheme, because most employees are offered an employer's final salary scheme, and it seldom makes sense to opt out of an employer scheme. In the future, however, there is likely to be a shift by employers to money purchase schemes.

Other benefits

Although it is natural to concentrate on your pension and the lump sum you get, there are other aspects of an employer's pension scheme that you should be aware of, in particular:

● What are the terms if you choose to retire early?

● What are the terms if you have to retire early because of ill-health?

● What benefits will your spouse and dependants get if you die before retirement?

● What benefits will your spouse and dependants get if you die after retirement?

● Is life insurance included?

You may feel that pension basics are hard enough to grapple with without going into all this as well. Unfortunately, that is not a sensible view. All these things matter because they affect how you should handle your investments. For example, if there is a lot of life insurance built into your pension package, you may feel that there is no need to take out any yourself. You can invest any free cash on something else. Also, if you transfer your pension, something I discuss in the next chapter, you will only be able to make a rational assessment if you know the value of all the factors I have just listed. I'll look at each factor in turn.

The idea of retiring early appeals to many people, and the Inland Revenue rules allow you to draw a pension from age 50, if your scheme permits. But for most people it's not practical. Think of a simple example. You start work at 20, retire at 65, and die at 75. You will have paid contributions for 45 years, and you will get a pension for 10. If you retire at 50, you will have contributed for 30 years and will draw a pension for 25 years. In the first case, you will have paid 4½ years of contribution for every year of pension, in the second case, you will have paid not much more than one. It should not be surprising that in most schemes your pension is cut dramatically if you retire early. Usually the amount you will get is determined by the scheme's actuary, who will aim to see that what you cost the scheme is the same no matter when you retire.

Inland Revenue rules, however, permit you to get two-thirds of your final salary, subject to a maximum of £54 800 if you joined your scheme on or after 1 June 1989, or before that date if the scheme was set up on or after 14 March 1989, and have 20 years' service (there are a few other complications I've omitted). You can take advantage of this in two ways. You may be retiring voluntarily, but your employer may also want you to go. In such a case you may be able to get your employer to pick up the cost of an enhanced pension. You may not do as well as the Inland Revenue limit, but you may do better than the actuary's sums. The second thing you can do is plan ahead and top-up your pension as much as possible with AVCs or FSAVCs (which are discussed later) so that you will get a higher pension and be able to retire early.

If you retire because you become permanently incapable of doing your job, you can get a pension from your date of retirement, whatever your age. The Inland Revenue maximum is two-thirds of your actual salary, but the years of service are reckoned as what you would have achieved with your firm had you been able to work to normal retirement age. Most firms' schemes are less generous.

If you die before you retire, your spouse or dependant can get a pension with a maximum of four-ninths of your salary at death under Inland Revenue rules. To get the maximum requires a "potential membership" of 10 years if you joined your scheme before 17 March 1987, or 20 years if you joined on or after 17 March 1987. If you joined after 1 June 1989 there is a maximum of 4/9ths of the earnings cap. "Potential membership" is the membership period you would have achieved had you lived until retirement age, although most schemes are less generous than the limit allows. Most pay the spouse's pension for life, but some stop it on remarriage. You can increase the spouse's pension by contributing to an AVC or FSAVC.

If you are a normal person, your mind will have glazed over as you read the previous paragraph. The only way to make the rules meaningful is to do the sums for your own situation. The applicable rules should be set out in your scheme details, a copy of which you will have been given by your employer. How much pension your spouse will get if you die is a factor that you should take account of in determining how much life insurance you need (see Chapter 23).

If you die after you retire, the maximum permitted pension your spouse or dependant can have is two-thirds of the pension you would have received had you not died and not taken a lump sum. Most schemes are less generous and typically pay about half.

Finally, you may get life insurance as part of your pension scheme. The Inland Revenue limit is for a tax-free lump sum of four times your salary at death (or a maximum of four times the earnings cap if you joined your scheme on or after 1 June 1989, or before that date if the scheme was set up on or after 14 March 1989) plus a refund of your pension contributions with interest. Once again, most schemes are less generous than the maximum.

AVC and FSAVC

You may find that your prospective pension isn't very good. That might be because you belong to a not very generous scheme, or because you have not been a member for very long. Or it could be the result of job-hopping as I discuss in the next section. Whatever the reason, you may wish to top up your pension.

Additional Voluntary Contributions (AVCs) and Free Standing Additional Voluntary Contributions (FSAVCs) are both ways of topping up your pension if you belong to an occupational scheme. As I noted above, you can pay up to 15% of your gross salary into your company pension fund each year, but most people are not required to pay this much. The difference between what you pay and 15% can be put in an AVC or FSAVC. If you joined your scheme on or after 1 June 1989, or before that date if the scheme was set up on or after 14 March 1989, an earnings cap will apply in addition, i.e., for tax year 1996–7, your total contributions must also not exceed £12 330 (which is 15% of £82 200).

Say you earn £50 000 and you pay 5% into your employer's scheme. Your earnings fall below the earnings cap so you can ignore that and you can contribute 10% (i.e., 15% – 5%) into an AVC or FSAVC. Be careful here. Your pension scheme will base its calculations on "pensionable earnings" as it defines them. These may not be your full earnings. It is common to count basic salary as pensionable earnings, but to exclude bonuses, and benefits-in-kind. If the £50 000 in my example consists of £25 000 basic and £25 000 bonus, and pensionable earnings are only the basic £25 000, your 5% contribution will be based on that. This means you will only be contributing 2½% of your total earnings to your company scheme, so you will be able to pay 12½% (i.e., 15% – 2½%) into an AVC or FSAVC.

Benefits from AVCs or FSAVCs and the company scheme together cannot exceed the maximum set by the Inland Revenue for a member's earnings and length of service. In other words AVCs and FSAVCs are a way of topping up the pension of those people with pension shortfalls, rather than a means of adding to an already substantial pension.

AVCs normally, and FSAVCs always, take the form of money purchase benefits. In the case of an AVC, the investment may be made in the main company scheme, although it can be into any scheme approved by the trustees, and the trend is away from using the main scheme. In the case of a FSAVC, the investment is made into any approved money purchase scheme available in the market place. Some AVCs take the form of an added years scheme. In this case you are granted credit for more years of service than you actually have.

Choosing between an AVC and a FSAVC is not easy. Generally an AVC will be cheaper because the provider's charges are usually borne by the company scheme. However, if you leave your company, your AVC is not portable. It will be lumped in with your company pension, although it can be used to increase its transfer value (discussed in the next chapter). A FSAVC is covered by the occupational scheme tax legislation, but is very much like a personal pension plan. If you leave your employment, your FSAVC is unaffected. You should probably consider a FSAVC in preference to an AVC only if you can contribute at least £100 per month.

JOB-HOPPERS GET LOWER FINAL SALARY PENSIONS

If you have an occupational final salary scheme and you have changed jobs often, you should be aware of the adverse effect that this may have on your pension.

Let's look at the experience of three men. All start work at 20 and earn £10 000. Steady Eddy stays with the same firm throughout his career and retires at age 60 on £50 000. His salary progression is shown in Table 27.1. Mobile Mike's career parallels Eddy's, but he has four employers. At age 30 Mike gets married to a girl who lives in a different town, so he switches to a firm in her home town. At age 40 Mike thinks the firm might be going bust so he switches to another firm. At age 50 Mike and wife move back to his home town to look after his ageing parents, so Mike changes

Table 27.1 Salaries at Various Ages for Three Men

Age	Steady Eddy	Mobile Mike	Fast-track Fred
20	10 000	10 000	10 000
30	20 000	20 000	20 000
40	30 000	30 000	36 000
50	40 000	40 000	52 000
60	50 000	50 000	72 000

employer again. Fred also starts out on £10 000 at age 20. But Fred is on the fast-track. He earns as much as Mike and Eddy at age 30, but then switches for a better-paid job. At age 40 and also at 50 he moves again for more pay.

I'll assume that all the jobs offer a pension based on the final year's salary multiplied by the number of years employed, divided by 60. (This means anyone working 40 years will get a pension of 40 ÷ 60, i.e., two-thirds final salary.) The relevant final years' salaries are shown in bold in Table 27.1.

Steady Eddy's pension is: $£50\,000 \times \dfrac{40}{60} = £33\,333$

Mobile Mike's pension is:

$$(£20\,000 \times \frac{10}{60}) + (£30\,000 \times \frac{10}{60}) + (£40\,000 \times \frac{10}{60}) + (£50\,000 \times \frac{10}{60}) = £23\,333$$

Fast-track Fred's pension is:

$$(£20\,000 \times \frac{10}{60}) + (£36\,000 \times \frac{10}{60}) + (£52\,000 \times \frac{10}{60}) + (£72\,000 \times \frac{10}{60}) = £30\,333$$

Steady Eddy gets a much higher pension than Mobile Mike. Although both had exactly the same incomes, because Mike has had several employers he retires on only 47% of his final salary, whereas Eddy retires on 66% of final salary. Fast-track Fred has switched jobs as often as Mike, but because he had higher salaries he retires on a higher pension. However, his pension may come as quite a shock, as it is only 42% of his final salary. In fact, despite earning much more than Eddy, Fred has a smaller pension.

Since 1986, all schemes of the type discussed here have had to provide to leavers a pension based on final salary increased each year by 5% or the RPI (Retail Price Index), whichever is the smaller, on that part of the preserved pension that is deemed to have accrued between 1 January 1985 and the date of ceasing employment until the date of retirement. For leavers who left after 1991, the revaluation applies to the entire period of service, not just since 1985. These rules obviously mitigate the pension problems caused by changing jobs, but only to a degree. First, the full benefit will take a long time to flow through. For example, if you were 50 on 1 January 1990, and changed your employer then, and you retire in 2000 having stayed with the same employer, you would only benefit from revaluation of five years of your pre-1990 preserved pension. Second, because of the 5% cap on increases, rapid inflation will still leave all job changers substantially exposed. Third, even if inflation remains below 5%, many early leavers will lose out because the deferred pension is linked to price inflation and not wage inflation, which is roughly 2% higher on average.

If you are in Mike or Eddy's position, you should consider boosting your pension by an AVC or FSAVC, or adding to your investments by buying a PEP (see "Alternatives to a Pension", p. 294).

SMALL SELF-ADMINISTERED SCHEMES (SSASs)

SSASs are approved occupational pension schemes with less than 12 members. There has to be some connection between the members, or between the members and the employer or trustee. If you are not in such a scheme and cannot be in one, you should skip this section.

SSASs are administered by an insurance company or other body, but the investments may be managed by the trustees. The assets may be invested directly in stocks and shares, cash, etc., or in insurance company funds, or in a mixture of the two. In small companies, where the fund members own the company, it is common for part of the fund to be invested in the business. For example, the fund can invest in property and lease it to the company at a commercial rent. The fund can also make loans to the company at a commercial rate (Base Rate plus 3%). In the first two years after setting up a SSAS, only 25% of the fund's assets may be loaned in this way, but after two years, up to 50% may be loaned. Normally only 5% of an occupational pension scheme's assets may be self-invested (i.e., invested in the company whose scheme it is), but this is waived if all members of the scheme are trustees, and all agree in writing to self-investment. It may be difficult to ensure fairness if all members of the SSAS are not owners of the company.

Additional tax planning opportunities arise in terms of the size of the pension contribution that the firm may make (to reduce profits and thus the amount of corporation tax). Apart from the effect on corporation tax, reducing profits will also lower the value of the company and its shares, which may be useful for inheritance tax purposes.

BEATING THE EARNINGS CAP

High earners who joined their employer's scheme on or after 1 June 1989, or before that date if the scheme was set up on or after 14 March 1989, will find their pension limited by the earnings cap of £82 200. You should skip this section if you don't earn that much. If you earn, say, £200 000 per year and are subject to the earnings cap, you will get a maximum pension worth about one-quarter of your salary. If you think you would like to retire on two-thirds final salary, you have a problem (but one most readers would be willing to have). If you have a personal pension you will encounter similar problems. How can you boost your pension?

In essence this is just the standard problem of investing outside of a pension fund to have money available at retirement age, although there are, in addition, unapproved pension schemes. I discuss non-pension means of providing income or capital at retirement in "Alternatives to a Pension" p. 294.

Unapproved Pension Schemes are a way of providing benefits in excess of those permitted in approved schemes. They come in two forms, funded and unfunded. While the details differ, the main point is that there is no special tax advantage. They are used exclusively for topping up funds. They are available only to employees (i.e., not the self-employed). If you have negotiating power and you are caught by the earnings cap, ask your employer about unapproved schemes. With a funded scheme, your employer's contributions will count as a benefit-in-kind, so your tax bill will rise.

APPENDIX: PENSION SCHEME LIMITS

The rules for pension schemes are complex. In addition there have been changes in the Inland Revenue requirements governing schemes. What follows is a brief outline of some of the limits for employer pension schemes. You should note that what is set out are maximums—your scheme might be operating well within the maximums so you might not get as much as the Inland Revenue allows. Most readers can skip the details here, but should read their own scheme's rules.

Employer schemes

It is important to know when you joined an employer scheme. There are three important dates:

- Before 17 March 1987

- On or after 17 March 1987 but before 1 June 1989 (and the scheme was set up before 14 March 1989)

- On or after 1 June 1989, or before that date if the scheme was set up on or after 14 March 1989

The limits differ for each of these three sets of dates. Read the section below which applies to you, but note that the rules applicable to the third situation may apply to you if joined before this date, and the members elected to be subject to these limits, and the scheme rules permitted it. There are special Inland Revenue limits for shareholding directors and people with benefits from previous employment or self-employment that I do not discuss.

Before 17 March 1987
- The maximum pension allowed by the Inland Revenue for these schemes is two-thirds final pay after a minimum of 10 years' service. If you take a lump sum, the maximum pension will be reduced.

- The maximum pension you can get varies with the years of service as shown in Table 27.2.

- The maximum lump sum you can get is $1^{1}2$ times your final pay after at least 20 years' service.

- The maximum level of contributions you can make and get tax relief is 15% of your earnings plus most benefits-in-kind. If you contribute less, you can invest the difference in an AVC or a FSAVC.

Table 27.2 Years of Service and Pension as a Fraction of Final Pay

Years of service	Pension as a fraction of final pay
1 to 5	1/60 for each year
6	8/60
7	16/60
8	24/60
9	32/60
10	2/3

- There are additional rules covering death in service lump sum, death in service spouses pension, death in retirement pension, early retirement, late retirement, etc.

On or after 17 March 1987 but before 1 June 1989 (and the scheme was set up before 14 March 1989)

- The maximum pension allowed by the Inland Revenue for these schemes is two-thirds final pay after a minimum of 20 years' service. If you take a lump sum, the maximum pension will be reduced.

- The maximum pension you can get varies with the years of service. It is 1/30th of your years in your scheme, but subject to a maximum of 2/3. (E.g., for 15 years' service: (15 ÷ 30 = ½ final salary.)

- The maximum lump sum you can get is 1½ times your final pay after at least 20 years' service, with a maximum money value of £150 000.

- The maximum level of contributions you can make and get tax relief is 15% of your earnings plus most benefits-in-kind. If you contribute less, you can invest the difference in an AVC or a FSAVC.

- There are additional rules covering death in service lump sum, death in service spouses pension, death in retirement pension, early retirement, late retirement, etc.

On or after 1 June 1989, or before that date if the scheme was set up on or after 14 March 1989

- The maximum pension allowed by the Inland Revenue for these schemes is two-thirds final pay after a minimum of 20 years' service, with a limit of £54 800. This sum is two-thirds of the earnings cap, which is usually increased each year in line with inflation. If you take a lump sum, the maximum pension will be reduced.

- The maximum pension you can get varies with the years of service. It is 1/30th of your years in your scheme, but subject to a maximum of 2/3 and the limit above.

- The maximum lump sum you can get is 1½ times your final pay after at least 20 years' service, with a maximum money value of £123 300, a sum usually increased each year.

- The maximum level of contributions you can make and get tax relief on is 15% of your earnings plus most benefits-in-kind, subject to a maximum of £12 330. If you contribute less, you can invest the difference in an AVC or a FSAVC.

- There are additional rules covering death in service lump sum, death in service spouses pension, death in retirement pension, early retirement, late retirement, etc.

READ 📖 WRITE 🖃 RING ☎

♦ The basics of the State pension system are set out in the mind-numbing *A Guide to Retirement Pensions*. To get a copy, visit your local Social Security office (address in the phone book under Social Security or Benefits Agency). You might get a copy in some Post Offices or your local public library. Or write to BA Distribution and Storage Centre, Manchester Road, Heywood, Lancashire, OL10 2PZ and request leaflet NP46, or call the Social Security Freeline, 0800 666 555. The form you need to get a pension forecast is BR19: write to Heywood or call Freeline.

♦ The Pensions Schemes Office (a department of the Inland Revenue) publishes useful booklets for pension scheme members including *Occupational Schemes: An Introduction*, and *Occupational Pension Schemes: A Guide for Members of Tax Approved Schemes*. Available from Tax Offices and Tax Enquiry Centres, or call 0115 974 1670.

♦ For a list of AVC and FSAVC providers see Linda Drake, "Building Up Pension Income", *Planned Savings*, November 1995, 55–69.

♦ If you want to find a financial adviser to help you with your pension planning, see the sources listed in READ 📖 WRITE 🖃 RING ☎ in Chapter 10.

28

Pensions: Part 2

Old age is the most unexpected of all things that happen to a man.
Leon Trotsky

In this chapter I continue my discussion of pensions. I look at personal pension plans (which will only be of interest to some readers, as I explain shortly), and also some general topics such as contracting-out, pension options when leaving an employer, and pensions versus alternative investments.

PERSONAL PENSION PLANS

You can have a personal pension plan if any of the following apply:

- Your employer doesn't have a pension scheme

- You have two jobs, one of which doesn't have a pension scheme

- You are self-employed

- You've chosen not to join your employer's scheme

- You've personally contracted-out of SERPs

- You've taken a personal pension plan to receive a transfer payment from another scheme

You should skip this and the next section if you are in an occupational pension scheme and don't have a personal pension plan, unless you have a FSAVC, in which case you should read the next section.

Personal pension plans are all money purchase, or defined contribution, schemes. What you get depends on the amount invested, the investment performance and annuity rates at the time your pension is purchased, and is not directly related to your salary. I discussed money purchase schemes in the last two paragraphs in the section "Types of Scheme", p. 269.

The discussion that follows relates to the first three reasons for having a personal pension plan. Subsequent sections deal with occupational versus personal pension plan, contracting-out and transfers.

Strictly speaking the term personal pension plans refers to a specific type of plan taken out on or after 1 July 1988. However, the term is also used to cover retirement annuity policies (RAPs), sometimes called Section 226 policies. RAPs pre-date personal pension plans. Existing plans remain in effect, but no new plans have been permitted since 30 June 1988.

The main details of the two types of policy are set out in the appendix to this chapter. The maximum contribution attracting tax relief is 17½% of earnings for younger persons and this increases to a maximum of 27.5% for RAPs and 40% for personal pension plans. After age 35, the percentage of earnings that may be put into a RAP is lower than for a personal pension plan. The earnings cap, however, does not apply to RAPs whereas it does apply to personal pension plans. This means for people age 36 or over, if incomes are sufficiently large, a greater contribution in money terms can be made via RAPs, despite the lower permitted percentage. For example, for someone in the 36 to 45 age group, more can be contributed via a RAP if their salary exceeds £93 943 (i.e., 17.5% × £93 943 = 20% × £82 200). This break-even rate rises to a peak of £127 867 for the 56 to 60 age group. There are other differences between RAPs and personal pension plans, such as the minimum permitted retirement age, the size of the tax-free lump sum, and so forth. If you have a RAP, you should take advice as to whether you should continue to contribute to it or whether you should start a personal pension plan.

For either type of personal pension, contributions are calculated as a percentage of your pay and the value of most benefits-in-kind if you are employed, or on taxable profits if you are self-employed. An employer may make contributions for you to a personal pension plan (but not a RAP) but, unlike a final salary scheme, these contributions count as part of your permitted contributions. You may make contributions to a number of plans providing your total contributions fall within the permitted limits. While contributing to several plans will reduce your investment risk through diversification, there are usually set-up costs and monthly minimum payments so that this strategy only makes sense for a high earner. How high is high? It depends on the charges for the plans you are considering, but you probably should be contributing at least £100 a month to each plan you set up.

Many people who are not in company pension schemes are lax about setting up a personal pension plan. An important consideration with personal pension plans is that you can carry back contributions and carry forward reliefs.

You can carry back contributions for one year. Thus, if you make a contribution in 1996–7, you can have it treated as though it were made in 1995–6. This enables you to fully use up the relief of the earlier year. If there were no net relevant earnings in that year you can go back to 1994–5. You can do all this before you use up 1996–7's relief. Tax relief is given at the tax rate applicable in the earlier year.

You can carry forward unused relief for six years, but in this case you must have first used up this year's relief. Thus if you have used up all the 1996–7 relief you can use any unused relief in the period 1990–1 to 1995–6. You use up relief from the earliest years first, and relief is given at the current year's rate.

If you do not have an occupational pension, and you have not been putting money into a personal pension plan, making use of your carry back and carry forward contributions could be one of the best investment decisions you ever make.

INVESTING YOUR PERSONAL PENSION PLAN

Mastering the rules of pension plans is hard enough, but with a personal pension plan, and FSAVC, you have to decide how to invest the money which will pay your pension. There are two main ways of doing this—you can give it to a life insurance company, unit trust or investment trust company, which I'll call external management, or you can manage it yourself in the form of a Self-Invested Personal Pension (SIPP).

External management

The vast bulk of personal pension plans are with life insurance companies, although this is likely to change because of increased competition from investment trust and unit trust companies. If you go to a traditional life insurance company for your personal pension plan you will usually be able to have it invested in the following ways:

- Deposit administration

- Unit-linked

- With-profits

- Without-profits

I have covered these types of investment—with the exception of deposit administration—in Chapter 23, but I'll briefly state the key points here.

Deposit administration   This is, in effect, a deposit account. Your cash earns interest, and is safe from actual loss. With high interest rates you will do well in money terms but you may not beat inflation. This type of plan is often taken up in the last few years before retirement to avoid the risk of a stockmarket crash.

Unit-linked   In a unit-linked plan you are in effect buying unit trusts, but these are unit trusts only available for personal pension plans. As is pointed out in the adverts, unit trust prices may fall as well as rise. Usually there is no guarantee as to what you will receive. You can sometimes spread the risk by investing in a number of funds; you can usually invest in cash, fixed interest stocks, equities, property and a managed fund, which will invest in all of these asset types. Most people who have a unit-linked plan opt for the managed fund, but you don't have to. The return you get will be a function of the funds you select, whose performance will in turn depend on the performance of the underlying markets, the investment manager's performance, and the costs.

With-profits   This policy is invested in a number of asset types by the manager. You will get a guaranteed minimum sum when you retire but you will expect to do better because of bonuses (the "profits"). These will depend on investment performance, a function of both the underlying markets and your manager's performance. There are two types of bonus, reversionary, which is usually annual, and terminal. Once a reversionary bonus is declared, you cannot lose it. As a result, these bonuses tend to be somewhat lower than fund performance justifies. At the end of the plan, a terminal bonus will reflect overall performance.

Without profits These policies give a guaranteed return. To ensure it can be achieved, it is likely to be low. This sort of policy is only suitable for someone close to retirement.

Although the life insurance companies dominate the market, some of the unit trust and investment trust companies have entered the market and investment is made in their various trusts. The risks—and opportunities—are similar to an insurance company's unit-linked policy.

Selecting a personal pension provider

You would be wise to get independent advice when you select a pension provider. As a minimum you have to consider:

- Your attitude to risk and return
- The charges
- Product flexibility
- Investment performance
- Financial strength of the provider
- Quality of service

I'll comment briefly on some of these points.

In the previous sub-section I discussed the various ways a fund can be invested. If you think unit-linked, investment trusts and unit trusts are too risky, you should be looking at with-profits or deposit administration. Neither would be my choice, but if that's what you feel happy with, you should be looking at product providers that offer those options.

Personal pension plans can be on a regular premium basis, where the premium is paid every month say, or on a single premium basis where only a single payment is made. It is possible to pay, say annually, what you would have paid in regular premiums over the course of a year, and each year you take out a new single premium policy. This approach can be cheaper (administration costs are lower), but many advisers feel that few people have the will-power to do it, and many end up with inadequate pension provision because they skip some years.

Product providers give an illustration of your returns by assuming an illustrative growth for your investment, but deducting their actual charges. Thus for an assumed regular premium investment of, say, £200 per month, or £2400 recurring single premium, for a 20-year period, it is possible to calculate what this would grow to in money terms at, say, 9% per annum, and what the actual money charges would be. The difference is the money value of the plan. Alternatively one can work out what the rate of growth to the policy holder would be after allowing for charges. For example, an assumed investment return of 9% per annum might be reduced to 8% after charges have been borne. In a survey of some of the major providers by the *Financial Times*, the growth after charges on a 9% pre-charges assumption varied between 8.3% and 6.7%. There is no obvious reason why anyone should buy a high-charge fund. Amongst the cheapest providers were some of the investment trust and unit trust providers.

A different way of looking at charges is to ask what transfer value you would get if you transferred your pension at various stages. Again the range is wide. For example, with a regular premium policy of £2400 and a 20-year term, assuming 9% growth, the *Financial Times* survey found that Foreign and Colonial would have given transfer values after 1, 3 and 10 years of £2477, £8194 and £37 440 respectively. Laurentian Life would have given values of £0, £3440 and £28 700 for the same periods.

Product flexibility is desirable. There are a number of issues here:

- You should consider the number of funds available to you in case you want to change your investment strategy and, in particular, want to switch from an equity fund to a more cash-based fund when you get close to retirement.

- You should be able to stop your premiums without penalty. Who knows if you will always be able to make contributions? You might lose your job, or join an employer's scheme.

- You should be able to retire earlier than you had planned without penalty.

- You should be able to have a number of pension plans (which is called segmentation) so that you can phase your retirement if you want, and take the benefits from some of your plans by stages.

If you believe my discussion about investment performance (Chapter 14) you will pay little attention to past performance and concentrate more on other factors. Low charges give a head start in the performance stakes. You might want to select a low-cost provider from the best performing half of the providers over the last five years. If you think I'm too sceptical, consider this. According to pensions consultant John Sheffield, the top managers in 1989 were Colonial Mutual, Provident Mutual, London & Manchester, British Life and Confederation Life. In 1994 they ranked 73rd, 60th, 8th, 77th, and 70th respectively out of 82 funds. London & Manchester had two personal pension contracts, and if you had selected the wrong one, you would have been 71st instead of 8th.

Most people will be unable to judge the financial strength of the provider and the quality of service. An independent adviser can help you.

Finally, to select your product provider, you will have to weigh up all the above factors. Again you may prefer to rely on an IFA. You may also find it helpful to look at some articles that attempt to rate product providers. Several are listed in READ 📖 WRITE 🖅 RING ☎.

Self-Invested Personal Pensions (SIPPs)

SIPPs are a specialized form of personal pension which may interest those people who have considerable investment expertise and who want to manage their own pension fund, or the sole trader or a partnership that wants to buy commercial property. The rules in terms of contributions and benefits are the same as for other personal pension schemes.

SIPPs were first allowed in October 1989, and there are still only a few firms providing them, with a very small number of plans in operation (see READ 📖 WRITE 🖅 RING ☎). The idea was to allow pension plan holders more control over how their plan is managed. The plan can be self-managed or given to a manager. In either case it will be administered by an insurance company, stockbroker or a specialist company. The Inland Revenue permits investments to be made in deposit accounts, stocks and shares quoted on UK and overseas recognized exchanges, unit trusts and investment trusts, insurance company with-profit and unit-linked funds, and commercial property.

Although SIPPs might seem like the ideal plan for somebody interested in investments, most of the conventionally managed SIPPs appear to have been given to stockbrokers to manage on a discretionary basis. That seems to me to negate the main attraction of a SIPP. In general you need a pension fund of at least £50 000, or to be making annual contributions of about £10 000, for a SIPP to be an economic choice.

For sole traders and partnerships, SIPPs provide a way of funding the business in a tax efficient manner. If the business wants to buy its own commercial property and has cash, the cash can be put into the SIPP, attracting tax relief, and the SIPP can buy the property and lease it to the pension holder's business. Alternatively, an existing pension scheme might be transferred into the SIPP and the proceeds used to purchase property. Despite the tax efficiency of these plans, anyone thinking of doing either should consider the wisdom of such action. Is a single property a wise investment for a pension fund? If your business is strapped for cash, is it wise to raid your pension fund? Do you want to risk losing both?

ANNUITIES

There are two reasons why you might have an annuity: you may have to—when you retire, money purchase pension schemes have to be converted to an annuity—or you may want to. If you are forced to buy an annuity because the money comes from a pension scheme, it is called a scheme annuity or compulsory annuity, and if you choose to buy it but don't have to, it is a purchased life annuity. I'll cover both types here, concentrating on scheme annuities.

So what is an annuity? It's like a reverse insurance policy. Instead of saving money each year to get a lump sum at the end, you pay over a lump sum for the right to an income for as long as you live, or some specified period. How much you will get will depend on the terms of the annuity, your age, sex and interest rates at the time the policy is taken out. A person who buys an annuity is called an annuitant.

When you purchase an annuity you will receive an income that consists partly of interest on your capital and partly a return of your capital. Obviously the younger you are, the longer the payments are likely to continue, so the smaller the income you will receive. Since women live longer than men, a woman will get a smaller income than a man of the same age. The usual benchmark annuity is an *immediate level annuity*. Here the income payments begin as soon as the annuity is purchased, and the payments are made at a constant, or level, rate.

For people who choose to buy an annuity, the Inland Revenue recognizes that part of the income from an annuity is a return of capital and only the interest element is taxed. Lower rate tax is deducted by the annuity provider, but non-taxpayers can reclaim the appropriate sum, and higher rate taxpayers will have to pay a further 20%. Although the interest and capital component of the annuity varies over the duration of the annuity, the interest payment is assumed constant for the purposes of tax. Its value is agreed between the provider and the Inland Revenue. If you get an annuity through a pension scheme, all the annuity income is taxed as earned income. (That's fair, you got a tax-break in your pension scheme when you were amassing the sum used to buy the annuity.)

There are three obvious problems with level annuities. The income is fixed, which will mean falling real income if there is inflation. Second, when an annuity is bought, the capital used is gone for ever. If you die tomorrow, your estate will not get anything. (Of course, if you live for much longer than average, you will do very well.) Third, a couple will want the income flow to last as long as either is alive. To overcome these, and other problems, a number of variations on the immediate level annuity are available. They all involve a lower starting income:

- *Escalating annuities* pay an increased sum each year: the escalation may be inadequate to match inflation

- *Index-linked annuities* pay a sum that increases in line with inflation

- *With-profit annuities* pay income which is dependent on the investment performance of a with-profits fund: there may be a guaranteed income, but this will be low

- *Unit-linked annuities* pay income which is dependent on the investment performance of a with-profits fund: there may be a guaranteed income, but this will be low

For each type of annuity, other variations are possible:

- *Capital protected annuities* make payments for a guaranteed minimum period (to the annuitant's estate if necessary)

- *Joint life/last survivor annuities* pay income until the death of the surviving spouse (at the same rate, two-thirds, or one-third of the original income)

Table 28.1 gives an indication of the income from three types of annuity.

Most annuities are immediate, and for life, but there are also:

- *Temporary annuities* which pay for a set number of years

- *Deferred annuities* which are purchased some time before the income is paid out

Purchased life annuities are usually only recommended for older people (say 70 for men and 75 for women). The older you are, the higher the income you will get, and the fewer the years you will be exposed to inflation. Age is less important in determining the income from a temporary annuity, and may be used by anyone to fund regular outgoings. A typical use of a deferred annuity is by a grandparent who might buy one when a grandchild is born, with the income to commence at the start of the child's education.

Timing an annuity purchase

I mentioned that the income you will get from an annuity depends partly on the level of interest rates. Obviously, the higher interest rates are, the more interest your lump sum will attract, and the greater the income the product provider can pay you. To make sure the books balance, all the calculations are based on the rates the provider

Table 28.1 Indicative Annuity Rates for Various Situations
£, for purchase price of £10 000, Autumn 1995

	Male 65	Male 70	Female 60	Female 65	Male 65/ Female 60	Male 75/ Female 70
Immediate Annuity	1195	1365	980	1030		
Escalating Annuity 5% Compound	820	1015	575	675		
Immediate Annuity Joint Last Survivor					885	1065

can lock into on the day you part with your lump sum. Since interest rates fluctuate, the terms for annuities bought only a few months apart may differ significantly. Over slightly longer periods the differences can be very large indeed: between October 1990 and January 1994, annuity rates fell by about 30%.

Such changes pose a problem for anybody wishing to buy an annuity, but were especially harsh on somebody in a money purchase pension scheme who had to purchase the annuity immediately on retirement. There was an offsetting factor, to some extent, in as much as the stockmarket would tend to be at a high level when interest rates were low, and vice versa, so that more money would be available to purchase an annuity when rates were low. But this is only a rough and ready relationship, and there was always the danger that an annuity had to be purchased at an unfavourable time. With personal pension plans there is freedom to retire at any time between 50 and 75, so you could choose to retire at a time annuity rates were favourable. But few people either think in these terms, or have the flexibility to retire when rates are favourable. Moreover, if you retire early, to take advantage of high annuity rates, there may be early surrender penalties that offset the benefit. However, the rules on pension annuities have recently been changed to give more leeway.

Now, personal pension plan holders can defer buying an annuity until age 75, even if they have retired. The option to defer purchasing an annuity has been known as a "flexible annuity", but the terms "income withdrawal" and "pension withdrawal" are now being used. With pension withdrawal, an income can be taken from the pension plan before the annuity is purchased. The maximum income is related to the yield on high-coupon 15-year gilts. There is a minimum income level that must be taken and this is 35% of the maximum level. The level of income has to be reviewed every three years. There are detailed rules relating to the treatment of the pension fund if the policy holder dies while drawing income, but before buying an annuity. If you elect for pension withdrawal, you must take your tax-free lump sum at the same time—assuming you intend to take a lump sum.

An example may be useful. A 65-year-old man has a personal pension plan and takes a lump sum on retirement, but defer purchasing an annuity. The rest of his fund is worth £100 000. In Autumn 1995, with high-coupon 15-year gilts yielding about 8.25%, the maximum annual income per £1000 was £116 (according to official tables) so his maximum income would have been £116 × 100 000 ÷ 1000 = £11 600, and the minimum would have been £11 600 × 35% = £4060. For a woman aged 65, the annual income per £1000 was £105, so the corresponding figures were £10 500 and £3675. If you retire early, the maximum income will be lower. For a man and a woman aged 50, the annual income per £1000 was £92 and £88 respectively.

Pension withdrawal is not without its risks. The value of the annuity eventually purchased will depend on the increase or decrease in the value of the investment fund from the retirement date to the date the annuity is purchased, as well as the annuity rate. One way to reduce this risk is by playing the averages, and to take staggered vesting or phased retirement. This allows part of the fund to be converted to an annuity (and up to 25% of that part of the fund to be taken as cash), and the process repeated periodically. Another way of reducing risk is by only taking pension withdrawal if you can wait at least five years before buying the annuity (recall the discussion about equities, risk and time in Chapter 21).

However a deferment in purchasing an annuity is effected, there will be set-up costs and costs in managing the portfolio. Most advisers suggest that it will only be economic to have pension withdrawal if your pension fund is worth more than £100 000, but some suggest much more.

The new annuity freedoms only apply to personal pension plans. They don't apply to retirement annuity plans (RAPs), or to money purchase occupational plans (see Chapter 27), although there are plans to include these. If you have one of these plans you will have to switch to a personal pension plan to benefit from the new rules. However, there may be a charge to make the switch, and the rules on tax-free lump sums differ between RAPs, occupational schemes and personal pension plans. In general, the older you are, the less attractive it will be to make a switch. Seek advice before making a move.

Getting the best annuity rate

If you are buying a purchased life annuity, you can obviously buy from any provider. If you are buying a compulsory annuity, you have the same option. Pension plans have an "open market option" which allows you to shop around for the best rate. The chances are that your fund manager will not be offering the best annuity rate available. Annuity advisers state that there can be a 10–15% difference in annuity rates amongst the large insurers, and an even greater difference amongst all insurers. Yet, less than 20% of all retirees exercise their open market option.

The weekend national press gives the names of companies offering some of the best annuity rates, but the lists are always very limited with regard to the types of annuities shown. It makes sense to get the help of an independent financial adviser who has a computer system listing the best rates. This is a one-time decision that could make a 20% difference in your pension's value. You are not allowed to subsequently change your mind and go to another insurance company. You should also get advice as to which of the various types of annuity is best for you.

Remember: *with a personal pension plan there are two investment decisions—investing the contributions, and buying an annuity. Most people focus on the first, and forget the second.*

OCCUPATIONAL VERSUS PERSONAL PENSIONS

Since 1988 you have been able to opt out of an occupational pension scheme and have a personal pension. It almost never makes sense to do so. The reason is simple.

In an occupational scheme you might make pension contributions of, say, 5% of your salary, and your employer might pay 10%. When you decide to opt out and have a personal pension, it is up to your employer whether to contribute or not. Most don't. This means you are giving up, in my example, a tax-free sum worth 10% of your income. No matter how bad your occupational scheme, you won't be able to use your 5% of contribution to outperform 15% of contribution. Indeed, with a non-contributory scheme you get the pension, no matter how bad, for free, and you can invest up to 15% in a FSAVC. That has to be better than a personal pension plan.

One reason companies seldom contribute to personal pensions is the burden of paying lots of different sums to different pension providers. Some companies have set up group personal pensions whereby they will make a contribution to a personal pension as long as you have it with a specified provider. In such a case it may be worth having a personal pension plan instead of an occupational pension if one is on offer.

In the coming years, group personal pensions are likely to become more common. The burden of final salary schemes on employers has been increasing, and the provisions of the Pensions Act 1995, which will take effect in April 1997, will further increase the burden. Some estimates suggest as much as a 25% increase in employer contributions will be required. Contracted-out money purchase schemes will also be affected. The result is that many companies are likely to close their existing schemes to new members and start group personal pensions. That way they offer a "company scheme" but escape some of the burdens. See READ 📖 WRITE 🖅 RING ☎.

CONTRACTING-OUT

In the previous chapter, I discussed the State Pension and SERPS. The idea behind SERPS is sound—people will want to retire on a pension that bears some relation to the salary they have been receiving. The problem with SERPS as it exists is that the government is unsure that the public purse can afford it. From the recipient's point of view the scheme doesn't really relate pension to final salary. There is no recognition of earnings above the upper band, and only part of earnings between the bands is considered, and the part that will be recognized in future years will relate to lifetime earnings and not the salary at retirement. Further, SERPS pension can only be taken at the statutory retirement age and there is no tax-free lump sum as there is with private schemes.

To reduce the burden of SERPS, the government allows firms and employees to contract-out of it. In return, employer and employees pay reduced NICs. In many cases you will not have a decision to make. Most company final salary schemes have contracted-out and the self-employed are not in SERPS at all, and so don't have to make a decision.

There are three main ways you can be contracted-out of SERPS:

● You are a member of a contracted-out final salary scheme

● You are a member of a contracted-out money purchase scheme (COMPS)

● You have personally contracted-out with an appropriate personal pension scheme (APPS) even though your scheme is contracted-in, or you are not in a scheme

In a contracted-out occupational scheme, both employer and employee pay lower NICs. The employers' contributions are reduced by 3% of each employee's middle band earnings and the employee's contributions are reduced by 1.8%. This reduction in contributions is called the "rebate" and is invested in a pension plan.

For a scheme to be able to contract-out, it must offer benefits in place of the SERPS pension. For members of a final salary scheme that has contracted-out, a member's and widow's pension must be offered which are as good as the SERPS pensions. In addition, the pensions must increase by the lower of the rate of inflation or 3% per annum. If inflation exceeds 3%, the State will pay the difference. These pensions are called Guaranteed Minimum Pensions (GMPs). GMPs cannot be commuted for cash (i.e., you can't take a tax-free lump sum).

This is a good deal for the employee. The pension may be better than SERPS, but won't be worse. This situation will change from April 1997, when the link between SERPS and employers' schemes will be broken. GMP will be abolished, and contracted-out final salary schemes will have to provide benefits based on 1/80th of final pay for each year of service. Final pay will be calculated by reference to 90% of the average of the last three years' earnings between the upper and lower earnings limits.

If you are a member of a contracted-out money purchase employer scheme, the NIC rebate is invested in a fund to provide "protected rights." As in the previous case, a member's and spouse's pension must be provided, and the annual increase will be the lower of the rate of inflation or 3%. The value of the protected rights will depend on the performance of the investments in the fund and the annuity rate when the pension is purchased. You could do much better than SERPS, or much worse.

Finally, if you are in a scheme that is contracted-in, or you are not in an occupational scheme, you can decide to contract-out. You do this via an appropriate personal pension scheme (APPS). Both employer and employee will continue to pay contracted-in NICs, but the APPS provider will reclaim the appropriate sum from the DSS. In addition there is tax relief on the employee's NIC rebate of 0.6%. To encourage contracting-out, the State at first offered a 2% bonus. This was subsequently reduced to 1% of band earnings for APPS members aged 30 or over. It will be changed again in 1997.

If you are in a scheme that has contracted-in, should you personally contract-out? It is hard to say, for the value of your pension could be better or worse than under SERPS, depending on your contracted-out fund's performance and the annuity rates at the time you retire. There is also a trade-off to be made between the rebate bonus and high personal pension plan charges. Also, you may change jobs and join a scheme that has contracted-out, so you will stop making payments into your plan. Some providers impose a penalty charge if you stop making payments. The most general advice is that the lower your income, and the older you are, the more likely it is that you should stay in the State scheme.

The fixed charges in an APPS will kill your return if you are not investing much. The usual advice is to stay in SERPS if you earn less than around £8000 to £10 000. With an income of £10 000, the amount available to be invested in an APPS is only about £400—a bit higher if you are 30 or over, a bit lower if you are under 30. The maximum that is available is £1311 (in 1996–7) for those earning £23 660 and above. As to age, the fewer years you have to work, the less time your money has to grow to offset the charges. Also the older you are, the higher your salary is likely to be. These are the years you want in SERPS to pull up your average earnings. All this means that young people have the greatest incentive to contract-out, but they should note the bonus is only given from age 30.

If you have contracted-out, you are permitted to contract back in. As a rule of thumb, men in their early 40s should contract back in, as should women in their mid-30s.

If, after reading this, you think you should contract back in, you should be aware that it is the Government's intention to make contracting out more attractive by providing age-related NIC rebates for both money purchase and appropriate personal pension schemes. These rebates will be higher for APPS than for COMPS, because of the higher charges levied by the former. The Government has announced that these rebates will be capped, but at a level that is likely to be lower than the rebate required on the basis of actuarial calculations for employees over 50 years of age. Thus it is likely that age-related rebates will raise the age at which you should contract back into SERPS, rather than completely remove the incentive to contract back in. Let's face it, deciding whether to contract in or out is a nightmare: get advice before you contract-out and get advice if you are contracted-out and are a woman aged 35 or more, or a man aged 40 or more.

Warning

Some people tell advisers that they have a personal pension plan so they are OK on the pension front. Sometimes it turns out that they mean that they have an APPS. This is indeed a personal pension plan, but it only replaces SERPS, and will give you a very modest pension. If you don't have an occupational pension and if your only personal pension is investing the rebate, you are making inadequate pension provision. Seek advice, today.

PENSION OPTIONS WHEN LEAVING AN EMPLOYER

If you leave your employer before normal retirement age, and you have an occupational pension, there are a number of ways your pension rights may be treated:

- You may get a refund of contributions if pensionable service is less than two years
- You may get a deferred or frozen pension (although "frozen" is not really an appropriate term since the pension must be revalued)
- You can take a transfer which must go into one of
  - Your new employer's scheme
  - A single premium policy from an insurance company or other provider (known as a "Section 32 buy-out")
  - A personal pension plan

It is important to make sure that all the rights under a final salary scheme are taken into account when making a decision. These rights will include the following (which are taken from FIMBRA Guidance Note 7):

a) Guaranteed pension at retirement
b) Spouses' and children's' pensions

c) Indexation of pensions in payment both guaranteed and discretionary
d) Guarantees under GMPs
e) Statutory indexation of preserved benefits and the history of discretionary increases provided
f) Risk benefits payable on death or long-term disability or illness
g) The "transfer club" rights applicable for members of public sector schemes
h) The beneficiaries' age and attitude to investment risk
i) The potential for loss on moving from "uncapped" final salary benefits to "capped" personal pensions for pre-1989 scheme beneficiaries
j) The prospect of the final salary scheme benefits increasing further as a result of the Pensions Act
k) The view taken on the financial security of the pension scheme, for example by reference to the Trustees' Report and Accounts and also the composition of the Board of Trustees.

This list should make you aware of the complexity of changing your pension arrangements and the value of getting advice. I'll look briefly at each of the options when you leave an employer.

Refund of contributions

If you have been in your employer's occupational pension plan for less than two years, you may get a refund of your contributions (less 20% tax). If the scheme is contracted-out, there will be a deduction to contract back into SERPS. Your employer's contributions will not be refunded.

Deferred or frozen pensions

It is possible to leave an employer, but stay in the pension plan. This option must be given to you if you have been in a scheme for more than two years. In a defined benefits scheme, what usually happens is that the entitlement you have earned, such as 10/60ths, is applied to your salary when you leave the scheme. Of course, if there is rapid inflation between the time you leave the scheme and when you retire, you will be substantially penalized on this basis. Some schemes have revalued leavers' salaries in some way to give a better pension, but this has been uncommon outside the public sector. Firms wonder why they should look after people who have left. Since 1 January 1991, benefits have had to be increased for leavers by at least the lower of the rise in the RPI or 5% each year over the period from leaving until retirement. With money purchase schemes, leavers must be treated in the same way as non-leavers.

Transfers

If, when you leave, there is at least a year to your normal retirement age, and you have worked for your ex-employer for more than two years, you have the option of having the cash value of your benefits transferred.

There will be some haggling over your pension transfer value. To give an example, if you have worked for 10 years in a scheme which pays 1/60th of your final salary, and your salary is £30 000 your frozen pension will be £5000 (i.e., £30 000 × 10/60). However, you would expect to be earning more than £30 000 when you retire. But, when your transfer value is calculated, the actuary for the scheme you are leaving will only look at the deferred entitlement and statutory increases (i.e., 5% or RPI, if lower). That will produce a lower final salary than you might expect, and a lower transfer value. That's where the haggling begins. Once a transfer value is determined, you pay it into any of the following:

- Your new employer's scheme

- A single premium policy from an insurance company or other provider (known as a "Section 32 buy-out")

- A personal pension plan

You can buy pension rights in your new employer's pension scheme. You might find that your ten years in your old scheme is valued at eight years in your new scheme. If your new employer is keen to get you, you might find you will get a full credit.

Section 32 buy-outs are used only for transfer of the "cash equivalent" of deferred benefits from the occupational pension scheme which an individual has left, and are not widely held. They retain some of the guarantees which must have been preserved within the previous employer's occupational pension scheme. Many insurance companies do not offer Section 32s and therefore will not be able to compare the three transfer options listed above. You should get independent advice as to whether a Section 32 would be appropriate for you, but you should be aware that few advisers are qualified to give advice in this area.

Finally, you can transfer into a personal pension plan. If you change your job again, you won't have to do anything with your pension plan. This also applies to a Section 32, but unlike a Section 32, you will be able to make new contributions to your personal pension plan if your new employer doesn't have a pension scheme, or if you become self-employed.

WERE YOU MIS-SOLD A PERSONAL PENSION?

As you are no doubt aware from press discussion, many people have been mis-sold a personal pension and SIB is taking action so that victims may get redress. You should skip this section if you do not have a personal pension which you joined from 29 April 1988.

SIB has split the five million people who had bought a personal pension since April 1988 into five categories:

- People who took money out of an ex-employer's pension scheme and put it into a personal pension plan or "buy-out" contract. SIB calls this a *pensions transfer*

- People who were in an employer's scheme but who transferred into a personal pension plan while still working for the employer—*pension opt out*

- People who would have been able to join an employer's scheme but instead took out a personal pension—*non-joiners*

- People whose employer did not have a pension scheme

- People who were self-employed.

SIB's concern is with the pension transfer, pension opt out and non-joiners who were advised to join a personal pension plan from 29 April 1988, when the Financial Services Act came into force. The following discussion relates only to these groups.

SIB is requiring investment firms to automatically review the pension arrangements for some personal pension policy holders; these people are in priority groups, which I

Table 28.2   SIB Pension Priority Groups

PENSION TRANSFERS

PRIORITY GROUPS	TARGET DATE for most cases to be reviewed
Priority Group 1	31 December 1995
<ul><li>Men over 55 at the time of transfer</li><li>Women over 50 at the time of transfer</li><li>People who have retired</li><li>Spouse and dependants of people who have died</li></ul>	
Priority Group 2 <ul><li>Men aged between 50 and 54 at the time of transfer</li><li>Women aged between 45 and 49 at the time of transfer</li></ul>	31 December 1996

PENSION OPT OUTS and NON-JOINERS

PRIORITY GROUPS	TARGET DATE for most cases to be reviewed
Priority Group 1	31 December 1995
<ul><li>People who are retired/spouses or dependants of people who have died</li><li>People who left an employer's scheme, were aged 35 or over at the time they took out a personal pension, and who are still with the same employer</li></ul>	
Priority Group 2	30 June 1996
<ul><li>People who decided not to join an employer's pension scheme, were aged 35 or over at the time they took out a personal pension, are paying their own money into a personal pension and are still with the same employer</li><li>People who left an employer's pension scheme, were aged 35 or over at the time they took out a personal pension, are paying their own money into a personal pension and who are still with the same employer</li></ul>	
Priority Group 3	31 December 1996
<ul><li>People who left an employer's pension scheme, were aged 35 or over at the time they took out a personal pension and who are no longer with the same employer</li></ul>	

Source: SIB, "The Pension Transfer and Opt Out Review", October 1994, pp. 4–5.

discuss below. If you qualify for redress, the aim will be to put you into a position equivalent to the one you were in before you took out your personal pension. You will only qualify for redress if the firm that advised you broke the then rules and you have suffered, or will suffer, a financial loss. Financial loss can cover things such as lower pension benefits and loss of extra benefits such as life insurance.

SIB feels that older people and people close to retirement should have their case reviewed first. Accordingly it has split *pension transfers* into two priority groups and a non-priority group, and *pension opt outs* and *non-joiners*, into three priority groups and a non-priority group. The various priority groups are shown in Table 28.2.

For *pension opt outs* and *non-joiners*, an insurance company or financial adviser may not be sure whether you left an employer's pension scheme or had the chance to join one, so you may be asked to complete a questionnaire.

When your case has been reviewed—by the firm that may have mis-sold you a pension!—it will either state that the advice given was sound or it may send you an offer of redress letter. You then have to decide if you accept the firm's conclusion, and offer, if any.

If you are not in a priority group, your position will not be automatically reviewed and you should ask the firm that arranged your personal pension to review your case. But don't hold your breath for a reply. SIB has asked that non-priority cases be reviewed within two years of any request. However, if your situation warrants a faster review you should say so—for example, if you are in ill-health and have lost out on ill-health benefits you would have got from your employer's scheme.

For priority groups SIB expects the advice provider to take the initiative. Many advisers think this unfair, as normally firms are not put in the position of having to check, at their own expense, to see if their advice was sound. You wouldn't expect a car salesman to check back on every deal as to whether he gave sound advice when he advised you to trade-in your existing car. If he misrepresented the car he sold you, then you would normally take the initiative. Some lawyers have suggested you do the same on personal pensions, either by contacting the adviser or going through the courts. So far, going through the courts has not been a successful course of action, and it also involves expense. Writing to the adviser, but then relying on the SIB procedures won't involve expense, but when this was written in November 1995, the PIA was struggling to get the reviews carried out. The insurance companies were nearly all complying, but only 50% of IFAs appeared to be, and the PIA was making various threats.

Whether or not you wait for your adviser to take the initiative, you should have an idea of whether you were badly advised. You were probably badly advised if your adviser:

- Did not tell you that occupational schemes benefit from employer's contributions, which you usually lose if you opt out

- Did not obtain details of all the benefits you would have got from your employer's scheme

- Did not check whether your employer's fund had a history of improving pensions above any required amounts

- Did not establish your attitude to risk, and explain that you bear the investment risk in a personal pension plan

- Did not take account of early retirement options under your occupational scheme

- Did not evaluate a transfer to a new employer's scheme

- Did not evaluate the merits of a Section 32 buy-out

- Did not explain the potential for loss from moving from an "uncapped" final salary scheme to a "capped" personal pension for pre-1989 scheme beneficiaries

For help, or general advice, you can ring the PIA Pensions Unit—see READ 📖 WRITE 🖃 RING ☎.

ALTERNATIVES TO A PENSION

Because of the tax-break, it is advantageous to save for retirement via a pension scheme. But once you have put money into a pension scheme, you can't get it back. You will get income at retirement, but you have lost control of your capital. Other forms of savings offer tax-breaks and most allow you to get your hands on your capital if you need it, although maybe with a penalty. So while investing in a pension will usually be a good investment, it may not be the best investment.

Much the best alternative to a pension is a PEP (see Chapter 20). Should you have a pension fund or a PEP? You may not have a choice, but self-employed people will, anybody not in an employer's scheme will, and anybody wishing to supplement an occupational scheme by AVCs or FSAVCs will also have a choice of going the pension or PEP route. High earners who are caught by the earnings trap should also consider PEPs.

A pension fund offers three tax advantages:

- Your contributions attract tax relief at your marginal rate of tax

- Your pension fund is not subject to CGT or income tax

- You can get a tax-free lump sum

but

- When you draw your pension it is taxed as income at your marginal rate

The tax advantages of a PEP are:
- Your PEP is not subject to CGT or income tax

- If you spend your PEP income or consume your PEP capital, it is not taxed

but

- The sum you invest in your PEP will have suffered income tax, e.g., if you pay income tax at 40%, you will need income of £10 000 to fund a £6000 PEP

Overall, the maths favours the pension route (assuming equal investment performance) because the tax-free lump sum means part of your pension totally escapes tax. You will have obtained tax relief when you invested, and suffer no tax when you get the lump sum.

However, you might also take into account your tax rate when you invest and retire. For example, if you pay higher rate income tax now but expect to pay basic rate when you retire, it makes sense to get the tax-break now, i.e., go the pension route, but if you pay little tax now, but expect to pay a lot when you retire, you might prefer to go the PEP route.

Even if you conclude that the maths favours pension over PEP, you should remember that a PEP is more flexible. When you take out a pension you have to follow your plan's rules and you have lost control of the money you invest until you are permitted to draw a lump sum and income. Should you die soon after retirement, your pension will cease, even though there will still be a pot of assets able to generate an income for you (of course there may be a pension for your spouse if you have one, but the same point applies if your spouse dies young). With a PEP you can change your mind at any time and decide that you will spend all the money at any age you choose and not wait until you are of pensionable age. If you die young, the PEP will form part of your estate, and not be lost in the way that a pension might be. Of course, if you live to be 100, you would have done better to have had a pension. With a pension, you may also be able to purchase, for extra cost, a guarantee that if you die in the first five years, the residual pension fund will be paid to your estate.

Before making a decision, you should make an honest appraisal of yourself. I have treated a PEP's flexibility as an advantage. But if you are the sort of person who can't be trusted with a credit card, the flexibility will be a disadvantage. If you can dip in at any time, you may be tempted to do so, and as a result underprovide for your old age.

So, which is it to be—PEP or pension? Well, there simply can't be one correct answer. Remember too that tax rules can change, and what looks sensible now, might not be in the future. Tax rates might go up or down, and perhaps both (tax cuts for the poor and increases for the rich, or the other way round if you are a Thatcherite). The lump sum might be taxed, and PEPs might lose all or part of their tax-breaks. On balance I prefer the PEP, because of the flexibility, but that's just my view. It would be reasonable to prefer the pension route, or subscribe to a PEP in all odd years and a personal pension in all even years. Because of the £9000 per annum limit on the two types of PEP, some high earners could have both a PEP and a pension top-up in the same year.

In Table 28.3, I show some other savings options. A **TESSA** may seem attractive as a pension top-up because it offers a tax-break. However, a maximum fund of £9000 is not going to go far for a high earner, and cash has not performed as well as shares over the long run.

Investment trusts and **unit trusts** have an element of tax shelter built in. Although income will be taxed when received, capital gains will only be taxed when realized, and then after the annual exemption and indexation allowance. Any transactions within the fund will not crystallize a capital gains liability. If you invest in general trusts, and especially index funds, you may feel that you need never trade them, and thereby postpone any capital gains liability for as long as you wish. Alternatively you may largely escape CGT by astutely bed and breakfasting your trusts.

Some **National Savings** products pay tax-free income or capital gains. The problem in terms of building up a nest egg is that there are limits on the amount you can invest. 8th Issue Index-Linked Savings Certificates are very suitable as a pension fund substitute. Index-linked gilts are nearly as good: while the income is taxed, an unlimited sum may be invested versus a maximum of £10 000 in the NS index-linked.

Table 28.3   Tax Status of Various Forms of Saving

Product	Tax Relief on Contributions	Tax-Free Roll-Up: Capital	Tax-Free Roll-Up: Income	Tax-Free on Maturity	Lump Sum Available
Employer Pension Scheme	✓	✓	✓	✗	✓
Personal Pension Plan	✓	✓	✓	✗	✓
AVC and FSAVC	✓	✓	✓	✗	✗
TESSA	✗	✓	✓	✓	✓
National Savings*	✗	✓	✓	✓	✓
Investment and Unit Trusts	✗	✓	✗	✓ and ✗	✓
Index-Linked Gilts	✗	✓	✗	✓	✓
Friendly Societies	✗	✓	✓	✓	✓
Qualifying Life Policies	✗	✗	✗	✓	✓

Key: ✓ = yes; ✗ = no; * Some products only

Friendly Society and insurance products offer some tax advantages. In the case of Friendly Societies the tax advantages match those of PEPs; insurance products offer fewer. Both types of product suffer from high surrender charges and, in the case of Friendly Societies, the sum you can invest is tiny.

APPENDIX: PENSION SCHEME LIMITS

The rules for pension schemes are complex. In addition there have been changes in the Inland Revenue requirements governing schemes. What follows is a brief outline of some of the limits for personal pension plans.

Personal pension plans

With personal pension plans there are two important dates:

- Before 1 July 1988

- On or after 1 July 1988

Plans taken out before 1 July 1988 were Retirement Annuity Plans (RAPs), and those taken out on or after 1 July were Personal Pension Plans (PPPs). The maximum annual contributions are shown in Table 28.4.

Table 28.4   Personal Pension Contribution Limits 1996-97

Age at start of tax year	Maximum contributions: % of net relevant earnings RAP	Maximum contributions: % of net relevant earnings PPP
35 or under	17.5%	17.5%
36–45	17.5%	20.0%
46–50	17.5%	25.0%
51–55	20.0%	30.0%
56–60	22.5%	35.0%
61–74	27.5%	40.0%
75 and over	0%	0%

- For the Personal Pension Plan, there is an earnings cap of £82 200 in 1996–7, an amount usually increased each year.

- The maximum pension that may be taken for either type of fund is determined by the size of the fund (affected by contributions and investment performance) and interest rates at the time of retirement (which determines the value of the annuity).

- The maximum lump sum that can be taken for a RAP is three times the amount of the remaining pension. (There is a limit of £150 000 per plan for plans taken out on or after 17 March 1987. This can be circumvented, so if you are caught by it, seek advice.) For a Personal Pension Plan, the maximum lump sum is 25% of the value of your fund at retirement.

- You can use up to 5% of your net relevant earnings to buy term insurance linked to a personal pension plan. This qualifies for tax relief, but comes out of your pensions contributions limit.

READ 📖 WRITE 🖃 RING ☎

♦ For a list of group personal pension providers, see Julia Dodds, "Strengths in Numbers", *Planned Savings*, July 1995, 56–64, or Mark Battersby, "Survey: Group Personal Pensions", *Money Management*, December 1995, 57–68.
♦ For a survey of personal pension plan providers and some recommendations see, Janet Walford, "Unlocking the Facts and Figures", *Money Management*, March 1995, 4–14, and "Will Your Pension Stand the Test of Time?", *Which?*, July 1995, 30–37. The *Financial Times* survey mentioned in the text is: Debbie Harrison, "Personal Pension Plans" in "Weekend Money", *Financial Times*, 31/12/94–1/1/95, 7–10.
♦ Some Section 32 buyout providers are listed in "Slow-Down for Buyout Bonds", *Planned Savings*, January 1995, 47–54.
♦ For a list of some providers of SIPPs and their charges, see "Do It Yourself", *Planned Savings*, December 1994, 49–53.
♦ For details of some of the various types of annuities and the names of product providers, see David Hunt, "The Workhorses of Income Generation", *Planned Savings*, May 1995, 51–57.
♦ A fax list of a variety of annuities on offer from 30 of the main providers is available from *Moneyfacts* Fax Service: calls are charged at 39p per minute cheap rate and 49p per minute at other times. Tel: 0336 400236.
♦ SIB has produced factsheets called "Pension Transfers", for people thinking of transferring out of an employer's scheme, and "Pension Opt Outs", for people thinking of opting out of an employer's scheme. For copies, send a large stamped addressed envelope to The Securities and Investments Board, Gavrelle House, 2–14 Bunhill Row, London EC1Y 8RA.
♦ If you think you might have been mis-sold a personal pension plan, request a copy of "The Pension Transfer and Opt Out Review" from Pension Factsheet, PO Box 701, Basildon, Essex SS14 3FD, enclosing a large stamped addressed envelope. For help, or general advice, ring the PIA Pensions Unit. Tel: 0171 417 7001.
♦ If you want to find a financial adviser to help you with your pension planning, see the sources listed in READ 📖 WRITE 🖃 RING ☎ in Chapter 10.

29

Coupling and Uncoupling

You don't know a woman till you've met her in court.
Norman Mailer

While the song tells us that love and marriage go together like a horse and carriage, and the marriage vows tie us till death, social statistics suggest something different. Love and cohabitation often go together, and marriage often ends with divorce rather than death. I'm going to reflect the world as it is and lump together cohabitation, marriage and divorce. All three are common.

About 94% of us get married at least once, and about 40% of recent marriages will probably end in divorce. The average age for marriage for a man is 28.2 years, and 26.2 for a woman. The average length of a marriage ending in divorce is 9.8 years. About a third of all marriages involve at least one divorced partner, probably a man. Divorced men and widowers are much more likely to get remarried than divorced women and widows. In 1992, nearly one in five of unmarried men and women aged 16 to 59 were cohabiting. In the early 1990s, nearly 70% of women getting married for the first time had pre-maritally cohabited with their future husband, whereas for women getting married for the second time, the figure was nearly 90%. For those marrying for the first time, the period of cohabitation was about two years.

Cohabitation, marriage and divorce each have financial implications and I'm going to consider some aspects here. I must stress that I consider only some aspects, and if you are considering divorce, you must get legal advice and not assume anything said here necessarily applies to you. I will begin with cohabitation.

COHABITATION

Cohabitation can be a prelude to marriage or an alternative. But if you are not married, you are single in the eyes of the law, at least in England and Wales, and usually in the eyes of the Inland Revenue. In Scotland you may have a chance of getting your union recognized as "marriage by cohabitation, and habit and repute", but this is beyond the scope of this book. The implications of being single are as follows.

Tax You will each receive a personal allowance and be taxed on your own earnings and assets. This is exactly how a married couple would be taxed, except they would also get a married person's allowance (see Chapter 8). If you have a child, the Additional Personal Allowance of £1790 can be claimed. If you are both single parents living together, only one additional allowance can be claimed. An unmarried couple can claim tax relief on the interest on a loan of up to £30000 on their only or main home. If they exchanged contracts before August 1988, they can each get tax relief on interest on a loan of up to £30000.

Home You should be careful about buying a home together. The costs of buying and selling are such that it will only make financial sense if you are confident you will be together for several years, so that an increase in the value of the home will offset the transaction costs. As we all now know, home prices can fall, and the problem of negative equity in the last few years has forced many cohabiting (and indeed married) couples to stay together when they would have preferred to part.

Because you are single, you may assume that none of your assets automatically go to your partner. However, if you jointly buy the home, the position will depend on how you jointly own it. If you hold an asset with someone as "joint tenants", on the death of one of you, the other will own the asset. If you own the asset as "tenants in common", each has a separate share which can be willed to whoever you wish. Married couples who jointly own assets are presumed to be joint tenants, whereas others are assumed to be tenants in common. However, it is possible to vary the normal presumption, so you should be clear on how you jointly own your home.

Often one partner will be buying a home, and the other partner will move in. If the partner moving in pays some of the bills, whether the household bills or some of the mortgage payments, you should be aware that this may give the partner an interest in the property.

Pensions Cohabiting women tend to lose out on pensions. (Pensions are discussed at length in Chapters 27 and 28.) Both married and single women can qualify for a State pension in their own right, but a married woman who does not have sufficient National Insurance Contributions may be able to qualify through her husband's contributions. Single women can't qualify in this way.

With regard to company pensions, the position can be complicated. I will give an explanation in terms of a man earning a pension, but it applies equally when a woman earns a pension. When a man dies, a widow's pension will usually be paid, but often only to a widow. If there is a widow, the single cohabiting partner won't get it, and even if there isn't a widow, she may not. However, if an "Expression of Wish" or "Nomination of Beneficiaries" form is completed, the pension fund trustees, who have discretion, may follow the stated wishes. In the public sector, however, the cohabiting partner will not be paid a pension whatever the stated wishes. All cohabitees should discuss their pension rules with their Pensions Manager who will have "Expression of Wish" forms.

Social security benefits The value of some social security benefits (see Chapter 26 for details) are affected by whether you have a partner, and your partner may simply be a cohabiting partner.

Separation   Single people can't divorce, so you might think that they can just pack their bags and move on, with no real problems. But it's not that easy. If there are children, the Child Support Agency (discussed below) will ensure that the absent parent contributes to the children's upbringing. And if the couple have been together for a few years, it is likely that their finances and assets will have become enmeshed, even if there are no children. One may have bought the home while the other paid the Council Tax, or one bought the home and the other the car and paid for holidays. If an amicable split can't be agreed, the divorce laws can't be used to enforce a reasonable split. The law can only be used to establish who legally owns what, and what contribution each partner has made. If the female partner has sacrificed a career to look after the home, this will not affect the split of assets, although it would in the case of divorce. However, if you cohabit for a long period, get married and then quickly divorced, the period of cohabitation probably will be taken into consideration in the divorce settlement. Women should think carefully about the financial wisdom of cohabiting instead of getting married.

Death   When a married person dies intestate (i.e., without a will), the spouse will automatically get all or part of the estate (see Chapter 33 for details). When someone cohabiting dies, their partner will get nothing unless there is a will (broadly speaking, and with the exception of the home as outlined above). If it can be shown that the survivor was being maintained by the deceased, a claim might be made under the *Inheritance (Provision for Family and Dependants) Act 1975*. If you want to be sure your cohabiting partner inherits your assets, make a will immediately. However, if you have had children with your partner, they will be entitled to a share even of an intestate partner's estate.

Assets passed on death to a spouse are exempt from inheritance tax—this is not the case for an unmarried couple. And assets passed before death between an unmarried couple will be liable for CGT, whereas assets passed between spouses are not subject to CGT.

Action?   Having outlined some of the financial aspects of cohabiting, the question is what action should be taken. Often, no action will follow. What I have discussed is pretty serious stuff. If you are a young woman who has been living with someone for six months, it may seem premature to say to your lover that since he could die at any time, and it would be a shame for the widow's pension to go to waste, could he pop down to the Pensions Manager and try and get you a cut. And if you are middle-aged and you have been living together for four years, it may well be that one of you hopes that you will get married, and one of you would prefer to carry on as you are. Sorting out long-term financial arrangements is equivalent to stating that the current arrangement is permanent. That may be something that both are unwilling to broach.

As well as the big issues that have been outlined, there are some basic domestic issues such as joint accounts that need to be discussed. I'll consider them in the following section.

MARRIAGE

The best friend is likely to acquire the best wife, because a good marriage is based on the talent for friendship.

Friedrich Nietzsche

There are two extremes in pre-marital financial planning. One is to do nothing, and the other is to demand a pre-nuptial agreement. The school of no planning can be carried to extraordinary lengths. When I was a child, it was common, especially amongst working class families, for the wife not to know what the husband earned—even after they were married. It is less common now, but still not unknown in families of all classes. Well, if you want that kind of relationship, it is up to you. But most people will want to talk through their financial assets, incomes, hopes and dreams, and commitments (e.g., to an infirm parent or a child from an earlier marriage). And I think you should make a couple of decisions concerning pre-nuptial agreements and joint property.

Pre-nuptial agreements Pre-nuptial agreements don't sound too romantic: they are basically contracts that stop one spouse getting all the loot when the other dies, or if you divorce. They seem like something for an ageing rock star and bimbo, or maybe for any Californian couple. But pre-nuptial agreements may have a more widespread application. Some people who have had a bad divorce experience may feel more secure with some form of agreement, and this may improve the new relationship, or at least stop it being undermined by unwarranted, but perhaps understandable, anxieties. And where there are children from a previous marriage it may be sensible to make provision for them by a pre-nuptial agreement, although it would be safer to put assets intended for such children into a trust (see Chapter 35).

The legal status of pre-nuptial agreements is somewhat uncertain, however, and although in 1988 the Council of Ministers recommended that such agreements be accepted, there are a number of ways they may be challenged, e.g., if there is an element of coercion involved. In any event, an agreement will have more value for those who don't get married than those who do. At the time of divorce, the divorce laws take precedence—in other words the divorce laws overrule the pre-divorce agreement.

Joint property Are you going to own your assets jointly or not? This can apply to all assets or to just some, like having a joint bank account, or to assets acquired after marriage. The romantic answer is that you should own assets jointly—isn't marriage a case of what's mine is yours and what's yours is mine? The practical answer is more complex.

- Joint property usually cannot be disposed of without both parties signing. This ensures that the husband's gambling debts, or the wife's spending sprees, don't go unnoticed until it's too late because the culprit has been secretly selling family assets. However, if one partner becomes senile or incapacitated by illness, it may not be possible to obtain a signature to sell an asset without having to go through various legal procedures. This will not be a problem if a power of attorney has been obtained in advance, but some people don't want to give such powers. And one partner may refuse to sign something out of spite, in which case there is little that can be done.

- A home owned as "joint tenants" will automatically pass on the death of one spouse to the surviving spouse (for implications, see Chapter 34).

- A joint bank account can usually be operated on the basis of one signature, so one partner can spend all the family's cash. When assets are held individually, the family cash (the only asset for some families) can't be entirely cleaned out by one partner.

- As mentioned above, you may feel that you should keep some assets separate if there are children from a previous marriage.

DIVORCE

The only solid and lasting peace between a man and his wife is, doubtless, a separation.
Lord Chesterfield

In this section I outline some of the key financial implications of divorce. These can be grim. For all but the rich, getting divorced will reduce your standard of living.

Maintenance and division of property

Divorce raises two major financial issues—maintenance and the division of property. The law lays down the same principles to govern the determination of both. Moreover, in many cases a clean break settlement is made (for spousal maintenance, but not for child maintenance) and this eliminates maintenance in favour of a lump sum payment which has an equivalent value to what any on-going maintenance might have had. Maintenance and property division are therefore looked at together. The law sets out guidelines for both the amount of financial provision, and its duration. Only where there is a dispute need the court be involved, but what the court might decide is a good benchmark for a voluntary agreement.

As to amount, the court has to have regard to all circumstances of the case and give first consideration to the welfare of any child under the age of 18. In particular, the court has to have regard to:

- The income, earning capacity, property and other financial resources which the parties have, or are likely to have in the foreseeable future

- The parties' financial needs, obligations and responsibilities

- The parties' standard of living prior to the marriage breakdown

- The age of the parties and the duration of the marriage

- The contributions of the parties to the family's welfare, including looking after the home and family

- Any physical or mental disabilities of either party

- The conduct of the parties

- The value of pension benefits that either party will lose

The problem with this sort of list is that it is quite vague—the court has to have regard to both the list and to all circumstances, and there is no guidance as to which factors weigh most heavily. All one can really do is look at how the courts have typically interpreted matters. It is worth stressing that the conduct of the parties seldom affects the financial settlement. Even if he really was a rat, it won't affect the settlement.

The law as set out above is contained in the *Matrimonial Causes Act 1973* and the *Matrimonial and Family Proceedings Act 1984*. The latter Act abolished the old—and usually unworkable—objective of trying to put both spouses in the financial position they would have been in had the marriage not broken down. (Note: these Acts apply to England and Wales, divorce in Scotland is covered by the *Family Law (Scotland) Act 1985.)*

With regard to duration of maintenance, the court must decide whether there is a case for on-going financial provision and, if so, whether there should be a time limit. Also, it must decide whether the spousal maintenance should be paid as a lump sum in the form of a clean break.

Child Maintenance   As I noted above, the court's first consideration will be for any children, and here the *Child Support Act 1991* has created a new framework for the assessment and collection of child maintenance. This new system came into effect on 5 April 1993 and is operated by a Government Agency, the *Child Support Agency*, or CSA. The key elements of the Act are that all parents, whether married or not, must support their natural children, with the amount of child support determined by a statutory calculation, assessed and enforced by the CSA. The Child Support Act is not specifically concerned with divorce—it is concerned with the maintenance of children irrespective of the marital status of the parents—but it obviously will be an important factor in divorce settlements.

The Act requires some parents to apply for child maintenance, while others can. If you are a parent with care of a child and either get Income Support, Family Credit or Disability Working Allowance, or you are the partner of someone who gets one of these benefits, you must apply for a child maintenance assessment. The other specified categories that can apply for child maintenance are:

- Parents living with the child or children, and the other parent living elsewhere

- Persons with care of a child whose parents live elsewhere

- An absent parent may apply to see what sum they should pay

- A child aged 12 or over living in Scotland with at least one parent living apart

  In working out the amount of child maintenance, the CSA takes into account:

- The cost of maintaining a child

- The incomes of the two parents after allowing for tax, NIC, rent/mortgage and basic expenses

- Any other children either person has

The calculation also looks at the amount of income the parent paying maintenance would be left with, to ensure that it is not too low to live on. The goal is to leave the parent paying maintenance better off than they would be on Income Support. If the child lives part of the time with each parent, the child maintenance will be shared. For details, see READ 📖 WRITE ✑ RING ☎.

The effect of the *Child Support Act* is that in many divorces the CSA will be setting the child maintenance so only that spousal maintenance will be in dispute. However, the Act does not cover all children, and in particular stepchildren, and here the court will look at the factors it would have applied in the past, and the sum that would be paid if the *Child Support Act* applied.

Spousal Maintenance After determining child support, the court will look at spousal maintenance. The old rule the court used was that wives might expect to receive a third of the combined gross incomes. That rule has been replaced by a needs and resources approach. The court focuses on the needs of the children and the spouse looking after the children. If the resources of the spouse looking after the children are inadequate, the court will set a level of spousal maintenance to bring the resources up to the required level. However, if the absent spouse has insufficient income or capital, the amount will be whatever can be afforded. The ultimate fall-back for the parent with the children will be State benefits.

To give a flavour of how the various notions might affect a real case, I'll outline the approach that might be taken in a few sets of circumstances.

Because women generally earn less than men, and generally look after the children, the principle of need usually results in payments being made to the woman so that she can meet her needs for somewhere to live, to have a car if she had one when she was married, and so forth. The spouse receiving the payment is expected to make some effort to find employment, although this is affected by whether there are children, and their ages. A young wife without children might receive payment in respect of only a few years, a young wife with children would receive a greater payment (perhaps maintenance until her mid-40s), whereas a woman in her 50s would have limited job prospects and a settlement might build in nothing for her own earning capacity.

In most marriages the home will be the principal asset, and this will create problems if there are children and the home is a standard sort of home. The court will look to ensure that the children and mother are adequately housed (assuming she is looking after them). It will rarely be possible to sell the home and buy two new adequate homes that are each worth half the value of the former home. Inevitably the court will allocate most of the value to the wife and children, and the husband may end up in a small flat. Perhaps three quarters of the assets will go to the wife. If the husband has to pay a mortgage on his former wife's new home, maintenance for the children and live in a tiny flat, he will no doubt feel hard done by.

With a short and childless marriage, the courts will prefer a clean break to on-going maintenance. This may amount to no more than the couple sharing the capital they have—usually a home. If the husband earns a lot more than the wife, she may get a larger share of the capital. If there is no capital at all, a lump sum payment will not be possible, so a high-earning spouse might have to make maintenance payments for a few years.

When the marriage has lasted a long time, and there are no children (or they have grown up and left home), the wife's salary or financial contribution to the marriage is still a relevant factor, but much less so than for a short marriage. Even if the wife has made no financial contribution, she can still expect to receive a higher standard of living than the wife in a short marriage. Although a clean break may be desirable in these circumstances, there will seldom be sufficient capital to provide two homes and a lump sum for the wife.

Divorce and Pensions   For any type of situation except a very short marriage, the larger earner's pension will be important. *The Pensions Act 1995* has recently changed the law on this, with Section 166 amending the *Matrimonial Causes Act*. It is worth beginning with a few words on the general problems arising with divorce and pensions.

The two basic types of pension are money purchase and final salary (see Chapters 27 and 28). In the case of money purchase there is an identifiable pot of money and it is fairly easy to work out the value of a share of the pot. Of course, working out what the share should be could be difficult. With a final salary scheme the problem is more difficult, as there will be many benefits. Valuing the benefits will be complex and involve many assumptions. There are three broad approaches that might be adopted:

- To fudge matters and just throw the pension into the pot of goodies to be divided, not to give the pension a specific value, but to give the wife more of other assets. The exact value will then be determined by general horse-trading. This is how matters have usually been decided, but the wife may have few years to build up a pension of her own. Until 1993, if there were few other assets that the wife might get, the pension was often ignored, but in that year Griffiths sued her solicitor for ignoring her pension rights and was awarded £20 000. Since then pensions have been treated more seriously.

- To legally split the pension at divorce (not necessarily an equal split) so both parties have independent pensions. Although this approach is favoured by the Law Society, the Pensions' Management Institute and the Equal Opportunities Commission, the government has refused to accept it on the grounds that with two separate, and therefore smaller, pensions, a divorced couple would pay less tax than they would if they had remained married.

- To require a husband to forgo part of his pension when he receives it—a sort of deferred maintenance. This is what was tacked on to the *Pensions Act 1995*, after intense lobbying by various pressure groups. The money will come directly from the Trustees and not via the husband. This is better than fudging matters, but means a clean break is not possible, may not fully cover all the types of value of a final salary scheme, and means the wife can only get her pension when her ex-husband does. This is unjust, and poses special problems when the woman is older than the man. The arrangement also comes to an end on the death of either party. In the worst case, the man might die at age 64, a day before retirement, and the wife would get nothing.

How exactly the new law will work in practice is unclear, and all the necessary regulations have not yet been published. Also, the Labour Party is committed to trying to get clean break legislation passed. What is clear, is that pensions will be a key item in any future divorce settlement.

Additional considerations

There are a huge number of financial aspects of divorce that could be discussed. I will simply make a list of a few important points—anyone getting divorced will need additional advice on each point.

Tax Until 1988, maintenance payments attracted tax relief. This is no longer the case (although it applies to pre-15 March 1988 agreements)—the only tax-break is that the husband can claim is the Married Person's Allowance if he is making enforceable maintenance payments. The husband therefore will pay maintenance out of his after-tax income but the wife will not have to pay income tax or NICs or her maintenance. In any negotiations, both parties should be discussing net amounts. Sales or transfer of assets may crystallize capital gains and CGT liability. However, transfers between the spouses are exempt when they are living together, so every effort should be made to agree, and make, any transfers that might otherwise attract CGT in a tax year in which the couple are living together.

When you are divorced, you are single again. After the year of the divorce you will get a single person's tax allowances. If you care for a child, you will get the Additional Personal Allowance.

Life Insurance If you get maintenance from you former spouse, you will have a financial interest in him (or her). You should consider taking out life insurance with your former spouse being the insured life and you the beneficiary. Term insurance would be the most sensible form. Although you have an insurable interest (see Chapter 23), because you are no longer married, you do not have an unlimited interest. You can only insure to the extent you would financially suffer on your former spouse's death.

I explain in Chapter 33 that if the maintenance payer dies before the recipient, a claim may be made upon the deceased's estate. The recipient may be able to persuade the maintenance payer to pay life insurance premiums to avoid this arising. In return, an agreement would have to be effected whereby the right to make a claim against the estate is waived.

State Pension A wife can qualify for the State Basic Pension on the basis of her own, or her husband's, NICs. On divorce, the ex-husband's contributions will only count for the period of marriage. This may adversely affect the woman's pension. A divorced woman should complete form BR19 (see Chapter 27) to see what her pension will be: in some cases voluntary Class 3 NICs should be paid to increase the pension.

Will Once you have started divorce proceedings you should change your existing will. If you don't have a will and you die before your divorce is finalized, part of your estate will go to your spouse. After the divorce you will need to change your will because references to your wife or husband will be invalid, but it is sensible to change it before the divorce is finalized, in case you die in the meantime.

Negotiation

I've discussed some of the financial aspects of divorce. No matter the cause of divorce, it will usually be a traumatic event for one partner, and probably for both. Agreeing an allocation of assets would probably be difficult in any event, but in an emotionally charged state it is even harder. Moreover, if one partner is unreasonable, the other will also become unreasonable, and nothing will be gained, and much might be lost. The last thing you want is to end up in the grip of competing solicitors, or fighting it out in court. You really should try to negotiate with each other in a rational way.

Most people are poor negotiators, and they are likely to be especially poor when negotiating a divorce settlement. However, because the stakes are so high, it is worth planning a sensible negotiating strategy. Fisher and Ury, who have written an excellent book on negotiating (see READ ⌷ WRITE ⌐ RING ☎), not specifically related to divorce, recommend a four-step approach to negotiating:

- You have to separate the people from the problem. You should accept the people as human beings, but not allow the relationship to get mixed up with the problem. Your focus should not be on the person, but the problem you are facing.

- You should focus on interests and not on positions. People often develop negotiating positions which don't reflect their real interests. What are your interests, and what are the other person's? Make a list, and while there may appear to be some difficult problems to be resolved, be tough on the problem and not on the people.

- Generate as many options as possible to meet the combined interests before deciding what to do. Identify any shared interests and try to establish differences in how various options are valued. Find out how the other party values particular options. If the other party cares deeply about something and you don't, and vice versa on something else, you can come to a much better deal than just splitting everything down the middle.

- Ensure that the decision is based on some objective criteria. These can include fairness to the parties, the interests of the children, monetary value, what a court would decide, and so on.

Following this sort of approach will be hard—divorced people assure me that it's impossible—but it is worth attempting, especially where a couple have just drifted apart over the years so that the divorce is not acrimonious. This approach doesn't waste time attributing blame and attempting retribution, it attempts to achieve a rational division of the financial assets which, once your marriage is over, is all you should focus on.

READ ⌷ WRITE ⌐ RING ☎

♦ A brief general guide on divorce is: F. Shackelton and O. Timbs, *The Divorce Handbook: A Step-By-Step Guide to the Divorce Process*. London: Thorsons, 1992. The book pre-dates the CSA and the reforms that are currently being considered, but is still useful, both on divorce in general and with regard to finance.

♦ For information on the Child Support Agency, write to it at PO Box 55, Brierley Hill, West Midlands, DY5 1YL, or call the Child Support Agency Enquiry Line: 0345 133 133. CSA publications may be available in your local Post Office or public library.

♦ The book on negotiating mentioned in the text is: R. Fisher and W. Ury, *Getting to Yes: Negotiating Agreement Without Giving In*. London: Hutchinson, 1984.

30

Children's Finance and Education

Children are poor men's riches.
English proverb

In this chapter I look at a few aspects of investing for children and then move on to what is, for most people, much more important—paying for education, both school and higher education.

INVESTING FOR CHILDREN

Tax is often a factor affecting children's assets. Children have personal tax allowances just the same as adults (i.e., £3525 in 1996–7). If they have less income than the allowance, whether from being a British Macaulay Culkin or from washing cars, they pay no tax. Thereafter they are taxed like an adult. The same rules apply if all or part of their income comes from bank interest or dividends, unless the money in the account, or which bought the shares, was given by a parent.

To stop parents avoiding tax by depositing money in their children's names, if income from gifts from a parent exceeds £100, the entire income is taxed as part of that parent's income. The £100 limit applies to each parent. However, if one parent does not work and has no income, that parent will have an unutilized personal allowance. That parent can give a large sum to a child because, although the income will be aggregated with the parent's, there will be no income tax payable up to the value of the parent's personal allowance.

If a parent or grand-parent has an estate large enough to suffer inheritance tax, and it is intended to give assets to a child or grandchild, it is advantageous to give gifts, tax-free, during the adult's lifetime (see Chapter 34). Even taxed gifts will suffer tax at a lower rate than if they passed at death.

Suitable investments

Which investments are suitable for a child will depend on the objective of the investment, whether the child is a taxpayer, and whether the gift is from a parent and, if so, whether the £100 income barrier will be breached.

If a child is not a taxpayer, it is worth looking at investments that pay interest without deduction of tax. Bank and building society accounts will pay interest without deduction of tax if form R85 is completed (see Chapter 5). The Halifax Building Society has reported that 45% of the children's accounts it has still have tax deducted. Most of these probably don't need to pay the tax.

Some banks and building societies have special accounts for children. Some offer the normal level of interest but add various goodies, such as a free piggy bank, a tee shirt and so on, while others offer unusually high rates of interest. For example, in Autumn 1995, Universal Building Society was offering children 7.05% for a minimum sum of £1 invested, with instant access. *Moneyfacts* lists special children's accounts (but not in every issue).

National Savings offers a very attractive product for children called Children's Bonus Bonds (discussed in Chapter 9). For the best return the bonds have to be held for five years. The return is tax-free, so this is especially attractive for rich children or children with generous parents.

As well as investments specifically designed for children, many other investments—such as investment trusts, unit trusts, or endowment policies—are also suitable.

Opening a child's account

The age at which a child can operate its own account varies with the product. For most Post Office based products, i.e., the various National Savings products, the child must be seven. For Premium Bonds and Children's Bonus Bonds, the child must be 16. For bank and building society accounts seven is the usual minimum age, and for shares and unit trusts it is 18. However, these ages usually relate to when a child can both deposit and withdraw, or buy and sell. In many cases accounts can be opened, or assets purchased, at a younger age (e.g., at birth), but withdrawals can either not be made or only made by a parent or guardian. Some products, e.g., unit trusts, can be bought in the name of an adult, but designated with the name of a child. For example, if Jane Smith has a son called Ben, the account might be designated as Jane Smith A/C BS. The adult operates the account, but the Inland Revenue will treat it as the child's.

In short, the details of opening a child's account vary, and you will have to check the details with the product provider. It is well worth opening a child's account, as it is sensible to train children in finance at an early age. Of course, if you allow children financial freedom, they may squander their assets (as do some adults). For modest sums that may seem a risk worth taking. If, however, the plan is to give the child a very large sum of assets, the risk may not be worth taking. In that case it may be worth setting up a discretionary trust or an accumulation and maintenance trust (see Chapter 35). These trusts will bear set-up costs and perhaps annual costs so they are only worth establishing for sums in excess of, say, £20 000, or smaller sums where it is thought the child definitely needs protecting against itself.

PAYING FOR EDUCATION

Education with socialists, it's like sex, all right so long as you don't have to pay for it.
                                                                                              Alan Bennett

Although financial planning books in the UK concentrate on school fees, higher education fees affect more families. This is because higher education is now available to a much larger percentage of the population than was the case 20 years ago, and because of a move by the State away from providing grants for higher education to providing loans. How many children will go on to higher education in the future is difficult to predict. Currently, about 30% of the population achieve some form of 18+ qualification. In France, the figure is nearly 50%, in Germany it is approaching 70% and in Japan it is about 80%. It seems likely that even more UK students will go on to higher education in the future than do today. About 7% of children go to independent schools, so higher education fee planning affects about four times as many families as does school fees planning. However, I'll be traditional and start with school fees.

SCHOOL FEES PLANNING

School fees planning is a great obsession of British middle-class financial planning writers, but there are few special breaks—tax or otherwise—for school fees. In essence, school fees planning is simply making sure you have money available to spend in particular years. There are a number of ways of achieving this:

- Invest a capital sum now to produce the required income in the future

- Save over the period prior to the commencement of the expenditure

- Pay fees out of income at the time by
  - Reducing savings
  - Increasing income

- Get somebody else to pay, e.g.,
  - Grandparents
  - State assistance

- Borrow at the time

Before looking at these methods it is worth noting that few parents plan, but school fees are steep. Mintel found that only about 35% of parents with children at independent schools planned ahead to meet the costs, and 80% financed school fees solely from salary and other income. Secondary school fees (in 1995) are about £3250 per term for boarders and about £1400 for day schools. Prep schools are cheaper. Extras such as school trips, uniform, sports kit etc. may add nearly £1000 a term at some schools. So, providing you have a calculator with lots of noughts, the maths is easy. Take one of my fees numbers and add a sum for extras, multiply by the number of terms per year, then by the number of years, then by the number of children, then adjust up for the rate of inflation, then adjust up a bit more (in recent years fees have risen faster than inflation), and then lie down in a dark room for an hour or two. Now let's see what you can do about it.

Lump sum

If you have a lump sum now which you can afford to invest to generate school fees, you have a number of options. These include specialist plans (see READ 📖 WRITE

⊑ RING ☎) and DIY plans. The specialist plans will involve investments and maybe some form of single premium insurance to provide a minimum guaranteed sum per term, year, or whatever. The insurance plans would be set up as a series maturing in different years. Obviously you can do the same thing yourself, by setting up a pool of investments concentrating on PEPs, TESSAs, investment and unit trusts, and various National Savings products and, if you think it necessary, taking out endowment insurance. Even deposit accounts will make sense for non-working wives who pay no tax. Single premium with-profits insurance provides a guaranteed sum, but it has the drawbacks that I discussed in Chapter 23. Of course, your exact mix of investments will depend on how far ahead of the school fees becoming due you are doing your planning. Qualifying insurance products need to be purchased at least 7½ years in advance, and equities should be held for at least five years to reduce your risks.

The non-insurance investments will not provide a guaranteed sum, but you may not feel that this is necessary. TESSAs are a cash-based investment and have a guaranteed minimum value (the cash you invest) and your PEP can contain bonds as well as equities. Your portfolio does not have to hit a specific value on a specific date—it has to provide enough over a period of years, so you can afford to play the averages, providing your lump sum is invested at least five years before the fees start to be paid. The markets are unlikely to be poor throughout all the pre-school and school years. Moreover, your portfolio would generate a reasonable income, so if you were forced to dip into capital during a poor market period, you would not be consuming much capital. You would also have the option of meeting part of the fees out of other income (e.g., your salary) in such a period, and leaving the fund untouched. After all, you may have earmarked it for school fees, but it is not written in stone that you have to use the fund for that.

Sometimes it is suggested that lump sums be invested in zero coupon bonds (see Chapter 19) or split capital investment trust zeros (see Chapter 32). Either of these will produce a known sum at a known date—providing they don't default. Stripped gilts (see Chapter 19) will be a much more suitable type of zero for school fees planning. But you have to remember that with any kind of zero you are vulnerable to inflation if it turns out to be higher than was expected when you bought your zero.

You can use educational trusts to guarantee school fees. You pay a lump sum to the trustees of an educational trust which buys an annuity from an insurance company. Annuities are explained in Chapter 28. When fees are due, the insurance company pays money to the trustees who in turn write out a cheque for school fees. No tax is paid within the trust, and payments from the trust are tax-free, but the returns are not necessarily compelling, and your money is tied up for a long time. The returns will be higher in periods of high interest rates. Of course, a future government could change the tax status of such trusts. You are not tied by these schemes to any particular school. Before taking out such a scheme, you should be aware of possible inheritance tax complications if you retain the right to recover the funds and the potential liability to CGT if you terminate the plan and are paid its value. Educational trusts are worth looking into, but do get advice before signing up.

Some schools allow you to make a lump sum payment in advance, known as a composition plan, which is used to pay fees and which either gives you a discount from the fees when your child goes to school, or freezes the fees at their current level. Be sure to calculate the implicit rate of return involved, and remember that this is a tax-free return so, when comparing it against other returns, make sure you gross up the return. Also, check that you can switch the fees to a different school if necessary.

Save in advance

If you don't have a lump sum, but are planning ahead, you can save in advance using endowment insurance savings plans, e.g., maximum investment bonds, or set up your own investment savings plan. If you do the latter, and you die while your children are still at school, there may be a fee shortfall. You might therefore wish to take out term insurance. If you go the endowment route, you would set up a series of endowments maturing at different dates. Remember, endowments need to be purchased at least 7½ years in advance of the fees being required.

Pay out of income

You might decide to make no special provision for school fees but reduce your savings, increase your income, or reduce your expenditure when your child goes to school. For example, if you are saving regularly, perhaps through a PEP or AVC, you might decide to simply stop saving and spend the same amount of money on school fees. Once the fees cease, you can start saving again. Alternatively, some couples will have scope to generate extra income by the wife starting work when the school fees start, so that she, in effect, pays the fees. And, of course, everybody can spend less.

Get somebody else to pay

You may be able to get somebody else to pay, usually the child's grandparents, or the State. If the grandparents are willing to fund school fees, this can best be done as part of their inheritance tax planning and in the form of a maintenance and accumulation trust. This particular legal structure is described in Chapter 35. If you have a low income, your child may get all or part of the fees paid through the Assisted Places Scheme (see READ 📖 WRITE ✎ RING ☎). The child must be as academically gifted as other children at the school, and the age of entry will usually be 11 to 13. The Scheme provides help only with day or tuition fees, but an assisted place may be given to children to attend boarding schools if the boarding fees are paid from other sources. In the 1995–6 school year, fees will be paid in full if parental "relevant" income is £9572 or less (in tax year 1994–5). As income rises, the parental contribution increases, e.g., parents will have to contribute £5187 for one assisted place holder if their income is £29 000. The maximum parental income at which children will be eligible for assistance will vary with each school's fees.

If the Conservatives stay in power, the Assisted Places Scheme may be expanded. If Labour assumes power, the scheme may be terminated.

Borrow

If you don't do any planning, or you simply haven't had the money to do any, you may have to borrow at the time the fees are due. You can probably best do this by using your home as security. But would that be wise? If you haven't saved the money, why will you now be able to foot the bills? Is it really worth sending your child to an independent school when you might lose your home? You may not feel under any great pressure because you may not have to repay the loan for a very long period, but you are probably just short-changing your retirement income. It is worth remembering that it is possible to be well educated in the State system, although the reason many children go to independent schools has nothing to do with education.

HIGHER EDUCATION FEE PLANNING

If a man empties his purse into his head no one can take it away from him, An investment in knowledge always pays the best interest.

Attributed to Benjamin Franklin

State finance for higher education is a mixture of grants, which are means-tested, and loans. The regulations are quite complex and what is stated here is intended only to give you a flavour of the issues involved, and not provide you with complete information. The information here relates to England and Wales.

Students get financial support from grants, loans and Access Funds. The last are available for students with particular financial difficulties and will not be discussed here (but see READ 📖 WRITE ✑ RING ☎).

Local authorities give awards for undergraduate degrees, HNDs, Diplomas of Higher Education and some other full-time courses. The awards include tuition fees, which are paid direct to the institution, and a grant for living costs. The maximum value of the grant for 1995–96 is shown in Table 30.1, and payment is made after means-testing. For most students it will be parental income that is means-tested, although for some students it will be the spouses' income that is relevant. In Table 30.2, I show the assumed total parental contribution for various residual income levels, which is income after certain deductions such as pension contributions. (The scale is different for spouses.) The grant will be cut by whatever the table suggests the parents should be contributing (there is a sliding scale for income levels that fall between the values shown). The cut is made whether or not the parent pays the sum. The actual deemed parental contribution may not be as high as suggested by Table 30.2, because the contribution *per child* cannot be more than the relevant grant e.g., £2340 for a student in London. Also, if parents have other dependent children, their contribution will be reduced by £75 for each child.

Students can also get loans from their college, and this is not means-tested. Loans are interest-free, but the sum to be paid back is the sum borrowed increased by the rate of subsequent inflation. The 1995–6 loan levels are shown in Table 30.3.

The important thing to be aware of is the shift that is taking place between grants and loans. In recent years the total of grants and loans has been rising, but within that

Table 30.1   Higher Education Grants: 1995–6

In London	£2340
Elsewhere	£1885
Living at parental home	£1530

Table 30.2   Means-Tested Parental Contribution: 1995–6

Parent's residual income	Parental contribution
below £15 510	nil
£15 510	£45
£20 000	£409
£25 000	£968
£30 000	£1550
£35 000	£2244
£40 000	£2939
£45 000	£3633
£50 000	£4327
£60 599 or more	£5800

Table 30.3   Higher Education Loans: 1995–6

	Full year	Final year
In London	£1695	£1240
Elsewhere	£1385	£1010
Living at parental home	£1065	£780

total, the main grant rates have been cut, while the loan rates have been increased to make up the total. In 1996–7 the main grant rates will again be cut by around 10% and the total will be adjusted. Clearly, UK higher education funding has been, and still is, moving away from grants to loans.

The implications vary for parents. For rich parents, the shift is probably advantageous. Rich parents have long been means-tested for student grants. When there wasn't a student loan system, it was difficult for students to pay their own way. Inevitably children of rich parents who received a small grant relied on their parents for support. As the UK moves to a loan system, students have a source of funds other than their parents and, if the parents wish, they can pay less and less, and the students pay more and more.

Students from poor families will pay more as the full grant falls in value and, of necessity, is replaced by a loan. Poor parents won't be affected.

Of course, it could be argued that it is unfair to saddle students with a debt at the start of their working life, and many parents will either want to, or will have to, take over the burden. With more students in higher education, this will be a dilemma for more parents.

Planning for higher education fees

How much parents have to pay for their children's higher education will depend on their income, and whether they want to repay any loans their children take. For parents paying school fees, higher education fees just mean that they will be paying for education for longer. Whatever strategy has been adopted for school fees can be adopted for higher education. However, since higher education fees have to be paid so far in the future, a more equity-orientated strategy will be warranted.

A much higher proportion of the population will go on to higher education than will go to independent schools. Thus a large number of parents will have to think about meeting higher education fees without having had to meet school fees. The strategy is easy, at least in principle. You will know when your child is very young whether it is likely to be able to go on to higher education. Start saving immediately, and buy equities, perhaps in the form of a PEP, but perhaps just as a regular savings plan into an investment trust or unit trust if you are not saving very much and the PEP charges would be onerous. You might save for ten years from, say, when your child is four through to thirteen, then you might start to withdraw your money year by year and switch it into a TESSA and high-yield cash fund. You could aim to be mainly in cash about the time your child goes to college. This may not be necessary, but makes more sense as a strategy than for school fees, because the period of higher education is relatively short compared to the period for school fees, and it is possible that the stockmarket could perform poorly for the three years of higher education.

If you plan to foot the bills, should your child take a loan? Yes. TESSA rates are currently much higher than the rate of inflation, so you would be better off if your offspring takes a loan (costing the rate of inflation) and you repay it (from an account earning more than the rate of inflation) rather than you giving your offspring the cash and not taking a loan. A non-taxpaying parent could simply use a savings account rather than a TESSA.

If, after all the planning, students end up with more debt than the student loan when they graduate, and their parents don't pick up the bill, they should make sure they have some form of graduate banking loan (offered by most of the major banks) where the rate of interest may be zero for a few months after graduation, and then about 9%, and which will be much cheaper than other sources of finance. All forms of debt such as overdrafts, credit card debt, etc., should be paid off and converted into a graduate banking loan.

READ 🕮 WRITE 🖃 RING ☎

♦ The Mintel study I cite is: "School Fees Planning", *Mintel: Personal Finance Intelligence*, Vol. 2, 1994.

♦ You can get information on school fees specialists, the Assisted Places Scheme and much more from: Independent Schools Information Service, 56 Buckingham Gate, London, SW1E 6AG. Tel: 0171 630 8793.

♦ For official leaflets on assisted places contact the appropriate office. For schools in England: Department of Education, Assisted Places Team, Mowden Hall, Darlington, DL3 9BG. Tel: 01325 392163. For schools in Wales: Welsh Office Education Department, SAD:3, Phase II, Government Buildings, Ty Glas Road, Llanishen, Cardiff, CF4 5WE. Tel: 01222 761456 ext. 5362. The Scottish scheme is significantly different: Scottish Education Department, Room 4/08, New St Andrew's House, Edinburgh, EH1 3SY. Tel: 0131 244 5521.

♦ For information on higher education grants see: *Student Grants and Loans*, available from the Department of Education, Publications Centre, PO Box 2193, London E15 2EU. Tel: 0181 533 2000. Student Awards Agency for Scotland, Gyleview House, 3 Redheughs Rigg, South Gyle, Edinburgh EH12 9HH. Tel: 0131 244 5823. Department of Education for Northern Ireland, Rathgael House, Balloo Road, Bangor, Co. Down, BT19 7PR. Tel: 01247 279279. Welsh Office Education Department, FHE1, 3rd Floor, Cathays Park, Cardiff, CF1 3NQ. Tel: 01222 825831. *Student Grants and Loans* briefly covers Access Funds—students can get details from their college.

31

Miscellaneous Investments

The time has come, the Walrus said, to talk of many things.
                                                    Lewis Carroll

In this chapter I make short comments on a variety of investments. Some of the investments discussed here could perhaps be discussed in Chapter 32 ("Investments to Avoid"), but as they are new, and nobody has any experience of them, I can't really justify a strong position. And some of the investments discussed here don't really fit into any other chapter.

PREMIUM BONDS

Gaming is a principle inherent in human nature. It belongs to us all.
                                                    Edmund Burke

Premium Bonds are not usually treated as a serious investment, but for the wealthy investor they may be a sensible investment. Premium Bonds can be cashed in quickly, so it is reasonable to treat them as a near-cash investment. Most readers would have been a bit startled, however, to see Premium Bonds right after the chapter on savings accounts, which is why I have relegated them to this chapter. The National Lottery, on the other hand, is just a flutter and I've allocated that to Chapter 32.

Premium Bonds are a government security issued by the Treasury in £1 units, although the minimum value that can be purchased is £100. The maximum holding is £20 000. Anybody aged 16 or over can buy Premium Bonds, and they can be bought for children under 16 by their parents, grandparents or guardians. They are free of both capital gains and income tax. They do not pay income but, after they have been held for a complete month, are eligible for inclusion in a monthly prize draw. The value of the prizes is currently 4.75% of the value of bonds sold. The structure of the prizes is shown in Table 31.1.

There are a fixed number of prizes per month—350 000. By far the largest number of prizes are the lower value prize of £50. These also account for most of the prize fund by value. There are few higher value prizes and, in particular, just one prize of £1 000 000 per month. National Savings estimate that in May 1996 the chances of winning a prize in any month will be about 1 in 17 200 per Premium Bond held. Because the number of prizes is fixed, the odds of winning a prize will decline as more

Table 31.1 Structure of Monthly Premium Bond Prizes

Prize	Percentage of Prize Fund
Higher value prizes (£1 million, £100 000, £50 000, £25 000, £10 000, £5000)	10%
Medium value prizes (£1000 and £500)	15%
Lower value prizes (£100 and £50)	75%

Bonds are sold. But since the size of the prize fund by value will grow (it's 4.75% of the value of sales), the odds of winning a more valuable prize will grow. Think of it this way. If your odds are 1 in 17 200 of winning a prize, with £50 by far the most likely prize, then if sales double, your odds of winning a prize will fall to 1 in 34 000, but the prize will most likely be £100. Currently, the odds of winning the £1 000 000 prize are about 1 in 5½ billion, or 1 in 460 million in the course of a year.

Are premium bonds a good investment?

A lot of people hold Premium Bonds: nearly a million hold more than £1000 worth, and about 35 000 hold the maximum of £20 000. For the people holding, say, £100 of Premium Bonds, the Bonds are probably best viewed as a flutter. The holders have entered a monthly lottery and they can always get their stake money back. With £100 of bonds, their chance of winning a prize in a year is about 1 in 14, and it will probably be £50.

For somebody holding £20 000 of Bonds, the flutter aspect diminishes. On average the holder should win slightly more than one prize a month, or 14 prizes a year. In any one year, the outcome could be very different—the holder might win only six prizes, say, or perhaps 24 prizes. The number will vary from year to year—it might even be no prizes. But over a few years, we might expect the holder to achieve pretty much the average number of wins. The average return is 4.75% tax-free, or about 7.9% grossed-up at 40%, so this appears to be a good return for what is effectively near-cash and government guaranteed. Throw in the chance of winning £1 000 000, and the deal becomes irresistible. Or does it?

The problem is that in calculating the 4.75% return, all the prizes are included. The big prizes are few in number but take up a significant amount of the prize money. The chances of even a £20 000 holder winning the big prize is still negligible. It's about 1 in 23 000 in the course of a year. It is likely that a large holder will win a prize most months, but the odds are the prize will be nearly always be £50, with the occasional £100. Although Premium Bond holders taken as a whole will get a 4.75% return, this will be made up of a few winners with astronomical rates of return, many small holders with a zero rate of return, and nearly all big holders with a rate of return somewhat below 4.75%. For example, if we expect our big holder to win on average 14 prizes a year, but to win say, 13 prizes of £50, and one of £100, then the return works out at 3.75%, or about 6.25% grossed up.

Is 6.25% a good return? Well, clearly it is for near-cash, but it is less than the grossed-up return from a TESSA. If we are now discounting the chance of hitting the jackpot, we have to ask whether it makes sense to have £20 000 invested in near-cash. If you have a million pounds in assets, having £20 000 (or 2% of your assets) in Premium Bonds isn't excessive. But if you have £100 000, having 20% of your money in Premium Bonds does seem excessive. You will presumably have some cash as well, and it would seem to me that you have too much in cash and near-cash, and not enough in shares, which will probably produce higher returns. But this view depends on your investment horizon. If you are young and we are talking about your long-term savings, what I have said is probably right. But if you plan to pay large university fees in a year or two, so you don't want to be exposed to volatile equities, Premium Bonds might be sensible. As so often with investments, it all depends on your investment horizon and attitude to risk.

One final comment. It is possible to be asset rich and income poor. You might not have an income except from your investments, and with only a few investments not paying out an income (e.g., you may be reinvesting tax-free PEP income), your taxable income may be modest and your tax rate may not be the higher rate. In that case, the grossed-up equivalent yield on your Premium Bonds will be lower than stated above, and the case for them correspondingly weaker.

BUSINESS EXPANSION SCHEME (BES)

The BES was a means of investing in small unquoted companies and obtaining tax relief to compensate for the risk. No new investments after 31 December 1993 qualify for tax relief, although existing investments continue to enjoy tax advantages. I have not listed the details of this scheme as no new investment is possible, and existing investors should know the rules (and in any case have little control over when, and whether, they can realize their investments).

The scheme was marked by the ingenuity of sponsors to exploit legal loopholes and to find companies that investors would support. While some sponsors had marketing skills there is little evidence that any of the larger BES managers had any skills in selecting good investments. I am not aware of any statistical study of BES returns. None of the leading managers has advertised its track record. Since they were good at making the mundane look marvellous, I assume the record is dire.

EMPLOYEE SHARE SCHEMES

Many companies offer their employees shares in their company by means of save as you earn schemes, profit sharing schemes, and share option schemes. These investments have tax advantages and should be considered, especially following the changes in the 1995 Budget.

In a **save as you earn (SAYE) scheme**, companies offer all employees who have been with them for a qualifying period, the option to buy shares at a fixed price in three, five or seven years' time, using the proceeds of a SAYE contract. The employees pay a monthly contribution (£5 minimum, £250 maximum). At the end of an agreed period the savings can be repaid with a bonus (or left to the next period for a bigger bonus) or used to buy shares at the fixed price, which can be as low as 80% of the price of the shares when the contract was begun. The bonus is tax-free, and there is no tax on any gain in the share price between the date the option was granted and the date exercised.

In an **approved profit sharing scheme**, all employees who have been with a company for at least five years are allocated free shares in the company. The number of shares allocated will depend on seniority, length of service, and so forth. The initial market value given to any for an individual in any tax year cannot exceed the greater of 10% of earnings (maximum £8000), or £3000. The shares have to be placed in a trust for two years, but can be removed and sold after that. If they are sold before the end of year three there is an income tax charge on the value of the shares. If the shares are sold after three years, there is no income tax to pay. Dividends received in the three-year period belong to employee, and are subject to income tax. CGT is chargeable on any gain made.

Approved share option schemes give employees the option to buy shares in their company. For tax relief to be obtained, there is a limit of £30 000 on the value of shares under option which may be held by an employee at any one time (the value calculated by reference to the value of the shares when the options were granted). Also, the options must not be granted at a discount to the share price at the date of the grant. If the option is exercised between three and ten years after it was granted, and not within three years of another option exercise, there is no liability to income tax. Any gains made on the options will be liable for CGT.

Are these good investments? An approved profit sharing scheme offers something for nothing, so it seems to be attractive. On the other hand, if there is the alternative of a cash bonus that can be spent on anything, the cash may be better. It could be tax-sheltered in an AVC, FSAVC, etc. Approved share option schemes will be worth having if you exercise the option and immediately sell the shares, but if you retain the shares you are then deciding to invest in a single company. It is usually better to diversify. A general PEP would seem to be more flexible than a SAYE scheme: there is a trade-off to be made between tying yourself to only one share versus the benefit of up to a 20% discount.

THE ENTERPRISE INVESTMENT SCHEME (EIS) AND VENTURE CAPITAL TRUSTS (VCTs)

The EIS was introduced in January 1994 and replaced the Business Expansion Scheme (BES). When you invest in a company that qualifies under the EIS, you get income tax relief at 20% on up to £100 000 in any tax year. Qualifying companies are those that are not quoted on the Stock Exchange or USM, do not deal in land or shares, are not in financial or legal services or invest in collectable goods (e.g., wines). You must not own the company, nor should your family or business partners own more than 30%. You may not be a paid director or employee of the firm, but can become a paid director after your investment, provided you had no relationship prior to your investment. Investments can be made direct or via funds. You need to hold the shares for five years not to have some tax relief clawed-back. The shares are exempt from capital gains tax on first disposal, and losses on first disposal may be offset against income or other capital gains in the year of disposal.

Venture Capital Trusts began in 1995. A VCT issues shares like a conventional investment trust and invests in unquoted companies. VCTs are quoted on the Stock

Exchange. No more than £1 million may be invested by a VCT in any company, and it must have assets of less than £10 million. VCTs offer 20% income tax relief at the time of investment, and must be held for five years to avoid clawback. The maximum investment you get income tax relief on in any tax year is £100 000. Providing you do not exceed this, you can get tax-free dividends.

Both types of investment offer a further tax advantage, capital gains tax (CGT) re-investment relief. If the capital gains from any investments are re-invested in an EIS or VCT, the capital gains realization is deferred. This has allowed some commentators to state that EIS and VCT are subject to 60% tax relief (20% income tax relief and 40% capital gains). This is misleading. CGT is charged at the tax rate applicable to the top slice of your income—this need not be as high as 40%. Further, the CGT saving is only a deferral—the tax has to be paid when the new investment is sold. Of course, this might be a very long deferral, or only occur on death. But it could occur when CGT is at a higher level than it is currently.

Are the EIS and VCTs worth investing in? Consider the case of an investor without CGT to defer. A 20% income tax inducement is not compelling when you consider that you will incur costs of perhaps 5% to 7% when you invest and suffer annual charges of perhaps 2½% to 4%. You may find that the manager gives himself an option to buy shares in five years' time at the issue price, so any gains will be partially diluted by the manager. Even with 40% tax relief (and 60% in the first few years) few BES investors have made a positive return, let alone done better than cash deposits, in any of the high risk ventures that EIS or VCTs will have to invest in. EIS or VCTs managed by the old BES sponsors are probably best avoided until they prove themselves with these new vehicles. There are, however, a number of managers of quoted venture capital investment trusts who will be interested in VCTs. Their record indicates they may be competent managers—but few have a record with companies of the size VCTs will be required to invest in.

It is hard to see why VCTs won't be like most other investment trusts and trade at a discount. To save 20% tax on a high risk investment that goes to a 15% discount does not seem especially attractive. Why not wait till the VCT sells at a discount? Because, alas, the initial 20% income tax-break goes to investors buying new shares and not to those buying in the market (although buyers in the market will still qualify for tax-free dividends). But you could reasonably argue that the short-run price doesn't matter—to keep the full tax-breaks you are locked in anyway for five years.

If the underlying investments are sound, VCTs offer high yields. Say a VCT yields 4%. After 20% income tax relief, a £100 investment effectively costs £80, raising the yield to 5%. Because this is tax-free, for a 40% income tax payer, this is equivalent to a taxable yield of 8.3%. For an investor with 40% CGT to defer, the effective purchase cost would be £40, so the taxable equivalent yield would be 16.7%. Of course, if the trust performs badly, and you lose all or part of your capital, and if dividends are not maintained, the picture changes. Also, I've ignored the managers' charges.

GUARANTEED EQUITY BONDS

Guaranteed equity bonds are offered by insurance companies, building societies and banks. They provide a guaranteed annual income or guaranteed accumulated income.

Table 31.2   Specimen Returns From £10 000 Investment in Equity Bond

Movement of relevant Index over 4 years	Accumulated income		
	Income reinvested	Capital return	Total
5% or more decrease	£4600	£6000	£10 600
2.5% decrease	£4600	£8000	£12 600
No change	£4600	£10 000	£14 600
Any increase	£4600	£10 000	£14 600

For, example, one issued in 1995 was offering 10% p.a. income for four years (paid monthly or annually) or 46% accumulated income over a four-year period. The capital return was not, however, guaranteed but depended on the performance of either the FT-SE 100 Index or the S&P 500 Index. In Table 31.2, I show the returns for the accumulated income version of the product.

The FT-SE 100 yielded about 4% when the bond was issued, so the income from the index over four years would be about 16%. Allowing for dividend growth of 5% per annum and compounding, this would increase to over 18%. In other words, the market could fall 18%, before an investor would suffer a return of 0%. To beat the return shown in the first row, the market could fall by up to 12%. The minimum return is therefore not especially attractive, but it would be in truly awful bear market conditions. For a market fall of 2.5% or no change, the bond's return beats the market's. But the bond caps returns on the upside. If the market rises by 6% p.a., or more, the market will give a better return. The tax treatment (16% for higher rate taxpayers on the income or increase in value) might be advantageous for some investors, but is less attractive than that for a PEP.

These products come in many versions, and are popular. But it is hard to see why they should appeal to most people. The problem is that while they remove some of the risks of stockmarket investing, they also remove some of the potential reward. To some people that may seem a fair deal. But surely conservative investors should be investing in deposit accounts and not taking any equity risk. It would be easy to find a safe investment that gave a return that was better than the worst outcome in Table 31.2 (although not as good as the best return). If you don't like risk, I don't think you should buy a guaranteed equity bond. If you are willing to accept risk, I don't see why you want to accept a cap to your returns—you should buy an equity investment. Any equity capital gains might fall within your CGT exemption, especially after indexation, or they could be taken tax-free within a PEP.

Guaranteed equity bonds are fixed term products and you may not get your capital sum back if you cash in early. The Age Allowance trap may also apply.

TRADED ENDOWMENT POLICIES

You get a poor return if you surrender an endowment policy. There are three reasons for this. In the early years the policy and commission costs are borne and so not much of the premium is invested. Second, insurance companies have given low surrender values to encourage policy holders not to cash-in the policy which would deprive the insurance company of a stream of annual charges. Third, there hasn't been much pressure to force insurance companies to offer better terms.

Despite the poor returns, most policies are surrendered early. However, a with-profits endowment policy holder doesn't have to cash-in a policy by surrender to the insurance company that issued it; the policy can be sold to anyone. In recent years there has been a rapid growth in traded endowment policies (TEPs), also known as second-hand endowment policies. Trade in TEPs is now probably in the order of £125 million per annum, against about £5 million in 1988. There are about 20 firms that trade in this market, with most of the business done by the largest half dozen. With most firms you ask for a list of the policies they have, and buy the one you want at the price indicated, but one firm holds a physical auction, and another holds a postal auction. (For the names of some firms in this market see READ 📖 WRITE ✑ RING ☎.)

How should you value a TEP? First, you look at what it will be worth on maturity. This will require assumptions about the reversionary and terminal bonuses. Most sellers will provide an estimate based on maintenance of current rates. Because reversionary bonuses once granted cannot be withdrawn, there is only uncertainty about future bonuses. This means that buyers will usually be most interested in policies that are through their early years of high costs, have a lot of reversionary bonuses locked in, and have perhaps six years to run to maturity. Next you look at the costs of the TEP. These will be the purchase cost and the remaining premiums, all of which will be paid by the buyer of the TEP. Finally, you can calculate the rate of return you will get. If this is attractive, you buy, if not you look at a different policy.

The above is just an outline of the decision process. You would also need to consider the quality of the life company that issued the policy, the size of the policy, the original term of the policy, and whether the policy is qualifying (in which case the gain is subject to CGT) or non-qualifying (the gain is liable to both income tax and CGT).

If you buy a policy you will be paid out either when the policy matures, or on the death of the original policy holder. Unfortunately you have to know when the original policy holder dies. You might find this by asking the original policy holder for the name of his executor or executrix and asking him to notify you on the death of the policy holder. The executor could, of course, be the person's spouse. Rather you than me.

Historical returns of 10–12% are quoted for TEPs and the calculations some traders make suggest current policies will yield 12–13%, or more. But historical returns achieved in a market worth £5 million per annum are not necessarily relevant to current conditions. Part of the terminal bonus comes at the expense of those cashing in early. If fewer people do this, and early surrender values are increased, as has been happening, future terminal bonuses will be smaller. Moreover, bonus rates are currently being cut because of lower underlying investment returns, and it seems unlikely that the illustrative 12–13% returns will be achieved on current purchases. If bonus rates are cut by 25% from the levels of 1994, many of the most commonly traded TEPs would give a return nearer to 9–10%. Prospective returns of perhaps 9–12% might be a realistic range.

While TEPs may be attractive for some investors, most people will lack sufficient knowledge to make an informed judgement about future bonus rates or be able to do the maths necessary to calculate the expected return. And don't forget that once the TEP is purchased, there will be a cash outflow until maturity because the premiums will have to be paid. If you are forced to sell the TEP you have bought, the costs will ensure you make little, if any, return.

TEPs are worth looking at if you wish to sell your policy. You should at least get some quotes from some of the firms trading in this market to set alongside the surrender value offered by the insurance company that issued the policy. If you cancel your policy in the first three years, you will find that the TEP market will not be interested in it. But if you have a policy of the kind that the market is interested in, you will probably get at least 10% more from the market than you would from the insurer, and perhaps substantially more.

As well as the TEP market, there is also a market for the policies of those with a known terminal illness. This is called the viatical settlements market. In the UK the market is dominated by three firms. They are interested in policies with a minimum death benefit of £10 000 and a maximum of between £85 000 and £200 000. The policy holder must have a terminal illness and a life expectancy of up to four years. The maximum purchase price will be around 70% of the death benefit. For more information see READ ▢ WRITE ▢ RING ☎.

OFFSHORE FUNDS

Any fund that is not based in the UK may be considered to be an offshore fund, and this would include many excellent US mutual funds. Some of these, e.g., the international index fund and extended US market index fund sold by the Vanguard Group, may well be worth considering. But the term offshore fund usually refers to a fund located in a tax haven such as the Channel Islands, the Isle of Man or Luxembourg and that is what will be discussed here. These funds operate in a manner similar to unit trusts, although some of them are technically companies. They may invest in equities, bonds, currencies and some more exotic investments. Offshore funds, often managed by UK household names, make good sense for people living abroad, but there are few advantages for UK residents. Most readers should skip this type of investment and also this section. Note that high interest offshore deposit accounts are not considered here, but in Chapter 5. They may make sensible investments for UK residents.

Why have an overseas fund?

Some investors show an unhealthy interest in offshore funds. These investors are scared of having assets in the UK, or hope to illegally avoid paying taxes or simply don't understand the nature of overseas investments.

Whenever there is a Labour government, or the prospect of one, some investors want to physically shift their assets to a foreign jurisdiction. The value of this is unclear. If the objective is to avoid British taxation, this will not work (subject to the comments later), because British residents are liable to tax on their world-wide investment income and assets. (It will work for those who are non-UK domiciled but UK resident, but few people fall into that category.) If the objective is to escape exchange control, the effectiveness will depend on the nature of the controls. Moreover, given Britain's membership of the EU, exchange control seems unlikely.

Some people do, of course, shift money overseas with the intention of concealing income and assets from the Inland Revenue. If you plan to do that, a word of warning. Don't turn up with a suitcase of money in the UK. UK financial institutions probably don't care about your attitude to taxes, but they are subject to strict regulations concerned with the prevention of laundering of drug money and will report you to the authorities if you have unexplained wealth.

Some investors believe that if they put their money abroad, or if it is denominated in a foreign currency, they have eliminated the risk of sterling depreciation. This is mistaken. The currency risk is solely dependent on the nature of the assets held, and is not dependent on their location or the currency in which the fund is valued.

To see this, let's assume you invest £1000 in a fund in the UK which invests in US cash, and that the fund's value is reported in sterling. Let's also assume that the exchange rate is originally £1=$1.5, but sterling subsequently depreciates to £1=$1. Your £1000 initially will be invested in $1500. When the exchange rate changes, your fund will still be invested in $1500, but at the new exchange rate this will be worth £1500 because $1=£1. So, even though your fund is in the UK and the value calculated in sterling, you have made a profit because you were invested in dollars when sterling depreciated against the dollar.

Now let's assume you invest in a fund based in the Bahamas, which invests in sterling cash, but reports its value in dollars. Let's assume the same investment and exchange rates as above. You invest £1000 which is in turn is invested in £1000 of sterling cash deposits, but the valuation is given in dollars and will appear as $1500. The exchange rate moves as before (to £1=$1), so your units invested in £1000 cash will now be reported in dollars as $1000. You appear to be worse off. But let's cash in your units valued at $1000. When you exchange this back into sterling at a rate of $1=£1, you will get £1000. In this example your money has been offshore and your fund valued in dollars but, because your underlying investment was in sterling, you have been unaffected by exchange rate movements.

If you still want an offshore fund to avoid exposure to sterling, re-read the last two paragraphs as many times as it takes for the urge to go away.

Two good reasons for holding offshore funds are that you intend to emigrate and you are doing some advance planning or that there are genuine tax advantages for you. A poor reason is that you want to invest in something that offshore funds can invest in, but onshore funds are not permitted to. I will mainly discuss the taxation issue here, after giving a few general details.

Offshore funds must satisfy certain conditions before they can be marketed in the UK. They can either apply directly for authorization or they must be registered in an area with regulatory standards as good as in the UK. This can be a country with "designated territory status", i.e., Jersey, Guernsey, the Isle of Man and Bermuda, or a fund with UCITS (Undertaking for Collective Investments in Transferable Securities) status, currently Luxembourg and Dublin. Because the funds are not subject to UK Department of Trade and Industry regulation, they can invest in a wider range of assets such as currencies, physical commodities such as gold, and derivatives. With the exception (perhaps) of currencies, I don't think you should want to invest in these assets.

With regard to compensation payments, Jersey and the Isle of Man have the same terms as the UK, Bermuda has very similar terms, and Guernsey is slightly less generous to investors with £50 000 and less invested, and more generous to the £100 000 investor.

Finally, with regard to cost, the stated management fees are often misleading. Many costs can be charged to the fund that a manager would bear in the UK. These potential charges will be indicated in the small print, but most investors will skim over that.

Taxation issues

Offshore funds in tax havens are generally exempt from taxation except perhaps for a low rate of corporation tax or some form of modest ad valorem tax (perhaps 1%). But your income may well suffer more tax than it would in a non-haven.

Many countries have some form of withholding tax on dividends paid abroad, often 10% or 15%, but double taxation agreements mean that these withholding taxes are recognized by the tax authorities of the persons receiving the dividends and count as a payment towards any tax due. Thus, if your money suffers withholding tax of 10%, and you pay tax at 40%, the Inland Revenue will only ask for 30% more. Tax havens do not usually have these double taxation agreements, so any withholding tax suffered by offshore funds is irrecoverable. If you receive a dividend from a tax haven which has suffered 10% withholding tax, and you pay tax at 40%, the Inland Revenue will still want 40% from you.

For UK residents it is important to distinguish between funds with distributor status and those without, for this affects their tax position. The main condition for distributor status is that at least 85% of the income arising in the fund is distributed. This status is granted (or not) every year, after the event, by the Inland Revenue.

Funds with distributor status   Dividends are paid gross and are liable to income tax at both lower and higher rates. Tax is assessed on a prior year basis, so there is an advantageous delay in paying. Capital gains tax is payable on disposal of fund units or shares in the same way as for onshore units or shares. Given the potentially higher tax bill because of irrecoverable withholding tax, and the somewhat higher costs off-shore funds often have, it is hard to see the attraction of most equity and bond distributor funds for UK residents. High income sterling cash funds for a non-taxpayer may be attractive.

Funds without distributor status   For these funds, the gross income accumulates within the fund and there is no tax liability until a sale is made. Compounding thus occurs on the gross income instead of the net income. When a sale occurs, the total gain—both capital and income—is taxed as income in the year of disposal. There is no capital gains liability. This means that the investor loses the benefit of indexation and the annual capital gains exemption. The gain is taxed under Schedule D Case VI and, if a loss arises, it can only be offset against other income taxable under Schedule D Case VI. Since such income is rare, the investor effectively loses the opportunity to use capital losses to offset capital gains. However, for an investor who realizes any gain during a period of low income, e.g., after retirement, or while not subject to

UK taxes, e.g., during a period of employment overseas, the tax treatment can be attractive.

Umbrella funds   These are mentioned here because they had tax advantages at one stage. Some management groups have marketed funds which have a number of equity and bond sub-funds (all under one umbrella) and which allow cheap switches between the sub-funds. This provided a way of making investment switches, but postponing crystallizing capital gains until the fund was disposed of. The 1989 Budget eliminated this tax shelter by treating each sub-fund switch as a disposal.

READ 📖 WRITE 🖹 RING ☎

♦ If you own Premium Bonds and you have moved home since you bought them, make sure National Savings knows your new address. It is sitting on lots of unclaimed prizes. To record your change of address, write to: Premium Bonds, National Savings, Lytham St Annes, FY0 1YN, stating your Holder's Number.
♦ For the names of some TEP dealers contact The Association of Policy Market Makers, Holywell Centre, 1 Phipp Street, London EC2A 4PS. Tel: 0171 729 5143. See also: "Trading Places", *Money Management*, December 1995, 57–68.
♦ For details of the viatical settlement providers, see Stephanie Spicer, "Terminal Bonus", *Money Management*, July 1995, 55–58.

32

Investments to Avoid

There are two times in a man's life when he should not speculate: when he can't afford it, and when he can.

Mark Twain

The investments to avoid are the ones that perform poorly. That much is easy—the hard part is knowing what they are. Even in categories of investments that have performed well, such as shares, some individual shares will go bust and prove to have been bad investments. Diversification within categories of investments that we think will do well is the way to get protection against the odd loser. But some entire categories of investments seem to be poor investments for the average person, and those categories are the subject of this chapter. Before you look down the list of investments I think best avoided, let's be clear as to what I'm saying. I'm not arguing that people can't or haven't made fortunes with these types of investments. They have. The issue here is whether *you* can make a good return and even if you can, whether it is worth the effort. You have to consider both risk and return, and make sure you add in all the costs involved in making an investment. Buying an investment trust or putting your money in a high interest cheque account is so easy that the returns from more exotic investments have to be really spectacular if they are to be worth the extra effort and risk.

Investments I think you can ignore are gold, commodities, art and collectibles, the National Lottery, warrants, options, futures, buying on margin, and split capital investment trusts. You can probably ignore property too. I'll discuss each in turn.

GOLD

There are three main reasons for buying gold and three main ways for private investors to do so. The reasons are as an inflation hedge, as protection against social or financial Armageddon, and as an investment. The methods of buying gold are as coins, bullion or shares. (Professionals also deal in the futures market.)

Although gold is always touted as the ultimate inflation hedge, this is simply untrue. Whatever the long-run figures might show—and in this case by long-term I mean centuries—during your investment horizon there is no guarantee that gold will be an inflation hedge. It hasn't been in recent years. Over the long haul, equities and property have been at least as good as inflation hedges, and index-linked gilts are the perfect investment for anyone obsessed by inflation. They give a real return, i.e., they give a return in money terms that will have increased by more than the rate of inflation.

Gold has often been seen as the ultimate protection against social and financial collapse. I've never understood what this means. Presumably if the entire financial system collapses, paper assets become worthless. That must apply to gold shares as much as engineering shares. So presumably it is gold coins or bullion that provides the protection. But would people really walk around with gold bars to do their shopping? How would they get change? Would they be a target for robbers? Where there has been a breakdown in a currency in this century there has been a tendency to substitute another currency (usually the US dollar, but maybe the DM in future) for international transactions and possibly for internal transactions too. When there has been a move to barter, cigarettes have usually been the closest thing to currency. I think you should ignore the possibility of the end of the world as you know it and worry more about paying your mortgage. But if you must worry about The End, you might as well hoard cigarettes or DMs as gold.

Is gold a good investment? When there is a major international scare, many asset prices will tend to fall. However, the price of gold may well rise. This characteristic of gold to do the opposite of other investments is attractive for purposes of diversification and may make gold attractive as part of a portfolio, irrespective of the total return it provides. It is hard to say what the total return from gold will be in the coming years. It will depend on the industrial demand for gold (affected by both world growth rates and technical innovations), the purchases and sales of the world's monetary authorities, the demand for jewellery (affected by the increasing wealth in the Far East), the discovery of new supplies of gold, sales from official and private stocks by countries in turmoil such as Russia and Iraq, and so on. You may have a view as to how all this will work out. However, would you make a big bet on your ability to forecast the price of, say, oil or molybdenum? If not, why make a big bet on gold? A few gold shares, a diversified mining company, or a retailer specializing in jewellery in a well-diversified portfolio might make sense, but a big gold bet doesn't.

I would pass altogether on gold coins and bullion. First, they offer no income. Second, you suffer insurance and possibly storage costs. Third, there is a spread of a few per cent on gold coins between the purchase and selling price, and a higher spread on the smallest gold bars. The spread is narrow on the standard size of gold bar, but unfortunately it weighs about $27\frac{1}{2}$ lb (inconvenient if you want to run when the looting hoards appear on the horizon), and costs over £100 000. Fourth, purchases are subject to VAT and sales may be subject to an assay fee to see that what you are selling really is gold. You can avoid VAT if you buy gold offshore and keep it there, but that will involve storage costs, and again is inconvenient if you want to run from the looting hoards.

COMMODITIES

Commodities fall into two categories: soft, such as cocoa, rubber and coffee and hard, such as tin, zinc and lead. Commodities seem to many people a natural inflation hedge, but they aren't. For example in the last 50 years, commodity prices as a whole rose during the Korean War, steadily fell until the early 1970s, soared, but not to the heights of the Korean War, and then tended down (all this is expressed in constant purchasing power terms, i.e., relative to other prices). Individual commodity prices have displayed very different patterns. You can buy commodities as a long-term investment or on a short-term view.

The long-term path for commodity prices is unclear. Rising world income will tend to push prices up, but technical change will tend to push prices down. This may be because new sources of supply are discovered (e.g., new oil wells in the Atlantic off the Shetland Isles), production made more efficient (the "green revolution" in agriculture), or alternative ways of meeting demand are invented. It is not obvious to me that you should make a big bet on commodities for the long term.

Commodity prices in the short term tend to be very volatile, because of some unusual supply and demand characteristics. For example, sometimes supply cannot be readily increased in response to new demand (new supplies have to be discovered or trees take years to grow), whereas in other cases supply can be readily increased without a change in demand (where there is potential excess supply—e.g., oil—which is only held back by a cartel agreement which may break down). In the short term prices will be affected by natural disasters and politics as well as by economic conditions. It is not obvious that you should want to play the commodity markets in the short term: the factors driving the markets do not seem to be the most predictable, and you will be competing against professionals who buy and sell for the world's major corporations, such as BP, Nestlé and Unilever.

Further, anybody with a well-diversified equity portfolio will have some exposure to commodities via mining, oil, agricultural and other shares. Exposure to some of the foreign stockmarkets will also give exposure to commodity companies or to economies which benefit from rising commodity prices. It seems unnecessary to make a further commodity bet. If you still want to invest in commodities, there are three routes. You can invest in physicals, futures or via a fund.

Investing in physicals means taking delivery of a commodity. This is not an option for most investors, as the size of order is far too large, let alone the problems of storage and deterioration. Investing in commodities by means of futures is just another form of futures trading, which is discussed in a separate section below.

Commodity funds take two forms. The authorized UK funds invest in shares of commodity companies. Some offshore funds do this too, but others invest in physicals and futures. These funds usually trade in a variety of commodities, giving an element of diversification. The fees, however, are often absurd. You could be charged a front-end load of 5%, an annual charge of 2% and a performance fee of up to 20% (i.e., the manager takes 20% of your gains, but does not rebate any of your losses). Some of these funds are run by managers who are also brokers, so that they make a further commission on transacting the futures trades. The fee structure is an inducement to high-risk rapid turnover. If things don't work out, you lose, but the manager doesn't, because he has taken his 5% on your original investment. If the manager deals frequently he makes brokerage commission and, should by chance things work out well, he'll dip into your profits with the performance fee.

Sometimes people are induced to buy a commodity fund with high performance fees by claims of superior past performance. Sometimes this performance is genuine (but probably won't last), sometimes it is a computer record of what would have happened if a certain strategy been followed. Such records are always suspect because there is always a strategy that would have worked in the past. Whether it will work in the future is another matter.

I don't think you need a commodity fund, but if you buy one, make sure you know what its strategy is and how it charges.

ART AND COLLECTIBLES

People often have mixed motives when they talk about art, furniture or other collectibles as an investment. If you buy a picture you like and add "and it will make a good investment", you probably aren't really investing at all. You are probably justifying spending the money. That's OK, but it's not really an investment. Alternatively, some people are interested in art and it is their hobby and they would really like to make it their job, so they start buying and selling pieces of furniture. That's OK too, but it is more a trade than an investment, and your profits may be taxed as income. For art and collectibles to be an investment, I think you have to be consistently adding to a portfolio of physical objects as a means of making capital gains, and as an alternative to more conventional investments. And I don't think that is a very good idea.

The problem is that if you invest in this area, you are competing against experts. Now there is no reason why you can't beat them, but art is liable to fashion fads, and people who are trading every day, and following every auction, are likely to be ahead of you. Second, these investments produce no income, indeed you will bear insurance costs and maybe storage costs too. Third, there are often huge trade mark-ups. If you buy something retail you may suffer a 100% mark-up. Thus for you to break-even, the price has to rise by 100%. If you buy from dealers, you will have to pay VAT. If you see a fancy chart showing indices of prices of various collectibles, remember to check whether it includes all costs. The returns after costs will bear scant relation to price movements. Fourth, depending on what you are investing in, there may not be a ready market when you wish to sell.

THE NATIONAL LOTTERY

The National Lottery sells itself with the line that "It could be you". Indeed it could, but it probably won't. The odds of winning the big prize—perhaps £40 million—are one in fourteen million. Look at it this way: to have an equal odds chance of winning the big prize, you will need to buy a ticket every week of your life and, if you live for 75 years and if reincarnation is true, you will need to keep buying through 3590 lifetimes. Of course there are smaller prizes, but your chances of winning even the smallest, a modest £10, are only 1 in 57, or one prize per year if you buy one ticket each week.

The basic problem with the Lottery is that for every £1 it takes in, it pays out only 50p. For gamblers as a whole, the Lottery promises to halve their money. While Premium Bonds may be an investment, the National Lottery isn't. Sadly, it is the poor who are the heaviest players, i.e., losers.

Ah, but the Lottery helps charities. Yes, but only to the extent of 28% of the ticket price. For the average player, over the years every £1 ticket will make you poorer by

50p, and charities richer by 28p. If you want to do good, give the charities 28p directly and you will only be 28p poorer, instead of 50p poorer if you give it via the Lottery. Better yet, give via a deed of covenant, and you will pay 28p but the charity will be able to get the income tax deducted before you got your 28p. You will also be able to give to who you think is deserving, rather than who someone else does.

Is there no case for the Lottery? Actually there is, but it is not an investment case. If you find the Lottery exciting, if you look forward to watching the numbers appear on television and checking your numbers, by all means play. There are many forms of entertainment that cost more, and return less pleasure. But if you take this view, remember you are not investing but buying entertainment. You will have to make separate provision for investment.

A justification for the Lottery that comes closer to an investment justification is that you won't miss a pound a week and it would not change your life if you invested it. On the other hand, if you won the Lottery, that would transform your life. While the odds of this happening are minute, the impact if it did would be immense.

I don't think this really is an investment justification because the odds of winning are so low. You don't really have any prospect of changing your life. Given the popularity of the Lottery, either a lot of people are short of entertainment, or they have an unrealistic view of the odds. I think that the latter is likely to be an important explanation. Remember my discussion in Chapter 14 of the psychology of the illusion of control? Because players pick their numbers, my guess is that they see themselves in a game of skill and not one of pure chance. They believe their odds of winning to be much higher than they really are. To put matters subjectively, you've "no chance" of winning, but I bet you believe you have a "reasonable chance" of winning. I think you would do better trying to transform your life via Premium Bonds. You won't win the £1 million either, but at least you will keep your stake money.

In addition to what most of us think of as the National Lottery, there are National Lottery scratch cards. You scratch a latex cover off a £1 card and, if you have three matching numbers, you win that amount. The odds of winning are 1 in 5, but as that includes prizes of £1 (your stake money), this is somewhat misleading. Your odds of winning £1000 are 1 in 480 000 and your odds of winning the top prize of £50 000 are 1 in 2 400 000. The advertising slogan is "Forget it All for an Instants." The arithmetic suggests: "Forget it."

WARRANTS

Warrants are securities which have the right to be converted into ordinary shares on specific terms. They have a limited life and, if not exercised, expire worthless. Warrants do not have to be held to their expiry date but can be sold in the stockmarket at any time. They produce no income. They are a geared investment and are best explained by means of an example.

I'll assume an ordinary share is selling at 90p and the warrant at 30p, with the right to subscribe to one ordinary share at 100p in five years' time. If you buy the share you will get dividends. If you buy the warrant you won't. With the warrant costing 30p and the subscription price 100p, it will cost 130p to get into the stock via the warrant. Why buy the warrant, which is a more expensive way into the stock?

- The immediate outlay is only 30p against 90p. This gives a chance to buy more exposure to the stock by buying more warrants, or to invest the difference in another asset such as a deposit account.

- The total downside is 30p versus 90p if the stock goes bust.

- The potential profit is high if the stock performs well. For example, if the stock rises to 200p over five years, a purchase of shares will produce a profit of 122%, i.e.,

$$\frac{(200p - 90p)}{90p} \times 100\% = 122\%$$

whereas purchase of the warrant will produce a profit of 233%, i.e.,

$$\frac{(200p - 100p - 30p)}{30p} \times 100\% = 233\%$$

(These are shortcut calculations. Strictly we should allow for the dividends on the stock and the interest on the 60p (90p − 30p) that could be put in a deposit account.)

Since there is no gain without pain, what's the catch? A small rise in the price of the share will not overcome the extra cost of investing via warrants. If the share rose to 120p, the share investor would make 30p, but the warrant investor would lose 10p (120p − 30p − 100p = −10p). If the price of the share stays at 90p, the warrant holder loses 30p, whereas the share holder loses nothing.

The problem with warrants is that the gearing works both ways, and you have to be very sure of your share selection. Further, not many shares have warrants and the market is quite small. On the plus side, however, is the fact that many investment trusts have warrants, and given that they hold diversified portfolios, it is not so necessary to have a wide spread of warrants. But then you have to be sure that the warrants are priced correctly in relation to the underlying share.

Warrants on investment trusts are not necessarily a bad investment, but I recommend that you give all warrants a miss. The gearing means you could lose a lot of money: you can even lose money when the share price has risen. Add to this the difficulty for most investors to find out what warrants are available and their terms, and warrants seem an unnecessary hassle for most investors. (But see READ 📖 WRITE 🖊 RING ☎.) Making geared investments in individual shares that aren't investment trusts is just foolish for most investors.

Although warrants are not a major market, I have gone through the mechanics because warrants are akin to call (or buy) options, with a longer maturity, but they are easier to understand. (The maths of valuing a warrant is actually much more complex than I have indicated because you have to allow for volatility and other factors. But you will have got a good enough idea for my purposes.)

Many investors find warrants exciting, and although they wouldn't buy any, love the idea of getting some for free. Thus, you often see new investment trusts launched with free warrants attached and brokers selling the fund (for a fat commission) stress the value of these warrants. I have explained why you should not buy a new investment trust in Chapter 16. Free warrants do not affect this decision. When you get shares with warrants, you are both a shareholder and a warrant holder. If you can trade your warrant in for a share at less than the fair price of the share, you gain as a warrant holder, but lose as a shareholder. Shareholders suffer dilution of their position since there are new shareholders with the same rights as the old shareholders, but who have paid less than the fair price for those rights. Since you are both warrant holder and shareholder, you are simply paying money into one pocket and taking it out of another.

However, investors often overlook what I have just explained, and share and warrant packages trade above fair value initially. This means you might make a small profit by applying for a new trust and selling quickly. Over time, this pricing anomaly is unlikely to last. That means if you are making a long-term investment, you would be better off buying a second-hand trust on a discount. If you want a quick speculation, there must be sexier plays than the warrants of new issues of investment trusts!

Wealth warning: exercising warrants   You may have warrants because they came free with investment trust shares. You didn't go out of your way to buy them, and make no pretence at understanding them. If you own warrants you will be told by the company when you can exercise them—usually it is only for a short period each year. But you don't have to exercise them. If you can exercise your warrant and pay, say, £1 for an ordinary share, you should check that you can't buy the share for less in the stockmarket. A lot of investors have been exercising warrants for various investment trusts that are trading at well under their warrant exercise price. They are getting the same sort of deal as they would if they bought 50p coins from me for £1 each.

OPTIONS AND FUTURES

Options

There are two forms of options, traditional options and traded options. When people talk about options, it is usually the latter they are referring to, and that's what I'll discuss here.

An option gives the right—but not the obligation—to buy or sell shares in a company or a market index at a fixed price up to a specific expiry date. The details of options trading are so complex that they would take up far too much room here. The key features of options are that they are highly geared investments (and you have seen the issues raised by gearing in the section above on warrants) and they have a short life. This means your timing has to be spot on. There are two main ways of using options. The first is highly speculative and there is the potential for unlimited gains or losses. The second is as a risk reduction strategy, where known losses and gains are involved, or where the options modify existing equity exposure.

I think options are very unattractive for the average investor and should not be used. There are a number of reasons for this:

- Options are inherently complex, and many investors don't understand what the true risks are. This applies to their brokers too.

- You incur large costs in trading options because the bid-offer spread is wide. You are competing against professionals such as market makers who use the options market to adjust their dealing book exposure. They know more than you, and have lower dealing costs.

- Options are valued on the basis of the life of the option to expiry, the volatility of the underlying stock or market, interest rates, and so forth. This is all pulled together in the Black-Scholes model, a very complex piece of maths, which gives the theoretical price of an option. All options professionals have this at their fingertips, via hand-held computers. You don't, and your stockbroker probably doesn't.

- The options market is a zero-sum game—for every winner there is a loser. However, for you it will be a negative sum game, because of the huge dealing costs (including the spread). If the average result is negative, and you are playing against professionals, in a game where you probably don't understand the rules, why play?

- There are more technical reasons why you shouldn't play. Anyone who still wants to trade options should read the article referred to in READ 📖 WRITE ✉ RING ☎.

Futures

A future is a contract that requires investors to buy or sell a given quantity of a specified asset on a specified future date at a specific price. Futures have traditionally been important for agricultural products, but now cover financial instruments and stock-market indices. Because no physical commodity underlies an index, stock index futures are settled by cash when the contract expires. Cash-settled stock index futures are on a daily marked-to-market basis, i.e., any gain or loss on a future must be settled daily.

Futures are bought and sold on margin. Only a small part of the total value of the future changes hands when the trade is made. The price of a future will be the current index value plus an allowance for interest earned on the cash that can be deposited because of the margined nature of the transaction, less the value of dividends that would be received on the underlying stock. Futures trade at close to the theoretical value, but not always exactly at it. Like traded options, futures can be used for speculative or risk reduction purposes. They are also a highly geared investment.

There are differences between options and futures, but I won't go through them. The only point worth making is that if you sell a traded option or a future you can lose more than the money you put up: your losses are potentially unlimited. If you buy a future, the same is true, but if you buy an option, the most you can lose is your entire investment.

I think you should ignore futures.

Am I Willie the Wimp?

Since your broker may tell you that derivative securities such as warrants, options and futures are attractive, you may feel I am unnecessarily negative. My defence is to remind you of some recent disasters. In the USA, Procter & Gamble is reported to have lost $157 million in this area; Paine Webber used fixed interest derivatives in its mutual funds and lost $268 million; Kidder Peabody bought back particularly risky derivatives and compensated the funds it managed; Askin Capital Management, a Wall Street hedge fund operator, went bust because its deals went wrong; Gibson Greetings lost $20 million; and Eastman Kodak closed positions and took a loss of $220 million. In Canada, Confederation Life, the fifth-largest insurer was driven into bankruptcy following massive investments in derivatives. In Singapore, Mr Leeson lost £860 million, and broke a bank. In the UK, Allied Lyons lost £150 million dealing in currency options, and Union Discount also lost millions.

MARGIN TRADING

Margin trading isn't an investment, but a way of borrowing, usually to make stock-market investments. It is very common in the USA, and may have been one of the causes of the 1929 stockmarket crash. Margin trading is not well known in the UK but is about to become common. At the time of writing, so few accounts exist that my discussion will reflect what will likely be the norm, rather than describe existing accounts.

Margin trading works like this. If your broker holds your assets (such as shares, gilts, cash) and you give him the power to sell them in certain circumstances, he will be willing to advance you a loan against the security of your assets. You will probably be able to get a loan of up to 50% of the value of your portfolio. You will be charged interest at perhaps 4% to 4½% above base rate.

I'll assume that you have decided to buy a share you read about in the Sunday press. You can invest your cash, or you can borrow from your broker, or both. You decide to use your £5000 cash, while your friend, Marvin the Margin, uses his £5000 and borrows £5000. The share is a winner, and rises by 10% in the first month. You will have made £500 while Marvin has made £1000. Marvin will be pleased, and will have benefited from gearing by having bought on margin. So, if the market goes up immediately, buying on margin seems to be a good deal. And it is, but my sums exaggerate the value. Let's fully cost the deal. Base rates are currently (November 1995) 6.75%, so margin interest might be 11%. I'll assume 12% to make the maths easier (i.e., 1% interest for one month). I'll assume 1% commission on buying and selling, ½% stamp duty on buying, 1% price spread (e.g., you can buy at 100p but sell at 99p). On these assumptions you'll have made 10% less buying and selling costs of 3½%, whereas Marvin will have made 10% less costs of 4% (the extra ½% is 1% interest on half the sum invested). So you will have made about £325 (£5000 × 6½%) and Marvin will have made £600 (£10 000 × 6%). (These numbers are approximate, for reasons I'll skip.)

What if the market rose 10% over the course of a year? In the previous example I ignored dividends. Chances are you wouldn't get one in a month. But in a year you would, so I'll assume a 4% dividend. You would now make £525 (£5000 × 10½%), but interest eats into Marvin's return. He would suffer dealing costs of 3½% but also bear interest costs of 6% (i.e., 12% on half his investment). So he would make £450 (£10 000 × 4½%), of which £400 comes from the dividend.

Now let's assume the market falls 10% in a month, and also in a year. You will lose £675 in a month (£5000 × minus 13½%) and £475 in a year (£5000 × minus 9½%). Marvin will lose £1400 in a month (£10 000 × minus 14%) and £1550 in a year (£10 000 × minus 15½%).

This doesn't seem a terrific set of outcomes for the margin trader. He does well if his investment performs well immediately, but not if it performs well over a longer period. And he gets murdered if he gets it wrong. Might you get it wrong? Of course, the stockmarket is notoriously volatile. But I've saved the best to last.

Any fall in the stockmarket will reduce the value of your holdings. If you borrow a large percentage of the value of your assets, you may find that with a large fall in the market, your borrowings as a percentage of your assets have risen above the agreed percentage, and you will be required to deposit more cash or assets—known as a margin call—or your broker may sell part of your position. So, even if your stock eventually performs well, you may not benefit, because your broker might have sold your position.

Margin accounts are great for commission-earning stockbrokers. If you want to make money out of margin accounts, become a broker; otherwise, ignore them.

SPLIT CAPITAL INVESTMENT TRUSTS

Split capital investment trusts are either a very useful financial instrument or they are a clever piece of financial engineering and marketing designed to overcome the problem of discounts. Perhaps they are both, although I think most ordinary investors should ignore them (despite being widely recommended for paying school fees). If you do not completely understand these types of shares—and you will need to read more than what follows to do so—you should not invest in them.

Split capital trusts, unlike conventional investment trusts, have different classes of shares, which have unique characteristics and entitlements. All split capital trusts have wind-up dates (as do a few conventional trusts) which means that at a specific date the trust's assets are sold and the proceeds given to the shareholders according to pre-determined rules. Different split capital trusts have different types of capital, but the most common are zero dividend preference shares, stepped preference shares, income shares, capital shares, and highly geared ordinary shares.

Zero dividend preference shares are shares which are entitled to a fixed sum when the trust is wound up but are not entitled to dividends. The rate of return can be calculated in terms of a gross redemption yield and this can be compared with the return from gilts and products offering guaranteed returns. Although these shares will usually be the first to be paid on wind-up, if the trust has insufficient assets, the shares will not be fully paid.

To assess the likelihood of a default, it is usual to calculate the cover the trust's assets currently provide and to calculate what growth in assets is needed each year to provide for the full amount to be paid. The required rate of growth of assets is called the hurdle rate. For example, a trust's asset cover may be only about 80% of the amount to be repaid, and if the wind-up date is in nearly six years, the assets will have to grow at about 3½% per annum to provide full cover. You might feel that this would be a risky investment, and the share's price would reflect this and offer a high gross redemption yield. If, however, the current cover is, say, three times the amount due at wind-up, the trusts assets can consistently fall and still pay off the shares. The prospective return will be lower in this case, but much safer.

Although many advisers recommend these shares for school fees planning and such like, you should be aware that the market is not large and you have little choice: e.g., there are only six shares that have a life of more than seven years. Once stripped gilts become available (see Chapter 19) most investors probably should use them for school fees planning, because they will be less risky.

Because these shares do not pay income, there is no income tax to pay, and they will be tax efficient for anybody with unused capital gains allowance.

Stepped preference shares offer a predetermined growth in dividends each year and growth of capital at the wind-up date. For example, the shares may be launched with a price of 100p and a yield of 2%, with a growth in dividends of 5% per annum (the annual step) and a wind-up capital value at a specific date of 150p. As with the previous type of share it is usual to calculate the gross redemption yield and the hurdle rate of growth necessary to ensure payment.

Income shares aim to produce a high income whereas **capital shares** aim to produce capital growth. If there are zero dividend or stepped preference shares as well, the situation will be complicated. The easiest case to understand is where there are just income and capital shares and where there are equal numbers of each share. In essence, the income shares get all the income from the trust's assets and the capital shares get all the capital growth. This may be complicated by the income shares getting a modest amount of capital growth or not getting repaid their initial value. In this case, income shares issued at 100p might have a wind-up value of 80p, a guaranteed capital loss. (This would provide some protection for capital share-holders, who have received no income, in the event of poor markets.)

Let's consider the income shares first. We can once again calculate a gross redemption yield using the purchase price, capital redemption value, and the stream of income received. The problem here is that the income stream is unknown. The value of dividends will not depend on a formula, but whatever the underlying equities pay. The way round this is to calculate the gross redemption yield on the basis of various assumed dividend growth rates. For example, for a particular trust, the income shares might have a gross redemption yield of 8.9%, 11% or 13.1% on the assumption of dividend growth of 5%, 7½% and 10% respectively. At the time of writing, a 13.1% return would be attractive, but 8.9% is little better than the return from gilts.

Capital shares are entitled to all the capital gains after all other types of shares have been paid at the wind-up date. After allowing for prior charges, it is possible to calculate the NAV of the capital shares. If various rates of capital growth are assumed, it is possible to compute various sums the capital shares might receive on wind-up. Using the current price and these various sums, possible gross redemption yields can be calculated.

Highly geared ordinary shares are shares which are normally offered in conjunction with zero dividend preference shares. The latter have no income rights and only a fixed capital right. The ordinary shares get all the income and whatever capital remains after paying off the zeros. Once again a gross redemption yield can be estimated, but now both dividend and capital growth rates have to be assumed.

Units are a combination of shares, rather than a class. For example, a trust with income and capital shares might arrange for each class of shares to be quoted and traded on the market, and also the two classes to be combined and traded as a unit. In effect, this enables a split capital trust to offer its shares as though it were a conventional trust as well.

Are split capital trusts for you? It depends on your objectives and your attitude to risk. If you want a specific sum at a specific date, there are alternatives to split capital trusts which you will probably find easier to understand and monitor. Geared positions on the market may well seem attractive. But remember that anybody who has held equities for long periods in the past has done very well. Do you really want to try to do even better, but at the risk of getting a very poor return? Gearing works both ways. Financial advisers often tout new issues of split capital trusts as the answer to all your problems. Make sure you know what the advisers are talking about and that they do too. Ask about the gross redemption yield and what assumptions in terms of asset cover, growth rate, hurdle rate, etc., that the adviser is making. If the adviser says that's all too technical and unnecessary, get another one.

Split capital investment trusts may have a useful role to play in Inheritance Tax planning, and I discuss this in Chapter 34.

PROPERTY

Property represents a major component of world wealth. Think of all the private residences, the property owned by corporations and also farmland. Some years ago, it was estimated that property formed about 55% of the world's physical and financial capital. Somewhat surprisingly, the proportion of property in institutional investment portfolios is quite small. Amongst the largest institutional portfolios it comprises less than 5% in the USA, about 8% in Canada and less than 10% in the UK. Recently property returns have been poor in all the major economies, but over the long haul returns have been attractive. These returns have been achieved with low volatility, although this is misleading. When the property market is weak, few transactions take place. Prices appear to be higher than they would be if a sizeable portfolio had to be liquidated. Even allowing for this, property offers worthwhile diversification potential. That's the positive case for investment. So why don't you need any property investments?

If you have a million pounds of assets, I would be surprised if your home is worth less than £250000. In the London area, it could easily be worth £400000. If you have £150000 in assets, your home probably makes up anywhere from 50% to nearly 100% of your assets. In short, I'd be surprised if your home was worth less than 25% of your assets and I imagine that it is much more. You are already more committed to property than the institutional investors. Do you need more?

You might argue that since you live in your home and you have to live somewhere, your home should not really be counted as part of your investments. Of course, you could use your home as means of raising cash, or you could move to a smaller home. In that case we could perhaps count part of your home as an investment. That still leaves your home as quite a big percentage of your investments, although not quite so dominating as before. However, all those folks with negative home equity probably see their home simply in terms of being a bad investment *in toto*. And you don't have to buy a home. You could rent. I don't think you can escape the view that if you are buying a house you have a large investment exposure to the property market.

So, is property sufficiently attractive that you should have more? While the potential returns and diversification characteristics of property are attractive, equities have given much better total returns in the UK. For example, the Jones Lang Wootton Property Index, which samples office, shop and industrial properties, has increased from June 1967 to 1995 by only just over half as much as has an equity index. I think you should stick to shares since they are easier to deal in and to get good diversification. It is not easy to get good exposure to the whole property market, and property is also difficult to sell in weak market conditions. You probably don't have enough money to buy an individual building, and even if you do, you probably don't have the time or expertise, and it is foolish to put a large sum in a single building. You should be diversified by region and by property type. If you insist on property, these problems force you into property trusts.

You have to be careful with property trusts, and be sure you distinguish between property investors and property developers. Property investors buy buildings and collect the rents. Property developers develop new projects, usually on the back of loans. They are highly geared, and if they develop schemes at the right point in the property cycle they make a fortune, and if they do it at the wrong time, they go bust. You have to be sure you know what type of property investment a trust you are buying makes, and make sure the fund is big enough to be properly diversified. All this can be done, but I doubt that except for the wealthiest investors it is worth doing, especially when you bear in mind that you will almost certainly have some exposure to property if you own equities.

When you buy a pooled equity fund you will get some exposure to property. Only 2% of the stockmarket (in terms of value) consists of shares of property companies, but many other companies have significant exposure to the property market. Brewers and hotel groups have significant property holdings and banks, through their loans, may have significant indirect exposure. If you have a personal pension plan or Section 32 Buyout, you should make sure you know what you are invested in. Many "managed funds" hold equities, gilts and property. You might find that about 20% of your pension fund is invested in property. I can't see the case for you having even more in the investments that you manage.

A special category of property consists of commercial property in Enterprise Zones, which can be bought either as individual buildings or in trusts, which usually have a minimum subscription of £5000. There is 100% Capital Allowance on the buildings. This appears to be a way of a higher taxpayer buying property at a 40% discount. Unfortunately, Enterprise Zone property tends to be overpriced when there are various incentives to firms renting in the Zones. When these incentives end, prices fall. In addition, the 100% Capital Allowance applies only to property, and not to land, which may mean the tax-break applies to only 85–90% of the trust. Add in huge promoter's selling fees, and also promoter's exit fees, and the true discount to asset value will be no more than that on a well-respected property company traded on the London Stock Exchange.

You are locked into an Enterprise Zone property for at least seven years, and possibly for ever. You should require quite exceptional returns to compensate you for your loss of liquidity. You should also be aware that if a trust is sold, both the trust and the investors are each liable to CGT. Many of the existing trusts have been financial disasters, but some have done very well. One problem with this type of investment is that investors often suffer from a lack of information and ability to control the managers. And much of the advertising puts a very favourable gloss on matters. One of the larger trust managers issued Offering Memoranda which made claims about estimated rental values on existing trusts which disappeared after I made a complaint to FIMBRA. Tread carefully with this type of investment.

Is property a bad buy? No, exposure to property in a well-diversified portfolio is sensible. But, given your exposure via your home, possibly your pension fund, and indirectly through shares, the case for additional property exposure is not compelling.

READ 📖 WRITE ✉ RING ☎

◆ In the text I say it is hard to get information on warrants. Warrant prices are not given in most newspapers, but the *Financial Times*'s London Share Service section shows many warrants, especially for investment trusts. Stockbrokers should be able to tell you warrant subscription terms. The terms for investment trust warrants are shown in the Association of Investment Trust Companies, *Monthly Information Service*. AITC, Durrant House, 8–13 Chiswell Street, London, EC1Y 4YY. Tel: 0171 588 5347. Fax: 0171 638 1803. Warrant terms are also shown for each company that has issued warrants in its Annual Report and Accounts.

◆ An excellent article which warns of the dangers of dealing in options is: R. W. McEnally and R. J. Rendleman, "How to Avoid Getting Taken in Listed Stock Options", *AAII Journal*, 12, February 1990, 8–13. The article is reprinted in: Stephen Lofthouse, *Readings in Investments*. Chichester: Wiley, 1994.

33

Wills

When you have told anyone you have left him a legacy, the only decent thing to do is to die at once.

Attributed to Samuel Butler

There seems little point in planning your finances and making provisions for others (e.g., through life insurance and school fees arrangements) and then not making a will. For, without a will, the State decides, through the intestacy rules, who gets your assets. Yet about two-thirds of us die intestate.

It is easy to understand why many people don't draw up a will. Most of us don't like the thought that we will die, or even become old, so we avoid thinking about anything related to death. And many people have additional reasons for not thinking about a will. Single people often assume that their possessions will automatically go to their parents, and then forget to make a will when their parents die. Married people often assume that their spouse will inherit everything, which is only true in specific circumstances, or if their estate is worth less than £125 000 or £200 000 (again depending on the circumstances). There are plenty of family homes in London that would take an estate over these sums. Some people plan to use up their capital before they die and figure it isn't worthwhile making a will. But of course they could be hit by a bus tomorrow, in which case they will leave assets.

You should draw up a will as soon as possible. It is the core of estate planning, i.e., drawing up plans so that as much as possible of your assets is passed on to the people or institutions that you want to benefit. Your will has no effect until you die, and you can change it whenever you wish. If you don't draw up a valid will, the intestacy rules determine what happens to your assets.

THE INTESTACY RULES

The man who wants to make an entirely reasonable will dies intestate.
George Bernard Shaw

The intestacy rules are the same for England and Wales, but are a bit different in Northern Ireland, and substantially different in Scotland. The rules outlined below are for England and Wales—I stress that the following is an outline only. The term "issue" includes both legitimate and illegitimate children, adopted children, but not step-children, grandchildren and any other lineal descendants.

Single people

The intestacy rules for single people are:

- The estate of a single person is shared equally among any issue

- If there are no issue, the deceased's parents inherit equally

- If the parents are deceased, then brothers and sisters, and the issue of any who have predeceased

- If none, then half-brothers and half-sisters (and their issue if any are predeceased)

- If none, grandparents

- If none, aunts and uncles (and their issue if any are predeceased)

- If none, half-brothers and half-sisters of the deceased's parents (and their issue if any are predeceased)

- If none, the estate passes to the Crown, the Duchy of Lancaster or the Duchy of Cornwall

Married people

The intestacy rules for married people are:

- If there is a spouse and issue
  - The spouse takes the chattels (your personal items such as furniture, jewellery, wine, car, but not money) and the first £125 000 (or entire estate where this is less). The remainder, or residue, is split in two with the spouse taking a life interest (i.e., income only) in one half, and the issue taking the other half. On the death of the surviving spouse, that half of the estate passes to the issue.

- If there is a spouse and no issue, but one of parents, brother/sister, nephew/niece
  - The spouse takes the chattels and the first £200 000 (or entire estate where this is less).
  - The residue is split in two with the spouse taking a half share absolutely, and the other half passing to the parents or, if none, the brothers and sisters of the whole blood, or their issue if any are predeceased.

- If there is a spouse, but no issue, parents, brother or sister, nephew or niece
  - Everything passes to the spouse

Draw up a will

These are the intestacy rules. You may find if you are single and haven't drawn up a will that your money will go to the Crown, or to your long forgotten deceased aunt's child, Norman the Nerd. If you don't like that, you should draw up a will. Leave your money to a charity, to an old flame, to Manchester United, or whatever. Married readers may decide that under the rules their children get too much relative to their spouse: again, the remedy is to draw up a will.

Even if the intestacy rules distribute your estate as you want, there are still reasons why a will is desirable. With a will, you can choose who will administer your estate, you can probably get it done at lower cost, and the estate may be distributed faster. Further, you may be able to reduce the amount of inheritance tax your estate suffers.

You should also be aware that substantial assets may pass on your death independently of whether you have a will or not. These include property held as joint tenants, life insurance written under trust policies, and lump sum pension payments payable on death where the trustees have discretion as to the beneficiary.

GET PROFESSIONAL ADVICE

You should get a solicitor to draw up your will. For your will to be valid, you must have the capacity and intention to make the will and you must follow various prescribed formalities. There are just too many traps for the unwary, and a "DIY will" runs the risk of being invalid, or in other ways fail to achieve your objectives. For example, you might know what you mean if you "leave all your money to your husband and two children equally", but how would "money" be interpreted, and are you giving your husband half and your children a quarter each, or all three a third each?

There are alternatives to using a solicitor, such as will-writing services and banks. *Which?* found the will writing services to be generally poor; they are probably best suited for very simple wills. *Which?* found banks to be as competent as solicitors, but two-thirds insisted on being the executor (see below). This is not acceptable. Overall, a solicitor seems to be the best bet.

A simple will should cost less than £100, but the costs may build up rapidly if you only think about all the issues when you are in the solicitor's office. However, don't be rushed by the solicitor. Make sure you understand what you are told and that you have got across your points. Before you visit a solicitor, you should have worked through the following issues.

You may wish to **specify how your body is to be disposed of**, e.g., burial versus cremation, organ donation, and use in medical research. Do you wish to be buried at a particular church? If you wish to be cremated, do you want your ashes to be kept or scattered? How will the funeral be paid for? While you can put all this in your will, you should also tell a close friend too. Your wish to be buried, expressed in your will, may be read after you have been cremated.

You should **list relevant personal matters** that a solicitor should know about. Are you: married, planning to get married, or divorced? If you are a single parent with a young child, do you want a guardian appointed, and has the guardian given consent? Even if you are married, you may wish to appoint a guardian in case you and your spouse die together, e.g., in a car crash. Do you have step-children? Do you have any joint property? Are you living with somebody, but not married? In this last case it is especially important that you have a will because a "partner" has few rights. If you are living as man and man, for example, your relatives may not do what you would consider to be the decent thing for your partner.

You should **choose executors**, and get their agreement. An executor is somebody who executes the will, i.e., carries out your wishes. Ideally the executor will be younger than you, and you may wish to have a substitute in case your first choice dies before you. Two executors would make sense, perhaps a professional person and a grown-up child if you have one, or a friend or your partner. Executing a complex will is time consuming and involves lots of letter writing. Do choose somebody likely to be able to cope, and not simply your best friend. You may have to get a solicitor, accountant or bank to be one of the executors, but this will involve costs. Banks are usually the most expensive—horror stories appear in the press from time to time—and should probably be avoided. The Law Society claims that banks charge about three times as much as solicitors. Solicitors may charge an hourly rate plus mark-up, plus a percentage of the assets, e.g., 0.5–1%. If you use a solicitor or accountant, they may charge for every letter written. Ideally, simple matters such as paying gas bills due will be handled by a friend or relative acting as an executor. If you get a friend or relative to act as an executor, do leave them something!

You should **produce a list of your assets**, their value and where they, or their documents of title, are held. This should not be a hard task if you followed my advice in Chapter 2 concerning keeping records. Only assets in your name can be left in your will. However, don't forget the assets that pass irrespective of your will (e.g., a life insurance policy written in trust, a lump sum death benefit under a pension policy). These, plus the assets you can leave in your will, should jointly achieve your desired distribution of assets.

You should **decide on the beneficiaries** of your will and what they should get. This can be a sum of money, a particular asset or possession, or a percentage of your estate. You should specify what happens if a beneficiary dies before you. You should have a catch-all beneficiary, e.g., a charity, which will receive anything that cannot be disposed of for whatever unforeseen reason. Otherwise, even with a will, there may be a partial intestacy. You can name your beneficiaries, but sometimes specifying a class of beneficiaries is better. For example, you can name your grandchildren or specify grandchildren as a class. The latter course will cover grandchildren born after your will is drawn up.

You should be aware that **your will can be challenged**. While in general you can do anything you want with your assets, under the *Inheritance (Provision for Family and Dependants) Act*, some relatives and dependants may make an application to the court that reasonable financial provision has not been made for them, and the court can override your will and ensure adequate provision. Since this will affect what your chosen beneficiaries receive, you may prefer to make provision in your will for dependants you dislike so that you ensure exactly what happens to your assets. (The categories of applicant are: the deceased's spouse; the former spouse of the deceased who has not remarried; a child of the deceased; a child of the family; a dependant.)

When you get a draft will from your solicitor, do check it. Make sure all names are spelt correctly, and that what is written achieves what you want. If the solicitor has written in his or her firm to administer the estate or be an executor, demand that it be removed if you did not request it.

AFTER YOUR WILL IS DRAWN UP

Keep the will in a safe place, and tell your executors where it is. Review matters every few years and decide whether to make changes as a result of changes to your circumstances, the tax laws or your preferences (maybe you've grown to like Norman the

Nerd). Marriage automatically revokes a will, and divorce disinherits the former spouse (unless, in both cases, the will was drawn up in a specific way that avoids this). Your former spouse can't remain an executor or trustee. Normally you would in any case want to change your will after such big changes in your life, so you are unlikely to get caught out. But change your will immediately: don't forget the proverbial bus that keeps hitting people at the wrong moment. Separation does not have the same effects as divorce. Again, review your will.

POST-MORTEM CHANGES

Finally, although your will may seem like the last word on your assets, your will can be changed after your death by four methods:

- Disclaimers

- Variations

- Flexible wills

- Orders under the *Inheritance (Provision for Family and Dependants) Act*

In 1819, Chief Justice Abbot stated that "the law is not so absurd as to force a man to take an estate against his will". Thus, a beneficiary under either a will or intestacy can disclaim an interest, but only if no benefit of any kind has been received. The effect is as if the beneficiary had predeceased the person whose will it is, or the intestate. Disclaiming is an effective way of avoiding an asset that has unattractive conditions, but will only pass an attractive (or unattractive) asset to a specific person if that person is naturally next in line in terms of the will or the intestacy rules. To pass an asset to a particular person requires a variation whereby the beneficiary gives instruction for the asset to be passed to someone else.

For capital gains and inheritance tax purposes the Inland Revenue will treat a disclaimer or variation as though the assets had been left by the deceased to the person receiving them. Certain conditions must be met for this treatment, the most important of which are that the changes must be made in writing, must be made within two years of death and, for a variation, the Revenue must be told within six months of the variation taking place. While for capital gains tax and inheritance tax the deed is retrospective to the date of death, it is not retrospective for Income Tax purposes, and this may mean some careful calculations must be made, and specialist advice should be sought.

In a flexible or discretionary will, the executors have the power to decide how to distribute the estate, although the spouse, for example, can be given a power of veto.

Orders under the *Inheritance (Provision for Family and Dependants) Act* were discussed in the previous section.

LIVING WILLS

Your will sets out what you want to happen to your assets after you are dead. You might like to make a so-called "living will" which states what you want to happen to you while you are still alive, but when you don't have all your faculties. You appoint someone to act for you and set out guidelines or "advance directives" for their decisions.

You might feel that if you were to suffer from Alzheimer's disease, for example, no heroics of surgery should be performed were you to develop other illnesses. You should be kept pain-free, but no more. In a living will, you state this preference.

The validity of living wills has been subject to some debate, but in April 1995, the British Medical Association set out its position. A request that treatment be withheld in certain circumstances is binding on the doctor because, were the doctor to force treatment, he would risk a court action for assault. But a doctor cannot be compelled to commit euthanasia (or mercy killing), which is against the law.

READ 📖 WRITE ✉ RING ☎

♦ The *Which?* survey mentioned in the text was reported in "Where There's a Will...", *Which?*, October 1994, 48–55.
♦ You can get information on living wills and copies of a standard living will for £3 from VES, 13 Prince of Wales Terrace, London, W8 5PG. Tel: 0171 937 7770, Fax: 0171 376 2648.

34

Inheritance Tax

Inheritance tax is, broadly speaking, a voluntary levy paid by those who distrust their heirs more than they dislike the Inland Revenue.

Lord Jenkins

Having drawn up a will, you have determined who gets what when you die. The exact amount the beneficiaries enjoy will depend both on what you have given them and any inheritance tax (IHT) that is payable. In broad terms IHT is payable if you leave more than £200 000 to anyone other than your spouse or a charity (and less if you have made large gifts in the previous seven years). Many people, especially in London and the South East, will fall into the IHT bracket simply by virtue of the value of their home and having a few modest investments, and it may be worth engaging in some planning to minimize the tax payable. About 1 in 45 estates will pay IHT in 1996–7.

If you have assets, it only costs you a solicitor's fee to determine who gets it—hence the desirability of having a will. But minimizing IHT can introduce conflicts. To reduce the tax bill you have to leave a smaller estate, which means giving it away before you die, or ensuring that any growth occurs outside your estate. Clearly this adversely affects you, especially in terms of reduced income, whereas the size of the IHT bill only affects your beneficiaries. It may be sensible to live well yourself and let your estate suffer tax, although, of course, by living well you will also reduce your estate and thereby reduce the IHT bill. The approach of looking after Number One applies especially to single people, or married couples without children. However, because by skilfully giving away your estate you can escape IHT, it is often called a voluntary tax.

I'll look at the IHT rules and provide a taste of how IHT can be minimized in case you are not the volunteering type. It is important that you should not act on the basis of anything in this chapter, but treat it as giving you an indication of possibilities, and which you might wish to get detailed advice about. I omit all reference to business property relief, woodlands, etc., which will not be relevant for most readers.

WHAT INHERITANCE TAX IS

IHT is a tax on the transfer of value, and may apply when you make gifts in your lifetime, or on death. Lifetime gifts will either be exempt from IHT, or non-exempt—a chargeable transfer. The latter are of two kinds, potentially exempt transfers and life-

Table 34.1   Inheritance Tax Rates

Value of estate plus gifts made in previous 7 years	Tax rate
Up to £200 000	Nil
Over £200 000	40% of the excess over £200 000

time chargeable transfers. On death, there is a deemed transfer, and this is cumulated with chargeable transfers made in the previous seven years to calculate the IHT due. Some of the transfers deemed to take place on death are exempt from IHT.

When you die your estate is valued along with gifts made in the last seven years and if the total exceeds £200 000, your estate is taxed at 40% on the excess. This is shown in Table 34.1.

I now discuss this in more detail.

Exempt transfers

The detailed rules on exemptions seem a bit silly, but the basic idea is simple. Without some claw-back on gifts, we could all escape IHT by making a death-bed gift.

The following gifts are not added to the value of your estate for the purpose of calculating IHT, irrespective of whether they are lifetime transfers or on death:

- Gifts between spouses (if the recipient is domiciled in the UK)

- Gifts to UK-established charities and recognized political parties

- Gifts to many museums and art galleries

The following transfers are only tax-free if made as lifetime transfers:

- Gifts up to £3000 per annum: an unused portion can be carried forward one year

- Any number of "small" gifts of up to £250 to different people (but you can't give the £3000 to one of the £250 recipients)

- Normal expenditure out of income (not capital) which is regular and does not reduce the donor's normal standard of living

- Wedding presents: parents can give up to £5000 each; grandparents £2500; others £1000

- Gifts for the maintenance of one's family, e.g., an ex-spouse, an infirm relative, a dependent child, mother or mother-in-law who is widowed, separated or divorced

The following transfers are tax-free on death only:

- A lump sum paid from an occupational pension scheme, providing the trustees have discretion as to who gets it (they will generally follow your wishes, even when they have discretion)

- A lump sum paid from your personal pension plan, again providing it is at the discretion of the trustees

For many of the exemptions or reliefs listed above there are specific rules that have to be adhered to. There are also special rules relating to business and agricultural property, woodlands and Lloyd's insurance market members, which are too complex, and not of sufficient general interest, to be discussed here. However, it is worth noting that the 1995 Budget relaxed the rules on shareholdings in unquoted companies by extending 100% business relief. Now any holding of a qualifying unquoted share, held for at least two years, can be passed on free of IHT. This means heirs to private companies will escape IHT. But, because USM and some AIM shares are qualifying unquoted shares, this will be of interest to investors in general.

Potentially exempt transfers

A potentially exempt transfer is a lifetime gift made to one of the following categories:

- An individual
- An accumulation and maintenance trust
- An interest in possession trust
- A disabled person's trust

If you live for seven years after making a potentially exempt transfer, no IHT will be payable on the gift. (Trusts are discussed in Chapter 35.)

Some gifts are given outright while others are gifts with reservation, i.e., the recipient does not fully enjoy the gift, or there is some string attached, e.g., if parents give their children their home, but continue to live in it rent-free. Were they to give the home, but continue to live in it and pay a full commercial rent, that would be a gift without reservation—the children would pay income tax on the rental income at their marginal rate. Gifts made with reservation are treated as part of the estate at death if the reservation has not been released. If it has, it is potentially exempt from the date of the release.

If a potentially exempt transfer becomes a chargeable transfer because of your death, it is taken into the assessment at the value when given. Any subsequent increase in value is ignored. While this makes lifetime gifts of chargeable assets very attractive from the viewpoint of IHT, the gift will be liable to CGT. Assets passing at death, are not liable for CGT.

Chargeable lifetime transfers

A lifetime gift which is neither exempt nor potentially exempt is a chargeable lifetime transfer: usually this will be a gift to a company or to a discretionary trust (see Chapter 35). Such gifts begin a running total of chargeable transfers. The running total is maintained over the most recent seven years. The tax rate is half the death-scale rate and is shown in Table 34.2.

An example may be useful. If a chargeable transfer worth £200 000 is made, this would fall in the nil tax band and no tax would be payable. If another transfer were made six years later, for £100 000, the running total would be £300 000, and £100 000 would be immediately liable for tax. If another transfer were to be made two years later, this time for £40 000, the first transfer would have dropped out of the running total (having been made more than seven years ago), and the new total, £140 000, would fall in the nil band.

Table 34.2 Chargeable Transfer Tax Rates

Running total of chargeable transfers	Tax rate
Up to £200 000	Nil
Over £200 000	20% of the excess over £200 000

Table 34.3 Taper Relief

Years between death and gift	Percentage of tax payable	Effective tax rate*
up to 3	100	40
3–4	80	32
4–5	60	34
5–6	40	16
6–7	20	8
more than 7	0	0

* This is the percentage of the 40% rate that is payable: e.g., 100% of 40% = 40%; 80% of 40% = 32%, etc.

The death estate

When you die, the deemed chargeable transfer at death is cumulated with the chargeable lifetime transfers and potentially exempt transfers within the previous seven years. IHT is charged as per Table 34.1. Any lifetime chargeable transfers within the seven years prior to death will have borne tax at half the rate applicable at death at that time (currently nil or 20%). As a result of death the amount of tax has to be recalculated at the rates applicable at death (subject to taper relief as discussed below) and taking into account potentially exempt transfers that have become chargeable. Credit is given for any tax paid, but if this exceeds tax due, the difference is not repaid.

When calculating the tax due on gifts made within the seven years prior to death, the tax is reduced if you have survived more than three years. The reduction is known as taper relief, and is shown in Table 34.3.

INHERITANCE TAX PLANNING

There are two basic strategies to reduce your IHT bill:

● Give your assets away—often called estate spreading

● Ensure that future growth takes place outside your estate—estate freezing

The second strategy essentially involves using pension and insurance products as well as trusts. Here are some specific strategies:

● Reduce your assets by spending your money on yourself.

● Give your assets away and live at least seven years. Even if you live for less than seven years, as long as you live more than three years the IHT bill will be reduced. While it may be possible to give assets away, there may often be complications. For example, giving away shares in a family business may lead to loss of control, or the beneficiary may be a child and therefore not be responsible. To overcome such problems, assets are often put into a trust. Trusts are discussed in Chapter 35.

- Give your assets away by using up the specific exemptions. Some of these can be quite substantial, e.g., it would be possible for grandparents to pay school fees.

- Equalize estates and draw up wills. If you have a spouse, you can give assets to each other without triggering IHT—and there may be favourable income tax implications from a more equal share of assets. You can now each use all the IHT exemptions and, more importantly, you will both have a £200 000 nil band. Of course, you have to have a stable marriage for this strategy.

  As an example of how the nil band might be used, consider a couple with £400 000. If the husband holds all the assets he can leave them all to his wife in his will. On his death the assets pass free of IHT, but on his wife's death, IHT of £80 000 will be payable (£400 000 – £200 000 = £200 000 taxed at 40% = £80 000). If the wife dies first, the IHT will be payable when the husband dies. If the assets are split, and each has £200 000, each could leave this in their wills to, say, a daughter. In this case each transfer falls in the nil band and no IHT will be payable.

  There are three snags with this strategy. The first, which applies to all strategies, is that the surviving spouse may need all the assets for the income they generate. The second is that one has to be careful to minimize the entire tax bill and not just IHT. In particular, one has to watch for adverse capital gains tax implications. For example, if shares are passed between spouses, the liability to capital gains tax can be rolled over, but the tax becomes payable when the shares are sold. This may result in a large capital gains bill if the shares have been held a long time or have performed exceptionally well. Indexation allowance and the annual exemption will reduce the bill, but it still may be substantial. If, however, the shares are passed in a will and then sold, the acquisition cost will not be the original cost plus indexation, but the cost at probate plus indexation. Clearly, detailed sums have to be made to establish whether you should be minimizing IHT or CGT.

  The third snag with equalizing assets is that for many people their home will comprise the bulk of their assets. You can't save IHT by giving your home away and then continue to live in it rent-free, because it would be a gift with reservation. Moreover, many couples will already jointly own the home as joint tenants: when one dies the interest automatically goes to the other. If you are not married, the value of your share of the home will go into your estate and there could be IHT to pay. If you are married your share passes tax-free, but on the death of your spouse, the whole home will form part of the estate. However, if the home were owned as a tenancy in common, each would own a separate share of the home and could leave it to anyone, e.g., to a child. On the death of either partner, their share of the home would form part of their estate, and it could be liable to IHT, but may fall in the nil band. However, when the second partner dies, there will be a smaller estate, and a lower tax bill.

- Put growth assets outside the estate. While this may be desirable, the donor may well need income. If the donor gifts the asset, but retains the right to income, this becomes a gift with reservation. Purchase of income and capital shares of a split capital investment trust provides one solution. The donor may retain the income shares, and hence an income, while gifting the capital shares and moving the growth element outside the estate.

- Move assets into trusts/life insurance. Life insurance products are often used as a means of moving assets outside an estate and also as a way of paying tax bills that cannot be avoided. The basic idea is that the insurance policies are written in trust for a named beneficiary. You pay the insurance premiums, but somebody else collects the benefit. The proceeds are not part of your estate and not liable for IHT. The premiums you pay are gifts, but this should not cause any problems because they should fall under one of the exemptions I listed earlier in this chapter. Even if some of the premiums are deemed to be gifts, if you survive three years there should still be some advantage from adopting this strategy.

  Different types of insurance products will be appropriate for different objectives. An endowment policy pays out a lump sum on the earlier of a specific date or your death. This can be used to give tax-free capital during your lifetime (or on death if you mistime things!). A whole-life policy pays on your death, and provides a means of paying IHT. If you are married, you can get policies which pay on the second death, i.e., when the tax bill is due on assets which passed tax-free between the spouses on the first death. A term insurance policy pays out only if you die before a specific date. If you survive, there is no payment. This could be used to pay an IHT bill that will become due on a potentially exempt transfer if you do not survive seven years.

  The actual implementation of some of these schemes can be quite complex. For example, if you are over 70, the premiums on a whole-life policy would be expensive, and you could live for far longer than average and end up paying a very large sum in premiums. One solution is to combine the life policy with an annuity. The annuity will generate an income for as long as you live, and you should get an income in excess of the life premiums. Buying the annuity reduces your estate, and gives a saving in IHT. The life policy, written in trust, does not attract IHT.

- Get advice. What I have outlined above is very basic, and much more complex planning can be undertaken. If you have a potential IHT problem, get advice.

35

Trusts

The trust is the guardian angel of the Anglo-Saxon, accompanying him everywhere, impassively, from the cradle to the grave.

Pierre Lepaulle

Trusts often seem like something for the very rich, but trusts are very common in Britain. Many life insurance policies are taken out in trust, and millions of people invest in unit trusts, which are genuine trusts (unlike investment trusts, which are not). Most company pension schemes are set up as trusts, and many charities are trusts. The pharmaceutical company, Wellcome, was until recently owned by The Wellcome Trust, a charity and trust. And there are more than 65 000 discretionary trusts and accumulation and maintenance trusts in the UK, the sort of trusts that readers of this book might set up.

WHAT IS A TRUST?

A trust is a legal relationship, created by a trust document, either during the life, or on the death, of a person (the settlor), whereby assets are placed under the control of trustees for the benefit of beneficiaries. The settlor is the person setting up the trust fund, usually by giving assets. The trustees are the people in whom the assets are vested, but the assets are not part of their estate. The trustees have to manage the assets in accordance with the terms of the trust deed or will, or otherwise by law. The trust property will consist of the original property, any subsequent additions, the growth of the property and any retained income. The beneficiaries are those who can benefit from the trust, and they may be named, e.g., John Smith, or be a class of beneficiaries, e.g., my grandchildren.

The key to a trust is the trustee–beneficiary relationship. In English contract law it is necessary to be a party to a contract to enforce it. With a trust, a beneficiary who was not yet born when a trust was established, e.g., a grandchild, and was thus not a party to the contract setting up the trust, can still enforce it because of the trustee–beneficiary relationship. Trusts are very flexible, which is why they are so widely used.

THE ADVANTAGES OF TRUSTS

Trusts may be used to save income tax, capital gains tax and inheritance tax. The potential for each type of tax saving varies with the trust, as will be discussed. This chapter gives an indication of the tax issues involved, but should not be relied upon for tax planning. Trusts are complex, and you must get specific legal advice if you wish to use a trust. Trusts are normally irrevocable, so once you have set one up, you can't usually change your mind. Get advice first.

As well as a means of reducing tax bills, trusts may also be used to effect suitable financial arrangements for family members. Examples include benefiting young children, or a handicapped person, unable to look after their own financial affairs; ensuring that the children of a first marriage are cared for if the parent dies and the second spouse remarries; providing funds for a specific purpose such as school fees.

To achieve either tax or general financial planning goals, one of the following types of trust may be set up:

- Off-the-shelf trusts

- Interest in possession trusts (fixed interest trusts)

- Trusts for mentally or physically disabled

- Discretionary trusts

- Protective trusts

- Accumulation and maintenance trusts

- Bare trusts

- Non-resident trusts

- Secret trusts and floating "trusts"

I'll briefly discuss each of these types, but first I'll discuss costs. You may find you don't need to read the rest of the chapter.

THE COSTS OF TRUSTS

A trust, other than an off-the-shelf trust is, unfortunately, expensive to set up and administer. There will be legal costs involved in setting up a trust, a minimum of £500, and possibly substantial costs in administering the trust. You will need a trustee, preferably two, and while one can be an unpaid friend, at least one should have experience in managing a trust. There are various administrative chores to be handled, and the trustee is personally liable for any loss. Solicitors, accountants or bank trustee departments may charge on the basis of, say, 1% of the value of the assets with a minimum fee of £1000. These charges are on-going, so a trust will have to be of sufficient size to make it an economic proposition. What is "sufficient" size will be a function of both the tax that a trust might save, and the value of the trust in stopping, say, a minor having control of an estate.

If a trust is not a sensible option for you, read only the first paragraph of the next section.

TYPES OF TRUST USED IN FINANCIAL PLANNING

Off-the-shelf trusts

Although one normally thinks in terms of having a trust drawn up to meet specific circumstances, it is possible to get an off-the-shelf trust. Technically it will be one of those listed below, but for most people that is of no interest. The most common use of an off-the-shelf trust would be in regard to life insurance where a policy would be in trust for other members of the family. Most insurance companies will have a standard form of trust document and this is a good way of reducing inheritance tax liability (see Chapter 34). It is the one occasion you do not need a solicitor to draw up a trust document for you and where there will be minimal costs.

Interest in possession trusts (fixed interest trusts)

In these trusts, at least one beneficiary (the life tenant) has a right to receive income from the trust assets. The beneficiary may also have use of an asset such as a home. These trusts ensure that the beneficiary receives income, but does not control the capital. Such a trust would be suitable to:

- Give income to a child whose marriage might not last

- Keep control of a family business by giving the trustees the voting rights on the shares of the company, but the income to family members

- Move assets out of an estate, but not give control of them to the beneficiaries until the settlor's death

- Save income tax if the beneficiary has a lower tax rate than the settlor

- Save capital gains tax if the capital gains tax rate is lower on the trust property than the settlor's or beneficiary's rate

The tax position is as follows (I have omitted the special rules if the beneficiary is the settlor's spouse). The trust income is taxed at the lower rate, and the beneficiary either pays no additional tax or a further 20%, depending on his or her income level. With regard to capital gains, a lifetime transfer of funds by the settlor to the trustees constitutes a disposal for capital gains tax, and tax will be payable if the indexed gain exceeds the exempt amount. If the trust is set up at death, there is no liability to capital gains tax. Capital gains on disposals within the trust will be subject to capital gains tax at 24% if the trustees' exemption of £3150 is exceeded.

A gift into a trust is a transfer of value, and a potentially exempt transfer. It is exempt if the settlor survives seven years. The beneficiary of a share of the income of the trust property is treated as the owner of that share of the trust for IHT purposes.

On the death of the life tenant, the trust funds, or a share thereof if there are several beneficiaries, is aggregated with the tenants' other assets for inheritance tax purposes. Distribution of capital to beneficiaries, in proportion to their income entitlement, does not give rise to IHT because that share is considered to be part of the beneficiary's estate. If the beneficiary surrenders interest in the trust during his or her lifetime, that surrender constitutes a potentially exempt transfer.

Trusts for mentally or physically disabled are a special form of interest in possession trust.

Discretionary trusts

Discretionary trusts are very flexible. They allow the trustees full discretion as to whether or not to make payments out of income or capital and to which beneficiaries. Such trusts allow:

- A settlor to pass capital to children, but to permit payments to be made if necessary to the spouse

- A settlor to pass assets to beneficiaries, but without knowing at the time of setting up the trust the extent of the benefit to each of the beneficiaries, e.g., control of a business might ultimately pass to the child that shows most business aptitude

- A tax saving if the rates of income and capital gains tax on the trust property are lower than the settlor's or the beneficiaries'

- Capital gains tax hold-over relief may be available on assets transferred into the trust

The tax position is as follows. The income in the trust will bear income tax at a rate of 34%. The beneficiaries will be able to reclaim tax or will have to make further payments, depending on their tax position. When funds are transferred into the trust, the transferor may make an election for hold-over relief, whereby any capital gains on the assets transferred may be held over until realized by the trustees. On realized capital gains, there is an annual exemption of £3150 and the capital gains rate is 34%.

The inheritance tax position is less attractive than for other trusts. The transfer of assets into the trust is a transfer of value but it is not a potentially exempt transfer. It is a chargeable transfer (see Chapter 34) and is immediately chargeable, but subject to the usual exemptions and reliefs. If it falls within the nil band, there will be no immediate charge, and it will be omitted from cumulative transfers after seven years. There is a further charge of 30% of the lifetime rate (30% × 20% = 6%) made every ten years, and when capital is distributed.

Protective trusts are a special form of discretionary trust used to protect the gullible or spendthrifts. Here the property in the trust is for the beneficiary for life, or until bankruptcy or another specified event occurs. At that point, the trust would become a discretionary trust, and it would be expected that the beneficiary would get sufficient for maintenance, with the spouse and children receiving the rest.

Accumulation and maintenance trusts

These trusts are used to benefit children under the age of 25. There must be a living beneficiary when the trust is established, but the beneficiaries can be a class such as the settlor's grandchildren. Until a beneficiary is 25, the trustees may accumulate income, or pay it out for his or her maintenance or education, and the trustees can pay out capital if they wish. Once a beneficiary reaches the age of 25, the income must be paid to him or her. The capital may also be paid out at the trustees' discretion, but it may also pass to another beneficiary (e.g., the parents). These trusts are valuable where:

- It is advantageous to reduce the value of an estate for inheritance tax purposes, but not to give the beneficiary control of the assets

- A grandparent wishes to pay school fees

- It is desirable for the trustees to control capital for a long period

Income received by the trustees before the beneficiary is 25 is taxed at 34%, and a rebate may be claimed depending on the beneficiary's tax position. If, however, the

beneficiary is an unmarried, under-18-year-old child of the settlor, the income distributed is assessed on the settlor. After the beneficiary is 25, the tax rate is 24%, with
that amount credited to the beneficiary and further tax is payable, or a rebate due,
depending on the beneficiary's income level.

When assets are transferred to the trust, or from the trust to beneficiaries, capital
gains tax may be payable, although hold-over relief may be available. On chargeable
capital gains the trustees will be taxed at 34% until the beneficiaries are entitled to all
the income, when the rate will be 24%. The annual exemption is £3150. The transfer
of assets into the trust is a potentially exempt transfer of value for inheritance tax
purposes. No tax is chargeable if the settlor lives for seven years. There is no liability
for inheritance tax once the beneficiaries are entitled to the income of the trust.

Bare trusts

A bare trust is one in which the trustees act effectively as nominees. The beneficiary is
entitled to the income and capital. The tax position is as though the beneficiary had
been given the assets. Bare trusts might be used to pass assets to a child or an adult
unable to manage his or her affairs.

Secret trusts

Secret trusts are a way of leaving money in a will to, e.g., a mistress or illegitimate
child, without the fact becoming general knowledge (a will is a public document).
Money would be left in the will to, say, John Smith, with Smith having previously
agreed to hold the money in trust for Ms X. A secret trust is a form of bare trust.

Non-resident trusts

A non-resident trust is one which has trustees resident outside of the UK. These trusts
were very popular prior to 19 March 1991 because they conferred significant capital
gains tax advantages. Since that date, when complex anti-avoidance provisions were
introduced, the use of such trusts has been reduced. They still have inheritance tax
and capital gains tax attractions for non-domiciled settlors, but such people are outside the scope of this book.

36

Pulling It All Together

The golden rule is that there are no golden rules.
George Bernard Shaw

In this chapter I am going to pull together much of what has been discussed in this book. I assume you have read the rest of this book and so this chapter just highlights some issues. For a more detailed discussion of any topic you will have to turn to the appropriate chapter.

DIY FINANCIAL PLANNING

To fix your finances you should go through the following steps.

The most important step is to know yourself and set goals

What is your attitude to risk, your financial resources and your personal circumstances? Do the boring tasks set out in Chapter 2, i.e., establish your cash flow and net worth and keep records. Then set your financial goals (Chapter 4).

Sort out your basic cheque account

Sort out your basic cheque account, get debit and credit cards if you want them, and make sure your account meets your needs. Is it cheap if you get overdrawn? Does it pay a good interest rate if you don't? If you are going to use Direct Debits, get them set up. Many firms that pay you money will agree to pay directly into your cheque account if you want. Get that set up if you want that. Your aim with your cheque account is to enable your financial life to run smoothly, not to become rich. But it will be nice if you can earn something, and if you can't, make sure you don't pay too much. *Moneyfacts* and *Which?* will be helpful in picking a suitable cheque account.

Set up an emergency fund

Put some money aside in a savings account. High interest is desirable, but immediate access is essential. Aim to have three months' after-tax income set aside to pay for the unexpected. Again, refer to *Moneyfacts* and *Which?* for product providers.

Think about protection insurance

Whatever your age, you will have a valuable collection of possessions. Even students have clothes, electrical gizmos, books, and so forth. Insure your home contents and, if you own a home, your building. If you go on holiday, protect yourself with travel insurance. *Which?* can guide you on all of these.

There are various forms of medical insurance that you can buy if you have the money. You should *think about permanent health insurance* (PHI). If you are too ill to work, who will look after you? Single people should consider PHI very seriously indeed.

Draw up a will

If you have an emergency fund and some home contents, you have assets. Now is a good time to draw up a will. You may not have much, but if you draw up a will now, you'll be sure to have one when you are really rich. Get a solicitor to draw it up.

Think about the big three—buying a home, getting life insurance, building up a pension

You should probably tackle these three in the order given, but this will depend on your circumstances. If you are single, and likely to switch jobs to a different area, postpone a decision on buying a home. The buying and selling costs plus the emotional turmoil aren't worth incurring if you will only be in a property for a short period. While the order you should tackle the big three items depends on your circumstances, I'll treat them in the order I listed them.

Think about buying a home I think buying a home is a sensible investment, as I explained in Chapter 24. If you disagree, don't buy one, look for rented property and move on to the next item. If you do buy a home, you will have to decide how much you can afford in monthly payments and the method of repaying the mortgage.

Don't overborrow—i.e., don't borrow an amount you can only just afford the payments on. If the cost of borrowing rises, and home prices fall in the short run, you could find yourself in a nasty position. Borrow as much as you can comfortably handle if interest rates rise. Ask the lender how much you would have to pay if interest rates rise by, say, 4%. If you overborrow and lose your home, the lender will not lose out because of insurance you will have been forced to pay for to protect the lender. It's desirable to put down a deposit.

You can repay your mortgage by a standard repayment mortgage, an endowment, a PEP or a pension. Most people will consider only the first three. Many people have no idea what an endowment or PEP mortgage really is. Basically you have some exposure to the stockmarket. If you are a risk-averse investor (nervous Nelly) who would not dream of investing any cash you have in the stockmarket, you probably should have a repayment mortgage. If you are willing to take more of a risk, an endowment or PEP mortgage will probably prove cheaper in the long run providing you don't have to surrender your endowment. If you do, the poor surrender values mean you would probably have been better off with a repayment mortgage. Most people with endowments do surrender them. If there is a reasonable possibility that you might, don't get one. Since the returns from the investments that produce an endowment's return are taxed, while those in a PEP are not, it is hard to see why a unit-linked endowment would be preferred to a PEP. With-profits endowments have less volatile returns than a pure equity PEP portfolio, but since a PEP can now hold bonds, a PEP's volatility can be reduced quite easily.

You may wish to get an independent financial adviser to help you select a method and a provider. Make sure you know how you will pay for advice.

Think about life insurance If you have dependants, who will look after them if you die? If there will be an income gap that needs filling, **think about life insurance**. Make sure you need it. If you are a non-earning spouse, you probably don't need cover (but your spouse does), if you are single and have no dependants, you don't need it either. You may get life insurance as part of your pension package, and there may be a spouse's pension if you die in service. That may eliminate or reduce your need for life insurance.

If you do need life insurance, you can get life insurance that provides protection only—term insurance—or life insurance that has an investment component—whole-life and endowment. Because insurance investments are taxed in the hands of the insurance company at a rate of 20% on income and 25% on capital gains, non tax-payers and lower rate taxpayers who don't pay CGT should not buy life insurance as an investment but instead buy term insurance and have separate investments. An investment trust or unit trust will be more tax efficient. Higher rate taxpayers who are not liable to CGT may find little difference in the tax efficiency of an investment trust or unit trust and life insurance as an investment, but the former will be more flexible. The trusts will be more tax efficient if held in a PEP.

Life insurance is expensive, and you need it when you have least money. Term insurance is cheaper than other forms of life insurance so you are more likely to be able to afford the cover you need.

Think about a pension as soon as possible If you are in a good company scheme, you may not need to do anything. If you are not in a good scheme (i.e., two-thirds final salary after 40 years), or you won't qualify for a full pension (perhaps because you won't work for 40 years or you have changed your job a lot), or you are not in a pension scheme, think about topping up your occupational pension by an AVC or FSAVC, or starting a personal pension plan if you don't have an occupational pension. Pension contributions get a tax-break, and you should put building up your pension high on your list of financial objectives. The sooner you start, the better.

That's the theory. But when you are young, and have been married a few years, there may be competing calls on your money, for example saving for school fees. You might prefer when you are young to save via PEPs. With contributions to a pension plan you can't change your mind and get your money back. When you retire you will get a tax-free lump sum and a pension which will be taxed as earned income. With a PEP you get no tax-break on your contributions, but income and any capital gains are free of tax. This works out nearly as tax-efficient as a pension. In addition, you have a choice as to whether you will keep the PEPs to boost your retirement income, or whether you will spend the PEP on school fees or something else. Of course, if you do spend the money, you will end up with no additional retirement money. If you are not in a pension fund, you probably should force yourself to go the pension route. If you are in a pension fund, you may prefer the flexibility of a PEP and run the risk you will have spent it before retirement.

Pension planning is difficult because there are so many rules and regulations. You should begin by establishing what your State pension will be (by completing form BR19) and by discussing your company scheme, and your entitlements, with the pensions manager at your firm. Whether or not you are in a company scheme, you may wish to get independent advice.

Establish a portfolio of investments

If you have any money left over you can think about constructing an investment portfolio. You should consider:

● Whether you have any debts

● When you will want to use the money

● Whether you are willing to risk the value of your capital

● Whether you are willing to have fluctuating income

● Whether you want a high immediate income

● Whether you want long-term growth of capital and income

● Whether there are any tax advantages for you

If you have debts, you will probably be paying a higher rate of interest than you can earn on your investments. It will usually make sense to pay off your credit cards, overdraft, and other debts before you invest. Mortgage debt is relatively cheap and it may make sense to leave that: but often it will be sensible to reduce your mortgage. Remember, though, once you have used the money to reduce your mortgage, you won't be able to get it back.

In Chapter 4, I showed that over the years equities have given a much higher return than cash or bonds. But I also showed that they give the most volatile performance. You could easily lose your shirt in one year, and while you might get it back over many years, this would be no consolation if you can only invest for a year. If you can only invest for a short period (say anything up to five years) it will be safer to avoid equities and go for cash-based products.

Many products—including cash-based products—will give a guaranteed return if held for a specific period—e.g. a conventional gilt with five years to maturity will give a guaranteed return over five years, or a National Savings Certificate, held for five years, or a two-year term deposit with a building society, and so on. But if you don't hold the gilt for five years, you won't necessarily get the sum you expected, and while in the other two cases you will get pre-arranged sums, these will be much less attractive than what you would have got had you held the investment to maturity. So while these investments are less risky than equities, you still have to make sure you can hold the investment for the entire period of any agreement to get the best return. If you think you might not be able to, you might be better off with a slightly lower return from an investment with no fixed term. You have to be especially careful of some guaranteed return products where you may lose part of your capital if you don't hold the product for the agreed period.

If you might want your money soon, you should stick with instant access savings accounts. If you won't want if for a year or two you might consider short-term (e.g. three or six months) savings accounts. If you won't want the money for at least five years, you can consider various National Savings products (some are especially attractive for higher rate taxpayers), guaranteed bonds, a TESSA, and equities. If you are not sure whether you will need the money in less than five years, a TESSA is attractive. You'll probably get a very competitive rate of interest and there need be no penalty if you don't last five years. If you do, you will get a tax-free income.

If you do not want to risk the value of your capital you should stick to savings accounts, National Savings accounts, and if you will hold the investment for a specific period, guaranteed bonds and gilts. If you are willing to risk your capital, equity-based products should be considered.

Some investors have an income requirement. This can either take the form of a desired immediate high income or a lower, but rising, income. You can get a high income from gilts, corporate bonds, PIBS, unit trusts investing in any of these, investment trust split capital income shares, high income equity unit trusts, savings accounts (especially for large sums), guaranteed income bonds, National Savings Income Bonds and, for older investors only, annuities. Equities offer a lower income than many other assets, but over the years equities have produced a growing income. Remember that when you read about stockmarket crashes, it's the price of your shares that is falling. Your income will be unaffected at the time, and probably subsequently too (refer to Figure 11.2). If you don't have to touch your capital, your day-to-day living standard will be unaffected.

Many people are attracted to savings accounts, especially during periods of high interest rates, because of the high income and safety. You should remember that when interest rates fall, your income will also fall and you will not be in a good position to increase it. Your capital will not grow, and while your investment is safe in the sense you can't lose your capital, you are still exposed to the inflation risk. Savings accounts can be risky long-term investments.

If you want long-term growth of capital you should consider National Savings Index-Linked Certificates, Index-Linked Gilts, equity-based products (such as shares, unit trusts, investment trusts, single premium investment bonds and endowment policies), and higher risk products such as Enterprise Investment Schemes, Venture Capital Trusts, and Enterprise Zone property trusts—although most investors can ignore these higher risk investments.

If you buy National Savings Index-Linked Certificates, you are guaranteed to get 2½% per annum more than the rate of inflation over the five-year life of the certificate. This is tax-free. If you buy Index-Linked gilts you will get about 3.5% per annum more than the rate of inflation if you hold the gilt to redemption (the exact amount varies with each gilt). The income is taxed at your marginal savings tax rate.

If you buy pure equity products, there are no guarantees as to the return you will get. Historically, however, the returns over long periods have been high. If you have an investment horizon of more than five years, equities should figure prominently in your portfolio—if you can live with the possibility of a stockmarket crash. You can buy individual shares or pooled products such as investment trusts and unit trusts. You will reduce your risk by diversifying your shareholdings, and the easiest way of doing this is by buying a pooled product. There are many fancy products based on equities such as split capital investment trusts, options, warrants and futures. Most investors would be well advised to keep things simple and buy a straightforward investment trust or unit trust. Insurance products will have varying degrees of exposure to equities, and will have some minimum value. Relative to investment trusts and unit trusts held in a PEP, the insurance products are not tax efficient.

Although much is made of investment performance, few fund managers show consistent ability. The distribution of managers' performance is very similar to what you would find if chance alone determined performance. Contrary to what advisers say, this isn't contradicted by finding a manager who has performed well for a few years, any more than finding a coin that has turned up heads five flips in a row refutes the fact that its an even money bet as to whether a coin comes up heads or tails. There is much to be said for buying index funds if you share this view.

If you live in the UK, the bulk of your expenditure will be in sterling. You should probably have the bulk of your investments in UK assets. Don't risk more than about 30% of your assets in non-UK investments such as US, European, Japanese and emerging market shares unless you want to take a very aggressive investment stance.

Although you can improve your returns by only holding stocks when there is a bull market, and by selling and holding cash in bear markets, few investors have these market timing skills. You would be sensible not to try to time the market. Even better, you should try to buy on a regular basis. That way you don't attempt to time the market, and you will get more shares for your money through pound cost averaging. Best of all, invest in equities for the long term and don't fiddle with them. If you keep dealing in your equities, and trying to get in and out of the market, your investment returns will be killed by costs.

Costs really do matter. Try to deal as cheaply as you can, and don't use high-cost product providers. If you are looking at an equity-based insurance product, select one with low costs first, and above-average past performance second.

Many people get confused as to which assets risk their capital and which have variable income. Table 36.1 provides a matrix summarizing the position.

Diversify and get the mix right

No one investment is the solution to all your requirements. Cash accounts are great for emergencies, but risky as a long-term investment. Shares are great for your retirement fund but inappropriate as a one-year investment. It's not a question of all or nothing, but how much of each you want.

In general, however, British investors seem to worry too much about the risks of equities and invest too little in them. For example, many people are warned to get out of equities about five years before they retire. This makes little sense, as it is based on the "retirement equals death" fallacy. Depending on the age of retirement, and the ages of both partners, the younger one may live anywhere from 20 to 30 years after the older partner retires. This is a long investment horizon, and equities are an appro-

Table 36.1   Matrix of Fixed/Variable Capital/Income

	FIXED INCOME	VARIABLE INCOME
FIXED CAPITAL	• Term accounts • Fixed annuities • NS FIRST Option Bond • NS Pensioners Bond • NS Capital Bond • NS Fixed Interest • Local Authority Fixed Term Loan	• Bank deposits • Building society deposits • TESSAs • Increasing annuities • NS Income Bond • NS Investment Account
VARIABLE CAPITAL	• PIBS • Conventional Gilts • Corporate Bonds • Preference Shares	• NS Index-Linked • Index-Linked Gilt • Investment trusts • Unit trusts • Unit trusts investing in bonds

priate investment. Remember, dividends for the entire stockmarket have seldom fallen, and when they have, it has usually not been by much.

Imagine that five years before retirement you buy a gilt at par value yielding 8%, and you hold it for 30 years, when both you and the gilt are redeemed. You would get 8% income in year 30, just as in year 1, and no capital growth. If you bought equities on a 4% yield and dividends grew by 5% per annum, you would be getting a yield of about 16½% on your original capital in year 30, and your capital would almost certainly have increased too. Now this isn't guaranteed, but it's not implausible.

For somebody who is retired and does not have much income, there is real pressure to get high-yielding investments. But even here equities should not be ruled out. The problem with cash savings is that your income can collapse if interest rates fall. Gilts protect you against this because your income is fixed, but you will get less and less in real terms as a consequence of inflation. If inflation increases, cash gives some protection because interest rates will rise. Clearly, holding gilts and cash deposits will reduce your risks—each asset offsets the other's major weakness. But there is no built-in growth of income or capital. While dividend growth is not guaranteed, it is likely. A high-yielding equity-based investment trust or unit trust would probably produce a steadily rising income, and perhaps some capital growth.

Somebody retired and looking for income would reduce their risks by having all three assets rather than just one. It's true the equities are riskier than the other assets in one sense—volatility of capital values—but they are less risky in other senses (less exposed to inflation and a better chance of income growth) so the portfolio as a whole is less risky than each of the parts. The point is this. Every asset has good and bad features. By combining assets with different characteristics, you will be able to reduce your risks. This example is just a "for instance". Don't view this as a model portfolio for retired people—it's just an example of diversification.

Table 36.2 overleaf lists some of the major assets and what they are best used for.

Which is the right mix of these assets for you? I don't know—it depends on your attitude to risk, your financial resources, your personal circumstances and your goals. Which is where I started. But the financial planning process isn't completed yet.

Table 36.2   Major Assets and Their Uses

ASSET	USE
Cash deposit type investments	• Emergency cash reserve • Saving for a holiday, stereo, car, etc. • Saving for a deposit on a home • Waiting for a good moment to invest elsewhere • Protecting the value of your capital before a known expenditure, e.g., school fees
Shares	• For a high total return over a long holding period (e.g., saving for expenditure in the far future—college fees for your toddler; building a retirement fund) • Growing income • Diversification
Conventional gilts and corporate bonds (with redemption dates)	• For a high immediate income • For a fixed sum on a specific date • Diversification (especially with shares)
Irredeemable gilts and PIBS	• High income • Speculation that interest rates will fall
Index-linked gilts	• Capital and income growth • Hedge against inflation • Guaranteed real return
Property (your home)	• Long-term capital growth

Estate planning

By now you should have your financial life in better order. As you get older, you will acquire more assets (even if it's only that you own more of your home and the lender owns less) and you should think about estate planning, i.e., how to pass on your assets in the most tax efficient way. This may involve attempting to minimize inheritance tax and establishing trusts.

Monitor

Things change; you, the markets, the tax laws, everything. Financial planning is a never-ending process—keep monitoring your affairs.

FINALLY

I hope you have found this book useful, and that it has helped you to fix your finances. But I hope you don't need reminding that money isn't everything. To put matters in perspective, I can't do better than John Locke:

A sound mind in a sound body, is a short, but full description of a happy state in this World: he that has these two, has little more to wish for; and he that wants either of them, will be little the better for anything else.

Glossary of Investment Terms

Accrued Interest. Interest earned on a bond since the last interest payment date. When a bond is traded, the buyer pays the Clean Price and the accrued interest.

ACT. See Advance Corporation Tax.

Active Investment Management. Investment management which aims to purchase or sell securities and assets which are not priced at their intrinsic value.

Actuary. Person who calculates insurance or pension risks and premiums.

Additional Voluntary Contributions (AVC). Contributions paid to a company pension scheme by an employee, in addition to any normal contributions, to obtain extra benefits. See also Free Standing Additional Voluntary Contributions.

Advance Corporation Tax. Companies pay a tax of 20% on dividends on behalf of shareholders directly to the Inland Revenue. It is treated as an advance part of the corporation tax companies have to pay.

Advance Directive. See Living Will.

Advisory Client. Client who requires an agent to act on his behalf only after his approval. The service provided may vary from execution of orders on instruction through to provision of substantial advice. Also called non-discretionary client.

After-Tax. Cost or return that is borne or obtained after allowing for any applicable taxes.

Agent. Person who acts on behalf of another, the principal. The agent is paid by a fee or a commission.

Agency Broker. Stockbroker who does not make a market in shares and acts solely as an agent and charges commission on transactions.

AIM. See Alternative Investment Market.

AITC. Association of Investment Trust Companies. Trade association for investment trusts.

Alternative Investment Market (AIM). New smaller companies stockmarket which opened on 19 June 1995. AIM companies qualify as "unquoted companies" and some are eligible for capital gains tax roll-over relief and are free of inheritance tax if held for two years. The Stock Exchange does not vet prospectuses, but the companies must have an approved adviser who has checked the company's financial figures.

American Stock Exchange (AMEX). Second largest US stock exchange. Sometimes abbreviated as ASE.

Analyst. See Investment Analyst.

Anomalies. An empirical finding relating share returns to a factor not predicted by an academic asset pricing theory, e.g., low price earnings shares and small capitalization shares. These seem to offer higher than average returns.

Annual Percentage Rate. See APR.

Annual Report and Accounts. Legal document issued by a company giving details of the business it is engaged in, its results and prospects, and audited financial statements including a balance sheet, profit and loss account, and cashflow statement.

Annuity. A lump sum paid to a financial institution in return for a stream of regular payments (comprising the principal and interest received) for a specified period.

Appropriate Personal Pension (APP). Formal name for a personal pension which is taken by an individual in a contracted-in scheme who personally contracts out (of SERPS), and which receives contributions from the DSS.

APR (Annual Percentage Rate). Annual return or cost which takes account of any charges, such as an administration fee, as well as interest. While lenders usually have to quote an APR, banks don't have to do this for overdrafts.

Arbitrage. Simultaneous purchase and sale of identical or similar assets in different markets for different prices. The objective is to earn a risk-free return.

Arithmetic Return. A type of average calculated by adding period returns (e.g. annual returns) and dividing by the number of periods.

Asset. Anything of value owned by an individual or company. The word "property" is sometimes used in this general sense.

Asset Allocation. The process of selecting the best allocation of an investor's portfolio amongst various asset classes.

Asset Allocation Fund. A pooled fund that invests in different types of assets such as cash, bonds, property, domestic and foreign equities and varies the proportion invested in each type depending on prospects.

Asset Value. Monetary value of an asset. Company asset values are often stated per share, i.e., the total asset value divided by the number of issued shares.

Auction (Gilt). Sale of new gilt issue at which successful competitive bidders pay the price bid. Non-competitive bidders (which usually includes all private investors) pay the weighted average of successful competitive bids.

Augmentation. Increase of benefits above the normal scale of a pension scheme.

Authorized Person. Person conducting investment business with authorization by appropriate regulatory body.

AUTIF. Association of Unit Trusts and Investment Funds. Trade association for unit trusts.

AVC. See Additional Voluntary Contribution.

Average Down. Buying more of an asset after its price has fallen, which reduces the average price paid.

Average Tax Rate. Total tax divided by total income or capital. See also marginal tax rate.

Balance Sheet. Statement of assets and liabilities of a company (or a person, trust, etc.) at a particular date.

Basis Point. One-hundredth of one per cent. Used to describe changes in bond yields; e.g., a move from 10% to 9.9% is a decline of 10 basis points.

Bear Market. A period in which asset prices are falling. A bear is an investor with a view that prices will fall.

Bearer Stock. Stock for which no central register of ownership is kept. The certificate is the instrument of value. To collect dividends or interest, the holder (i.e., bearer) cuts off coupons attached to the stock and presents them to a designated paying agent. Not common in the UK.

Bed and Breakfast. Sale of a security one day and repurchase the next to achieve a disposal for capital gains purposes. Brokers usually waive the repurchase commission.

Benchmark Portfolio. A portfolio against which investment performance can be evaluated.

Beneficial Owner. Person or institution which enjoys benefits of ownership although the asset may be registered in another name. See Nominee Account.

Beneficiary. Someone who benefits from a financial contract, inherits from a will, etc.

Bequest. Disposal of assets by a will.

Best Price. The highest price available to sellers of shares or the lowest price available to buyers at the time of dealing.

BES. See Business Expansion Scheme.

Bid Price. Price at which a market maker will buy shares and at which investors can sell.

Blue Chip Stock. Shares of a large company with a record of steady growth of earnings and dividends over a long period. (Origin: highest value poker chip.)

Bond. (1). An IOU issued by a borrower, usually a government or company. The purchaser usually receives a set sum of interest twice a year and repayment of the principal at a specific date. Usually described as a fixed income or fixed interest investment. Bonds issued by the government in the UK are called gilts, those by the US government are called Treasury bonds. (See also Zero-Coupon Bond and Index-Linked Gilt.) (2). The word bond seems to imply safety to many private clients, and numerous quite dissimilar financial products have been described by their promoters as bonds, e.g., broker bonds, single premium bonds, guaranteed bonds, etc. These are not bonds in the sense of definition (1). When the press reports that falling or rising bond prices have affected the equity market, they are referring to bonds in the sense of definition (1).

Book Value. Aggregate value of ordinary shareholders' equity, i.e., ordinary share capital plus reserves.

Book Value per Share. Book value divided by number of issued ordinary shares.

Broker. A person who handles buy and sell transactions in return for a commission, e.g., a stockbroker or insurance broker.

Bulldog Bond. A sterling denominated bond issued in the international markets by a non-UK entity.

Bull Market. A period when asset prices are rising. A bull is an investor with a view that prices will rise.

Business Cycle. The regular swings of economic activity between boom and recession.

Business Expansion Scheme (BES). Scheme which ended in 1993 (although pre-existing issues continue). Set up to encourage investment in small unquoted trading companies. Individuals could invest between £500 and £40 000 per year. Received tax relief at top rate of tax. Shares had to be held for five years.

Buy and Hold Strategy. A strategy whereby assets are purchased and held without any trading or asset rebalancing to the original mix.

Buying Price. Price at which an investor buys units from a unit trust manager.

Capital Gain. A profit made on the sale of an asset when the sale price exceeds the purchase cost. For tax purposes, capital gains are treated in a different way from interest, dividends or other income.

Capital Loss. A loss made on the sale of an asset when the sale price is lower than the purchase cost. For tax purposes, some capital losses may be offset against capital gains, but not against income.

Capital Gains Tax (CGT). Tax charged on realized capital gains, after any indexing permitted for changes in the retail price index. Some assets (e.g., gilts owned by an individual or trust) are exempt from capital gains tax.

Capitalization-weighted (or Value-weighted) Index. A market index in which each security is weighted according to its market capitalization.

Cash. Coins, bank notes and current account deposits. More generally, cash or near-cash is any immediately, or very quickly, realizable asset of known value.

Cash Flow. Income from all sources in a particular period.

Certain Annuity. Annuity for a specified number of years. Often used to pay school fees.

Certificate of Deposit (or CD). A tradable bank deposit, i.e., an investor (usually an institution) makes a deposit for a specific period with a bank but can sell the deposit in the money market if its requirements change.

CGT. See Capital Gains Tax.

Chattels. Personal possessions including home contents, but excluding cash.

Clean Price. Price of a gilt which excludes accrued interest or rebate interest.

Client Agreement. Document all clients who get investment advice must sign, specifying client objectives and terms of trading.

Closed-End Investment Fund. Investment fund with fixed capital, e.g., an investment trust.

Closet Indexing. The practice, unwittingly or otherwise, by active managers of keeping their portfolio close to the asset distribution of a benchmark index.

Coincident Indicators. Economic indicators which move at the same time as the business cycle.

Collateral. Assets used as security for a loan, and which may be sold to realize the sum owed if the borrower defaults.

Commission. The fee paid to an agent for advice, or transacting a purchase or sale. The rate of commission often varies substantially between agents.

Commutation. See Lump Sum.

Compliance Officer. Person in a financial firm responsible for seeing that industry regulations are adhered to.

Compounding. Reinvesting income to earn additional income on that income. Compounding may take place daily through to annually.

Compound Interest. Interest earned on the original deposit or investment and on previous interest earned.

Composite Leading Indicator Series. Economic indicators which move in advance of the business cycle.

Contracting-out. Occupational pension schemes may contract-out of the earnings-related part of the State pension scheme (SERPs). Final salary schemes must provide a Guaranteed Minimum Pension, and money purchase schemes must pay contributions equal to or better than the State rebate into an approved pension scheme. Individuals may contract-out of SERPs even if their occupational scheme is contracted-in.

Contrary Opinion. Investment strategy based on trading against the crowd.

Conventional Gilt. Gilt on which interest payments and principal repayment is fixed in money terms.

Convertible. A share or bond that can be converted into another share or bond at a specific time and under set terms.

Convertible Term Insurance. Term insurance with option to convert to whole-life insurance.

Correlation Coefficient. A measure of the degree to which two variables move together. Correlation coefficients range from -1.0 to $+1.0$. A coefficient of $+1.0$ means the variables move in perfect lockstep, -1.0 means they move in perfect negative lockstep and 0.0 implies that they are completely unrelated. Correlation coefficients measure the strength of a relationship, but do not imply causality.

Coupon. The percentage interest a bond pays on its nominal value (the value printed on the bond), which will probably not be the market price the bond trades at.

CREST. Equity settlement system that is being developed to replace the current Talisman system. Will enable shareholders to hold shares in electronic form if they wish.

Critical Illness (or Dread Disease) Insurance. Policy which pays out if a specified illness is suffered.

Cum. Means "includes" and is used in, e.g., "cum dividend" (cd), which means with a recently declared dividend. See Ex.

Current Yield. Annual interest payable, expressed as a percentage of the market price of the asset.

Cyclical Stock. Stock that is strongly affected by the course of the business cycle.

Debenture. A corporate bond, which may be secured against specific assets, or the company's assets in general.

Decreasing Term. A term insurance policy in which the sum assured declines over time. Used with repayment mortgages.

Deferred Annuity. An annuity which makes its regular payments some time after purchase.

Deferred Pension. (1). A pension due at normal retirement age to someone who has left a scheme early. (2). A pension where payment commences after normal retirement age.

Defined Benefit Pension Scheme. See Final Salary Scheme.

Defined Contribution Pension Scheme. See Money Purchase Scheme.

Dependant's Pension. Pension paid to a pensioner's dependant(s) on pensioner's death.

Derivative Security. Security such as option or future whose value derives from another asset such as a share or bond.

Discount. (1) The amount by which a bond sells below its par, or stated, value. (2). The amount by which an investment trust's price sells below net asset value.

Discount Broker. Stockbroker who deals at low commission rates and provides no advice.

Discount Rate. (1). The rate of interest used to discount a stream of cash flows to a present value. The discount rate reflects both the time value of money and the riskiness of the cash flows. (2). In the USA, it is the rate of interest at which the Federal Reserves lends to other banks.

Diversification. The spreading of assets in a portfolio to reduce its risk.

Dividend. Money paid by a company to its shareholders. Ordinary shareholders receive a dividend that may fluctuate with the company's profits. A unit trust also pays dividends, in effect passing on the dividends of the shares it holds.

Dividend Cover. The number of times a company's earnings exceed its dividend.

Dividend Payout Ratio. Percentage of earnings paid out as dividends.

Double-dated Gilt. A gilt, such as 8% Treasury Loan 2002–06, which has two redemption rates. The Government has the option to redeem the stock at par any time after the first date (2002) and must redeem it by the second (2006).

Dow Jones Industrial Average (DJIA). Best known US index. A price-weighted index of 30 leading industrial shares: its construction makes it less useful for portfolio analysis than the S&P 500.

Earned Income. Income earned from a job.

Earnings Cap. Maximum earnings on which a pension may be calculated in approved schemes and personal personal pension plans set up after certain dates. Cap in 1996–7, £82 200.

Earnings Per Share (EPS). A company's earnings divided by its number of issued shares. The earnings used in the calculation may be the last reported earnings (sometimes called historical or trailing) or forecast earnings (sometimes called prospective).

Earnings Surprise. Difference between reported earnings and analysts' prior expectations.

Earnings Yield. Earnings per share divided by the price per share: reciprocal of the price–earnings ratio. Also called earnings–price ratio.

Efficient Market Theory. The theory that security prices fully reflect all available information. The theory is sometimes stated in three versions. The weak-form of the theory states that prices reflect all past price information. The semi-strong version states that prices reflect all publicly available information. The strong-form states that prices reflect all information, both public and private.

Endowment Insurance. A life insurance policy that pays on death within a stated period, or on survival at the end of that period. The policy may be with-profits (or bonus), non-profits, or unit-linked. See also Low Cost Endowment Insurance.

Enterprise Zone Property Trusts. Trusts investing in property in designated Enterprise zones. The sum invested in property (but not land) attracts tax relief at investor's top rate. No limit to the amount that may be invested.

Equities. Another name for Ordinary Shares.

Equity (in property). The ownership proportion held in a property, i.e., the difference between the value and any mortgage outstanding.

Equity-Linked Annuity. Annuity in which the underlying value is invested in units of an equity fund with the beneficiary withdrawing a fixed number of units each year.

Equity Risk Premium. The difference between the return on equities and a riskless asset. Often used in the UK by practitioners as the difference between equity and gilt returns.

Escalating Annuity. Annuity which offers payments which rise each year.

Escalation of Pension. Increase of pension paid out; usually annually and the lower of a fixed percentage or the Retail Price Index.

Estate. All of a person's assets less liabilities.

Estate Planning. Drawing up plans so that as much as possible of your assets is passed on to the people or institutions that you want to benefit.

Eurosterling Bonds. A sterling denominated bond issued by a UK company in the international markets.

Ex. Means "excluding", e.g., "ex dividend" (xd) means excluding a recently declared dividend. See Cum.

Execution-only. Stockbroking service in which the broker executes client orders without giving advice. May or may not be discount broker.

Executor/Executrix. Male/female who carries out the terms of a will.

Exit Charge. See Sales Redemption Charge.

Expected Return. The return anticipated by an investor over a particular holding period.

Face Value. See Nominal Value.

Factor (or Attribute) Screening. Process of searching through stocks seeking those possessing factors that are thought to be associated with high returns.

Federal Reserve. US central bank: US equivalent of Bank of England.

FIMBRA. Financial Intermediaries, Managers and Brokers Regulatory Association—see Financial Services Act.

Final Salary Scheme. Pension scheme in which the benefits are specified in relation to salary; e.g., 40 years' employment might produce a pension two-thirds of the average salary earned in the last three working years.

Financial Adviser. Person who gives financial advice. See IFA, and Tied Adviser.

Financial Planning. The process of determining financial goals and the steps necessary to achieve them.

Financial Services Industry. General term that covers individuals and firms involved in giving financial advice and providing financial products to individual investors.

Financial Services Act 1986. Act which regulates investment business carried out in the UK by individuals or firms. Sets out statutory framework in which self-regulation, controlled by Self-Regulating Organizations (SROs) and Recognized Professional Bodies (RPBs), takes place. The lead regulator is SIB (Securities Investment Board). The SROs are: IMRO (Investment Management Regulatory Organization); SFA (The Securities and Futures Authority); and PIA (Personal Investment Authority), which took over the functions of FIMBRA (Financial Intermediaries, Managers and Brokers Regulatory Association) and LAUTRO (Life Assurance and Unit Trust Regulatory Organization) in 1994 and replaced them in 1995.

Fixed Income Security. American term for Fixed Interest Security.

Fixed Interest Security. A security such as a gilt or debenture which pays a fixed rate of interest.

Fixed Term. Some investments must be held for a fixed period of time, which is stipulated in the contract.

Flat Yield. See Current Yield.

Floating Rate Note (or FRN). A type of bond which periodically resets its interest rate in line with money market rates.

Free Standing Additional Voluntary Contribution (FSAVC). Contributions paid by an employee, in addition to any contributions paid to a company scheme, to a money purchase scheme not organized by the employer, to obtain extra pension benefits. See also Additional Voluntary Contributions.

Front-end Charge. Unit trusts typically charge an acquisition fee—the front-end charge or load—of between 5% to 7½%, although this can be much lower on specific types of fund, e.g., index funds or gilt funds. A few managers have abandoned these charges or have very low charges, and most will discount the charge for large purchases.

Frozen Pension. A pension due at normal retirement age to someone who has left a scheme early.

FSA. See Financial Services Act.

FSAVC. See Free Standing Additional Voluntary Contribution.

FT-SE-A All-Share Index. The major UK capitalization-weighted index consisting of about 920 of the largest shares and broadly representative of the UK market. Covers over 98% of the UK market by capitalization.

FT-SE 100 Index. Capitalization-weighted index of the 100 largest London-listed stocks. Accounts for about 72% by value of the London market. Usually referred to as "Footsie".

FT-SE Mid 250 Index. Capitalization-weighted index of the 250 London-listed stocks that come below the 100 largest listed stocks. The index comes in two forms, including and excluding investment trusts.

FT-SE-A 350 Index. Capitalization-weighted index of the stocks in the FT-SE 100 Index and the FT-SE Mid 250 Index. Accounts for about 92% by value of the London market.

FT-SE Actuaries Fledgling Index. Capitalization-weighted index covering stocks too small to be in the FT-SE-A All-Share Index. Includes about 800 companies with full listings on the Stock Exchange or on the USM. It covers 1.8% of the market. Only companies which meet certain liquidity standards are included. The index comes in two forms, including and excluding investment trusts.

FT/S&P Actuaries World Indices. Group of capitalization-weighted indices for individual countries and groups of countries.

FT-SE SmallCap Index. Capitalization-weighted index consisting of all companies in the FT-SE-A All-Share Index not large enough to be in the largest 350 shares. It comes in two versions, including and excluding investment trusts.

Fund Manager. Person who manages the assets of an investment fund or portfolio.

Fundamental Analysis. Evaluation of firms and markets and possible security mispricing (i.e., assets not priced at intrinsic value) based on analysis of economic and financial factors.

Futures. Contracts, traded on recognized exchanges, which give the holder the right to buy or sell a specified currency, stock, index, interest rate or commodity at a specified price on a specified future date.

Gartmore MicroCap Index. Index of about 676 companies comprising the smallest 1% by capitalization of the main UK equity market. Excludes investment trusts. Heavy weighting in manufacturing sector. Almost no overlap with FTSE-A All-Share Index.

Gearing. Gearing is a way of magnifying investment results, either up or down. E.g., investment trusts can borrow money to invest in equities, and this gears the effect of market movements for shareholders; futures are bought on margin, i.e., only a small amount is spent to gain a large exposure to a market; companies gear up by increasing their borrowings.

Geometric Mean Return. The compounded per period average rate of return over a particular period, i.e., the rate of return which makes the initial value of an investment equal to its end period value.

Gilts or Gilt-edged Securities. Fixed interest securities issued by the UK government. Interest payments may be made quarterly or semi-annually. Gilts are classified by their redemption dates. "Shorts" have less than 5 years to redemption, "Mediums" have between 5 and 15 years, and "Longs" have more than 15 years. "Irredeemables" have no redemption date.

Gross. Before tax (or other charges) is deducted.

Grossed-up Dividend. Value of dividend before tax is deducted. For example if a dividend is worth £100 after tax of 20% has been deducted, the grossed-up value is £125.

Growth Stock. The shares of a company expected to achieve above-average growth of profits.

Guaranteed Income and Growth Bonds. Lump sum investment usually in a non-qualifying life insurance policy providing a fixed rate of return.

Guaranteed Minimum Pension. Minimum pension required to allow a final salary scheme to contract-out: must offer at least the same as the earnings-related part of the State pension.

Hedge Funds. Inaccurate name used for certain offshore funds which are not subject to financial regulation and use aggressive trading strategies. These may include selling assets they do not hold, or borrowing to gear up or leverage the fund. Generally use futures and options. Better name would be leverage funds. About 800 such funds, managing about $45 billion, and mainly oriented towards US investors.

Hoare Govett Smaller Companies Index (HGSCI). Index comprising the smallest 10% by capitalization of the main UK equity market.

Hoare Govett 1000 Index. Index comprising the smallest 2.5% by capitalization of the main UK equity market.

Holding Period Return. The total return from an investment over a specified holding period expressed as a percentage.

Home Income Scheme. Scheme allowing elderly people to unlock the value of their property and enjoy an income while still living in their home.

Hurdle Rate. Rate at which an investment trust's assets must grow at to achieve a specific return.

IFA. Independent Financial Adviser, i.e., adviser not tied to a particular company.

IHT. See Inheritance Tax.

Immediate Annuity. Annuity which pays an income for life, commencing on the purchase of the annuity.

IMRO. Investment Management Regulatory Organization—see Financial Services Act.

Income Tax. Tax on income from salary, self-employment and investments.

Independent Financial Adviser. See IFA.

Independent Taxation. Since 1990, the incomes of husbands and wives have been assessed independently.

Index. (1). A measure of the level of a stockmarket. (2). Process of relating the value of a sum to changes in a price index.

Index-linked Gilt. A class of UK gilt which has both coupon payments and principal indexed to the Retail Price Index during the life of the gilt.

Index Fund. A passive investment fund which aims to achieve the performance of a particular index.

Indexation Allowance. Indexation allowance reduces the amount of CGT payable on the sale of an asset by notionally increasing the cost of the asset by any rise in the RPI that has occurred between acquisition (or 31 March 1982 if that is later) and disposal.

Inflation. Increase in the level of prices.

Inheritance Tax (IHT). Tax payable on transfer of assets on death or on gifts when these are chargeable transfers.

Insider and Inside Information. Insider and inside information have specific legal meanings in the UK and US and trading on the basis of inside information is illegal. However, often used in a more general sense to assess the activity of investors (such as company directors) with access to information not generally available to the public.

Institutional Investor. Investor acting on behalf of an institution such as a pension fund, insurance company or pooled fund such as an investment trust or unit trust.

Insurance. Premium paid to secure sum of money in event of loss or damage to life, property, etc .

Interest. Sum a borrower pays a lender for the use of money.

Interest Yield. See Current Yield.

Intestate. Not having made a will.

Investment Analyst. Investment analysts are employed by stockbrokers to research companies and make recommendations on their shares. The research is sent to institutional investors. Some of these have their own in-house analysts.

Investment Horizon. The period over which an investor makes investment plans.

Investment Manager. See Fund Manager.

Investment Trust. A company which invests in the shares of other companies and perhaps also in bonds. A form of pooled investments which offers good diversification. Traded on the stock-market at the market clearing price, which may be above or below the company's net asset value. See also Unit Trust.

Irredeemable Bonds. Bonds that do not have a date by which they must be redeemed, e.g., Consols 2½% have a redemption date of "1923 or after".

LAPR. See Life Assurance Premium Relief.

Lagging Indicators. Economic indicators which follow movements in the business cycle.

LAUTRO. Life Assurance and Unit Trust Regulatory Organization—see Financial Services Act.

Leading Indicators. Economic indicators which lead movements in the business cycle.

Legacy. Money or item bequeathed.

Life Assurance. Correct name for life insurance. This book follows the popular usage, except for proper names.

Life Assurance Premium Relief (LAPR). LAPR was available on policies taken out before 14 March 1984. LAPR was abolished for new policies, but it remains in force for premiums on old policies which have not had the benefits increased or the term extended. Currently the rate is 12½% of the gross premium. The relief is limited to the greater of premiums of £1500 or one-sixth of your income.

Life Insurance. See Endowment Insurance, Term Insurance and Whole-Life Insurance.

Life Tenant. Beneficiary of trust with a right to income from assets for a period, usually life, with the capital passing to others at the end of the period.

Liquid. (1). An asset that's easy to trade at a stable price—see also Marketability. (2). A market in which there are many buyers and sellers and where trades can be readily made. (3). An investor with mainly cash is said to be liquid.

Listed Stock. Stock traded on a recognized stock exchange.

Living Will. (or **Advance Directive**). This specifies who can make medical decisions on your behalf, and within what guidelines, if you are not capable of making them yourself.

Loan Stock. Corporate bond, usually unsecured. In the event of liquidation, ranks behind secured stock (e.g., debentures), equally with general creditors, and ahead of shares.

Low-Cost Endowment Insurance. Combination of term insurance (low-cost factor) and endowment insurance. Used to repay property loans. The endowment cover is insufficient to repay the loan, but should be sufficient with the addition of profits. The term insurance provides repayment of any shortfall if death occurs prior to loan maturity.

Lump Sum. Sum of tax-free money taken in lieu of part of a pension entitlement. Subject to limits set by Inland Revenue.

Marginal Tax Rate. Tax rate paid or due on the last pound of income or capital. This, not the average tax rate, is the important tax rate for decision-making.

Marketability. A marketable security is one that can be readily traded, but not necessarily at a stable price. Can be distinguished from Liquid (see also), but often the terms are used as synonyms.

Market Maker. A company or individual who facilitates trades by acting as a principal and holding an inventory of stocks. The market maker attempts to make a profit by the difference in the bid and offer prices and by being long (i.e., owning stocks) or short (i.e., having sold stocks he doesn't have) when the market rises or falls.

Maturity. The length of time until the principal on a bond is repaid.

Maximum Investment Plan. Insurance/savings product which has the minimum sum insured that is necessary to obtain "qualifying" status and the bulk of the premiums go into unit trusts and other investment funds.

Middle Price. The price mid-way between the bid and offer prices: price shown in the newspapers for stockmarket prices.

Minimum Price Tender. Method of selling new issues of gilts at which those tendering for stock must do so at or above a minimum price. All successful tenderers receive stock at the same price.

MIRAS. Mortgage interest relief at source.

Modern Portfolio Theory. Widely used term, but without precise definition. Usually implies a belief in the efficient market theory and an asset pricing model which quantifies the relationship between risk and return.

Money Market. Market in which money or short-term assets such as Treasury bills (government borrowing) and commercial paper (company borrowing) are traded. The size of transactions makes this a market for institutional investors. But see Money Market Fund.

Money Market Fund. Fund which invests in money market securities and is open to private investors.

Money Purchase Scheme. Pension scheme in which the contributions are specified and the benefits are wholly dependent on the value of the investments that have been purchased with the contributions and on annuity rates at the time of pension purchase.

Morgan Stanley Capital International (MSCI) Indices. Group of capitalization-weighted indices for individual countries and groups of countries.

Mortgage. A loan made with property as the collateral. Technically, the lender takes a mortgage using the property as collateral, although in everyday usage the loan is thought of as the mortgage.

Mortgage Indemnity Insurance. Covers the lender against loss if the borrower cannot pay: the borrower may be liable for any losses.

Mortgage Protection Insurance. Repays the whole loan if the borrower dies prematurely.

Mortgage Repayment Insurance. Insures monthly payments for a short period if the borrower cannot pay because of illness or redundancy.

NAV. See Net Asset Value.

Neglected Firm Effect. Empirical finding that stocks neglected by analysts or investment institutions provide superior returns.

Net. After tax, fee, commission or other charge.

Net Asset Value. Ordinary share capital plus retained reserves; usually expressed on a per share basis (i.e., divided by the number of ordinary shares in issue).

Net Cash Flow. Difference between cash inflows and outflows.

New Issue. Initial share sale by a firm.

New York Stock Exchange (NYSE). The largest US stock exchange.

Nikkei-Dow Jones Average. Arithmetic average of prices for 225 stocks on the First Section of the Tokyo Stock Exchange. This section consists of large capitalization stocks.

No Load Fund. Pooled fund that does not charge a front-end fee, but does charge an annual management fee.

Nominal Value. (1). The amount returned to a conventional gilt or bond holder at maturity or redemption. The amount to which indexing will be applied to calculate an index-linked gilt's redemption value. (2). The stated face value of an equity. This normally has little relevance to the current value of the share and the share cannot be redeemed at the nominal (or par) value.

Nominee Account. Account held with a nominee. Banks and brokers often act as nominees, holding assets registered in their nominee name and collecting income on behalf of the beneficial owner.

Non-discretionary Client. See Advisory Client.

Normal Retirement Date. Date on which the normal pension will start to be paid.

OEIC. See Open Ended Investment Company.

Offer Price. Price at which a market maker will sell shares and at which an investor can buy.

Offshore Fund. Usually refers to a fund set up in a tax haven.

Open-Ended Investment Fund. A fund which will issue or redeem units at net asset value (usually subject to a sales charge). UK unit trusts are open-ended investment funds. See also Open Ended Investment Company.

Open Ended Investment Company (OEIC). Already available in Continental Europe, OEICs (pronounced oiks) will be permitted in the UK in 1996. They are an investment company which has a variable share company. Many unit trusts are likely to convert to OEICs.

Open Market Option. Option that allows the annuity which is purchased at retirement to be purchased on the open market and not just from the life company which wrote the pension policy.

Option. A financial instrument that gives the holder the right, but not the obligation, to buy or sell a specific share, currency or market index, etc., within a specified time at a specific price. "Calls" give the right to buy, "puts" the right to sell.

Ordinary Share. A unit of ownership in a company. For example, anybody owning 100 BP shares owns part of that company. Shareholders usually have voting rights and receive dividends. Ordinary shares are often called equities.

OTC (Over-The-Counter) Market. The market in stocks not listed on recognized exchanges. Some listed stocks are also traded on the OTC. The security dealers act as market makers.

Overdraft. Withdrawal of an amount from a bank account greater than the balance in the account. Generally used to refer to a negative balance.

Overreaction Hypothesis. Hypothesis that investors tend to overreact to news causing asset prices to deviate from their intrinsic value.

Overweight. A fund is said to be overweight in an asset when it holds more than the appropriate index or benchmark weight.

Paid-up Pension. Pension policy on which no further contributions are payable.

Paid-up Policy. Insurance policy on which no further premiums are to be paid. The original term will remain unchanged, but the sum assured will be reduced.

Par Value. See Nominal Value.

Partly-paid Stock. Stock (either a bond or equity) which when issued requires the purchaser to pay only part of the total price, with the remainder due on specified dates in specified amounts.

Passive Investment Management. An investment strategy that does not involve trying to find mispriced assets. Usually will involve some use of an Index Fund.

PAYE. Pay As You Earn—employees have income tax deducted before they receive their wages or salary.

Penny Stock. Low-priced stock.

Pension. Periodic payment by employer, government or other institution. May be in consideration for past service or attaining a certain age. Usually paid on retirement.

Pension Fund. An institutional portfolio of assets established to provide pension benefits.

PEP (Personal Equity Plan). Tax-exempt investment in equity and fixed interest stocks. Maximum in 1996–7 tax year of £6,000 per General PEP and £3000 per Single Company PEP.

Permanent Health (or Disability) Insurance. Contract which provides an income until retirement age if the insured becomes disabled and unable to work.

Personal Equity Plan. See PEP.

Personal Net Worth. An individual's total assets less total liabilities.

Personal Pension Scheme. Pension arrangement made direct between an individual and a pension provider. May be used by self-employed and by employees who do not wish to join an occupational scheme or do not have one.

PIA. Personal Investment Authority—see Financial Services Act.

PIBS. Permanent interest bearing shares. Undated loan capital of a building society paying a fixed rate of interest.

Pooled Fund. Fund that pools many investors' money together, allowing greater diversification at lower cost than an individual investor could achieve. The investments are held in the name of the fund, and managed by a professional. The best known forms are investment trusts and unit trusts.

Portability. Term usually applied to pension funds when they can be readily transferred from one job to another.

Portfolio. The collection of assets held by an investor.

Potentially Exempt Transfer. Transfers of value that are subject to IHT if the transferor dies within seven years of making them.

Pound Cost Averaging. Buying an asset, usually ordinary shares, at regular intervals (e.g., monthly) in equal monetary amounts (e.g. £100). This eliminates the risk of buying only at the top of the market.

Power of Attorney. Power given to someone to be able to make decisions on behalf of another. May only apply in specific circumstances such as incapacitation.

PPP. See Personal Pension Plan.

Preference Share. Type of share that ranks ahead of ordinary share for dividend payments or repayment in case of liquidation. Benefit comes at cost of not fully sharing in rewards enjoyed by ordinary shareholders in good times.

Premium. (1). The amount by which a bond sells above its par, or stated, value. (2). The amount by which an investment trust's price sells above net asset value. (3). The sum paid to an option seller.

Premium Bonds. National Savings version of a lottery. Monthly prizes, and the stake money is never lost and can be encashed.

Present Value. The present value is the equivalent value today of future income streams. It is calculated by discounting future income by an appropriate discount rate.

Preservation. Pension benefit of an early leaver of a scheme with two or more years of service may be preserved until retirement.

Price Earnings Ratio. Share price divided by earnings per share.

Price-to-Book Value Ratio. Share price divided by the book value of assets.

Price-to-Cash Flow Ratio. Share price divided by cash flow, usually calculated as earnings plus non-cash expenses, the largest of which is depreciation.

Price-to-Sales Ratio. Share price divided by the company's sales.

Principal. (1). Amount of money borrowed or lent. (2). Person who takes a risk position—see Agent.

Private Medical Insurance. Insurance policy provided by private company to provide health care in a private hospital or to provide income while receiving National Health treatment.

Privatization. Sale of shares of a nationalized industry to the public and financial institutions.

Prospectus. Document which describes a security, fund or company being offered to the public.

Protected Rights. Minimum rights required to allow money purchase schemes and personal pension funds to contract-out of SERPS.

Qualifying Policy. Insurance policy so structured that it escapes tax on the policy proceeds.

Quality Spread. The difference in yields on corporate and government bonds.

Random Walk Theory. When applied to share prices, the theory asserts that the next percentage price change of a stock cannot be deduced on the basis of past changes.

Rate of Return. The percentage return from an investment, over a specified holding period, which includes both income and capital gains or losses, whether realized or unrealized.

Real Return. The inflation-adjusted return on an investment.

Rebate Interest. Interest paid by a seller of a bond to a buyer when the bond is bought ex-dividend.

Redemption Date. Date on which a bond or preference share is repaid.

Redemption Price. The price at which a bond is redeemed.

Redemption Yield. The pre-tax return from a bond if held to redemption. Technically, the discount rate which equates the present value of all future cash flows from a bond to the current price. In the USA this is called yield-to-maturity.

Renewable Term. Term insurance that may be automatically renewed at the rate for the age without medical examination or other conditions.

Repo Market. The repo market is one in which two participants agree that one will sell securities to another and make a commitment to repurchase equivalent securities on a future specified date, or on call, at a specified price. Effectively a way of borrowing or lending stock for cash, with the stock serving as collateral.

Required Rate of Return. The minimum expected return necessary to induce an investor to invest.

Reserves. When used in the context of a firm's balance sheet, it includes the profits kept in the business and the revaluation of any assets. The reserves belong to the ordinary shareholders.

Retail Broking. Private client stockbroking.

Retail Price Index (RPI). An index measuring consumer inflation.

Retirement Annuity Plan. Predecessor of personal pension plans and broadly similar. Existing policies can be retained, but new policies cannot be started.

Return. Amount received from an investment.

Reversionary Annuity. Annuity which commences on the death of another person: e.g., annuity payable to a widow on the death of her husband.

Risk. The uncertainty that an asset will earn its expected return. Usually measured by the variability (or volatility) of past returns.

Risk-averse. Investors are said to be risk-averse if they dislike risk. They will choose between two investments with equal returns the one with least risk. They will incur additional risk only if they expect additional return.

Risk-adjusted Return. The return on an asset adjusted for the risk it bears.

Risk-free Asset. An asset whose holding period return is known with certainty. Treasury bills are usually used as a proxy for this rate.

Risk-free Rate. The return on a risk-free asset.

Risk Premium. Rate of return above the risk-free rate required as compensation for bearing risk.

Risk Warning. Warning that must be attached to certain risky investments, e.g., "The price of units can go down as well as up".

Rolling Settlement. Settlement of a Stock Exchange equity bargain used to be made on a fixed account day. Now, settlement takes place 5 days after a transaction. This is a requirement for institutional investors, but currently many private investors still settle after 10 days.

RPI. See Retail Price Index.

Rule of 72. Short-cut and approximate method for finding how long it will take for an investment to double at a specific rate of return. The rule consists of dividing 72 by the rate of return. Thus, an investment earning a return of 9% will double in about 8 years ($72 \div 9 = 8$).

Rule of 113. Short-cut and approximate method for finding how long it will take for an investment to triple at a specific rate of return. The rule consists of dividing 113 by the rate of return. Thus, an investment earning a return of 9% will triple in about 12½ years ($113 \div 9 = 12.6$).

Running Yield. See Current Yield.

Sales Redemption Charge. A few unit trusts make a sales charge when the trust is sold. May be stepped, e.g., 3% if sold within one year of purchase, 2% within two years, 1% within three years, and none thereafter.

S&P 500. US capitalization-weighted share index published by Standard and Poor consisting of 500 shares. The 400 industrial shares included also form a separate index, the S&P 400.

Screening. Process of searching through stocks seeking those possessing factors or attributes that are thought to be associated with high returns.

SEAQ. Stock Exchange Automated Quotations: screen-based price and dealing service.

Securities. General name for stocks and shares.

Securities and Investment Board. See SIB.

Self-assessment. New tax system which will come into effect in 1996–7. Essentially, your tax assessment will be based on figures that you provide. You can calculate your own tax liability or let the Revenue do that from the figures you provide. In the first case you must complete your return by 31 January of the year following the year being assessed, in the second, by the previous 30 September. You will pay twice a year, half on 31 January and half on 31 July. These payments will be based on the previous year's income. The first payment will include an adjustment to bring the previous year's payments into line with the actual tax liability.

Self-Regulatory Organizations (SROs). See Financial Services Act.

Self-Invested Personal Pension. Personal pension plan in which the assets are managed by the policyholder.

Selling Price. Price at which an investor sells units to a unit trust manager.

SERPS (State Earnings Related Pensions). A State pension, additional to the Basic Pension, which is based on a defined slice of earnings.

Share Capital. When used in the context of a firm's balance sheet, the money put into the company by its shareholders.

SIB. Securities and Investment Board, chief UK financial services regulator.

Single Premium Bond. Non-qualifying life policy with small amount of life cover and most of the capital invested.

Single Pricing. Unit trusts currently are bought and sold at different buying and selling prices. When OEICs are introduced in 1996, they will be bought and sold at a single price, although a sales charge will be added to purchases. Unit trusts are likely to be allowed to move to single pricing.

Size Effect. Empirical finding that over long periods small capitalization stocks have outperformed large stocks.

Small Stock Effect. See Size Effect.

Speculation. Term not used in a consistent manner, or easy to distinguish from investment. Generally, any investment that offers high returns, but at great risk, or an investment made without adequate knowledge.

Split Capital Investment Trust. Investment trust whose capital is split to offer different risk/ return combinations to different investors.

Spread. Difference between buying and selling price.

Stamp Duty. Tax on documents associated with a change in ownership, e.g., purchase of a home and purchase of shares.

State Earnings Related Pensions. See SERPS.

Stepped Preference Shares. Shares that offer dividends that rise at a pre-determined rate. Usually offer a fixed value on redemption.

Strategic Asset Allocation. Asset allocation that is appropriate given an investor's liabilities and objectives. The benchmark portfolio from which Tactical Asset Allocation deviation may be made.

Stripping. Process of separating a standard coupon bond into its constituent interest and principal payments. E.g., a three-year bond with two interest payments per annum would have six interest strips and one principal strip.

Surrender Value. Amount payable to policy holder who terminates a policy.

Tactical Asset Allocation. Tactical asset allocation determines what departure, based on current market valuations, should be made from the Strategic Asset Allocation.

Tap Stock. Gilt held in official portfolios for sale to market makers when conditions are appropriate.

Tax Deferral. Taxes due are deferred until a later period. Usually applies to capital rather than income taxes, e.g., capital gains are usually charged on disposal of an asset and not on an annual unrealized basis.

Tax Exempt Special Savings Account. See TESSA.

Tax Haven. Country or political jurisdiction where no, or low, income tax is levied, e.g., Channel Islands, Bermuda, Isle of Man.

Tax Shelter. Structure that allows income or capital to escape taxation that would otherwise apply, e.g., shares held in a PEP.

Taxable Benefit. Benefit received in non-cash form, to which the Inland Revenue attributes a cash value which is then assessed for tax.

Taxable Income. Total income less any tax-exempt income and allowances and reliefs permitted by the Inland Revenue.

Technical Analysis. A form of security and market analysis which uses past price movements and volume levels plus other indicators to forecast future price movements.

Term Deposit. Interest paying deposit made for a specific term.

Term Insurance. Insurance that pays if death occurs in a specified period, but has no value otherwise.

Term Spread. The difference in yield between bonds with different maturities, e.g., three-month and ten-year bond yields.

TESSA. Tax-exempt cash account offered by a bank or building society. Maximum of £9000 may be deposited over a five-year period.

Tied Financial Adviser (Company Representative). Financial adviser who is tied to one company and can only recommend its products. Acts as an agent of the company.

Total Return. Return that includes both capital and income return.

Transferability. Ability to transfer pension rights from previous employer's scheme to current employer's.

Transfer Value. Payment made from one scheme to another which undertakes to provide pension benefits in respect of previous employment.

Treasury Bill. A security issued by the UK or US government which has a maximum maturity of one year. The bills are issued at a discount and redeemed at their nominal value.

Treasury Bond. A US government fixed income security with a term to maturity of over ten years. Income is paid semi-annually and the principal is returned at maturity. Term usually used to cover Treasury Notes too.

Treasury Note. A US government fixed income security with a term to maturity of between one and ten years. Income is paid semi-annually and the principal is returned at maturity.

Trust. Legal instrument which places assets under control of trustees, to be administered for the benefit of another person or persons.

Trustee. Person who administers assets held in a trust.

Undated Bonds. See Irredeemable Bonds.

Underweight. A fund is said to be underweight in an asset when it holds less than the appropriate index or benchmark.

Unearned Income. Income from sources other than a job, e.g., dividends and interest.

Unit Trust. A trust, available to the public, which invests in the shares of companies and/or bonds. A form of pooled investments which offers good diversification. See also Investment Trust.

Unlisted Securities Market (USM). UK market for smaller stocks, traded on the International Stock Exchange. Listing requirements are less onerous than those required for a full listing. Due to close end-1996.

Value-Weighted Market Index. See Capitalization-Weighted Index.

Venture Capital. Money invested in higher risk investments. An equity stake is acquired in an unquoted investment.

Volatility. The variability of an asset's return over time.

Warrant. Gives the owner the right to buy a security at a specific price during a specific period.

Whole-Life Insurance. Insurance that pays on death; also has a cash-in value.

Widow's/Widower's Option. Option for a married person to take a smaller pension so that the surviving partner may have a pension on the scheme member's death.

Will. Legal document setting out how a person's possessions should be distributed on death.

Withdrawal Option. Options (usually preserved benefits or a transfer) available to a member of an occupational pension scheme who leaves before the normal retirement date.

Winding-up Date. The date when an investor will be repaid the value of the net assets of an investment trust. Most trusts do not have such a date.

Yield. Interest or income divided by current value of asset, expressed as a percentage.

Yield Curve. A graph of the redemption yield of fixed income securities plotted against maturity.

Yield-to-Maturity. US term for Redemption Yield.

Zero Coupon Bond. Bond which does not make periodic interest payments. The bond is issued at a discount to its nominal value and redeems at the nominal value.

Zero Dividend Preference Shares. Shares of a split-capital investment trust which pay no dividends, but offer a fixed sum on winding-up.

Index

Index compiled by Geoffrey Jones